VOICES OF BLACK FOLK

ADVISORY BOARD

David Evans, General Editor
Barry Jean Ancelet
Edward A. Berlin
Joyce J. Bolden
Rob Bowman
Susan C. Cook
Curtis Ellison
William Ferris
John Edward Hasse
Kip Lornell
Bill Malone
Eddie S. Meadows
Manuel H. Peña
Wayne D. Shirley
Robert Walser

VOICES OF BLACK FOLK

THE SERMONS OF REVEREND A.W. NIX

TERRI M. BRINEGAR

UNIVERSITY PRESS OF MISSISSIPPI / JACKSON

The University Press of Mississippi is the scholarly publishing agency of
the Mississippi Institutions of Higher Learning: Alcorn State University,
Delta State University, Jackson State University, Mississippi State University,
Mississippi University for Women, Mississippi Valley State University,
University of Mississippi, and University of Southern Mississippi.

www.upress.state.ms.us
The University Press of Mississippi is a member
of the Association of University Presses.

Any discriminatory or derogatory language or hate speech regarding race, ethnicity,
religion, sex, gender, class, national origin, age, or disability that has been retained
or appears in elided form is in no way an endorsement of the use of such language
outside a scholarly context.

Copyright © 2022 by University Press of Mississippi
All rights reserved

First printing 2022
∞

Library of Congress Cataloging-in-Publication Data

Names: Brinegar, Terri, author.
Title: Voices of Black Folk: the sermons of Reverend A. W. Nix / Terri Brinegar.
Other titles: American made music series.
Description: Jackson: University Press of Mississippi, 2022. | Series:
American made music series | Includes bibliographical references and index.
Identifiers: LCCN 2021055866 (print) | LCCN 2021055867 (ebook) | ISBN
978-1-4968-3925-1 (hardcover) | ISBN 978-1-4968-3930-5 (trade paperback) | ISBN
978-1-4968-3927-5 (epub) | ISBN 978-1-4968-3926-8 (epub) | ISBN 978-1-4968-3929-9
(pdf) | ISBN 978-1-4968-3928-2 (pdf)
Subjects: LCSH: Nix, A. W. | Baptists—Sermons. | African American
Baptists. | Sermons, American—African American authors. | African
American gospel singers. | Gospel music.
Classification: LCC BX6455.N59 B75 2022 (print) | LCC BX6455.N59 (ebook)
| DDC 286/.1092 [B]—dc23/eng/20220110
LC record available at https://lccn.loc.gov/2021055866
LC ebook record available at https://lccn.loc.gov/2021055867

British Library Cataloging-in-Publication Data available

To Jim, for all you do, for all you are, for being my rock

CONTENTS

ACKNOWLEDGMENTS AND RESEARCH METHODOLOGY
- IX -

INTRODUCTION
- 3 -

CHAPTER 1: Rev. A. W. Nix Historical Background
- 13 -

CHAPTER 2: Class Divisions during the Modern Era
- 64 -

CHAPTER 3: The Sermons
- 101 -

CHAPTER 4: Vocal and Musical Analysis
- 189 -

CONCLUSION
- 264 -

NOTES
- 272 -

SELECTED BIBLIOGRAPHY
- 302 -

INDEX
- 313 -

ACKNOWLEDGMENTS AND RESEARCH METHODOLOGY

Interviews with living consultants, especially the two surviving adult children of Reverend Nix—Genester and Elwood—and one other family member, allowed me to gather firsthand personal information about the lives of members of the Nix family. I have never met a more loving and generous woman than Genester Nix. In the few short days we spent together, I found her to be kind, open-hearted, intelligent, and passionate about her family's history. I hope I have provided a thorough tribute to her father's life and legacy. Elwood Nix made me laugh almost constantly. For a man who became totally blind in adulthood and had to sacrifice so much, his heart was light and playful, and he was a joy to be around. I am thoroughly grateful to have met him. I would also like to thank Genester's son, Dr. John Wilson, who provided me with valuable information regarding modern preaching practices. I would like to thank the Association of Recorded Sound Collections (ARSC) for granting me a travel award, which provided the opportunity to travel to Philadelphia to interview Genester and Elwood Nix.

I consulted genealogical records, including census material, marriage and death certificates, and land ownership records, which I found online, in public libraries, and in the county clerk's offices in Longview, Texas, and Henderson, Texas. Archival research at Columbia University's Union Theological Seminary in New York City gave me access to the 1921 National Baptist Convention minutes, which revealed significant information concerning Andrew Nix, William Nix, Sutton E. Griggs, and Thomas A. Dorsey. In New York, I visited Harlem for a firsthand view of Nix's former church, Mt. Moriah Baptist Church. I also conducted archival research at St. George's United Methodist Church in Philadelphia and at the University of Louisville where the archives for State University (now Simmons College) are housed. In addition, I visited Georgetown, Kentucky, where Nix first preached. Because of the race riots in Chicago in 1919 and numerous racial inequalities directed towards African Americans in the 1920s and 1930s, multiple studies were conducted by the Works Progress Administration (WPA), the Chicago Commission on Race Relations, and the Illinois Writers' Project (IWP) to study these inequalities.[1] Later works, including Allan H. Spear's *Black Chicago: The Making of a Negro Ghetto* (1967) and E. Franklin Frazier's *Black Bourgeoise* (1957), helped me to understand the racial tensions in Chicago in the 1920s.

Sermons and sound films released in the 1920s are particularly relevant to my study, as these are primary sources that have allowed me to access the actual vocal sounds of preaching and singing of Nix, his "services" as recorded on phonograph records, and the Black voices represented on audio sources and in film. One film in particular, *Hallelujah*, released in 1929, features a version of one of Reverend Nix's sermons as well as an authentic representation of a folk church service. The recordings of Nix's sermons, available on reissues through Document Records, preserved the sound of Nix's voice, his choice of repertoire for musical selections, and his sermon texts. I have notated and analyzed these sermons. Numerous newspapers articles helped me to piece together missing information about Nix's life, and newspaper advertisements of Nix's sermons also helped to determine their relevance and popularity at the time.

For my analysis of vocal timbre and other qualities, I used the software program Sonic Visualizer.[2] This program allowed me to view and analyze images of the spectrogram, including harmonics, frequency and amplitude graphs, dynamics, and time points, and to play back audio at various increments of tempo for transcription purposes.

It is a pleasure to acknowledge the kind and generous support I have received from numerous scholars, colleagues, and friends. I could not have written this book without the support, guidance, friendship, and amazing knowledge of Dr. Larry Crook. He stood by me every step of the way and continuously amazed me with his level of insight and knowledge. I am grateful for his guidance, his brilliance in all types of ethnomusicology, and his talent as a musician. Dr. Welson Tremura provided invaluable expertise in the field of vocal pedagogy and ethnomusicology. Dr. Jennifer Thomas always set the bar high, which forced me to do my best, but I am grateful for the challenge. Dr. Paul Ortíz urged me towards a more thorough understanding of African American cultural history. He stands up for the rights of minorities every day, and it was an honor to have worked with him. I would like to extend my thanks to Dr. Sandra Jean Graham for sending me preview chapters for her book, *Spirituals and the Birth of a Black Entertainment Industry*, before its official release. Her research on the Fisk Jubilee Singers was invaluable to me. I am grateful to blues and gospel historian Dr. Guido van Rijn for referring me to valuable sources, for his support and assistance, and for providing photographic images of the original Nix recordings. I would like to thank Dr. David Evans for checking over my transcriptions of the Nix sermons for accuracy. This was a huge task, and I am grateful for his listening skills. I would also like to thank Dr. Evans for his editorial assistance with this book. He spent countless hours advising me on revisions, and for this I am grateful. I would like to thank everyone at University Press of Mississippi, especially Craig Gill and Carlton McGrone, for their support and guidance through this process. Dr. Melvin Butler was a great help to me in reading through the preliminary manuscript and offering suggestions. I am very grateful to Dr. Butler for his scholarly expertise and insights. Dr. Portia Maultsby gave me guidance on multiple occasions, and I am grateful for her expertise. I would also like to thank Dr. Lerone Martin for reading through parts of the manuscript and offering his opinions and expertise. Thank you to Dr. Cedric Dent for assisting me in searching for the sources of Nix's hymns and spirituals. I would like to thank my dear friend Debbie Gasho for her assistance in making the graphs.

Lastly, I could not have written this book without the love and support of my wonderful husband, Jim. He stood by me through the tears, exhaustion, and frustration. He balanced me and forced me to keep my feet on the ground and never to give up. I don't know how I could have done this without him.

VOICES OF BLACK FOLK

INTRODUCTION

In *The Souls of Black Folk*, African American sociologist W. E. B. Du Bois describes a "Negro revival" in the South in which the "people moaned and fluttered, and then the gaunt-cheeked brown woman beside me suddenly leaped straight into the air and shrieked like a lost soul, while round about came wail and groan and outcry, and a scene of human passion such as I had never conceived before."[1] At the revival, the preacher inspired his congregants into spiritual "frenzy," which included moans, shrieks, shouting, stamping, and the "wild waving of arms, the weeping and laughing, the vision and the trance."[2] These religious traditions of the "black folk"—the term Du Bois used to describe the critical mass of rural African Americans from the South[3]—were propelled into the early twentieth century as record companies began recording sermons by Black ministers in the 1920s.

Rev. Andrew William (A. W.) Nix, an African American Baptist minister originally from Texas, recorded fifty-four sermons on the Vocalion label in Chicago between 1927 and 1931 and was one of the most successful recording preachers in the early twentieth century. On his recordings, Nix chanted his sermons and shouted with a ferocity unequaled by any other phonograph preacher, while his studio congregants sang spirituals and shouted "Amen!" and "Preach!," vocalizing many of the same traditions that had been essential parts of the early Black folk church. An examination of Nix's recorded sermons reveals the values that were important to him and presumably to those who purchased his records. The sermons offer primary source evidence of the expressive traditions of southern Black Baptists—Black folk whose vocal traditions were frequently dismissed by many upper- and middle-class African Americans who viewed these traditions not only as an unwanted reminder of the slavery past, but also as an example of uncontrolled emotionality, backwardness, and ignorance. These vocal traditions were also dismissed and often parodied by many white people. Recorded sermons by Nix and others highlighted the traditional vocal techniques of the Black folk and presented them in new modern contexts that became symbols for advancement, cultural autonomy, empowerment, and agency. Recordings also superseded the written form, such as notated works, granting power to the oral transmission of Black voices and creating new ideas of modernity.

While copious attention has been paid to the folk spirituals, arranged spirituals by university "jubilee" groups and formally trained soloists, blues, jazz, and other Black musical forms prominent before and during the 1920s, only a scant amount of scholarship exists that discusses the use of vocal timbres, styles, and inflections (henceforth described as voices, vocalisms, or sounds) that serve as an expression of African American racialized identity and pride.[4] Preferred vocal timbres and inflections can be learned from other members of one's culture, passed down from generation to generation by means of oral traditions. While no single sound ideal in African American vocal expressions exists, culturally agreed-upon values and meaning are placed on sounds and are associated with specific cultural traditions. And because there is not a single, unified sound ideal, despite past assumptions of a homogenous vocal sound of Blackness idealized as "the Black voice," I will be discussing Black voices in the plural.

Vocal sounds have often functioned as an index of one's status, education, upbringing, and level of sophistication. Sacred vocal expressions were often associated with working-class Black churches, such as Holiness/Sanctified, Baptist, and Methodist churches, that set up in storefront locations in the marginalized poor Black neighborhoods of large northern metropolises.[5] The larger, urban Black middle-class Baptist and Methodist churches tended to criticize the vocal expressions of the working-class churches for their loud, demonstrative exhibitions of spiritual ecstasy, which included shouting, hand-clapping, foot-stomping, and congregational responses. However, I propose that the traditional expressions of the folk church were not limited to working-class congregations and their ministers, but instead were also valued by African Americans of varying class statuses. In other words, despite outward declarations by the middle class that Black people should reform their traditional expressions, the popularity of recorded sermons that feature vocal aesthetics of the folk, such as those by Nix, suggests that these sounds were more widely accepted than previously understood.

The sounds of the folk were and are sometimes associated with the sound of vocal timbre or vocal inflections, such as melismas, moans, and shouts. Although issues associated with vocal timbre are frequently linked to racialized understandings, timbre is not a biological feature of race or ethnicity, but instead is a cultural construct.[6] In other words, individuals such as Nix could and can choose—sometimes unconsciously—which sounds, including vocal timbre and expressions, have meaning and express group identity. Outsiders can also assign identity to individuals based on their interpretation of vocal sounds, and in response, insiders may alter their vocal sound to be perceived one way or another.

These differences exist not only between "Black" and "white" ways of speaking or singing, but also between African Americans from different socioeconomic classes and backgrounds. The differing class structures in the 1920s led to a multilevel dynamic within the African American community.[7] I argue that Nix's vocal utterances and texts exemplified the differences between the upper and lower classes in Black Chicago, not in the typical dual framework of Black and white so often discussed in African American scholarship.

As a significant component of "the Black experience," the enslavement of African Americans, along with the history and historical consciousness of Black oppression in the United States, has been integral to the development of African American vocal styles and sounds. Even contemporary vocalizations by Black Americans are closely intertwined with experiences of oppression, with ensuing emotionalism often developing as a cathartic reaction from pain.[8] Definitions of "Black music" often refer to the experiences of African Americans as foundational aspects of these sounds.[9] These vocal sounds have been appropriated by generations of non-Black singers, rappers, and speakers, who assert that the sounds are learned techniques, often ignoring the cultural residue of the historical past. While the vocal sounds of African Americans do have a historical background and have served as a cathartic release, essentialized notions based on skin color and ethnicity continue today, often equating African American vocalisms with a fixed, homogeneous vocal sound. However, while some common features link these expressions to genres and styles originated by African Americans, heterogeneous differentiations continue to develop, creating a myriad of vocal sounds. The purpose of this study is to delve into the hybrid nature of Nix's voice as a mixture of what has been considered part of African American vocal traditions—those traditions of the past that link various musical genres with common features—and modern voices that were conceptions of advancement, uplift, resistance, and progress.

Reverend Nix employed many vocal traditions through his use of moans, shouts, and chanting. Speech-song in his chanted sermons is a highly stylized use of gestures that move the sermon from the simple delivery of words into the zone of performance in which his congregants vocally participate, thus creating a participatory performance. Nix's vocal delivery, with his use of harsh vocal timbres, shouts, moans, congregational responses, and singing, profoundly affects the sermon content. Without the inclusion of these vocal practices, the listener would be left with only the sermon's words. Speech, or, in Nix's case, speech-song and singing, manifests as performance through the pre-planned stylization of sounds and words. Nix's recording-as-performance includes not only Nix's voice, but also the voices of several female congregants who interject, shout, and sing throughout his performance, simulating a live performance in the Black church to connect listeners to the experience.

The vocal sounds of the Black folk minister were transferred onto the modern phonograph and disseminated to African American consumers in the early twentieth century, bringing sounds that were linked simultaneously to the South and to the modernizing North. Recorded sermons thus blurred the demarcation lines between real and imagined spaces that separated lower- and middle-class African American communities and offer valuable insight into the lives of African Americans in the 1920s during a period of rapid change in American society.

The 1920s in which Nix recorded his sermons coincided with the migration of thousands of African Americans from the South to urban metropolises in the North, including Chicago and New York. During the first wave of the Great Migration, as it was called, from approximately 1916 to 1930, the rural, southern roots of the Black church moved along with them. The sounds that had typically been associated with the church of the rural South and that evoked home for displaced northerners entered into urban church enclaves via the African American minister. The recorded sermons by African American ministers such as Nix, also a southern émigré, brought Black vocal traditions into public awareness and spaces, alongside the popular expressions of the secular music of blues and jazz. The new media of the phonograph and sound film, and the voices they carried, created a bridge between the old and the new as the sound of tradition was propelled into the modern age.[10]

The 1920s, an era rife with dichotomies, saw a shift in the representation of Black voices. On the one hand, the stripping away of Reconstruction-era political, racial, and economic advances caused setbacks and injustices that instigated race riots throughout the US, from small, rural communities of former slave states in the South[11] to large, urban metropolises in the North.[12] On the other hand, technological advances provided opportunities for the sounds of the Black folk to be transported into the modern era through the development of the phonograph and sound films and the marketing of records of African American performers to African American consumers, which came to be termed "race records."

Middle-class ministers such as Nix deserve attention for their dissemination of vocal traditions on recorded sermons and their influence on subsequent musical styles. Sociologists and historians have discussed the distinct class divisions among African Americans in the 1920s, which included their church affiliations and practices.[13] While economic and moralistic standards assigned people to certain classes,[14] overlap between the classes in matters of cultural practice resulted in diversity within African American communities.[15]

Understanding the class and racial dynamics that existed for African Americans in the 1920s is crucial to understanding how Black voices have been identified as expressions of class.

RACIAL UPLIFT

The struggle for equality in the last decades of the nineteenth and early decades of the twentieth centuries created rifts and tensions between members of the emerging Black middle class, the elite class, and the Black folk.[16] Members of the Black elite, such as W. E. B. Du Bois and Booker T. Washington, disagreed, often publicly, on which methods best suited the advancement of the race.[17] Most believed, despite these contradictions, that a strategy of self-help, idealized as *racial uplift*, based on the improvement of African Americans' behaviors, lifestyles, and material conditions, would help to diminish white racism. Despite their best intentions to create a positive Black identity, Black elites created a racial hierarchy that privileged bourgeois standards of respectability.[18] The demonstration of themselves as "civilized," they hoped, would overcome racism from the dominant society and help to achieve their status as equal citizens.[19]

In the 1920s, African Americans were faced with numerous race leaders, musicians, and record company owners who encouraged assimilation to the dominant culture's vocal aesthetic values as one possible avenue to achieve race equality. It must be clear that, without racism in the first place, assimilation to dominant vocal styles would not have been necessary.[20] The use of particular vocal timbres and inflections represented choices that some African Americans used to project racial identity in the midst of these pressures. Class struggles in which the elite and middle classes castigated members of the lower class for their public behavior, including their vocal sounds, may have been the upper classes' attempt to separate themselves from not only traditions of the past and their association with slavery, but also the people who continued these traditions. As the upper classes sought to identify with the protocols of the dominant culture, they also sought to survive by participating in a society that was unequal and unjust.

Racial uplift during the late nineteenth century was originally understood as a way to transcend worldly oppression and misery, with education as its primary means to achieve these goals. A shift in racial uplift's objectives occurred after Reconstruction's promises were reversed, forcing African American leaders to establish new means for dealing with persistent racist practices in the United States. As historian Kevin K. Gaines explains, in the post-Reconstruction era, for many black elites, uplift came to mean an emphasis on self-help, racial solidarity, temperance, thrift, chastity, social purity, patriarchal authority, and the accumulation of wealth. . . . Amidst legal and extralegal repression, many black elites sought status, moral authority, and recognition of their humanity by distinguishing themselves, as bourgeois agents of civilization, from the presumably undeveloped black majority; hence the phrase, so purposeful and earnest, yet so often of ambiguous significance, "uplifting the race." . . . uplift, among its other connotations, also represented the struggle for a positive black identity in a deeply racist society, turning the pejorative designation of race into a source of dignity and self-affirmation through an ideology of class differentiation, self-help, and interdependence.[21]

Despite the best intentions of African American elites to aid the race in gaining autonomy, many Black elites were themselves dependent on white political and business professionals, which often required their accommodation to the demands of the dominant society. In addition, class and gender inequalities resulted in "unconscious internalized racism," a hierarchal system with Black elite men at the top of the pecking order and Black women and the lower classes beneath.[22]

On the one hand, some African American leaders fought for integration through legal attacks on segregation, laws for civil rights legislation, and open discontent with and protests against the abandonment of equal rights for Black people.[23] Elites argued against segregation, except in certain cases such as the separate Black church, which had been established with its own traditions since the pre-Civil War era.[24] Those African American leaders who fought for integration, such as W. E. B. Du Bois (1868–1963), were members of the cultural elite and had leanings toward assimilation. Du Bois and his followers also supported a classical liberal arts education, which he himself acquired from his New England teachers who espoused a middle-class, Victorian sense of morality, temperance, chastity, thrift, and piety. He insisted that students educated according to these standards would be the ones to lead the drive for economic independence of all members of the race. He dubbed this group the "Talented Tenth," establishing an elite vanguard of the most educated members of the community that would be responsible for uplifting the masses.

On the other hand, some southern African American leaders followed the tenets of Booker T. Washington (1856–1915), who encouraged economic segregation, the building of strong Black communities, property ownership, and industrial education rather than a traditional liberal arts education, which he considered unproductive, favoring instead education funded by the manual labor of the students. Washington also encouraged the Black masses to learn from whites: "Practically all the real moral uplift the black people have got from the whites—and this has been great indeed—has come from this observation of the white man's conduct."[25] His supporters believed that, to achieve their own goals, they must work within the framework of the dominant white society and accommodate to its demands. There were also those, such as Nix, who stood on the middle ground between the assimilationists and the segregationists, choosing certain tenets from one group but not from others.

The Black elite were not the only voices of racial uplift; racial uplift ideologies were disseminated through a variety of institutions, including churches, academic conferences held at Black colleges such as Hampton Institute, meetings of Black clubwomen, books, and Black newspapers and periodicals.[26] Black newspapers in the North and the South frequently published articles on racial issues, including racial uplift. One article by the Associated Negro Press claimed, "to-day, the average home receives not only one race periodical, but usually two or more, and the exceptional home, office, store, the schools and churches and libraries, receive from six to more than a score. This is PROGRESS; this is SUCCESS."[27] An article from 1919 described the prevalence of publications that discussed racial issues:

> To these numbers must be added the publications of churches, societies, and schools. For example, Mississippi has eleven religious weeklies, eight school periodicals, and two lodge papers, making a total, with the nineteen newspapers, of forty periodicals. And all classes of these contain articles on racial strife, outcries against wrongs and persecutions. You cannot take up even a missionary review or a Sunday school quarterly without being confronted by such an outcry.[28]

The *Memphis Times*, like some other newspapers, claimed to speak out "for progress, reform and the highest development of the race on all lines; speaks out against injustice and corruption; it uses its influence for equal rights to all. 'All men up and no man down.' It is a factor for social uplift, mental, moral and spiritual development, as well as commercial and financial."[29] The Associated Negro Press on January 1, 1920, also listed "Agencies for Uplift," including churches, schools, the National Urban League, and the National Association for the Advancement of Colored People. Apparently, racial uplift was a visible topic for African Americans of varying class status, not restricted to Black intellectuals or the college educated.

Suggestions for how to uplift the race also included elimination of self-deprecating behavior in the arts, such as the practice of "Blacking up" for minstrel performances, and the "burlesquing of the Negro," which was "doing almost as much to keep down high ideals among the rising generations as the most radical Negro-hating white journal."[30] Instead, it was suggested that attention be directed towards artistic representations, "with Negro characters as heroes," rather than as "clowns, servants, and petty criminals."

As one aspect of racial uplift, elite Black people encouraged "cultured" vocalizations as demonstrations of the artistic value of African Americans for the prospect of equality with white society. In other words, elite individuals such as James M. Trotter believed that assimilation to white, European cultural aesthetics, including the performance of Western classical music, could indicate one's intelligence, cultural sophistication, and social status. Trotter sought to bring attention to Black classical musicians, believing that by demonstrating African Americans' superior accomplishments in European classical music as equal to or surpassing those of their white contemporaries, Black people could "prove their worth" and achieve racial equality.[31]

Attention to classical performers was well documented in printed sources with the spread of Victorian-era vocal principles that used music to maintain class boundaries and uphold class distinctions.[32] Some elite and middle-class African Americans rejected traditional folk vocalizations in favor of Europeanized vocal aesthetics, influencing creation of the "New Negro" and "high art" during the Harlem Renaissance of the 1920s.[33] Ultimately, racial uplift attempted to alleviate racial inequalities between Black and white people, but inevitably it created class hierarchies and tensions between upper- and lower-class African Americans.[34] The voice often served as the determining factor of one's status.

Musical assimilation provided Black elites what they believed to be viable proof of a "better class" of African Americans, used to contest racist views of them as biologically inferior and uncivilized.[35] Du Bois and other African American elite leaders considered the "cultured" voices of the Fisk Jubilee Singers and the written, notated versions of the arranged spiritual as signs of African American advancement, modernity, and self-consciousness.[36] For centuries, the voices of marginalized Black people were insulted and ridiculed by white people, and criticized and shamed by African American elites.[37] The white majority contended that the "folk" voice of the Black masses exemplified the uncultured and uneducated status of African Americans; Black elites and the Black middle class associated the voices of the folk with the slavery past and as a source of embarrassment and shame. As a result, Black folk voices were often dismissed or ignored altogether, until the commercial production of race records in the 1920s promulgated the sounds of the folk in the national marketplace.[38]

My analysis demonstrates that Nix employed vocal traditions that had been present in African American communities since the era of slavery and that those traditions continued to be performed and valued by twentieth-century African American audiences. While I agree that African Americans who excelled in Euro-American classical repertoire and the creation of "sophisticated" versions of the old Negro spirituals represent profound moments of encounter with modernity in the late 1800s, I suggest that recorded sermons (and blues and jazz) of the 1920s provided an alternative entry point into modernity for many African Americans. These recordings allowed Black mass audiences a sense of connection to and identification with traditional vocal practices of the African American past, presented in a modern technological context. Black vocal traditions, as modern expressions on phonographs, countered the notions that African Americans must "uplift" themselves through association with the vocalizations of the dominant culture.

A primary concern of this study is to show how the sounds associated with Black voices served as indices of race, class, and the regional origins of the vocalist (i.e., northern/southern). This study also contests the binaries that have often existed in scholarly studies on African American music, which have consistently framed discussions as Blackness vs. whiteness, but have often avoided discussions of diversity within African American communities. I chose this subject because I was interested in the voices I heard on these records—Nix's gravelly shouts and the background singers' spiritual melodies and commentary—and how these sounds may have intersected with racial uplift themes and with notions of modernity.

This study is based on ethnographic interviews with two of Andrew Nix's surviving adult children, Genester Nix and Elwood Nix, musical analyses of Nix's recorded sermons, and a close reading of historical and contemporary literature that focuses on the vocal elements of African American musical genres in general and specifically those of Black churches, including preaching by African American ministers. A complete analysis of the rich traditions of African American preaching is not within the purview of this book; however, I focus on defining the vocal features common across these expressions. The terms I will use to describe African Americans and their vocal processes are those currently preferred by members of the community: "African American" and "Black," rather than the outdated terms of "Negro" and "colored."[39]

As a case study, Nix represents a middle ground between the old and the new and the South and the North. Chapter 1 reveals Nix's life history and career. I wanted to give a complete picture of Nix's life since few know about him and, indeed, little has been known about him. As part of the biographical study, this chapter also presents new archival information that clarifies misleading information written by other authors about Andrew, his brother, William, and their contributions to and influences on the "Father of Gospel Music," Thomas A. Dorsey. I also include a discussion of the film *Hallelujah*, in which a version of one of Nix's sermons was featured. An in-depth study of the voices and sermon in this film is relevant to this study. I conclude the chapter with a discography of Nix's recordings.

Chapter 2 explores the so-called "modern era" of the 1920s and specifically Chicago, where Nix resided and recorded his sermons. This chapter focuses on class divisions that developed in both the Black churches of Chicago and the vocal and musical expressions of the "New Negro." I begin with a brief history of vocal traditions and the African American church, followed by a discussion of Chicago Black churches. Modern voices and their association with class and uplift ideologies are examined as contrasting with the traditional sounds of the "Old Negro." Technology developed in the 1920s, including in the phonograph industry, aided in the dissemination of new, modern Black voices. A study of the impact of the commercialization of recorded sermons reveals the value placed on African American vocal traditions.

Chapter 3 addresses Nix's sermons themselves and includes the textual transcription of ten specific sermons. I discuss the textual themes associated with each sermon and the textual form. The analysis of the sermon texts clearly demonstrates their basis in older religious material and Nix's affiliation with uplift themes. I link the main themes and their relationship to both traditional topics and current social issues.

Chapter 4 analyzes the specific vocal and musical styles and repertoire used by Nix and his congregants on his recordings and discusses any spirituals or hymns that are included. Vocal and musical analysis of the sermons demonstrates Nix's unique vocal characteristics and how they compare with traditional sounds of the folk spirituals and other early vocal practices and serve as markers of traditional African American vocal aesthetics.

Chapter 1

REV. A. W. NIX HISTORICAL BACKGROUND

Rev. Andrew William (A. W.) Nix was an African American Baptist minister who recorded fifty-four sermons on the Vocalion label in Chicago between 1927 and 1931. His history is significant because it illuminates issues important to so many who migrated from the rural South to urban cities in the North in the early part of the twentieth century. Born in a farming community in Texas and schooled in Kentucky, Nix eventually migrated north to New York, Chicago, Cleveland, and Pittsburgh before finally settling in Philadelphia. Nix's recorded sermons offer primary source evidence of the expressive traditions of southern Black Baptists—Black folk whose vocal traditions were frequently dismissed by many educated African Americans who viewed these traditions not only as a reminder of the slavery past, but also as an example of uncontrolled emotionalism, backwardness, and ignorance.

A review of the life of Reverend Nix provides not only genealogical and census data on his family's history, but also illuminates Nix's involvement with and knowledge of contemporary ideas about racial uplift or "advancement of the race," as it was sometimes called. As the son of a formerly enslaved man and farmer from Texas, Nix eventually settled in northern metropolises and in many ways paralleled the experience of the thousands of African Americans who ventured north in search of more favorable conditions and opportunities. However, as an educated man and college graduate, he broke the mold of the stereotypical southern, rural preacher. His life became a contradiction of sorts, in that he continued the vocal traditions of the rural South while simultaneously adopting practical solutions for his congregants to overcome racial and self-imposed barriers and advocated standards identified with racial uplift philosophies. He can be described as a "middle-man" in that he never abandoned his traditional southern roots, but sought to uplift his fellow African Americans through his practical sermons, which he recorded on modern, cutting-edge technologies of the 1920s.

Andrew William (A. W.) Nix was born on November 30, 1880, in Harmony Hill, Texas, in Rusk County,[1] later moving with his family to Longview, Texas, in

Gregg County.[2] His father, William Sr. (1853–1927), was a farmer and a preacher, who married Ida Peterson (1854–1929) in Rusk County, Texas, on April 28, 1876. William Sr. was born in Georgia, and his mother was from Georgia; however, census reports from 1880 to 1920 provide conflicting information about the birthplace of William Sr.'s father: South Carolina (1880), Georgia (1900), Virginia (1910), and Georgia (1920). It is possible that William Sr.'s parents were Albert Nix (b. 1820) and Charlotte Nix (b. 1830), who with their children including William were born into slavery in South Carolina.[3] William Nix Sr. died on January 22, 1927. A brief article in the *Longview News-Journal* stated, "Wm. Nix, the old negro preacher, who lived at Nix's station on the Port Bolivar railroad, died Saturday. He was a good humble, negro having a great many white friends."[4] William and Ida had three children together: William Jr. (1878–1941), Andrew William (1880–1949), and Emma (1883–?).

After abolition, William Nix Sr. moved to Rusk County, Texas, later moving to the adjacent Gregg County. On December 17, 1898, he purchased ninety-nine and a half acres of land for $477.50 in Gregg County,[5] which was an enclave for freedmen's settlements. These settlements, also called freedom colonies, provided newly freed African Americans with not only land, but also autonomy away from the control of racist white society in Texas. Between 1870 and 1890, the rates at which African American farmers acquired land in Texas rose from 1.8 percent to 26 percent.[6] Many formerly enslaved people acquired cheap or neglected land, and it was during this time that William Sr. probably settled in the area called "The Ridge." The Ridge, also known as "Freedman's Ridge," was located at the intersections of farm roads 449 and 2751. Farm Road 2751 (also named Airline Road) was the exact location of William Sr.'s address in 1910.[7] Thus, the evidence suggests that he probably did choose to settle in The Ridge as a freedman.

The county seat of Gregg County is Longview, Texas, established in 1871, in which both cotton and railroads were thriving businesses. The Texas and Pacific (later named the Southern Pacific) railroad's terminus was in Longview, destined to extend to Dallas; the International and Great Northern Railroad reached the adjacent community of Longview Junction.[8] According to the Longview Chamber of Commerce, passengers could "board the Sunshine Special at Longview at 6:40 p.m. and be in St. Louis at 10:30 the next day, in Chicago at 7:25 and in New York the following day at noon, with only a few stops in between at the larger places."[9] William Sr. likely chose to settle in Longview for its Freedmen Settlements, inexpensive land, and accessibility to railroad lines. The rail system gave the booming cotton industry access to nearby markets that were previously difficult and time-consuming for farmers, such as William Sr., to access via wagons.[10] Because William Sr. was a farmer and had migrated as a formerly enslaved individual from South Carolina, he possibly farmed cotton.

Figure 1.1. School Building, 1888. Used by permission of Gregg County Historical Museum.

William Nix Sr. was a minister in addition to being a farmer, but little is known as to which denomination he belonged or in what capacity he practiced his ministry.[11] He is listed in the "1890 Marriages in Rusk County" report as officiating a marriage, with his denomination recorded as "N. R." for "no record." The Pleasant Hill Colored Methodist Episcopal Church, founded in 1870, was the main cultural artery for African Americans living in Gregg County and may have been the church where William Sr. attended and/or preached.

The first inhabitants of the area that would become Gregg County were American Indians from the Caddo and Cherokee tribes. According to Andrew Nix's daughter Genester, Ida Nix was Native American, which could explain Ida's relatively light complexion.[12] William Sr. probably met Ida in Rusk County and married her there. The Rusk County census of 1880 lists William Sr. and Ida along with their children William Jr. and Andrew as "mulatto" probably due to Ida's light complexion. This same census lists both William Sr. and Ida as not being able to write; however, by the 1900 census both were listed as being able to read and write. It is possible that upon William Sr.'s arrival to Texas and acquiring his freedom, he seized the opportunity to become educated and encouraged his wife to do the same. The Nix children most likely attended the local school for African American children on East Marshall Avenue in Gregg County, which had been constructed in 1888. They may be included in a photograph (Figure 1.1) from the same year. Andrew Nix would have been eight years old at the time of the photograph.

A family photo from c. 1898 (Figure 1.2) shows the entire Nix family dressed in fine clothing: William Sr. is sporting a gold chain; Ida is wearing an elegant gown. Although William Sr. was a farmer, the family has the appearance of

Figure 1.2. Nix Family Photo. Standing from left: William Jr., Emma, Andrew; seated from left: William Sr., Ida. Used by permission of Genester Nix.

wealth. In the 1900 census, a young boy of fourteen named Tim Taylor is listed as a "servant" in the Nix home. If Tim Taylor were indeed a servant, this could suggest that the Nix farm was a successful one and required the help of additional farm workers and/or a servant. In addition, both of Nix's sons attended college, which would have required substantial financial resources from their parents.

EMMA NIX

Daughter Emma Nix, at the age of sixteen, chose married life over college (if she even had that choice) and married Colonel Baker (his real name) in Gregg County, Texas, on January 5, 1899. The 1900 census lists Emma and Colonel with one son, Oddie, living in the same precinct in which Colonel was born. Colonel is listed as a farmer who rented his land, thus implying that he was probably a tenant farmer. Little is known of Emma Nix, except that she was reported to have been a singer.[13] Emma likely sang in the local church but did not have a professional career as a singer.

WILLIAM NIX JR.

William Nix Jr. (1878–1941) was a singer, minister, and choral director who was born in Harmony Hill (Rusk County), Texas (Figure 1.3).[14] By 1909, he was living in Ardmore, Oklahoma, and was serving at the First Baptist Church. An

Figure 1.3. William Nix Jr. From *The New York Age*, September 27, 1919, 7.

article in the *Baptist Rival*, a Black newspaper, mentioned William Jr. leading the choir and traveling to nearby towns to perform "sweet music" at local churches.[15] Between 1915 and 1919 he lived in Chicago and travelled to other cities to sing or deliver sermons. He was mentioned in the *New York Age* in 1917 for presenting a sermon in Florence, South Carolina, and in the same paper in 1919 he was named as "an Evangelist gospel singer."[16] The 1920 census lists him living at 719 42nd Street in Chicago, in the heart of the Black community nicknamed "Bronzeville."[17] He was married to Emma Nix and had two children, William and Emma, named after their parents.[18]

In 1921, he sang at the National Baptist Convention where he "thrilled" both the convention attendees and future gospel composer Thomas A. Dorsey with his rendering of "I Do, Don't You?" as a promotion for the newly published *Gospel Pearls*.[19] Nix travelled to Longview, Texas, in 1926, apparently to visit his parents, where he gave a concert at the Bethel Baptist church. He was named in the *Longview News-Journal* as "Evangelist Singer and Chorus Director Prof. W. M. Nix, Jr."[20] By 1930, he was living in Dallas at 1719 Ball Street, and the census lists him as a "minister" in the business of "gospel," remarried to a woman named Pauline, at least eleven years his junior.[21] They lived in Dallas as boarders with six other people in the same house. Boarding was common for African Americans in the early twentieth century, often a necessary means for both accommodations and affordability. By 1934, William and Pauline were living in California. In January of that year, Nix provided "inspirational worship" at the Second Baptist Church in Monrovia with Pauline directing the choir.[22] As reported in the *California Eagle* on June 5, 1936, William sang at the Second

Baptist Church on Griffith Avenue in Los Angeles, a prominent Black church with a long legacy of Black empowerment. The 1940 census lists William and Pauline as living alone in a rented house on 924 E. 25th Street in Los Angeles; however, William was not employed, while Pauline worked as a seamstress but claimed zero income. It is likely that William was ill and possibly bedridden because he died the following year on September 1, 1941, in Los Angeles. His illustrious contributions at the 1921 National Baptist Convention and as a committee member of the Sunday School Publishing Board, which published *Gospel Pearls* and *The Baptist Standard Hymnal*, may have been his great successes. After 1921, his lack of prominence in the gospel music industry, the infrequent newspapers articles about him, his itinerant lifestyle, and the lack of employment in the last stages of his life signal that he may have had financial and health problems before he passed.

ANDREW (A. W.) NIX

Andrew (A. W.) Nix, also born in Harmony Hill (Rusk County), Texas, was converted and baptized at Friendship Baptist Church in Longview, Texas, at the age of twelve, where both he and his siblings sang in the church choir.[23] No details of his life as a youth exist; however, we can assume that he most likely worked on his parents' farm. It is likely that the Nix family endured hardships as a result of the boll weevil infestation that overtook parts of Mexico and Texas in the late nineteenth and early twentieth centuries, which may have inspired A. W. to invest his talents in opportunities other than farming.[24]

In 1906, at twenty-six years of age, Andrew was licensed as a minister, beginning at Shiloh Baptist Church in Topeka, Kansas, under the direction of Rev. C. G. Fishback.[25] An article in the *Topeka Plaindealer* published on March 13, 1908, reported that "Rev. A W Nix preached an able sermon Sunday night. Rev. Nix is doing a grand work in Horton [in northeast Kansas]. He is lifting as he climbs." "Lifting as we climb" was a well-known slogan of the National Association of Colored Women,[26] who believed it was the job of the Black middle class to promote values that would benefit the race as a whole. Thus, it is evident that, as a young minister, A. W. Nix preached uplift goals and/or participated in organizations that supported the uplift of the race. In April 1908, Nix was reported in the *Horton Headlight-Commercial* as providing the invocation and singing "Far on the Mountain" for a program of music at the Second Baptist Church in Horton, Kansas.[27] Although Nix left Kansas in 1908, his mentor, Reverend Fishback, was involved in standing up for the rights of local African Americans. In 1914, Fishback was reported as "uniting the blacks into a body to fight Jim Crow laws . . . building up the race individually and collectively."[28] Nix's previous apprenticeship with Fishback could have resulted in an exchange of ideas about racial uplift between the two men. An article in the *Topeka Plaindealer* in 1909 confirmed Nix's impression of racial injustices:

> Rev. and Mrs. A. W. Nix[29] returned from Longview, Texas last Monday morning. They tell of a joyful trip and lovely visit with relatives and friends. They think that the jim crow [*sic*] car law is a disgrace to the better class of the race and that if the white people will enforce such a law they should give the colored people some nice, respectable cars and they hope that the state of Kansas and executive heads will maintain the right spirit and not emulate the example of Oklahoma and Texas. Rev. Nix will start soon to Louisville, Ky., to finish his theological course in the state university.[30]

At this early point in his career, Nix was conscious of not only racial segregation and the injustices directed towards African Americans, but also of his status as a member of the "better class of the race." Although only a young man still in his twenties and studying in college, the fact that he was interviewed by the Topeka newspaper for simply returning from a family visit implies that Nix was well respected and well known in the community. His experience riding in the Jim Crow car through Texas and Oklahoma must have made a profound impression on him.

Racism touched Nix's life in other ways as well, and in a story told by his son Elwood, Reverend Nix did not let racist words get the best of him. Elwood stated that, in a visit down South, his father ventured into a restaurant where he was refused service based on his skin color: "He went into this restaurant, and this is when he first got on the [police] force in New York, and he said, 'can I have some ham and eggs and some home fries,' and the guy told him, he said, 'we don't serve n-----s.' And my father said, 'I won't eat 'em either. Can I have some eggs, bacon, and home fries?' He got served."[31] Even when faced with racism such as this, he instructed his children, "anything you do, do your best ... [and] always do the right thing."[32] The philosophy that he instilled in his children was to treat everyone with respect.

Andrew was ordained in 1908 at the age of twenty-eight[33] and began his studies at Western Baptist College in Macon, Missouri.[34] For unknown reasons, he transferred to State University in Louisville, Kentucky, in 1909. The students of State University were primarily from low-income homes or farm homes and had to be of "good moral character."[35] The General Association of Colored Baptists, formed in 1865 by "messengers of regular Missionary Baptist Churches in the State of Kentucky,"[36] founded State University in 1879 "for the purpose of training and preparing young men and women for service, especially teachers, pastors and preachers."[37] The 1914 association meeting minutes reported that Nix served on committees, said prayers at meetings, and was introduced to the association at large as a "Corresponding Messenger" of the "Consolidated Association" thus allowing him to serve in the greater forum of Black Baptists.[38] At the time of the meeting in 1914, Nix would have been thirty-four, older than most other State University students, and was already pastoring at First Baptist Church in Georgetown, Kentucky. His older age and status as a pastor probably gained him respect and admission to the association and its meetings.

In the address at the 1911 association meeting, the moderator, R. Mitchell, D.D., apparently was well aware of the philosophies of racial and moral uplift and supported several of these doctrines, recognizing the demand for "consecrated manhood and womanhood," the importance of voting as a "weapon" to safeguard the rights of citizenship, and the need for temperance. "Manhood," said Reverend Mitchell, could be achieved through the attendance of men in church and was recognized as an act that had great impact on the lives of boys: "When men go to church the boy question is solved, for he loves to be where men are, do what men do."[39] Therefore, men were encouraged to set examples for their sons by attending church. Moral codes for Black Baptists also included the sanctity of marriage as "the foundation of the home."

Citizenship, according to Mitchell, was "the only weapon at our command with which we may be able to protect our liberties." However, voting rights were compromised by the practice of buying and selling votes among Black people. Ministers were encouraged to use their power to influence the masses of the "evil" of this practice. Although Mitchell understood that "the Negro ... is on trial and will be for the next fifty years," he also exhibited a naïve hope that, through the daily newspapers' pleas for equality and just treatment and through "the efforts and endeavors of our friends North and South," "we [can expect] a great change in our favor."[40]

As stated in the minutes of the association's forty-third session, temperance, although strongly supported by the association, was an "opportunity of our people to line up with the sober Christian element of the white race. We should always seek to be in line with the white people who strive to live the teachings of the Bible, for our safety in this country depends upon the Christian people of the country."[41] Perhaps Mitchell referenced white people as the example for temperance because of the strong moral reforms established in the late nineteenth century in which the emerging middle class in England during the Victorian era emphasized "competition, thrift, prudence, self-reliance and personal achievement."[42] The obvious similarities between the uplift goals of elite African Americans and the Victorian-era goals of middle-class English and white Americans relate to larger issues that are outside the purview of this book. Presumably, the adoption of some of the values held by Euro-American culture offered a shield of support by white Christians from the dangers that faced African Americans in the early part of the century, especially those from the South. In addition, the association had pleaded with the General Associations of White Baptists for the allotment of funds to be used for struggling Black Baptist churches. Although the association's board was "embarrassed" by having to make the request, white people were among those who supported the association and State University.

The association was concerned with themes of "amusement" and "revelry," including dancing. According to the association's 1914 meeting minutes, "the dance has invaded the church . . . [and] has killed the prayer meeting in many places and is sapping the Spirituality out of the church."[43] It is not known if "dancing" was referring to male-female dancing as an extra amusement activity, or to the physical responses, such as hand-clapping, foot-stomping, and ecstatic behavior, common in the services of post-Emancipation Black churches.[44] Because of the reference to dancing as an impediment to spirituality that had "invaded the church," it appears that the reference is to in-church physical responses rather than dancing for mere amusement. "Holy dancing" was characteristic especially of the holiness/Pentecostal churches, which were experiencing great growth at this time.

Daniel A. Payne (1811–1893), senior bishop of the African Methodist Episcopal Church (AME), had also expressed his disdain for the physicalized expressions of some Black worshipers. At a church service at Old Bethel Church in Philadelphia in 1878, which he called a "bush meeting," he described how practitioners formed a ring, "clapped their hands and stamped their feet in a most ridiculous and heathenish way. . . . I told him [the pastor] also that it was a heathenish way to worship and disgraceful to themselves, the race, and the Christian name."[45] Apparently, dancing and physical movement in the church setting had been associated with "heathenish" behavior long before the Kentucky Baptists expressed their disapproval of it.

REV. SUTTON GRIGGS

Rev. Sutton E. Griggs (1872–1933)[46] was the son of a formerly enslaved person, a college-educated Baptist minister, and an author who wrote over thirty books and pamphlets during his life (Figure 1.4).[47] I have included information on Griggs in the context of Andrew Nix's history for the simple reason that their professional lives intersected at various stages. First, Griggs was present at the 1911 meeting of the General Association of Colored Baptists in Kentucky, and Nix, as a student at the association's foster school, State University, possibly could have been present at the meeting or read the minutes at a later date;

Figure 1.4. Sutton E. Griggs. From *Alexander's Magazine* 2, no. 4 (August 15, 1906): 8.

second, both Nix and Griggs were present at the 1921 National Baptist Convention in Chicago; third, Nix served on a committee at that 1921 convention, which supported and distributed Griggs's book, *Guide to Racial Greatness or The Science of Collective Efficiency*; and fourth, both Nix and Griggs recorded sermons on race records in the late 1920s. It is therefore possible that Nix supported Griggs's writings and aspirations for uplift. While Nix's vocal practices were drawn largely from the Black folk traditions associated with the "Old Negro," Griggs's voice and writings represent the cultured voice associated with the "New Negro." Thus, although both Griggs and Nix wanted to uplift the race, Griggs serves as a contrast to Nix, not only in voice but also in approach. A brief history of Griggs will partially explain his ideologies as presented in his writings, as well as his role as an elite minister who worked to further the goals of racial uplift.

Griggs pastored the Tabernacle Baptist Churches in Memphis and Nashville, Tennessee, and because of his contact with his congregation, he developed an empathy for the plight of the working poor and sought to assist them through his own philosophy of racial uplift. Griggs was a well-known Black nationalist and, according to Wilson J. Moses, was the first Black author who spoke directly to the Black masses through literature that stressed an Afrocentric philosophy.[48] Du Bois acknowledged Griggs's "racial novels," which "spoke primarily to the Negro race."[49] In his most popular book, *Imperium in Imperio* (1899), Griggs was also one of the first to use the term "New Negro," although Alain Locke is usually credited with coining the term.[50] In the book, Griggs introduced a "new Negro, self-respecting, fearless, and determined in the assertion of his rights."[51]

At the 1915 Southern Baptist Convention, Griggs spoke of his appreciation for his white supporters: "The white people of the South have helped the negroes far beyond their calculations. They have given the negro new unity and new conceptions. They are helping him to self uplift and helping him to come to himself. There is a new relationship between the two races, and the work of the white people is affecting the negro not externally, but in the real emancipation of his race."[52] Around 1920, Griggs planned to convert the Memphis Tabernacle Baptist Church into an "institutional church [that] would teach domestic science to make better cooks for white Memphis homes . . . and provide the white community with well-trained black labor."[53] Because of his conservative strategies, some white people supported Griggs, praising him as "a thrifty, intelligent, self-respecting Negro,"[54] and endorsed his work through sponsorship of speaking engagements and financial contributions to the building of the church. Because of the labor shortage caused by the Great Migration, some white Memphis business owners and industrialists tried to keep African Americans from emigrating to the North and used Griggs as a spokesperson against emigration. As a result, some members of Black communities believed he was inhibiting the advancement of the Black race and labeled Griggs an "Uncle Tom" and accommodationist.

At the 1921 National Baptist Convention in Chicago, Reverend Nix was appointed to the committee formed to distribute Griggs's book *Collective Efficiency*. Therefore, not only did Nix have access to Griggs's convention report on interracial relations and probably heard it delivered in person; he also supported Griggs's publications and other endeavors. This connection suggests that Nix may have supported or was at least minimally involved in the era's racial politics of "advancing the race."

By 1928, Griggs had written several novels in which he promoted Black pride, Black separatism, and Black independence and self-reliance. When Griggs's novels failed to generate sufficient sales from within Black communities, he abandoned his strategy to direct his literature towards the race, and instead turned to support from white financial backers. This action caused him to be called "accommodationist," "marginal man," a "confused mulatto,"[55] and the "Negro Apostle to the White Race."[56] Griggs recorded six sermons in 1928 on the Victor label,[57] and preached in a calm, reserved manner, atypical of the emotionalism characteristic of southern Baptist ministers.[58] His limited recording history suggests that Griggs's vocal style apparently did not resonate with the Black masses to whom he preached and did not encourage future recordings. More will be said about Griggs's recordings in Chapter 3.

Figure 1.5. State University Campus, 1913.

NIX'S EDUCATION

In 1909, Andrew Nix transferred to State University (Figure 1.5)[59] in Louisville, Kentucky, graduating with a normal school degree in 1913 and a Bachelor of Divinity (B.D.) in 1915.[60] The 1909 university catalogue described State University as "An Institution for the Training of Colored Young Men and Women."[61] Normal schools had originally been established in the late nineteenth century by the American Missionary Association and other organizations, philanthropists, and educators.

Most of the students attended State University to earn teaching, ministry, or domestic science degrees. The fees for students were moderate: for the 1914–1915 school year, tuition registration cost four dollars; tuition plus room and board cost ten dollars per month; and the graduation fee plus diploma was five dollars for the normal school, seven dollars for the theological course. A normal school degree would have given Andrew the ability to become a schoolteacher; however, he had already been ordained to preach and obviously wanted to pursue this career path. Several of the officers and trustees of State University were also life members and served on boards of the 1921 National Baptist Convention (which was attended by Andrew Nix, William Nix Jr., Sutton Griggs, and Thomas A. Dorsey); thus, it appears that the officers of the university were well-established ministers within not only Kentucky but also the larger convention system. For example, W. H. Steward, Rev. W. H. Craigshead, and Rev. H. W. Jones all represented Kentucky at the national convention in 1921: Jones served on the Board of Trustees, while Steward served as chairman, and Craigshead as secretary of the board at State University in 1915, the year Andrew graduated. Andrew would likely have received the mentorship of these senior ministers, and they possibly could have been influential in his admission to various boards within the national convention system.

The college also offered a degree in instrumental music, which focused on European classical music masterworks and included the study of Mozart, Czerny, Mendelssohn, Haydn, Clementi, Chopin, Liszt, Schumann, Beethoven, and others. The preference for classical music studies with a focus on the great masters demonstrates adherence to European cultural traditions.

The Domestic Science School offered courses in Household Economics, including cooking, sewing, dressmaking, millinery (hat making), household values, applied housekeeping, and home furnishing and decoration. These courses were intended for the female students only. The pragmatic tenets associated with Domestic Science were similar to Booker T. Washington's philosophy of industrial education in which he encouraged Black people to

> Cast down your bucket where you are [including] in agriculture, mechanics, in commerce, in domestic service, and in the professions.... keep in mind that we shall prosper in proportion as we learn to dignify and glorify common labor, and put brains and skills into the common occupations of life.... No race can prosper till it learns that there is as much dignity in tilling a field as in writing a poem. It is at the bottom of life we must begin, and not at the top.[62]

Washington in 1895 supported the economic development of the working class in a segregated society. His Tuskegee Institute was supported by white philanthropists, leading him to be labeled an accommodationist and called the "Benedict Arnold of the Negro race" by William Monroe Trotter,[63] who himself promoted the Black musical elite.

Membership in the Literary Society of State University and attendance at its meetings were required for all students. The importance of the Literary Society was detailed in State University's 1908–1909 catalogue: "It secures an admirable training in self-restraint and self-command, in parliamentary procedure, and in aptness of studied and impromptu speech."[64] The Prentice Research Club, a literary organization, studied African American authors and purchased books by them for the school library.

Normal schools were the training institutions for teachers, with a four-year curriculum that was divided into three terms per year and included a rigorous program of classes. In the 1910–1911 catalogue, the academic year in which Nix was in his second year at the normal school,[65] the courses included Latin, German, French, Physics, Botany, Rhetoric, Orations, Bible studies by books, periods, and doctrines, Greek Testament, the works of Cicero and Virgil, and the reading of the *Iliad*, *De Senectute*, and *Anabasis*. Nix graduated with a normal school degree in 1913 and continued into the theological program the following year. The Theological Department had a two-year program and included courses on Hebrew, New Testament Greek, Ecclesiastical Latin, Homiletics, Biblical Geography, Missions, Church History, Systematic Theology, and Bible studies, among other courses. In the 1914–1915 catalogue, Nix

Figure 1.6. Rev. A. W. Nix Graduation Photo.

was the only student listed as a senior in the Regular Theological program out of a total of twenty-eight ministerial students at the school.[66] Thus, it is quite likely that he would have had one-on-one instruction and attention from the senior ministers.

The university stressed certain aspects identified with racial uplift theories and Victorian modes of behavior, such as those associated with quietness, cleanliness, moral virtue, and hygiene. For example, "Boisterousness will not be tolerated on the grounds," "Keep beds CLEAN," "Loud talking and laughing at meals or any other disorder will result in dismission from dining room," "Avoid all conversation from windows. Do not communicate therefrom," "The association of the sexes is not allowed, and there must be no communication without permission,"[67] and as stated in the catalogue: "The Sanitary Committee pays special attention to students' teeth, all students are requested to see their dentist before entering State University."[68]

Unfortunately, State University suffered serious financial crises and, by 1914, was not able to pay its instructors. Attempts at fundraising failed, and the university eventually closed in 1930. The association's minutes of the 1914 meeting claimed that they had

> assurance from an organized movement from our white friends that they would raise an amount sufficient to pay the indebtedness on the University if our brethren would raise $5,000 for our work. This was more than fulfilled on our part and when the demand was made for the redemption of this pledge, we were surprised to learn the details for the campaign had not been arranged and they were not prepared to make this pledge good. . . . The most embarrassment at present grows out of the fact that we are unable to pay the salaries due the teachers.[69]

Nix, as a soon-to-be graduating student from State University in 1915 (Figure 1.6),[70] and as a member serving on the association's committee, would surely have been aware of the university's financial difficulties and the promises made, but not kept, by its white benefactors. In short, State University replicated many of Booker T. Washington's philosophies regarding industrial education as well as his adherence to Black elites' accommodation to white philanthropists, depending on those donors for their very survival. The university encouraged strict Victorian moral rules, showed a preference for European classical music, and even stressed cleanliness and good hygiene. Andrew Nix would have been fully aware of the school's underlying ideologies.

NIX'S CAREER

Between 1914 and 1918, Nix was a pastor at the First Baptist Church in Georgetown, Kentucky, where he "built a strong Sunday School in 1914."[71] In 1912, prior to Nix's taking his position at the church, it did not have a pastor but still had a membership of 506.[72] When he became pastor there in 1914, the church had a membership of 550 and property valued at $10,000.[73] Also in 1914, Nix attended the association's annual meeting in Winchester, Kentucky, serving on a committee of six ministers and providing prayers for some of the sessions.

In 1915, Nix was a recipient of the Golden Jubilee Certificate from the General Association of Colored Baptists. The Golden Jubilee was a celebration of the anniversary of fifty years of the Kentucky Baptists' work from 1865 to 1915 and included a book published in 1915 with the Golden Jubilee title. The book provided an opportunity for the association to not only bestow recognition on its members, but to also promote its ideologies, achievements, desires, and suggestions. Nix's acceptance of a distinguished certificate from the association testifies to his involvement in its ideologies, which included racial uplift. Racial uplift stressed self-help as exemplified in the Golden Jubilee's suggestions of "some things we must do for ourselves," which included practical religion, honesty, personal hygiene, care and cleanliness for the home, moral behavior, and interracial encouragement. The association's alignment with racial uplift ideologies was evident in its recommendation to "be loyal and helpful to our race, by encouraging all worthy efforts put forth for its uplift." The association's quote from an article in the January 15, 1915, *Continent* made clear what its members desired to accomplish for the race, by which Black people would be judged by their progress, not their skin tones:

> Summed up in a word, what the black people do want is that with them, just as with the white people, every man shall be rated in estimation of

Figure 1.7. Mount Moriah Baptist Church (Harlem). Photograph by Terri Brinegar.

Figure 1.8. Ida Anita Burcher (c. 1920).

his neighbors on his own individual merits, character, efficiency, and mental caliber—with no discount taken off for the color of his skin.... He knows the average of his race is low, but when an individual climbs above the average, he ought to be credited for it with an honest measure of respect.

In addition, the association recommended to its members that "We must behave ourselves better on the streets and in public carriers and stop talking so much and so loud." Loudness was associated with low-class behavior, thought to keep African Americans from being respected by the dominant society. Andrew Nix, a student at State University in 1915 when the book was published, would most likely have been exposed to these documents and philosophies of racial uplift.[74]

After graduating from State University in 1915, Reverend Nix began his career as a college-educated minister. In this sense he was a contradiction of the stereotypical Black Southern migrant of the day in that he was college-educated with two degrees. His life goal, as described by his daughter Genester, was to move from church to church and build up church membership while simultaneously improving the physical structures of the churches themselves and reducing their debts.[75] Between 1914 and 1940, the Nix family lived in Georgetown, Kentucky; Pittsburgh, Pennsylvania; New York, New York (Harlem); Maywood, Illinois; Chicago, Illinois; Cleveland, Ohio; Pittsburgh, Pennsylvania (he was recalled to the same Pittsburgh church); and finally Philadelphia, Pennsylvania.

In January 1919, Nix accepted the position of pastor at the Tabernacle Baptist Church in Pittsburgh,[76] serving only one year in this position until 1920. However, in this short period, Nix reduced the church mortgage from $27,000 to $17,000 due to an increase in church membership under his leadership. In 1920, he resigned to accept a position as pastor at Mt. Moriah Baptist Church at 2050 5th Ave., New York City (Harlem) (Figure 1.7), where he met his future wife, Ida Anita Burcher (1902–2001) (Figure 1.8), an immigrant from Bermuda, twenty-one years his junior.[77] Nix served as pastor of Mt. Moriah until 1923 while simultaneously serving as a policeman in New York City. He moved to Chicago in 1923 amidst torrential racial strife.

CHICAGO

The General Association of Colored Baptists' recommendation in 1915 to "stop talking so much and so loud" was similar to the *Chicago Defender*'s 1917 admonition to southern migrants whose loud talking was deemed a sign of "low breeding" in the northern cities. According to the *Defender*,

There is entirely too much loud talking on the street cars among our new comers. . . . Such actions show low breeding. People of Chicago do not engage in such. Preachers should take up a few minutes of Sundays and instruct these new comers on how to act in public places and should take off a day and visit the plants, yards, and mills and tell them how to act. . . . Cut this out, dear reader, and whenever you see one talking loudly hand it to him.[78]

The link middle-class northerners made between vocal loudness and low-class behavior by migrants is evident. The *Defender's* recommendation for preachers to visit "plants, yards, and mills" speaks directly to the locations of work done by southern migrants, who capitalized upon unskilled jobs in Chicago that became available with the onset of the US entry into World War I. The *Chicago Defender*, a well-known and popular Black newspaper, took it upon itself to "educate" new migrants to Chicago about northern etiquette and the "right" way to behave. The *Defender* provided "instructions" to those who were deemed "undesirable" by "certain classes of citizens." The accusers based their prejudices on the modes of conduct by the new southern migrants, who were causing "humiliation of all respectable classes of our citizens," granting license to white Chicagoans to commit "unlawful acts" against the new migrants.[79] Thus, in the minds of the old settlers of Chicago, it was imperative that southern migrants improve their standards as a matter of safety from white retaliation. Racial uplift espoused "sophisticated" values as a means to achieve equality, and the very act of controlling the volume of one's voice was interpreted as accommodating to white aesthetic standards.

Many factors led to the mass influx of southerners into northern cities, especially during and after the World War I years between 1916 and 1919.[80] Despite the abolition of slavery after the Civil War, southern states continued with de facto slavery in the form of sharecropping, in which African America farmers were often bound to the land through debt peonage.[81] Southern states were also notorious for their continued practice of lynching, mob violence, and racial intimidation. However, general dissatisfaction with the South was also brought on by environmental factors, such as the infestation of crops by the boll weevil and massive flooding. By 1915, both types of natural disaster had caused major destruction for southern farmers. In addition, prior to World War I, companies manufacturing war supplies required more labor than was available, and Chicago became a major destination for southern migrants because of numerous employment opportunities in industry.[82] Advertisements in the *Chicago Defender* encouraged southerners to head north to escape the racist environment in the South, despite the rumors of the cold climate in Chicago causing death by freezing:

If YOU CAN FREEZE TO DEATH in the north and be free, why FREEZE to death in the south and be a slave, where your mother, sister and daughter are raped and burned at the stake, where your father, brother and son are treated with contempt and hung to a pole, riddled with bullets at the least mention that he does not like the way he has been treated.

Come north then, all of you folks, both good and bad. If you don't behave yourselves up here, the jails will certainly make you wish you had. For the hard working man there is plenty of work—if you really want it. The Defender says come.[83]

Southerners envisioned the North as free from Jim Crow segregation and as able to provide their children with better schools and other facilities.[84] Enticed by the lure of a better life in the North, many southerners—including Andrew Nix—ventured to resettle in northern cities such as Chicago.

The summer of 1919 brought an explosion of racial tensions in Chicago and other locations in the United States. One such riot took place in Longview, Texas, the city in which Andrew's parents resided and where Andrew had lived as a youth. Longview, in 1919, was a small community in Gregg County, Texas, with 5,700 people, in which 31 percent of the city population and 48 percent of the county population were Black.[85] The riots began in response to the alleged advances of a Black man, Lemmel Walters, to a white woman, leading to the abduction and lynching of Walters by white mobs. A local Black schoolteacher reported the incident to the *Chicago Defender*, which published an article on July 5, 1919, that conflicted with the opinions of white residents. The article stated, "Walters was taken to the outskirts of the town and shot to pieces. His nude form was thrown near the roadside. He was buried by people of his Race. White people here are angered because our people have been leaving this part of Texas in droves, and since this lynching all the farm hands have left."[86] Angry white mobs responded by attacking African Americans and burning the houses and businesses of several Black citizens. The hostility between bloodthirsty gangs of both white and Black individuals erupted to the point that martial law had to be imposed by the governor of Texas on July 13, 1919, lasting until July 18, 1919.[87]

Because Longview in 1919 was a small community, undoubtedly William Sr. and his wife, who still lived in Longview, would have been aware of the lynching and ensuing riots by virulent mobs. They probably feared for their own lives as mobs of violent white people paraded through the streets. Possibly they informed their children as to the situation in Longview, raising concern for their safety due to the racial violence there. Andrew's awareness of the racial strife in Texas thus could have been one of the motivating factors that inspired his move to the North.

African American migrants like Andrew Nix were faced with numerous conflicts as they adjusted to their new lives in northern cities. Despite the hope for a new "Promised Land," there were many discriminatory and racist practices in Chicago that were similar to those in the South. For instance, most businesses in Black neighborhoods, such as on State Street, were owned by white people. Established European immigrant communities, such as those inhabited by the Irish and the Poles, reacted to the sudden competition in the job market, feeling threatened for jobs by new Black migrants. In 1919, manufacturing jobs were on the decline as wartime needs came to an end.

Between 1890 and 1915, the population of African Americans in Chicago rose from 15,000 to over 50,000, and many were forced to live in the "Black Belt," paying higher rents than white renters for similar accommodations.[88] The Black Belt was a district thirty-one blocks long and four blocks wide in which 90 percent of the Black population lived, with State Street as the main thoroughfare. In 1917, as migrants flooded into the city, "in a single day there were 664 Negro applicants for houses, and only fifty houses available. . . . At the same time rents increased from 5 to 30 and sometimes as much as 50 per cent. . . . Forty-one of . . . seventy-five families were each living in one room."[89] As overcrowding in Black enclaves caused by the migration pushed African Americans into white neighborhoods, white residents responded with violence, bombing realtors who sold homes to Black buyers and the homes of Black residents.[90] Violence erupted on July 27, 1919, at the Twenty-Ninth Street beach after a seventeen-year-old Black boy, Eugene Williams, drowned after being stoned as he unknowingly crossed an unmarked barrier into "white" waters. Police did not make any arrests, which set off a barrage of violent clashes between Black and white Chicagoans, first at the beach, then later in the city, lasting a total of six days, killing twenty-three Black people and fifteen white people, and injuring 342 Black people and 178 white people. Despite efforts by the Chicago Commission on Race Relations to understand the reasons that inspired the riot, racism and discrimination continued in Chicago, with many claiming that segregation was the only means acceptable to quell racial tensions. As white residents reacted to job losses, the movement of Black residents into white immigrant areas, and the rise of African Americans in politics, fifty-eight residential buildings inhabited by Black residents were bombed between July 1, 1917, and March 1, 1921.[91] African American leaders, including those in the church, encouraged self-help through the initiation of Black-owned businesses to lessen the dependence on those owned by white people. By the 1920s, the Black Belt regions became almost exclusively African American as those within its areas intentionally separated themselves from white Chicago, creating a self-sufficient "Black Metropolis."[92]

Andrew and Ida moved to Chicago in 1923 and were married on August 9, 1923.[93] Whether Nix moved his family to Chicago to better their opportunities or to accept a position as pastor is not known. The Nix family lived at 2075 Ogden Avenue in the 18th Ward,[94] sharing a house with another family of eight[95] (most likely in a separate apartment), approximately five miles from Bronzeville, an important hub in the Black arts movement in the South Side of Chicago. Andrew's brother, William, lived at 719 42nd Street in the heart of Bronzeville.[96] A *Chicago Defender* article from 1910 described the activities of the main thoroughfare of Bronzeville known as "the Stroll": "With the coming of real summer weather 'The Great Light Way' [State Street] has blossomed forth in all its glory. From 26th street south it has become the popular promenade for the masses and classes. . . . From the merry-go-round in an open lot to the pretentious summer garden at 53rd street it is one continuous round of fun. It is the poor man's paradise."[97]

Despite Bronzeville being "the second largest Negro city in the world," it was subjected to segregation similar to that in cities of the South.[98] Bronzeville, as an all-Black community contained within a racial boundary, was a small universe within itself, consisting of diverse class structures of "acceptables" and "shadies." With the lower class in the majority, it became known as a center of prostitution, gambling, and illegal hustling.[99] Although Andrew and Ida were both conservative in their values, demonizing alcohol consumption, jazz, and the blues, the lively atmosphere of Bronzeville must have greatly impacted their understanding of city life. The *Chicago Defender* regularly advertised the activities on the Stroll in a column titled "On the Stroll by Ace," which described the "worldly" atmosphere that Andrew and Ida tried desperately to avoid. Ace described the "things I see . . . [including] a girl, whose color is rich chocolate and whose bright red hat gives her a saucy air, swings smartly along on high-heeled shoes," continuing, "Buster had been doing a little bootlegging and he was pretty smart about his comings and going. But finally police got on to him and chased him as he emerged from a flat with a gallon of alleged 'corn' under his arm."[100]

The people and activities on the Stroll, besides "saucy" girls and bootlegging, included jazz and theater, with over a thousand professional entertainers— more than "the combined states of Louisiana, Mississippi, and Tennessee, where the blues and jazz were said to have originated."[101] Thomas A. Dorsey played piano at the clubs on State Street at the same time Andrew and Ida were likely avoiding such establishments. Notable jazz and blues artists such as King Oliver, Jelly Roll Morton, Bessie Smith, and Louis Armstrong set up shop in Chicago, as did record companies that advertised in the *Chicago Defender*.

Andrew and Ida had four of their five children in Chicago: Andrew Jr. (1923–2011), Theophilus (1925–2008), Genester (b. 1928), and Elwood (b. 1930). While in the Chicago area, Nix pastored two churches: Second Baptist Church at 436 S. 13th Avenue in Maywood, Illinois, and Mt. Olive Baptist Church in

Figure 1.9. Parsonage in Maywood, Illinois, where Genester Nix was born.

Chicago.[102] At Second Baptist Church in Maywood, Nix conducted revivals, increased church membership, and "built a $7000 brick parsonage and almost paid for it before he left" (Figure 1.9).[103] He also initiated the remodeling of the interior and exterior of the church building. During his tenure, more than eighty new members were added. At Mt. Olive Baptist Church, Nix reportedly "saved the church property and secured the deed for the church building."[104] Newspaper articles called Nix a "national evangelist," even before he started recording sermons.[105] Thus, he apparently was building a name for himself as a singing-preacher, which may have been one reason Vocalion chose him to record on its label.

Between 1927 and 1931 while in Chicago, Reverend Nix recorded fifty-four sermons for the Vocalion label. Recordings would allow for opportunities of mass exposure to the public via the medium of new phonograph recordings and their accompanying advertisements. This exposure also created the potential for additional income for the recording artist. Despite the increased income Nix may have accrued through his recordings, Genester told me she remembers her father mentioning his losses in the investments that he had made.[106] The Great Depression swept away most acquired income for thousands of people during this time, so it is likely that Nix could have lost those earnings because of the stock market collapse. The recording industry was also seriously affected by the Great Depression, which could have been an impetus for the

Nix family to leave Chicago. Therefore, it is unremarkable that Nix stopped recording his sermons in 1931. The Depression forced many record labels out of business, and recordings were no longer as profitable as they once had been.[107] Nix, presumably aware of the Depression's widespread devastation, probably would have gone where work and income were secure.

NIX'S POST-1931 LIFE

Although this book focuses primarily on Nix's life in Chicago in the 1920s when he recorded his sermons, his two surviving adult children, Genester and Elwood, were not born until 1928 and 1930, respectively, and have only a faint memory of their father's early life. They discussed with me their lives in the 1930s and 1940s, and I felt it necessary to add their memories of their father shared in the interview process.

In 1931, the Nix family moved to Cleveland, Ohio, where Reverend Nix pastored the New Light Baptist Church. The fifth child, daughter Verolga (1933–2014), was born in Cleveland. At New Light, the church membership increased from forty members to 150.[108] The family returned to Pittsburgh when Nix was recalled to the ministry at Tabernacle Baptist Church, serving in 1935–1936 to "finish his work there."[109] While under the leadership of Nix, Tabernacle's membership doubled, and the church building was remodeled. By 1938, the church building could accommodate more than three thousand people; however, the new building caught on fire and burned to the ground, leaving the congregants without a church building. Because of the devastation of this event, Nix, overcome with emotion, moved his family to New Jersey to live with his wife's father and stepmother for a brief respite. He took a break from pastoring and instead worked in a factory. However, in the fall of 1939, Reverend Nix's preaching and singing caught the attention of the congregation of Mt. Zion Baptist Church in Philadelphia on Erdrick Street, leading to his acceptance of the pastorate there in March 1940.

Philadelphia is where the Nix children grew up. They were all very close and were raised in a strict conservative environment. As preacher's kids, PKs as they were called, they were forbidden from going to movies, playing cards, dancing, or going to parties. Of course, alcohol was strictly forbidden, and neither Andrew nor Ida partook of it. These activities were "of the world," that is, "part of the world—what the sinners were doing out there in the world."[110] Blues and jazz music were "of the world" because they were considered music of the devil, and this music led to dancing, which led to girls being close to boys and then, ultimately, to sexual relations. Thus, blues and jazz were strictly forbidden, and only religious music was allowed to be played on the family phonograph or radio. The Nix family listened to jubilee groups, quartet gospel groups, Mahalia Jackson, and the Ward Singers, for example.

The Nix family children were all required by their mother to play a musical instrument in school, and the three youngest children also sang in church together. Nix's daughter Verolga, who was a talented pianist, started the Intermezzo Choir in 1967, which is still in existence today (under new direction after her passing).[111] Verolga was also coeditor of the *Songs of Zion* hymnbook, published in 1981, a significant hymnal on par with Richard Allen's 1801 hymnal and the *Gospel Pearls* of 1921.[112]

Although their upbringing was strict, on Saturdays Reverend Nix and the children would play dominoes or checkers together. Nix hummed while he played and was a fierce competitor in board games. Sundays were church day, with a total of five services throughout the day: 9:00 a.m. Sunday school, 11:00 a.m. Sunday service, 3:00 afternoon church, 6:00 p.m. Baptist Young People's Union (BYPU), an opportunity for teenagers from twelve to eighteen to socialize, and then night church. The Sunday service could last for two to two and a half hours if "things got spiritual," as Genester said. The 3:00 service was an opportunity for the intra-church organizations to celebrate anniversaries, such as the pastor's anniversary, the choirs' anniversaries, ushers' anniversaries, and so forth. If Nix's church did not have an afternoon service, the family would accompany him to other churches where he would preach as a guest minister.

The church provided a safe haven from the temptations and the sinners that were what Genester called "out in the world." It was the source of most of the activities of social life for the African American community, including the Nix family. The church was the center of the community and often educated its congregants about social issues, including racism, which, as Genester explained, was "because they wanted us to understand what the whites were doing to us. And we learned black history in the church because the schools didn't teach it."[113] In the African American communities of Philadelphia in the 1940s, education about Black leaders such as Frederick Douglass came from the church. The young people were particularly interested in Black leaders, who were the focus of much discussion.

The Mt. Zion church is situated in an area of Philadelphia called Holmesburg, which at the time, was "out in the country."[114] Genester said she remembers that the sidewalks were not paved and that people had to walk in the street, "like you were down South. It was weird growing up. . . . They acted country-like. They worked in factories, and they did not think about furthering their education. High school was their limit." Class relations in the environment of Holmesburg were not strictly economically oriented. Although much of the congregation at Mt. Zion was not poor, Genester said "their mindset was not geared toward progress" and they were used to accepting the limitations that came along with racism and second-class citizenship. She claimed, "There wasn't much of anything to be, other than factory workers, because out there where we lived, there was nothing to do, nothing to strive for. There wasn't anything that showed them that they could strive for higher things." She remembered her neighborhood as strictly middle-class with no elite or "high falutin'" people living in close proximity.

Reverend Nix wanted to help the people, and because his travels had exposed him to much of the nation, he knew, according to Genester, "what could be, what was out there."[115] His goal was to "educate and to build them up so that instead of working menial jobs, they would strive for better, to be something better than just factory workers." As a result of Nix's desire to bring out his congregants' potential, Andrew and Ida became active in the church, forming a junior church in which young people acted as deacons, trustees, and members of the junior choir. He also brought in seminary students from the nearby theological schools, providing them the opportunity to preach before a live congregation. He entrusted the young people with responsibility and involved them "in working in the church and what the church was like and [what] Christianity was like and that it wasn't just a building where you come hear the grownups take charge and [then] you go back home."

Nix's vision of education included not only the encouragement of higher education for his congregants, but also setting a good example by being college-educated himself and by sending each of his children to college. Although Nix was college-educated, he never distanced himself from his working-class congregants but rather welcomed people of all classes to his church, treating all people with importance. As Genester said,

> He would call all the men "professor." He would sit on his porch at times and anyone coming down Erdrick Street he would have a hearty hello for them. He even made the drunks feel like somebody, so much so that whenever they would see him, they would apologize for their condition, and he would talk to them about it. This happened to the extent that many of them became saved.[116]

Reverend Nix believed in formal education and promoted the values of education to his children and his congregation alike.

Nix also believed that home ownership was a necessity and encouraged his congregants to purchase their homes. In an interview, Genester boasted, "When we came to Philadelphia and he became pastor of Mt. Zion, everybody rented. Nobody owned a home. My daddy was way ahead of his time. He got the folks together; called the meeting of the members and everything. And he would discuss ownership, home ownership." She added that the Nix family was one of the first Philadelphia Black families to own a home and go to college: "He was for education, and he was for being a part of the community—leadership, voting."[117]

Reverend Nix provided for his family in a way that satisfied their needs and created a feeling of prosperity and fulfillment in their lives. When they first moved to Philadelphia, they rented a home until Nix found a house to purchase.[118] According to the 1940 Philadelphia census, the Nix family rented a house at 233 Coulter Street, which was divided into apartments rented by four other families, including several boarders.

Renting rooms or entire floors to boarders was a common occurrence for African Americans in the early twentieth century. For example, after the influx of thousands of migrants from the South to fill job vacancies in the industrial centers of Chicago in the pre-World War I era, housing shortages became a way of life. The Black populated areas became overburdened as more African Americans struggled to find adequate housing. Black residents were often forced to stay within the confines of the neighborhoods of the Black Belt as racial tensions flared among white residents, who frequently turned to violence in objection to the influx of Black migrants in white-designated territories. Renting available space to boarders allowed the principal renter, such as Nix, to earn additional income and was sometimes the only option for new migrants to find available living quarters.[119]

The 1940 census lists Nix as having worked for only half of the preceding year, earning a meager $300 for twenty-six weeks of work.[120] However, the Nix portion of the rent was $32 per month, equaling $384 per year. He probably earned substantial (unreported) income from travelling to other churches around the country to conduct revival meetings or rented rooms to boarders for additional income. The incomes of the other residents on Coulter Street and the adjacent W. Earlham Terrace were between $240 per year (houseman) to $2900 (executive director), with the average yearly salary totaling $910.[121] Most of those on the census were working-class African Americans and are listed as having employment as waiters, housemen or servants in private homes, porters, chauffeurs, domestics, truck drivers, or school teachers.[122] However, Genester remembered that they "were middle class" and "didn't know anything about being poor." So regardless of the family income and their class status, Reverend Nix had the mentality of success and accomplishment, which he imparted to his family and congregation. All the Nix children attended college on his pastor's salary; several earned graduate degrees, and many went on to accomplish major feats in their fields, including owning their own businesses, becoming lawyers, or working in higher education.

Nix's philosophy of self-help also aided in reducing Mt. Zion's mortgage to $6,000 through his keen negotiations with the Fidelity Mortgage Company.

Genester said she remembers that her father had learned Hebrew while in college and negotiated in Hebrew with the Jewish broker, influencing the reduction of the mortgage. The remaining $6,000 debt was raised by church members through a combination of fundraisers such as plays, dinners, and other programs. In addition, Reverend Nix persuaded the local tavern owner to contribute to the church fund hundreds of dollars that congregant members had spent on alcohol at the establishment.[123] While at Mt. Zion, Nix's leadership led to improvements of the church, including a remodel of the interior and installation of a two-manual organ as well as liquidation of the $19,000 debt.[124] Furthermore, Nix created opportunities for ministerial students from Lincoln University to preach before the congregation at Mt. Zion.[125]

Music was an essential part of Mt. Zion, with multiple choirs participating in the music offerings. Hymns were the standard repertoire for the congregation, usually those from *Gospel Pearls* and the *Baptist Hymnal*. Sheet music of gospel songs, including those by Thomas A. Dorsey, was occasionally purchased from the local Theodore Presser music store for use in the church. The congregation of Mt. Zion participated in the traditional aspects of Black church music, such as shouting, verbal interjections, hand-clapping, singing, and swaying back and forth. The only musical accompaniment was provided by piano or organ and sometimes tambourine. Genester described the church as being an "emotional" church in which none of the music was "straight," but was "jazzed up." Reverend Nix was the inspiration for the congregants through the emotional delivery of his sermons. He "got you all riled up and you had to stand and clap and 'hallelujah' and all that."[126] There were many "fiery" preachers at this time who preached fire and brimstone sermons that often caused a lot of "crying and hollering and falling out," she said. Although Andrew Nix was Baptist and many of the old-line established Baptist churches in Chicago in the 1920s preferred a nondemonstrative or mixed style of worship that incorporated hymns similar to those found in white churches, Andrew kept alive the traditions usually associated with the Holiness and Sanctified storefront churches of the working class, which included hand-clapping, shouting, and body movement. Even Nix's son Elwood compared his father's vocal and preaching style to the Pentecostal tradition, exclaiming, "Instead of being Baptist now, I think he would be Pentecostal," adding, "They [traditional preachers] really hollered and screamed and shouted."[127]

Genester described her father as a heavyset man who "loved to eat," often in the company of church members whose dinners he frequented. He died on January 10, 1949, from an internal hemorrhage of the small intestine and is buried in Fairview Cemetery in Philadelphia (Figure 1.10). His death came as a shock to the church community.[128]

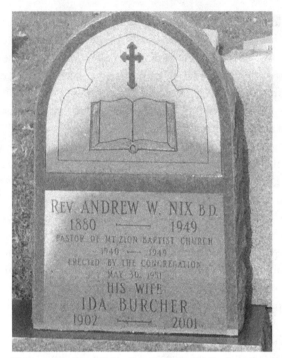

Figure 1.10. Tombstone for Rev. Andrew W. Nix and Ida Burcher. Photograph by Terri Brinegar.

ANDREW NIX, WILLIAM NIX, AND THOMAS A. DORSEY

Just two years after the Chicago riots, in 1921, both Andrew and his brother, William Jr., attended the National Baptist Convention in Chicago, which was held that year September 7–12. It is at this convention that the famous gospel music composer Thomas A. Dorsey expressed his enthusiasm for the singing of William's "I Do, Don't You?" The confusion between brothers Andrew (A. W.) Nix and William (W. M.) Nix has been prevalent in the scholarship, with practically every mention of each brother clouded in erroneous information. Scholars have often misidentified which brother sang at the 1921 National Baptist Convention, an event ultimately leading to Thomas Dorsey's initial conversion and his first gospel compositions.[129] Some have even viewed William and Andrew as the same person. Even Thomas Dorsey was confused about the two brothers and who sang at the convention, remarking that it was either "A. W. Nix, or if it wasn't him it was his brother. There was two Nix[es]. One was a great singer and then one was a preacher."[130]

One key source of the confusion between the two Nix brothers and which of them actually influenced Dorsey at the 1921 convention is Michael W. Harris's book, *The Rise of Gospel Blues: The Music of Thomas Andrew Dorsey in the Urban Church*. Harris correctly credits William Nix as the singer who inspired Thomas A. Dorsey to write gospel music; however, Harris states that it was "the sudden notoriety of the sermon records of the Reverend W. M. Nix (listed as 'A. W. Nix' on recordings), the singing evangelist who inspired Dorsey at the 1921 National Baptist Convention."[131] According to Harris, A. W. Nix's recorded sermons inspired Dorsey to seek like-voiced singers to represent his songs after his second conversion experience. Harris proceeds with an in-depth analysis of Andrew Nix's recorded sermons, treating the two brothers as the same person, believing that the sermons are actually by William Nix, rather than Andrew Nix. Another key source that has led to years of misrepresentation of Andrew Nix is Paul Oliver's *Songsters and Saints: Vocal Traditions on Race Records*. Oliver claims that A. W. Nix was from Birmingham, Alabama, was a miner and a piano player, sang "I Do, Don't You?" at the 1921 convention, recorded in New York, and was a man "with considerable wisdom, if little formal education."[132] In fact, Andrew was a minister from Texas who did not play piano, recorded in Chicago, and had a college education with two degrees. These two sources have led to numerous other sources' providing incorrect information. One of the purposes of this chapter is to rectify these misconceptions.

It matters who influenced Dorsey at the convention for the simple purpose of setting the record straight for future researchers by distinguishing between the two brothers and giving proper credit where it is due. Combining archival research with an analysis of the two brothers' vocal styles helps in correcting these misconceptions. While William's voice did contribute to Dorsey's first conversion and initial gospel compositions, Andrew's voice likely stood as the exemplar of African American vocal traditions after Dorsey's second conversion and subsequent success as the main progenitor of the new gospel composition style. The traditional "down-home" qualities of the voice of Andrew (A. W.) Nix, as heard on his recorded sermons, demonstrate the sonic qualities of the southern Black minister-singer that Harris claims Dorsey sought to represent in his songs.

Thomas A. Dorsey originally was a blues pianist who went by the names of Georgia Tom and Barrelhouse Tom and recorded songs with a guitarist called Tampa Red. The duo of Georgia Tom and Tampa Red had several big hits in the 1920s with their style of "hokum" blues, which were blues songs with sexually suggestive themes. One song, "It's Tight like That," was such a huge hit that several versions of the song were recorded.[133] The song catapulted Dorsey to fame and fortune, bringing his name into the national spotlight. Dorsey, as Georgia Tom, made a living playing in Chicago, performing and recording with some of the greats in the blues such as Gertrude "Ma" Rainey. Dorsey's blues background played a pivotal role in the development of his gospel style and compositions, which were initially inspired by William Nix's singing at the 1921 National Baptist Convention.

William Nix was born only one and a half years earlier than Andrew and was also a preacher and singer; hence, the confusion between the two brothers is understandable. Even Andrew's daughter Genester claimed that it was her father who inspired Dorsey due to Andrew's constant singing of "I Do, Don't You?" around the house. In a personal interview, Genester emphasized to me the distinction between the two brothers by describing her father, Andrew, as a preacher who sang and her uncle, William, as a singer who preached.[134] William had already established a reputation as a singer by 1920, as is evident in an article from the *Chicago Defender* advertising an upcoming concert, in which he was described as "one of the most powerful gospel singers in the country today.... this man is rated among the best evangelistic singers, and there is no doubt but that he will come up to all press reports, and will give the full house the thing they will be expecting."[135]

Despite the confusion between the two brothers, the minutes of the 1921 National Baptist Convention clearly distinguished between Andrew and William, their titles, and the roles they served at the convention. William was addressed as "Professor Nix" and called a "national evangelistic singer," while Andrew Nix was identified as "Rev. A. W. Nix, D.D." The 1921 National Baptist Convention minutes listed both brothers as pastors: William in Chicago (without a specific church, probably because he sang more than he preached), and Andrew in New York at Mt. Moriah Baptist Church. While Andrew served on several boards of the convention, William conducted devotionals and sang. William and Andrew were clearly distinguished in the minutes as holding separate duties and responsibilities at the convention.

The 1921 convention is significant because it is the year the music committee of the Sunday School Publishing Board of the National Baptist Convention, of which William was a board member,[136] published its first songbook, *Gospel Pearls*.[137] Musicologist Eileen Southern considers this hymnal to be of great historical importance and at the same level of excellence as Richard Allen's 1801 hymnal, *A Collection of Spiritual Songs and Hymns Selected from Various Authors*.[138] The "Spirituals" section of *Gospel Pearls* contained multiple songs arranged by brothers John Wesley Work and Frederick J. Work, who were notable contributors to the field of Black music: John Work led the Fisk Jubilee Singers and in 1915 published *Folk Songs of the American Negro*, and the Work brothers together published *New Jubilee Songs as Sung by the Fisk Jubilee Singers*.[139] They both served, alongside William Nix, on the music committee of the Sunday School Publishing Board, which published *Gospel Pearls*. William's name, listed as Prof. W. M. Nix, is clearly written after the two names of the Work brothers on the title page. Every song that William sang at the convention was from *Gospel Pearls*; hence, he was obviously promoting the new hymnal and performed the songs as a marketing device to bring attention to the musical material. The convention minutes listed "Prof. Wm. Nix, the popular evangelist," as singing "I Am Going Through, [Jesus]," "I Do, Don't You?," "Throw Out the Life Line," and "Take Your Burden to the Lord and Leave It There."[140] According to the minutes, William's singing of "I Am Going Through" "thrilled the convention."[141] The preface to *Gospel Pearls* used William's name to market the songbook as "a boon to Gospel singers, for it contains the songs that have been sung most effectively by . . . Prof. Nix . . . and other prominent singers."[142] *Gospel Pearls* thus established William Nix as a "prominent singer," making it apparent that he was already well known in 1921 for his singing abilities, not his preaching skills.

Thomas A. Dorsey also attended the National Baptist Convention in Chicago in 1921. It was here that Dorsey heard William Nix's performance of "I Do, Don't You?" and exclaimed: "My inner-being was thrilled. My soul was a deluge of divine rapture; my emotions were aroused; my heart was inspired to become a great singer and worker in the Kingdom of the Lord—and impress people just as this great singer did that Sunday morning."[143] Dorsey was so impressed with William's performance that it "led virtually to his conversion,"[144] inspiring Dorsey to write religious music. Dorsey claimed, "The thing that sold the song ["I Do, Don't You?"] was the personal pronoun, *I*; Nix made it [the song] popular at the Convention." However, I contend that it was more than the use of the pronoun "I" that inspired Dorsey. It was the way William Nix inflected the notes with "turns and trills"—improvisatory embellishments not written into the music. Dorsey claimed William's voice was unique because of his use of "turns and trills, [that] he [Nix] and a few others brought . . . into church music. Hymn singers, they couldn't put this stuff in it. What he did, I wouldn't call blues, but it had a touch of the blue note there. Now that's the turn and the feeling that really made the gospel singers."[145] William Nix's use of embellishments may have been more than the standard use of improvisation in religious music and was what "thrilled" both Dorsey and the convention attendees.

Dorsey's commentary on William's voice not being a blues voice implies that William was using vocalizations, such as melismas and embellishments, not characteristically considered a part of the blues idiom in the 1920s. Dorsey said, "All the blues pretty near sound alike unless you got a rare voice and put turns and trills in it."[146] William apparently was one of those rare voices. He changed the basic melody of "I Do, Don't You?" into an improvised and embellished version.

No recordings of William's voice exist, so the only evidence we have of what his voice sounded like is Dorsey's remembrance of it. The song "I Do, Don't You?" that William sang at the convention was clearly embellished and contrasted with the original printed version of the song. The original version of "I Do, Don't You?," by E. O. Excell, is a simple melody in 6/8 time with a range of an octave, and would be relatively easy for the average church congregation member to follow. Dorsey's instrumental version of William's interpretation of the song, transcribed by Michael Harris, altered the simple, written version of "I Do, Don't You?" into an improvised version that added sixteenth-note runs between notes (melismas), flatted thirds ("blue" notes), and appoggiaturas and altered the rhythmic values throughout. The improvisatory changes made to "I Do, Don't You?" by William Nix give evidence of his technical abilities and his possible voice type. He apparently sang melismas with ease and most likely was not a "shouter," as Andrew was. Although improvisation was standard for the singing of Black sacred music, Nix's use of embellishments was surprising and unique for both Dorsey and the convention.[147]

William's voice, according to Dorsey's description as not what he would "call blues," was either somewhat light with a clear vocal timbre or implemented a lighter mechanism to manipulate the notes, add embellishments, and sing in a style that we could possibly describe as R&B or contemporary gospel with its fast-moving embellishments and runs. In contrast, Andrew's voice was heavy, and in all of the recordings on which he sang, he never added vocal embellishments in this manner. It is doubtful that he would have been capable of "turns and trills" by the sheer weight and volume of his voice and his consistent use of a gravelly timbre.

An analysis of Andrew's voice provides evidence of his vocal characteristics, revealing a clear distinction between his voice and William's voice. Andrew's voice, as heard in "Hush, Hush, Somebody's Callin' My Name," in his recorded sermon "It Is a Strange Thing to Me" was heavy and with relatively few embellishments, "turns," or "trills" and had a gravelly timbre (Musical Example 1.1). In the recording, Andrew sang the basic melody without the addition of melismas, blue notes, or embellishments, and the notation of his singing looks quite different from the descriptions of William's embellished singing. Thus, the differences between William's and Andrew's voices are sufficient in themselves to know that it was William, not Andrew, who inspired Dorsey's first conversion and his initial gospel compositions.

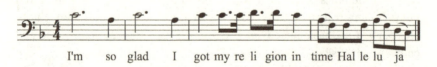

Musical Example 1.1. "Hush, Hush Somebody's Callin' My Name" in "It Is a Strange Thing to Me," (2:54–3:02), recorded June 29, 1927, on Vocalion (Vo 1125), reissued on Document Records (DOCD-5328).

DORSEY'S SECOND CONVERSION

In addition to the confusion as to which brother influenced Dorsey at the 1921 National Baptist Convention, Harris again confuses the two brothers by analyzing the recorded sermons of Andrew Nix, believing that he and William were the same person. If Dorsey was seeking a melismatic voice like William's for his gospel singing style, then the question remains why Harris would analyze the blues-like voice of Andrew. Harris knew Dorsey had been inspired by William's singing at the National Baptist Convention and obviously did not understand that there were two Nix brothers, each with differing talents and voices. However, it is not known if Dorsey—after his second conversion—was indeed searching for a voice similar to Andrew's or if Harris simply confused the two brothers' voices.

In August 1932, Dorsey experienced a monumental tragedy in his life when both his wife and newborn died in childbirth. This tragedy impacted him so severely that he experienced his second conversion in which he decided to devote his life entirely to God and gospel music composing, abandoning his previous blues career.[148] After writing several sacred songs, he realized that he needed a voice to sing and market his songs to the public.

Dorsey realized, through trial and error, that the right singer needed to possess a voice that was not sweet or high-class, such as the voices he had worked with previously.[149] In other words, Dorsey sought a voice that could produce not only melismas and embellishments similar to William Nix's, but "a voice similar to the ones known for singing gospel songs—the itinerant evangelistic singer or the blues artist."[150] Dorsey was apparently looking for a voice rooted in tradition. He himself claimed that he wanted to "get into the gospel songs, the feeling and the pathos and the moans and the blues."[151] The implication is that Dorsey sought a voice that could wail, moan, and cry—vocal characteristics associated with not only the blues of the 1920s, but also with the folk spiritual and chanted sermon of the antebellum era. Andrew Nix may have "provided Dorsey," writes Harris, "floundering with his spiritual blues—a salient link between his downhome and gospel blues," serving as the example of the traditional vocal elements Dorsey needed to find success with his gospel compositions.[152]

Dorsey was an expert and experienced blues musician who knew through experience what the blues sounded like. Despite Dorsey's opinion that William's voice was not what he would "call blues," and the voice on the recorded sermons by Andrew had blues qualities, there is an obvious misinterpretation of whose voice is on the recordings. Dorsey's lifelong experience in the musical world afforded him numerous opportunities to hear and work with a multitude of professional singers, including the greats such as Ma Rainey, granting him familiarity with many styles of Black singing. What Dorsey was seeking in the right singer was most likely not a unique singer such as William, but a traditionalist in the style of Andrew, whose voice had the qualities that Dorsey deemed appropriate for his gospel compositions—a voice type that was familiar to the Black folk and one that expressed Black vocal traditions.

Although I have not been able to confirm that Dorsey actually heard Andrew's voice on recordings of sermons or in church services, it is likely that their paths did cross. Elwood Nix claimed that "whenever Thomas Dorsey could go to hear him [Nix] preach, he would." Elwood remembered, "Tommy Dorsey said to him [Nix] one time, 'You almost as famous as I am.' My father responded to Dorsey with 'I'm striving to get there.'"[153] Genester Nix also remembered that "his name [Dorsey's] had been spoken so much in the house," and that Nix and Dorsey were friends.[154] Other reasons point to the possibility that Nix and Dorsey knew one another. Both Dorsey and Andrew lived in Chicago at the same time: Andrew from 1923 to 1931, and Dorsey from 1916 until his death there in 1993.[155] Nix lived only three and a half miles from State Street where Dorsey often performed.[156] Dorsey travelled from church to church attempting to market his songs, and possibly ventured into Andrew's church and heard him preach. Andrew was the only Black Baptist minister in Chicago whose recordings were commercially successful,[157] thus again suggesting that Dorsey may have heard his recordings; and most importantly, both Dorsey and Nix recorded on the Vocalion/Brunswick label in the Chicago Brunswick studios on November 1, 1930.[158] Because their sessions were back-to-back, they probably encountered each other in the studios. In addition, Andrew recorded three sermons that were titled identically to Dorsey's songs, all released on Vocalion: Nix's "The Dirty Dozen, Part 2" based on Dorsey's "The Dirty Dozen No. 2," both recorded in June 1930 (exact dates unknown); Nix's "Jack the Ripper" (March 28, 1931) with a title similar to Tampa Red and Georgia Tom's "Jack 'The Ripper' Blues" (January 15, 1931); and Nix's "It Was Tight like That" (ca. February 18, 1930) based on Dorsey's very successful "hokum" blues composition "It's Tight like That" (October 8, 1928). The lyrics to Dorsey's version, although tame by today's standards, were risqué for their day (partial lyrics):

Chorus

You know it's tight like that, beedle um bum
Boy it's tight like that, beedle um bum
Oh you hear me talking to ya,
I mean it's tight like that

There was a little black rooster met a little brown hen
Made a date at the barn about a half past ten

Chorus

I went to see my gal all across the hall
Found another mule kickin' in my stall

Blues music, and especially blues sung by Black female performers, was considered a part of "low" culture, associated with the sexuality of the working class. Although Andrew demonized blues and jazz for their connections to "the world" (i.e., the world of sin),[159] he still recorded his sermon of "It's Tight like That," in 1930, with text that reflected on the hardships caused by the Great Depression, not sexual themes. It is possible that Nix was inspired to record a sermon with the same title as Dorsey's blues song because of a friendship with Dorsey.[160] Lastly, Dorsey, as Georgia Tom, accompanied blues singer Victoria Spivey on several of her recordings. Spivey also recorded on Vocalion and had a leading role in the film *Hallelujah*, which also featured a version of Reverend Nix's sermon "Black Diamond Express to Hell." Therefore, it is possible that Dorsey, Spivey, and Nix were at least familiar with each other.

Whether or not Dorsey and Andrew Nix were friends, acquaintances, or simply knew of each other is a moot point. What is more significant is Dorsey's search for a voice that offered vocal traditions familiar to African American churchgoers. Possibly Dorsey was aware of Andrew's voice and was inspired by it. For Dorsey, a voice with heavy vocal weight was the key to his success. Dorsey claimed that a successful voice must possess the quality of being

> a heavy voice. If you want to make a good blues singer, the texture of the voice, the heavier the voice, woman or man, the better the blues. If you goin' to be a good gospel singer, the choice of texture of the voice is heavy. The heavier the voice, the better singer you make.[161]

Dorsey claimed that once he realized the importance of a heavy voice, he found the "right" singer to sing and, ultimately, market his songs. Initially, Dorsey had hired Louise Keller, but soon realized that she was not the right choice because she "sang in the 'hymn style; she was one of them high-class singers—had a lovely voice.'"[162] The significance of the association of the hymn style and vocal "sweetness" with high-class standards and aesthetics demonstrates the divisions between what was considered vocally appropriate or suitable for the working class associated with rural southerners and the middle class associated with northern urbanites, many of whom chose to assimilate to vocal aesthetics associated with white churches. Thus, a "sweet" voice, usually associated with classically trained voices in the Western European style, was deemed to be detrimental to the marketing of Dorsey's songs. Instead, he needed a voice similar to Andrew's that was heavy and employed the traditional or "down-home" characteristics of Black vocalisms, which included not only blue notes and improvisation but also moaning, shouting, and chanting. Dorsey's ultimate choice for a singer was Rev. E. H. Hall, whose voice, according to Harris, had the "same quality and impact as Nix's."[163] Hall was a singing preacher in the Baptist tradition who was able to captivate an audience with a style and quality that could not only stir the congregants' emotions, but also inspire them to extemporaneously improvise in response to his lead, as Andrew did on his recorded sermons.

The traditional vocal and performative qualities of Hall, apparently similar to those of Andrew Nix, were able to "authenticate" Dorsey's gospel songs.[164] The voice alone served as the carrier of African American traditions, inspired by both William Nix and possibly Andrew Nix, which opened the door to Dorsey's success. Therefore, the evidence from the 1921 National Baptist Convention minutes and analysis of Andrew's and William's voices make clear their distinctions and influences on Dorsey: William's melismatic voice influenced Dorsey to start writing gospel music and was the catalyst for his first conversion; Andrew—possibly a friend or acquaintance of Dorsey—may have influenced Dorsey after his second conversion and his search for a voice rooted in tradition. The voice of the folk preacher may have thus served as an influence on and a precursor to Dorsey's initial gospel compositions and the larger genre of gospel music as a whole.

HALLELUJAH

In addition to recorded sermons on phonographs, which will be discussed in more detail in the later chapters of this book, one of Andrew Nix's sermons was featured in the sound film *Hallelujah*, released by Metro-Goldwyn-Mayer (MGM) on August 20, 1929, and directed by white film director King Vidor (his real name). The film featured actress Nina Mae McKinney (1912–1967) in the leading role and blues singer Victoria Spivey (1906–1976) in a supporting role. The film is significant for several reasons: first, it was the first all-Black film produced by a major Hollywood studio; second, it featured a recreation of Nix's "Black Diamond Express to Hell"; third, like Nix's phonograph recordings, it propelled Black vocal traditions into the modern age via new technologies; and fourth, the film inspired McKinney to record on two of Nix's sermons.

Nina Mae McKinney made a total of fifteen films between 1929 and 1950, *Hallelujah* being her first.[165] She became "the first love goddess of color" and a "trailblazer" through her depiction of "black-as-beautiful."[166] She was sometimes called the "Black Garbo" and the "Dusky Clara Bow," both names referring to white sex symbols of the 1920s. Irving Berlin wrote two songs for *Hallelujah*: "Swanee Shuffle" and "The End of the Road," both of which were used in the nightclub scene of the film. McKinney was only sixteen when she starred in *Hallelujah*, achieving great success as a result of the film and her performance. She travelled to Chicago to play the wanton female character in two of Nix's sermons, the fifth and sixth parts of "Black Diamond Express to Hell," just eight months after the release of *Hallelujah*. In the sermons, she portrayed a similar character to her film character, that of the hardened sinner.

Hallelujah is truly a modern marvel in that it was one of the first sound films that featured not only audio of spoken dialogue, but also traditional Black voices in secular and sacred contexts. Director King Vidor filmed on location in Tennessee and Arkansas and featured African American musicians, including the Dixie Jubilee Singers and Curtis Mosby's band, the Blue Blowers, performing in scenes in nightclubs, riverside baptisms, religious revivals, and church services. While the film showcased African American actors and musicians, it was obviously trying to appeal to both Black and white audiences through a balance of authentic realism and stereotypical depictions.

The film included other examples of traditional Black voices with the inclusion of folk spirituals such as "Git on Board, Little Chillen," sung by the lead character, Zeke, and "Swing Low, Sweet Chariot" and "Old-Time Religion," sung by the group. According to film critic Donald Bogle, King Vidor asked ordained Black ministers for their advice on an accurate representation of African American culture.[167] Vidor consulted culture-bearers and attempted to recreate the songs and singing of Black voices as performed in the Black church service. In this sense, the film is similar to the hybrid nature of Nix's recordings that carried the voices of tradition into the modern era via technology.

According to Judith Weisenfeld, sound films "would finally allow black actors to appear on the screen in dignified ways," shifting the focus from the physical body, which was often portrayed as the comedic "fool," to the voice and sound. She adds, "Those critics who focused on the ability of the talking pictures to provide a showcase for African American culture also hoped that the new technology would necessitate the end of blackface performances in film, imagining that 'black voices' would require actual black people."[168]

African American audiences gave the film mixed reviews. For example, Earl A. Ballard, a "race writer," commented that "it is a flagrant and misleading mockery of the race's religion. Some say it is blasphemous and had any other race been involved, never would have passed the Board of Censors."[169] Another "well known Harlem leader" claimed that *Hallelujah* portrayed "the group as moral morons and religious barbarians."[170] John T. Sherman, a writer for the *N. Y. News*, stated, "King Vidor of Texas has revealed only the worst and most discreditable phases of levee, slum and backwoods life in the picture. There is a cultured, respectable devout christian [*sic*] progressive life there which Vidor probably never saw."[171] Some appreciated the attention to Black actors being featured in leading roles in a major Hollywood film, while others felt Vidor had presented stereotypical images that perpetuated racist myths, such as Uncle Tom figures and the hypersexualized Black male. The "shouting" in the praise house scene was also criticized. However, the film's musical director, Eva Jessye, defended the expressions in the shouting scene:

> There has been a lot of bitter comment on the part of Negroes concerning this "shouting" scene. Many foolishly contend that it was exaggerated. Many say that it is a reflection upon the race. Opinions may differ, but facts are facts. That shouting scene is a mild duplication of what takes place nightly in many Negro churches. I was raised up among shouters and have seen that very thing in my hometown, Coffeyville, Kansas, with my own relatives leading the gyrations. You can see shouting equally uncontrolled in certain churches in New York city—so why pretend?[172]

The praise house scene in the film incorporates vocalizations in which the practitioners cry out in wails. Eva Jessye described the cries that were uttered by "a spare, black woman of fanatical countenance."[173] She explained, "When the 'shout' began, she let loose a cry that was the most hysterical, savage sound I have ever heard. It was startling." If this scene was indeed a presentation of a 1920s church service as it was typically executed, then we have audio evidence of the vocalizations, including cries, moans, and wails, re-created in the film. A short clip of this scene demonstrates moans, wails, shouting, and the "wild waving of arms," as Du Bois may have experienced in the late nineteenth century.[174]

The wails, as vocalized by the mother in the film during the "wake" scene, are high-pitched scoops with the range of a fifth or more. As shown in the transcription, some of the pitches scoop up to a short note; others are held longer and scoop back down (Musical Example 1.2). According to Bogle, the "wails are part of the symphony that King Vidor orchestrated" in that they were intentionally added to bring the element of authenticity to the film.[175] Du Bois reviewed the film in *The Crisis*, praising it for its depiction of Black life, yet stated, "The music was lovely and while I would have preferred more spirituals instead of the theme-song [by Irving Berlin], yet the world is not as crazy about Negro folk songs as I am."[176]

The film featured the struggles between rural and urban life and between sacred and secular activities that Andrew Nix often depicted in his sermons.

Musical Example 1.2. Wails as heard in *Hallelujah* (43:08–48:38), directed by King Vidor (Metro-Goldwyn-Mayer, 1929), DVD (Warner Brothers Entertainment, 2013).

Figure 1.11. Victoria Spivey. "'Hallelujah' Ingénue! Celebrated Blues Singer and Phonograph Artist." From the *California Eagle*, April 12, 1929, 11.

Nix portrayed city life as one of sin, which included sinful women and jazz music. *Hallelujah* featured exactly that: McKinney as the sinful city woman who takes advantage, both sexually and financially, of the rural farmer. The jazz scene in the film is portrayed as a den of transgressions with live music, gambling, dancing, singing, and sexuality. McKinney sings and dances and swindles Zeke out of his family's earnings for the entire year of toiling in the fields. Blues singer Victoria Spivey (Figure 1.11) plays, ironically, the pious female to whom Zeke returns. The two female stars represent two sides of a coin: McKinney as the sinner, Chick, an urbanite who participates in gambling and the reckless lifestyle in jazz bars; Spivey as the religious woman, Missy Rose, a rural country girl, who is faithful to both her religion and love. The symbolism is overt. Nix utilized these themes repeatedly in his sermons.

Figure 1.12. Rev. Nix and Nina Mae McKinney. From "The Reverend Nix, Creator of the 'Black Diamond Express,' presents Nina Mae McKinney with a Bible on Her Revent [sic] Visit to the Brunswick Recording Laboratory," the *California Eagle*, May 18, 1930, 10.

Numerous scholars have debated whether the revival scene in the film (at 55:15) was based on Nix's recorded sermon "Black Diamond Express to Hell" or on a similar train-themed sermon by Reverend J. M. Gates, "Death's Black Train Is Coming." An article in the *California Eagle* (1930) reliably confirmed that Reverend Nix was indeed the inspiration for the revival scene of *Hallelujah* and that McKinney's familiarity with the sermon influenced her portrayal of a "wanton woman" in Nix's two sermons: "Through her familiarity with the 'Black Diamond Express,' as used in the revival scene from her recent picture 'Hallelujah,' Miss McKinney was able to inject into the recording a degree of realism which, according to Harry Kruse a Vocalion sales manager, is going to make of it the outstanding record of the year."[177] Apparently, McKinney was familiar with "Black Diamond Express to Hell" prior to her role in *Hallelujah*. An accompanying photograph of Nix presenting a bible to McKinney at the Brunswick/Vocalion studios in Chicago (Figure 1.12), presumably from their recording session on April 8, 1930, presents further evidence of their professional relationship.

The revival scene in which the film adaptation of "Black Diamond Express to Hell" is featured shows the lead character, Zeke, performing a soft-shoe dance, emulating the sounds of the train in his sermon about the "Cannonball Express." This type of dance, called "sand tap-dancing," was made popular by Bill "Bojangles" Robinson and, according to Bogle, was representative of the rhythmic aspect of 1920s preaching.[178] The rhythmic and chanting style of the sermon by Zeke represents King Vidor's idea of the origins of the chanted sermon:

> When the slaves were brought to America, they brought their strange chants with them, and so ingrained were they that they were a sort of second nature. The "blues" partake of this form of music. Then, introduced to the white man's religion, the negro fitted his chants to it, and in doing it often preserved a trace of the white man's hymns. These are the spirituals, one of the oddest and most haunting forms of music. The negro is a natural singer. He will toil along the levees or in the cotton fields, talking to himself in a sort of native chant, improvising as he goes along. He will do this by the hour.[179]

Zeke "travels" through several stops of the train and announces to the rural people at the revival to "get on board" to have their souls saved. Zeke urges "some of you bootleggers, and some of you gamblers," to "take hold of Faith," the first city on the Cannonball Express's stop to hell. Chick, McKinney's character, responds tearfully with "don't leave me." The references to bootleggers and gamblers, as well as Chick's pleas of "don't leave me," all refer to exact textual references in Reverend Nix's sermons, implying that they may have influenced both McKinney in her future recordings with Nix and King Vidor's screenplay of this scene. Ironically, Daniel Haynes, who played the character of Zeke, "was for a short time an itinerant preacher and revivalist, tramping from one town to another throughout the Southern States."[180] Another character, Parson Johnson, played by Harry Gray, was an eighty-six-year-old formerly enslaved person who did not learn to read or write until he was thirty-five.[181] Both Haynes's experience as a travelling minister and Gray's life in slavery brought authority to the film's portrayal of authentic, traditional voices.

Nina Mae McKinney became so popular in *Hallelujah* and subsequent films that she was featured in skin-lightening advertisements[182] and in gossip columns. In the June 29, 1929, issue of *Chicago World*, she reportedly "wouldn't have Stepin Fetchit, no sir. She wants a man that gives a fifty-fifty break, must shovel it home and not always use the rake. Must not always want the best go and 'sweetbacks' haven't even got a show, Hot Ziggety!"[183] She became the glamorized ideal woman for her light skin, her beauty, and her sexualized persona as represented in *Hallelujah*, and presumably, her vocal presence would have been a huge asset to the popularity of Nix's recordings. McKinney's spoken dialogue in Nix's sermons created a physicalized embodiment of the sinful urban woman that he often condemned. In the sermons, Nix successfully converted her from a life of sin to one of salvation. The characterizations of McKinney in *Hallelujah* and in Nix's sermons are almost identical.

For Ace's column in the *Chicago Defender*, he interviewed Black audience members who suggested that they would have preferred to have "seen a picture wherein the dark actors were garbed in fine clothes and drove big cars, and made love in lavish settings, or, in other words, conducted themselves much as their fairer brothers." Ace asked, "Why should that be? Has the American of color no individuality? Is not this 'Hallelujah' picture an important contribution to American art? It certainly records faithfully a small drama of Race life which all of us know is highly plausible, and it does it in a sympathetic, yet vivid, manner."[184] The comments by the audience members suggest that they would have preferred not to be reminded of the visual and aural past, including "Negro spirituals," but rather to be represented as sophisticated and wealthy, similar to white and elite Black people. Their desires hearken back to the New Negro's desires for equality via a rebranding of the image of Black lives (and Black voices).

According to Ace, Vidor specifically did not "show how much progress the Race was making, or how well they imitated the white man," so as not to offend "The South, the hypocritical, Race-conscious South." Instead, Ace claimed, Vidor attempted to portray "Race folk doing things that are generally conceded to be indigenous to them: such as . . . singing spirituals . . . [and] seeking God in churches with much loud shouting," without the presence of a white person in a single scene. Ace explained that while the film did not do well in the South due to the racist mindset there, "A series of scenes unroll without once aping anything that the white man does, except, perhaps, the very poor 'cracker' down South, and even the upper class whites in 'Bam [Alabama] scarcely consider him in the human category."[185] In Ace's opinion, Vidor avoided portraying Black characters as racial caricatures of white life, as was done regularly in blackface minstrelsy. However, Vidor was not entirely successful in his musical representations of "authentic" Blackness—Vidor did include two songs written by white Tin Pan Alley composer Irving Berlin that were meant to emulate the folk "feel" of the film. Although there were various criticisms of *Hallelujah*'s representation of the Black folk and their music, the film and its actors provided re-creations of folk performances and religious scenes to the public that would otherwise have remained segregated in private spaces. The film also propagated the sounds and themes associated with Reverend Nix's recorded sermons, providing an alternate form of the dissemination of traditional Black voices.

In Table 1.1, I have included a complete discography of Nix's recordings, so that the reader may observe the breadth and scope of his sermons.

Table 1.1. Discography of Rev. A. W. Nix							
Order	Date Recorded	Title	Matrix Number	Record Number	Biblical Text	Song Included	Background Voices	Theme
1	April 23, 1927	"Black Diamond Express to Hell—Pt. I"	C810-1 E22740-1 E5056-57	Vo 1098 Me M12545 DeE F3850, F9720	Matthew 7:13		5 women*	The Black Diamond Express Train. Sinners on the way to hell on the train. Nix condemns drunkards, liars, deceivers, conjurers, confusion-makers, and fighters. Themes of temperance and behavior.
2	April 23, 1927	"Black Diamond Express to Hell—Pt. II"	C812-3 E22742-3 E5058-9	Vo 1098 Me M12545 DeE F3850, F9720		"My Sins Been Taken Away"	5 women*	More sinners on the Black Diamond train: dancers, gamblers, thieves, plotters, parkers. Aligned with Victorian morals and uplift.
3	April 23, 1927	"Goin' to Hell and Who Cares"	C814-5 E22744-5 E5068-69	Vo 1108 Spt S2240	Matthew 25:46	"I Got Mah Swoad in Mah Han'"	5 women*	If you're a sinner, nobody's going to care if you die. Jesus cares for all the sinners. Sinners: liars, drunkards, "loose" women, gamblers. Short story on Jesus' resurrection.
4	April 23, 1927	"Hiding Behind the Stuff"	C816-7 E22746-7 E5070-71	Vo 1108 Spt S2240	Samuel 10:21–22	"Nowhere to Hide"	5 women*	Story of Jonah and the whale. You can't hide from God. Jonah tried to hide from God and got swallowed by the whale.
5	June 29, 1927	"The White Flyer to Heaven—Part 1"	C1000-1-2 E6166-7-8 E24088-89-0 E7137-8-9	Vo 1170 Br 7020 Spt S2252 Ba 33284 Me M13251 Or 8410 Ro 5410 Pe 0306	Matthew 7:14	"O the Blood"	5 women	The White Flyer train to heaven. Stops at Mount Calvary where Jesus was on the cross.

Order	Date Recorded	Title	Matrix Number	Record Number	Biblical Text	Song Included	Background Voices	Theme
6	June 29, 1927	"The White Flyer to Heaven—Part II"	C1003-4-5 E6169-70-71W E24091-92-93 E7140-1-2	Vo 1170 Br 7020 Spt S2252 Ba 33284 Me M13251 Or 8410 Ro 5410 Pe 0306		"Look for Me"	5 women	The White Flyer train on its way to heaven. Reference to the hymn "Amazing Grace."
7	June 29, 1927	"The Seven Rs"	C1006-7 E6172-73	Vo 1125	Luke 15:18	"When the Saints Go Marching In"	5 women	Story of the Prodigal Son returning home.
8	June 29, 1927	"It Is a Strange Thing to Me"	C1008 E6174	Vo 1125	John 3:9	"Hush, Hush, Somebody's Callin' My Name"	5 women	The story of Nicodemus and his actions are a strange thing, but we can learn from them.
9	June 30, 1927	"The Prayer Meeting in Hell"	C1017-8 E6175-6	Vo 1124	Luke 16:23		5 women	Story of Lazarus: the poor man vs. the rich man who ends up in hell where it is too late to repent.
10	June 30, 1927	"After the Ball Is Over"	C1019-0 E6177-8	Vo 1124	Matthew 14:6		5 women	Story of Herod's ball at which Salome dances and then asks for the head of John the Baptist.
11	October 12, 1927	"Mind Your Own Business (A New Year's Sermon)"	C1295/96 E6730-31	Vo 1143 Spt S2247	1 Thessalonians 4:11		5 women*	Mind your own business. Biblical references.
12	October 12, 1927	"Death Might Be Your Christmas Gift"	C1297/98 E6732-33	Vo 1143 Spt S2247			5 women*	Christmas message: death may come at any time, even on Christmas, so be prepared.
13	October 28, 1927	"Watch Your Close Friend"	C1299/300 E6755/56W	Vo 1149	Judges 16:18		5 women*	Story of Samson and Delilah. Can't trust anyone, not even your best friend. Only trust Jesus.

Order	Date Recorded	Title	Matrix Number	Record Number	Biblical Text	Song Included	Background Voices	Theme
14	October 28, 1927	"Deep Down in My Heart"	C1301/02 E6757/58W	Vo 1149		"Deep Down in My Heart"	5 women*	Religion is a love deep down in your heart.
15	January 11, 1928	"Generosity" (unissued)	C1430/31	Vo Unissued			N/A	N/A
16	January 11, 1928	"Throwing Stones" (unissued)	C1432/33	Vo Unissued			N/A	N/A
17	January 18, 1928	"Your Bed Is Too Short and Your Cover Too Narrow"	C1565/66 C6977/78W	Vo 1159 Spt S2253	Isaiah 28:20		5 women	You need a solid foundation on which to stand: Jesus. You can't cover up your sin from God. Mentions the "lodge" as an excuse for men to lie to their wives and stay away from home.
18	January 18, 1928	"The Matchless King"	C1567/68 C6979/80W	Vo 1158	Revelation 19:16		5 women	Compares Jesus to other great figures in history: Socrates, Plato, Napoleon, Hannibal, Moses; but Jesus is the only one who is "matchless."
19	January 18, 1928	"Three Boys in a Strange Land"	C1569/70 C6981/82W	Vo 1159 Spt S2253	Daniel 3:17		5 women	Biblical story of Nebuchadnezzar and his golden idol and the refusal of Shadrach, Meshach, and Abednego to bow down to it.
20	January 18, 1928	"Your Time Is Out"	C1571/72 C6983/84W	Vo 1157	Genesis 7:1		5 women	Story of Noah and the ark and the destruction of the world. Find Jesus before it's too late.

Order	Date Recorded	Title	Matrix Number	Record Number	Biblical Text	Song Included	Background Voices	Theme
21	January 18, 1928	"Robbing God"	C1573/74 C6985/86W	Vo 1157	Malachi 3:8		5 women	By avoiding church and not tithing or participating, you are robbing God. Some Biblical references. Nix mentions the theater as "robbing God" and mentions "old-time religion" as the remedy.
22	January 18, 1928	"Done Found My Lost Sheep"	C1575/76 C6987/88W	Vo 1158	Luke 15:6	"Done Found My Lost Sheep"	5 women	For the sinner who's wandered away, come back and we'll take you in (like a lost sheep). Bible parable. Mentions "leaders" as in politicians.
23	January 18, 1928	"Deep Down in My Heart" (unissued)	C1563/64 C6975/76W	Vo unissued			N/A	
24	January 18, 1928	"Generosity" (substitute for test recordings on 1/11/1928)	C1577 C6989W	Vo 1156	Luke 6:38		5 women	Be generous and give to the church because you reap what you sow. Some people tight-fisted with the church. Nix mentions the lodge, sport, and worldly pleasures.
25	January 18, 1928	"Throwing Stones" (substitute for test recordings on 1/11/1928)	C1578 C6990W	Vo 1156	John 8:7		5 women	Story of Jesus and those who wanted to stone the prostitute. Don't throw stones as they did.
26	October 26, 1928	"Begin a New Life on Christmas Day—Part I"	C2479 A-B	Vo 1217			5–7 women*	Begin a fresh new life on Christmas, change your ways, stop sinning, and turn over a new leaf. Nix discusses couples living together, gambling, and bootlegging.

Order	Date Recorded	Title	Matrix Number	Record Number	Biblical Text	Song Included	Background Voices	Theme
27	October 26, 1928	"Begin a New Life on Christmas Day—Part II"	C2480 A-B	Vo 1217		"What a Great Change Since I've Been Born"	5–7 women*	Christmas message (continued). Themes of gambling and alcohol consumption.
28	October 26, 1928	"Hang Out Your Sign"	C2481 A-B	Vo 1247	Luke 2:12		5–7 women*	The "sign" you wear reveals who you are on the inside, so wear a sign from God, not from the devil. Nix gives advice on basic things and discusses modern dresses of women and women as "loose."
29	October 26, 1928	"Sleeping in a Dangerous Time"	C2482 A-B	Vo 1247	Jonah 1:6		5–7 women*	Wake up and pay attention to what's going on around you and in your home and in your family. Nix discusses daily life: roomers in one's house, lodge meetings, women as "loose," and infidelity.
30	August 24, 1929	"The Black Diamond Express to Hell—Part 3"	C4158 A-B	Vo 1421			7 women	The Black Diamond Express Train. Nix discusses immoral and dishonest women, murderers, and hypocrites on their way to hell. He encourages chastity and financial responsibility.
31	August 24, 1929	"The Black Diamond Express to Hell—Part 4"	C4159 A-B	Vo 1421		"Hide Me Over in the Rock of Ages"	7 women	The Black Diamond Express Train (continued). Nix discusses women's fashions as too sexy and causing temptation to men.
32	August 24, 1929	"Love Is a Thing of the Past"	C4160 A-B	Vo 1431			7 women	Love isn't what it used to be; now people just use each other and don't marry for love. Nix discusses bad women and marriage/family.

Order	Date Recorded	Title	Matrix Number	Record Number	Biblical Text	Song Included	Background Voices	Theme
33	August 24, 1929	"That Little Thing May Kill You Yet (Christmas Sermon)"	C4161 A-B	Vo 1431	James 3:5		7 women	Christmas message: little habits, such as drinking and lies, might be your undoing and downfall.
34	December 12, 1929	"What's Wrong with the Church Today?" (missing track)	C4925 A-B	Vo 1548			N/A	N/A
35	December 12, 1929	"You Got the Wrong Man"	C4926 A-B	Vo 1448			5–7 women*	Slow down and take your time, so you won't end up with the wrong man. Nix discusses marriage, family, bad women, and women who can't cook.
36	December 12, 1929	"You're Flirting with Death" (missing track)	C4927A C4928 A-B	Vo 1548			N/A	N/A
37	December 12, 1929	"A Country Man in Town"	C4929A-B C4930A	Vo 1448			5–7 women*	Rural people don't know how to handle themselves in the big city and get manipulated by city women. Discusses pig meat and hog meat, country people, "loose" women, and class associations.
38	Mid-January 1930	"Who Dressed You Up for Easter"	C5196 A-B	Vo 1470			5 women*	Easter message: dress up for Easter, clean up, take a bath, and take on a new life. Nix discusses bad women.
39	Mid-January 1930	"Pay Your Honest Debts"	C5197 A-B	Vo 1470			5 women*	Pay your debts, don't buy on credit, don't buy what you can't afford, and don't borrow and not repay. Nix discusses financial responsibility, drinking, and gambling.

Order	Date Recorded	Title	Matrix Number	Record Number	Biblical Text	Song Included	Background Voices	Theme
40	Mid-January 1930	"Some Folks Don't Know What They Want"	C5198 A–B	Vo 1659			5 women*	People are never satisfied with what they have.
41	Mid-January 1930	"The Fast Life Will Bring You Down"	C5199 A–B	Vo 1659			5 women*	Slow down or the fast life will kill you.
42	February 18, 1930	"It Was Tight like That"	C5523 A–B–C	Vo 1505			5–7 women*	Great Depression has brought hard times to many. You should have prepared for these hard times. Religion is fine, but you need real practical solutions. Nix discusses financial responsibility and "loose" women. He uses long words such as "gastronomical propensities."
43	February 18, 1930	"How Long—How Long"	C5524 A–B–C	Vo 1505			5–7 women*	How long will you continue with bad behavior, cheating on your wife/husband, sexual debauchery in the church, and women bickering? Nix discusses "loose" women, lodge meetings, corruption in the church, and preachers who sin.
44	April 8, 1930	"The Black Diamond Express to Hell—Part 5"	C5584 A–B	Vo 1486		"Free at Last"	1 man and 7 women* + McKinney	The Black Diamond Express Train. Nix discusses "high-class" sinners, those with money on their way to hell, "scientific gamblers," and streetwalkers. He tries to convince Miss Hard-Boiled to stop sinning.

Order	Date Recorded	Title	Matrix Number	Record Number	Biblical Text	Song Included	Background Voices	Theme
45	April 8, 1930	"The Black Diamond Express to Hell—Part 6"	C5585 A-B	Vo 1486		"Come and Go with Me to That Land"	1 man and 7 women* + McKinney	The Black Diamond Express Train (continued). Say goodbye to all the sinners who are now leaving for hell.
46	June 20, 1930	"The Dirty Dozen—No. 1"	C5868 A-B	Vo 1526			5–7 women*	Lowdown men: the alcoholic, the wife beater, the gambler. Nix discusses moral responsibility.
47	June 20, 1930	"The Dirty Dozen—No. 2"	C5869 A-B	Vo 1526			5–7 women*	The Dirty Dozen (continued). More lowdown men and women. Nix discusses deceit, infidelity, lack of self-respect, and chastity.
48	c. June 20, 1930	"You Have Played the Fool"	C5870 A-B	Vo 1542			5–7 women*	Nix discusses chastity, infidelity, wife abuse, financial responsibility, dishonest preachers, and drunkards.
49	c. June 20, 1930	"Too Much Religion"	C5871 A-B	Vo 1542			5–7 women*	Too much of anything, even religion, is not good. Nix discusses laziness and humility.
50	November 1, 1930	"How Will You Spend Christmas?"	C6468 A-B	Vo 1553 Spt S2242			1 man + 5–7 women*	In these hard times during the Great Depression, nobody has money, and people are hungry. Religion is okay, but money is necessary. Save your money. Nix discusses financial responsibility and drinking.
51	November 1, 1930	"Slow This Year for the Danger Signal"	C6469 A-B	Vo 1553 Spt S2242			1 man + 5–7 women*	Slow down, pay attention, and stop living the fast life. Nix discusses drinking, "loose" women, and modern dresses.

Order	Date Recorded	Title	Matrix Number	Record Number	Biblical Text	Song Included	Background Voices	Theme
52	November 1, 1930	"There's Something Rotten in Denmark"	C6470 A–B	Vo 1578			1 man + 5–7 women*	Be aware and pay attention to things that don't appear "right," such as infidelity. Denmark quote is from Shakespeare. Nix discusses family responsibilities, infidelity, chastity, patriarchal family, and morals.
53	November 1, 1930	"You Low Down Rascal" (missing track)	C6471 A–B	Vo 1578			N/A	N/A
54	March 28, 1931	"Jack the Ripper" (missing track)	VO153 A–B	Vo 1609			N/A	N/A
55	March 28, 1931	"Hot Shot Mamas and Teasing Browns" (missing track)	VO154 A–B	Vo 1609			N/A	N/A
56	March 28, 1931	"Strange Things Happening in the Land" (missing track)	VO155 A–B	Vo 1634			N/A	N/A
57	March 28, 1931	"Downfall of Man" (missing track)	VO156 A–B	Vo 1634			N/A	N/A

Note: In the Background Voices column, the asterisk (*) signifies those tracks that are an approximation based on my listening; for the others, the number of voices is reported in Ross Laird's *Brunswick Records: A Discography of Recordings, 1916–1931*, Vol. 3: Chicago and Regional Sessions (Westport, CT: Greenwood Press, 2001). Laird had access to many of the actual file cards for Brunswick and the notes included therein. In the Record Number column, abbreviations of record labels are as follows: Vocalion (Vo), Melotone (Me), Decca-British (DeE), Supertone (Spt), Brunswick (Br), Banner (Ba), Oriole (Or), Perfect (Pe), and Romeo (Ro).

Chapter 2

CLASS DIVISIONS DURING THE MODERN ERA

The period from approximately 1880 to 1920, which is known as the modern era, effectively and legally disenfranchised African Americans by taking away the rights they had acquired during the Reconstruction period.[1] For example, from the 1870s to the turn of the century, African Americans' representation in Congress declined from sixteen Black members to zero; organizations such as the Ku Klux Klan emerged to assist white Southerners to regain control of their states; African Americans became victims of brutal violence and were often targeted simply for attending school or financially advancing; lynchings increased in the South; and whites instilled "Black Codes," such as literacy tests, to ensure that African Americans would lose their right to vote. In addition, Jim Crow laws kept the races separate, and the Supreme Court legalized segregation as "separate but equal" in *Plessy v. Ferguson* in 1896.

In this hostile environment, visual and musical representations publicly demeaned African Americans. Blackface minstrelsy depicted Black people as lazy and ignorant, reinforcing prejudices of working-class white people who feared for their jobs as a result of increased Black migration to industrialized cities in the North. White actors painted their faces black using burnt cork and performed "comedic" musical skits that showed African Americans in demeaning representations. The first decades of the twentieth century were also a period of racial turmoil, which included race riots in multiple US cities, including Reverend Nix's hometown of Longview, Texas, and his adopted city of Chicago, Illinois.[2]

Nix's perspective as a southern migrant—who left Texas and moved to New York and Chicago to create a better life for himself—was probably similar to the thousands of other migrants who expected the North to be a safe haven and a chance for new opportunities. However, many issues came to affect the lives of African Americans during the 1920s: North-South and urban-rural dichotomies, "highbrow" and "lowbrow" forms of musical expression, the Great Depression, the creation of the "New Negro," artistic expression during the Harlem Renaissance, and new technology that produced race records and recorded sermons. Ideas varied by class on how best to uplift African Americans, especially new migrants such as Nix.

In order to understand the 1920s, it is necessary to understand what came before. Thus, I begin with a brief discussion on the meaning of tradition, the importance of vocal traditions, the emergence of the modern era, and the dichotomies of old versus new in terms of thought, musical expression, and church affiliations. I focus on class divisions during the modern era, beginning with a discussion of Black Chicago churches, followed by a brief discussion of the elite artistic expressions of the "New Negro" during the Harlem Renaissance, and how both attempted to uplift African Americans through an association with highbrow art forms. I focus on the issues that were in direct correlation with Nix's sermons and thus evident in his life.

TRADITION

The word "tradition" is frequently intertwined with the idea of the folk, who can be understood as "the people sharing the common culture of a nation."[3] Ethnomusicologist Philip V. Bohlman explains that the folk created music that reflected the conditions of their lives, allowed them a literal and figurative voice, and expressed their culture and heritage, which resulted in the "invention of tradition."[4] In the United States, the enslaved population (Black folk) created their own music and sermons that reflected their values, their conditions, and their own cultural identity. For this book, I am concerned with the African American vocal practices that emerged during slavery and became conceptualized as Black folk traditions.[5]

In performance practices, tradition in itself is an abstract idea that exists in the mind of performers and their audiences, with the performance itself an opportunity to re-create the experiences and feelings associated with the tradition.[6] No prescribed sets can determine the meaning of tradition; rather, tradition is contingent upon the many experiences that are shared by cultural groups as expressions of their particular perspective. In other words, there is not an "authentic" practice at the root of any tradition. Rather, the ideas of tradition in folk performance adhere to shared customs, habits, and shared values.[7] Tradition is therefore a cultural construct, in that people choose which practices have value for them based on their ideas of how these practices represent their lives and their ideas about themselves. By repeatedly choosing certain practices, groups create canons that come to represent who they are. They then can claim ownership of these practices: "These are *our* traditions." Eventually, these practices are conceptualized as having existed forever, although they have been, in fact, constructed, based on the continual and repetitive choices of the group. Naturally, cultural groups choose those practices that represent what they believe are the most significant practices and integral to group identity.

Vocal traditions can serve as indices of one's culture and include verbalized as well as nonverbalized sounds, such as moans, cries, and shouts.[8] For enslaved individuals, oral sounds, more than visual texts, were important markers of tradition. As individuals generally excluded from the literate world, they relied on the oral transmission of songs and tales to give credence to their world and existence.[9] Thus, the *sound* of the voiced word, rather than the *written* word of texts, became identified with African American vocal traditions. The voice was important for not only communicative purposes, but also spiritual experiences.

The importance of the voice in slave culture provides a window into a world that placed high value on the religious experience. Spiritual conversions demonstrated one's death and rebirth and were often instigated by the hearing of the voice of God or some other spiritual entity. As spoken by one enslaved American, "I kept praying till I heard a voice. A voice told me, 'I've chosen you before the dust of the earth.' . . . I heard a voice, 'If I call you through deep water, it won't cover you; if I call you through fire, come on.'"[10] Common conversion experiences included seeing light, travelling through the air as if in flight, visiting heaven or hell, or meeting demons or angels, but most usually concluded with a voice affirming protection against all odds and often encouraging the person to pursue preaching and spread the message of God. Another enslaved person said a voice told him, "You are born of God. My son delivered your soul from hell, and you must go and help carry the world. You have been chosen out of the world, and hell can't hold you."[11] The phrase "God struck me dead" was used to describe the conversion experience, in which one felt deep inner feelings of joy and acceptance.[12] The voice itself became the means by which to achieve salvation, not just in death, as had been sung in many of the spirituals and preached by slave preachers. For enslaved African Americans, the voice offered the promise of protection and instilled a new awakening and meaning to life. Although the sounds of specific voices are unknown, the power the voice held over those converted provided an intuitive, inner, God-given experience that rejected intellectual effort or works. The hearing of a voice is one sign that conversion has occurred.

Theologian Henry H. Mitchell explains that God uses the voice in singing, praying, and preaching to supply one's experiential encounter and that "worship, especially the sermon, is under the control of the Holy Spirit, which is how the gift is given and not earned."[13] Mitchell's theory is an example of the practice of antinomianism, in which faith alone is necessary for salvation, not moral laws or works. The intuitive nature of the preacher, who is guided in his sermon by Spirit, draws upon deep emotional feeling, rather than intellectual words, to appeal to his congregation through his voice. Mitchell contends,

"The sermon that fails to reach the emotion fails to reach the very heart of faith. . . . The preacher does not 'use' emotion; holy emotion uses the preacher." Thus similar to the conversion experience, spirit is conceptualized as speaking through the voice of the minister in his sermon.

The conversion process was more important than intellectual learning, with overt emotional expression as a necessary sign of deliverance. The emotionalism of revival camp meetings, beginning in the mid-1700s, appealed to both Black and white believers, and allowed for congregational responses to the preacher's appeals. As Radano explains, among participants, class similarities often trumped racial differences of emotional expressions in religious settings:

> Because the unusual array of behaviorisms present at revivals—seeing visions, hearing voices, dancing to unsung melodies, wailing, shouting, and falling into trance states—had precedents in Europe as well as in Africa, lower-class whites could have engaged in these expressive practices and still considered them 'their own.'[14]

Radano designates ecstatic expressions, both vocally and physically, as a class-based distinction, not necessarily associated with race.

Although attended by both Black and white participants, camp meetings were usually segregated, which allowed enslaved African Americans the opportunity to express themselves freely away from the watchful eyes of white slaveholders and to join together in solidarity. Sometimes thousands of Black and white Baptists and Methodists practiced their faith in open air settings, and free and enslaved African Americans not only participated, but they also served as exhorters and preachers.[15] Revivals in Kentucky drew great crowds and were attended by members of both races, possibly explaining the shared tradition of the chanted sermon in the Black Baptist and the (white) Kentucky Baptist churches.[16] Borrowing between white and Black congregants may have led to the adoption of the chanted sermon by white participants and the adoption of fire-and-brimstone sermon themes by African Americans.[17]

For Baptist and Methodist clergy members, the most significant feature, more than training or education, was the possession of a voluble tongue. Converted enslaved persons with a knack for exhorting were allowed to preach to both Black and white audiences, with some travelling to plantations to minister to enslaved populations. Black Harry (Harry Hosier, Hoosier, or Hoshure), George Liele, and Liele's student Andrew Bryan were all known to be excellent preachers in the late 1700s. With the influx of Black converts attending Baptist and Methodist churches, separate services were often needed to accommodate the swelling number of congregants. Baptist churches allowed for more independence than other protestant denominations, offering Black members more control over their churches and opportunities for conducting business and official church operations, leading to the growth of independent churches after emancipation.[18] The opportunities for self-governance for Black preachers and churches during the slavery era were empowering to those who had no opportunities for authority positions in the white world. Baptist and Methodists were more lax than other denominations, allowing Black freed and enslaved preachers in the 1770s and 1780s to minister to their own people. As a result, these "African churches," as they were sometimes called, many without white supervision, led to separate Black congregations.[19]

The African American minister's voice, as Dolan Hubbard explains, functioned as "the collective voice of his people, who were once 'silent' and absent from the historical realm. Through his speech acts, he provides the vehicle by which the entire community of faith may participate in shaping its own history and in restructuring cultural memory."[20] Because most enslaved preachers were illiterate, they relied on their voices to capture the attention of their congregants and asserted leadership in the early church by embodying charismatic qualities, rather than through Biblical reading. Most used the emotional style featured in the chanted sermon, which stirred these early congregants' feelings, inspiring responsorial interjections of "Amen!" or "Preach it!" similar to those that would be used in Nix's sermons in the 1920s.

The chanted sermon, as a foundational element in Black preaching, may have been originally influenced by the emotional renderings in Puritan sermons by white preachers from New England, such as George Whitefield (or Whitfield) (1714–1770), leader of the Calvinist Methodists. In the 1740s during the beginning of the first Great Awakening, white revivalists, such as Whitefield, took notice of enslaved persons' adherence to their preaching, leading to slave converts preaching their own sermons in the 1770s.[21] African American preachers expressed themselves in "vivid imagery and dramatic delivery," and according to one white traveler, "a habit is obtained of rhapsodizing and exciting furious emotions."[22]

The chanted sermon was also a hybrid mixture of European and African influences. During the religious revival movements, the physicalized expression of the congregants was similar to many African-based religious traditions that include dancing as a means of achieving religious fulfillment through spirit possession. African practices involving spiritual possession may have influenced the chanted sermon through style switching in speech, which acts as "code signaling" that ritual spiritual possession is about to occur. Albert J. Raboteau explains, "the stylistic switch is commonly perceived as a change from order to chaos, from music to noise, or from speech to gibberish. What in fact is really happening is a shift from one type of order to another: from a non-rhythmic to a rhythmic, or rather, increasing rhythmic, performance style."[23] In the same regard, the African American minister switches from conversational prose to rhythmic and tonal chanting, signaling the connection with spirit. In some denominations, such as Pentecostal, speaking in tongues signals the onset of spirit, taking the form of "divine possession," also replicating African rituals. In the African American chanted sermon at the onset of the arrival of spirit, the minister's voice becomes hoarse, gravelly, constricted, and tonal, leading congregants to clap, shout, and sway their bodies, mimicking the ritual activity in many African-based religions.

Raboteau describes the folk sermon as spoken by African American ministers in the 1880s:

> The style of the folk sermon, shared by black and white evangelicals, was built on a formulaic structure based on phrases, verses, and whole passages the preacher knew by heart. Characterized by repetition, parallelisms, dramatic use of voice and gesture, and a whole range of oratorical devices, the sermon began with normal conversational prose, then built to a rhythmic cadence, regularly marked by the exclamations of the congregation, and climaxed in a tonal chant accompanied by shouting, singing, and ecstatic behavior. . . . The dynamic pattern of call and response between preacher and people was vital to the progression of the sermon, and unless the spirit roused the congregation to move and shout, the sermon was essentially unsuccessful.[24]

The early sermons were in a simple language, yet were dramatic and musical. An example of the chanted sermon's early history, in an 1897 article, described

> a member of the [Hampton Folklore] Society who had in early childhood attended many night meetings in the little log meeting-houses in one of the most thickly-wooded counties of Virginia, was able to reproduce verbatim from his own memory, several of the sermons and prayers of the night-hawks, as the night preachers were called. This report was rendered possible by the fact that the same sermons and prayers are used over and over by the same preacher, and that they are *intoned* [italics mine] in such a way as to remain in the memory like a song.[25]

Thus, the evidence shows that the chanted sermon was firmly established by the late 1800s.

The churches that became the most popular in African American communities were Baptist, African Methodist Episcopal (AME), and other Methodist denominations. They inspired their congregations through highly emotional and passionate renderings in their sermons, which allowed for a release of the anxiety felt by Black communities due to racial and economic injustices. The church was the one institution completely within the control of African Americans, although many parts of its ritual were derived from white church practices; yet these were adapted to conform to the particular needs and expressions of Black congregants.[26] However, African American communities were not homogeneous in their preferences for religious styles of worship.

By the post-Emancipation era, some educated African Americans began to express their disdain for the traditional practices of the folk church. In 1870, Elizabeth Kilham, a white woman who visited a meeting of the Freedmen's Bureau that convened at "Old Billy's church" in Richmond, Virginia, wrote:

> The distinctive features of negro hymnology, are gradually disappearing, and with another generation will probably be obliterated entirely. The cause for this, lies in the education of the younger people. With increasing knowledge, comes growing appreciation of fitness and propriety, in this, as in everything else; and already they have learned to ridicule the extravagant preaching, the meaningless hymns, and the noisy singing of their elders. Not perhaps, as yet, to any great extent in the country; changes come always more slowly there, but in the cities, the young people have, in many cases, taken the matter into their own hands, formed choirs, adopted the hymns and tunes in use in the white churches, and strangers who go with the expectation of something novel and curious, are disappointed at having only ordinary church music.[27]

Education and knowledge were viewed as the models of "fitness and propriety," while "extravagant preaching ... meaningless hymns ... [and] noisy singing" of the uneducated were in direct opposition. As education became the norm for the freedmen, the association with traditional forms of vocal and physical behavior in preaching and singing declined. Robert Russa Moton, a Black student who attended Hampton in 1872–1875, argued, "I had come to school to learn to do things differently; to sing, to speak, and to use the language, and of course, the music, not of coloured people but of white people."[28] Moton's comments reflect the growing tendency of some to dismiss Black vocal traditions and to favor instead assimilation to white vocal aesthetics. Harriet Beecher Stowe called the new singing by the assimilationists "solemn, dull and nasal" and went on to describe how the singing of spirituals had gone from an emotional expression to a "more dignified style ... a closer imitation of white, genteel worship."[29]

In addition, traditional Black folk expressions were often demonized for their association with the era of slavery. As mentioned previously, Bishop Daniel A. Payne described the emotionalized practices at a folk church as "ridiculous and heathenish ... [and] disgraceful to themselves, the race, and the Christian name."[30] Payne, as an educated, elite minister, reprimanded the northern freedmen who continued the traditions of their forefathers. His admonitions suggest that any reference to practices associated with the slavery era was "heathenish." Payne most likely attributed the practice of ring-dancing, called the "ringshout," to African practices, in which possession trance through singing, dancing, and drumming manifested the present of spirit.[31] Through the comments by Kilham, Moton, and Payne, we can begin to see the gradual decline and rejection of traditional Black vocalisms by certain segments of the Black community. However, the traditions of the Black folk church that evolved during slavery did continue into the early twentieth century and included emotional preaching, the conversion experience, singing, and shouting. As Raboteau explains, "these traditions helped poor black people to hold onto a sense of value and a degree of hope in a bleak social setting of discrimination, segregation, and racial violence."[32] As migrants moved from the South to the North, they brought their traditions with them, including vocalized traditions.

By 1901, class divisions in Black churches were already apparent. Ernest Hamlin Abbott, a white man who wrote about his visits to Black churches in both the North and the South, described a split in the style and delivery of services, with some churches moving away from emotionalism, typically associated with folk performance, toward quiet services. He described the differing opinions and expressions of the two classes: "those which believe that the emotional character of the negro ought not to be suppressed, but educated and guided; and those which believe that that emotional character should be minimized by the magnifying of the intellectual and ethical."[33] The "emotional character" was also present in the Black preachers and their presentation styles. For example, in a Charleston church, Abbott encountered a preacher who "felt it necessary to spend a good part of his sermon on very plain speaking concerning moral conduct," while an Atlanta preacher delivered an address that was "violent [in] manner." We can assume that Abbott's commentary of a "violent" address implied the speaker's use of vocalized shouts, moans, and other expressive devices known to be common in Black folk churches.

During his research, Abbott encountered W. E. B. Du Bois, who told him "that all such churches give similar evidence of two factors: one, the old-style darkey whose religion is of the hallelujah order; the other, the younger generation who are ashamed of these emotional outbreaks."[34] According to Du Bois, the split was based on generational identity, with the older members affiliating with Black vocal traditions and the youth moving towards assimilation. Abbott's driver, whom he described as "a young colored man of twenty-two," commented "that even in his short experience he had noted an improvement toward quietness and good order." In other words, quietness was equated with progress, which was opposed to shouting and the emotionalism associated with the traditional Black folk church.

One reason for these splits was class hierarchies in which economic and educational levels impacted which type of service one attended. Abbott visited an upper-class Black Episcopal church, which included "regulated appeal by means of the liturgy of the High Church service" (i.e., formalistic rituals), and where the Episcopalian minister informed him that "the fact that the Episcopal Church among the colored people [is] composed of the better-paid and better-educated class made it difficult . . . to reach 'the masses;' for the negroes have very well defined class distinctions among themselves."[35] In other words, the higher class could not (or would not) stoop below their class level to reach the masses. This minister added that, of the white Northerners who were doing charitable work in Black churches, "we want their advice, not because it is white, but because it is right." Abbott revealed that some Black churches chose to imitate the behavior of white churches to "give dignity to the service," believing that the dominant society's ways were what was "right."

The upper-class, educated ministers often associated assimilation as the "social foundation" for African Americans.[36] Thus, the homiletical style of Black ministers coincided with the "sophisticated" music chosen for middle-class churches. Abbott's visit to a Christian Endeavor prayer meeting at a church in Baltimore revealed "its success in imitating the most perfunctorily respectable meeting of white 'Endeavorers,'" which was "almost perfect."[37] Both the music and the preaching styles reflected the greater concern for proper decorum and restraint.

CLASS DIVISIONS IN CHICAGO CHURCHES IN THE 1920S

Traditions that first emerged in the rural South during the era of slavery were carried to both working-class and middle-class churches in northern metropolises by southern migrants, such as Rev. A. W. Nix. The adherence to tradition allowed African American migrants in the North, and specifically Chicago, a sense of familiarity and "home" as reminders of their rural, southern past. In their study of Black life in Chicago during the 1930s and 1940s, St. Clair Drake and Horace R. Cayton Jr. discussed the tendency of the lower class in Chicago's Bronzeville area to adhere to these traditions that originated during the slavery era:

> The prevailing attitude of Bronzeville's lower-class church people is expressed in an old spiritual: "Gimme that old-time religion, it's good enough for me." Drawn into the Baptist and Methodist evangelical

tradition by white missionaries during and immediately after slavery, Negroes have preserved on a large scale the religious behavior which was prevalent on the American frontier between 1800–1890. Since, however, the Negro church has evolved in isolation from the white church, certain distinctive modifications and colorations have grown up which give Negro religious services a flavor all their own. The fountainhead of the old-time religion is the rural South—the Bible Belt.[38]

These "modifications" and "colorations" stemmed from the rural South and entered the urban consciousness through church services of the 1920s and through the recorded sermons by African American ministers like Nix.

Because the new migrants were previously only familiar with rural forms of religion, they encountered "new, difficult, depressing problems" that they were not prepared to solve,[39] according to Rev. L. K. Williams, minister of Olivet Baptist Church, who pastored one of the largest Black congregations in Chicago.[40] In a 1929 *Chicago Daily Tribune* article, Williams concluded that the migrants were not prepared for these problems due to the unfamiliar urban environment and the cultural standards expected of them.[41] The adherence to tradition allowed the migrants a way to acclimate to their new environment while simultaneously holding onto their past.

Booker T. Washington noted the challenges that lay ahead for new southern migrants to Chicago: "When the colored man comes from the South he finds he is face to face with new conditions, as to climate and as to methods of labor. He also finds he is surrounded by increasing temptations. No race under such circumstances, without help and guidance can adjust itself to those new conditions."[42] Aid organizations and social welfare programs, such as the Urban League, supplied migrants with meals, educational programs, and employment assistance.

By the mid-1920s, when thousands of southern migrants had already arrived in northern cities, religion continued as the centerpiece for urban African Americans. A study of Chicago life in the 1930s by the Works Progress Administration (WPA) revealed, "In the nearly eighty years from the date of the establishment of the first Negro church in Illinois [1847], religion was without rival as the leading force and attraction in the life of the race in the state."[43]

The migration also created distinct classes, each with their own religious affiliations. Many of those in the lower class and lower middle class affiliated with traditional forms of worship such as those in which they had participated in their southern Baptist and Methodist churches. Once they migrated to northern metropolises, members of the rural Black middle class of the South were often relegated to the lowest-paying jobs and joined the lower-class churches. The upper middle class and elite class preferred Episcopal, Presbyterian, and

Congregational services, which were "ritualistic and deliberative."[44] The focus of the churches also changed from their "other-worldly" preoccupation with salvation in the afterlife to the everyday conditions of the here and now. This shift is defined as the "secularization" of Black churches because of the shift in attention from spiritual topics to the secular.

Class divisions do not always conform to economic conditions, but can also express social behaviors. Anthropologist Hortense Powdermaker's study of southern life in the 1930s revealed that, for rural southerners, class was based on "adherence to forms of expected behavior and, where relevant, the associated material symbols that they can afford. . . . The mores and patterns of conduct which are taken to represent proper family form, gender relations, female chastity, and male fidelity according to a model of white middle class culture are those that determine the acceptability of Negro individuals of varying economic statuses into the same class stratum."[45] Her study showed that of the three classes that existed in African American communities in the South—an upper, a middle (with borderline divisions into upper and lower), and a lower class—the upper class adopted the largest number of white cultural standards, and the lower class the fewest. Powdermaker included ministers in the middle class, not the elite professional class, because most rural southern preachers did not have much formal education and thus did not adhere to elite class standards. She added, "The main strength of the church is the middle class. Almost everyone in it is a church member. . . . From the middle class as a whole come the 'shouters' and the loud 'amens.'"[46] As previously mentioned, while issues of class are associated with church traditions, no singular mode of expression existed for all working-class African Americans with an opposing mode for those in the middle class. However, class lines were particularly marked in the churches of Chicago during the 1920s.

Class issues had affected church membership in Chicago as early as the late 1800s, with three main groups: the "respectables," who were low- or median-income people who were "unrestrained in their worship"; the "refined," educated people who looked down on the emotionalism of the respectables; and the "riffraff" and "sinners," who did not attend church. Prior to the arrival of southern migrants, Chicago had a handful of churches attended by the "old settlers"—African Americans who lived in Chicago prior to the Great Migration. Between 1900 and 1915, the number of churches doubled as thousands of migrants flooded the city, with most joining Baptist or AME denominations.[47] Reportedly, there were 170 churches in the Black communities of Chicago in the early 1920s, with the number of storefront churches more than twice those of "regular" churches.[48] The Black churches of Chicago provided a safe haven: as one woman described it, "a place where my people worship and ain't pestered by the white men."[49] Even in a northern city such as Chicago, racial violence, segregation, and discrimination were real issues African Americans faced.

The old settlers of Chicago believed that the new migrants, with their "uncivilized" behavior, were diminishing the respectability of all African Americans in the eyes of white observers. The migrants were judged unfavorably by many in the Black middle class and were thought to be the cause of the loss of jobs for those already established. Name-calling was frequent, in which the established settlers accused the newcomers of having poor etiquette, being prone to gambling, begging, stealing, and committing other purported crimes. The *Chicago Defender* offered help to the migrants with words of advice in the form of twenty-seven points on how to acclimate themselves to their new northern environment, which included:

> Don't get intoxicated and go out on the street insulting women and children and make a beast of yourself—some one may act likewise with your wife and children.

> Don't live in insanitary [*sic*] houses, or sleep in rooms without proper ventilation.

> Don't use vile language in public places.

> Don't appear on the street with old dust caps, dirty aprons and ragged clothes.

> Don't throw garbage in the back yard or alley or keep dirty front yards.[50]

Apparently, the established Chicagoans believed that the migrants were uncouth, unclean, and needed to be educated on the ins and outs of "proper" decorum. In this regard, the old settlers of Chicago resembled Du Bois's Talented Tenth, who believed they, as educated and elite leaders, were responsible for the uplift of the masses.

The vocal and musical practices of the African American church in Chicago in the 1920s also included separate practices based largely on class standing. Some churches adopted white performance practices; others continued the distinct performance practices that had emerged in Black churches during earlier periods, essentially choosing the continued segregation of the Black and white churches; and some churches employed practices that mixed elements from both. Robert Lee Sutherland studied the African American churches in the primarily Black residential areas of Chicago during the 1920s and found that most fit within five class-based categories.[51] Another classification of churches was made by Reverend Kingsley, as reported in the WPA's study of Chicago in the 1930s. Kingsley's classification is also grouped into five categories.[52] Both Sutherland's and Kingsley's categorizations can be simplified into three distinct class-based divisions: storefront and "fringe" churches of the lower class; old-line churches associated with the mixed-type church of the middle class; and liturgical and "intellectual" churches of the upper class. Drake and Cayton also used three class divisions:

1. Lower-class churches: Small churches in storefront locations in the poorer areas, uneducated, individual minister. Examples: Holiness, spiritualist, some small Baptist churches. Music consists of the singing of spirituals, interjections by congregation members, dancing, shouting, emotional demonstrativeness.

2. Middle-class/mixed churches ("old-line" churches): The larger Baptist and Methodist denominations in church buildings. Some demonstrative displays to appeal to the old settlers, but the younger congregants prefer subdued services and hymn-singing over spirituals.

3. Elite class/Assimilationist churches: Members and ministers are formally-educated, located in desirable neighborhoods. They meet "white standards" in that there are not emotional outbursts or interjections by congregants, and the music and service are subdued. Singing of "white church" hymns, not spirituals. Examples: Congregational, Presbyterian, Roman Catholic, Lutheran, and Protestant Episcopal.[53]

I also include the category of "hybrid" to discuss Nix's church, which was of a mixed type, but of a different sort than those discussed by Sutherland and Kingsley.

Working-Class/Lower-Class Churches

A study by the Chicago Commission of Race Relations (CCRR) after the 1919 riot revealed that the racial climate created an environment in which African Americans were isolated and felt ignored by the dominant society. The study determined that this environment created an "increasing sensitiveness to slights, and keeping Negroes forever on the defensive. Extreme expressions, unintelligible to those outside the Negro group, are a natural result of this isolation. The processes of thought by which these opinions are reached are, by virtue of this very isolation, concealed from outsiders."[54] As African Americans became more isolated and pushed to the fringes of society, according to the CCRR, their need to express their bound-up emotions increases. An educator interviewed for the post-riot Chicago study noted the importance of singing as a way to alleviate the pressures associated with living a life of social isolation:

> Many white men of high intellectual ability and keen discernment have mistaken the Negro silence for contentment, his facial expression for satisfaction at prevailing conditions, and his songs and jovial air for happiness. But not always so. These are his methods of bearing his troubles and keeping his soul sweet under seeming wrongs. In the absence of a spokesman or means of communication with the whites over imagined grievances, he has brightened his countenance, smiled and sung to give ease to his mind.[55]

Drake and Cayton explained that the lower class,[56] or "lowers" as they were called, was divided into two groups, consisting of "church folks and those families (church and non-church) who are trying to 'advance themselves'" and "the pimps and prostitutes, the thieves and pick-pockets, the dope addicts and reefer smokers, the professional gamblers, cutthroats, and murderers."[57] It is this second group of "shadies" that Nix so often addressed in his sermons. The members who attended church, usually of the Baptist or Methodist denominations, were opposed to gambling, card-playing, dancing, "improper" sexual behavior, and drinking. Reverend Nix's daughter Genester confirmed that her father never allowed these activities in their home. For our purposes here, we will be discussing the churchgoing lower-class members.

Although Baptists ranked as the denomination with the highest membership, a full 65.9 percent of Baptist churches were housed in storefronts in the 1920s, and these structures were typically on the poorest and most undesirable streets of the all-Black neighborhoods on the South Side, called the "Black Belt."[58] Storefront churches, attended by lower-class recent migrants from the South, were predominantly Holiness, Spiritualist, Pentecostal, and some smaller Baptist churches, which exhibited "uninhibited worship [in an] informal atmosphere."[59] The storefront churches, most led by uneducated ministers who preached part-time, were prone to shouting and emotional and uninhibited worship.[60] Southern migrants were unaccustomed to the decorum of the elite and middle-class churches, and instead brought their demonstrative and emotional church practices with them to churches in the North. They also felt more comfortable in churches that were not attended by those more highly educated, including the minister, as is demonstrated by one Chicago woman who had temporarily attended a large, mixed church, but said she "couldn't understand the pastor and the words he used" and complained that

"I couldn't sing their way. The songs was proud-like."[61] Her criticism reflects the attitude toward education of many in the lower class that educated ministers and their "Book learning, while good, is worldly and got nothing to do with being borned of God."[62] A minister in Chicago with less than a sixth-grade education was also known to declare, "God prepares a man to preach; he does not have to go to school for that. All he must do is open his mouth and God will fill it. The universities train men away from the Bible."[63] Contrasting with "manuscript" preachers who write out their sermons, "spiritual" preachers speak when inspired by the word or voice of God, needing no advance preparation, demonstrating their ability to improvise.[64] Nix, while educated, was a spiritual preacher in that he did not write out his sermons but improvised from an outline of the main points.[65]

The Holiness and Pentecostal churches and other "sanctified" churches with low-income congregants typically expressed themselves in emotional outbursts, with "shouts, jerks, dances, and speaking with tongues."[66] While many in the Black community sought to distance themselves from the sounds of the past and turned instead to hymns and arranged spirituals,[67] Holiness churches were prone to spontaneous singing and exhortations, allowing congregants to take up the singing of spirituals during the service, including hand clapping, body swaying, and tambourine playing. Traditional practices also included "rhythmic moans from the congregation, interjections of *Amen*, *Praise the Lord*, and *Hallelujah*," and "getting happy," also known as "shouting," in which congregants would cry, run down the church aisles, or flail their arms wildly.[68] The power of the minister's voice alone could inspire congregants to start shouting. The preachers of Sanctified and Holiness churches often "vocalized their sermons to the point of hoarseness, sometimes evoking a near-scream with their enthusiasm."[69] Zora Neale Hurston quoted one man describing the importance of a strong voice in the Black church: "Dis preacher was a good man, but de congregation was so tough he couldn't make a convert in a whole year. So he sent and invited another preacher to come and conduct a revival meeting for him. De man he ast to come was a powerful hard preacher wid a good strainin' voice. He was known to get converts."[70] Although these traditions were typically associated with Holiness churches, Baptists and Methodists shared some of these traits and would also express themselves with emotional displays, including shouting and "falling out," emphasizing the fact that there were not clear demarcation lines around any one denomination or means of expression. Nix's Baptist church was one of the churches that emphasized ecstatic behavior; however, his church was not in a storefront location but in a permanent, physical building.

The lower-class ministers demonized the upper classes and their ministers just as the upper classes looked down on the lower. A higher-class church member commented, "Religion ceases to be the focus of lower-class life. The vast majority organize their behavior around 'good-timing,' fixing their attention on the cheaper forms of commercial recreation."[71] In contrast, a member of Elder Lucy Smith's All Nations Pentecostal Church, a lower-class church, commented, "I don't like these preachers standing up saying things, and you don't know what they're talking about, all hifalutin'. I like the preaching like we had it down in Alabama."[72] Regarding the music in her church, Smith reportedly claimed, "The singing has a 'swing' to it, because I want people to swing out of themselves all the mis'ry and troubles that is heavy on their hearts."[73] Brother Brown, a Baptist minister of a church in Bronzeville, also criticized the ministers and their music: "They even have all high-class singing and not the old-time soul-stirring songs that furnish the soul with happiness. . . . The larger churches are too high-toned to serve God."[74] In the view of the lower-class congregants, the music associated with Black folk traditions was considered the means to happiness and spirituality, while education and "high-toned" status were deterrents to spirituality.

Among the ministers categorized as lower class were itinerant evangelists, also called "jack-leg preachers." They were typically uneducated, lacked a regular church home of their own in which to preach, often sang or preached on street corners, and were associated with the lower classes of Black society and the Sanctified/Holiness churches. According to Drake and Cayton, only 3 percent of "high-status" African Americans were in favor of jack-leg preachers, while a full 46 percent of storefront church members favored them.[75] A minister in a Congregational church noted that, due to these preachers' understanding of the struggles of the lower class, "The 'jack-leg' preacher fills a need. He may be ignorant and utterly uninformed in the respects that we think a preacher should be trained, but he has a useful role."[76]

Some believed that the emotional and demonstrative behavior of uneducated ministers mimicked minstrel performance. In 1895, African American Methodist minister R. R. Downs wrote of the minister "who turns the house of God into a low class circus or minstrelsy, telling old stale jokes . . . rolling his eyes . . . and to crown it all by having his church christened a theatre by the young people."[77]

Andrew Nix was not an itinerant evangelist due to his educated status and his pastoring of specific Baptist churches with physical buildings. He did often travel to give guest sermons at other churches, even though he had a home base. Nix's church in Maywood, Illinois, included a parsonage where he and his family lived. A jack-leg preacher would have neither a church nor a parsonage. Nix's son Elwood explained that jack-leg preachers were self-made preachers or "deacons one week and ministers the next."[78] Jack-leg preachers, according to Elwood, were not called to preach as ministers were. He believes that ministers often hear "some kind of voice" or "know it and feel it" as opposed to jack-leg preachers who were "just trying to make a buck" and would often sing and preach on street corners, busking for loose change.[79]

Many itinerant ministers were wanderers, similar to renowned bluesmen of the day, who did not have access to economic opportunities or basic education.[80] Because blues music was considered "of the world," many blues musicians concealed their identities on their religious recordings to disassociate themselves from their secular successes. For example, blues musician Blind Lemon Jefferson recorded several religious recordings under the pseudonym of Deacon L. J. Bates, and Charley Patton recorded spirituals as Elder J. J. Hadley.[81] The demarcation lines between sacred and secular genres were often blurred, with practitioners in one genre frequently borrowing practices from the other.

One of the few requirements for becoming a minister of a lower-class congregation was a good voice. The vocal abilities of preachers associated with the lower classes were noted as having power with loud dynamics and the ability to carry over distances, emphasized by shouting. A diatribe from a pastor with formal training emphasizes the power of the voice of jack-leg preachers: "A huckster used to sell vegetables; he used to go down the alley shouting his wares. And one day his wife said to him, 'You sound just like a preacher.' He got the idea, and decided if he sounded that good to his wife he could preach; so he started a church."[82] During the Great Depression, Chicago became home to many jack-leg preachers trying to become established with their own churches or sitting in as visiting ministers. They were familiar with the preaching of established ministers, such as Nix, and may have copied popular sermon themes and vocal characteristics of the more popular ministers in order to establish names for themselves.

Middle-Class/Mixed Churches

The middle class's ambitions included a stable family life, respectability, and economic upward mobility in an effort to "better their condition." Home ownership was of great significance to those who were descendants of formerly enslaved persons and sharecroppers, such as Nix. Education continued to be a symbol of class mobility, especially for those in the lower middle class. Outward manifestations of class were reflected by keeping up "front" through the "right" clothes, home, and club associations. In Bronzeville, these people were called "strivers" and "strainers." Although the lower middle class may not have had the means to do so, they often demonstrated conspicuous consumption— the outward illusion of status and class—while also juggling the long-term goals of education and property ownership. Sometimes, as Nix often preached, middle-class members focused more of their attention on conspicuous consumption than on church and family.[83]

Middle-class church members also learned "proper" behavior from the social clubs or lodges to which they belonged. Social clubs were an important addition to life for the middle class, offering opportunities to serve on committees and develop respectability.[84] Proper decorum was often a deciding factor for one's eligibility to join a particular club. In his sermons, Nix often discussed club membership and lodge meetings, which he believed were deterrents to the stability of the family.

Members of the middle class often looked down on those who attended sanctified churches, associating those members with "low-status." Conversely, the middle class also condemned those in the upper classes who attended Episcopalian or Congregationalist churches as "dicty" or as strainers or strivers. The Baptist and Methodist denominations associated with middle-class congregants were also split into separate churches based on class. Some of the Baptist and Methodist churches were considered "high-toned," while others were lower-class storefront churches. The mixed-class churches often tried to appease the sensibilities of both their lower- and middle-class members by incorporating both traditional musical elements of the folk and "sophisticated" music, typically associated with white churches. Drake and Cayton explained,

> When dealing with church rituals [i.e., traditions] "lower-class" in Bronzeville almost becomes synonymous with "old fashioned" or "southern" and in modern southern communities, or a generation ago everywhere, such prayers were common in colored Baptist or Methodist churches of *all* status levels. Therefore, an elderly person or an "old-fashioned" person in a Bronzeville middle-class congregation may pray in a manner which is *typical* of Chicago's lower-class congregations. A congregation cannot be stratified by any single item such as type of prayers or sermons [italics in original].[85]

Some of the Baptist and Methodist churches were considered "high-toned," while others were lower-class storefront churches.

The largest churches in Chicago in the 1920s—Bethel A.M.E., Quinn Chapel, and Olivet Baptist—tried to appeal to middle-class respectability while maintaining some of the emotionalism of the lower classes to attract a broad spectrum of the community. Although emotional displays were allowed in mixed churches, they were most often restricted so as to not become overzealous and thus label the minister as "uncultured." There were exceptions to these rules, and some ministers of the larger Baptist middle-class churches allowed their congregants to "get out of hand, with people falling out and running up and down the aisles hysterically."[86]

The mixed-class churches also tried to appease the sensibilities of both their lower- and middle-class members by incorporating traditional musical elements of the folk along with the "sophisticated" music typically associated with white churches. The larger, mixed churches, such as Olivet Baptist and the A.M.E. churches, whose choirs performed oratorios, anthems, and Sunday afternoon musicales by noted directors, presented "dignified" services in line with middle-class respectability. These churches were known to cater to "the more intelligent type" and were often avoided by southern migrants. The newer, younger members of the middle class rejected the folk spirituals and sermons and were more interested in the accumulation of wealth, believing that a respected business status would earn them equality in the white world.[87] Some music directors of old-line Black Chicago churches also rejected the folk spiritual because of its association with "backwardness," favoring instead complex choral works in the European classical tradition.[88]

Although Reverend Nix typically used traditional vocalisms and folk spirituals in his recorded sermons, he also occasionally presented Sunday afternoon musicales with trained vocalists as soloists in his live church services. An article in the *Pittsburgh Courier* in September 1927 reported that Nix hosted a Sunday afternoon musicale featuring a "dramatic soprano."[89] Genester Nix informed me that most contemporary Black churches sponsor musicales to raise money; however, they typically feature a variety of musical genres, including classical, gospel, and even jazz. Although she was too young to remember the music from her father's church in Chicago, the church in Holmesburg (Philadelphia) sponsored musicales featuring spirituals and gospel music.[90]

Most notably, ministers of mixed churches would present "intelligent" sermons that included themes addressed to "advancing the Race" and discussed the noble work done by race leaders.[91] Their attention to uplift was a necessary requirement to appeal to the more educated upper-class members. However, the mixed church minister was also responsible for the "molding" of the lower-class members, changing their behaviors into middle-class behaviors, and "advancing the Race."[92] The uplift goals associated with the middle class exemplify Du Bois's theory of the Talented Tenth and the need of the educated upper classes to uplift the masses.

Most of the educated ministers in the middle-class or mixed churches used a natural tone of voice and delivered practical sermons, in contrast to the lower-class uneducated ministers who prompted emotional outbursts from congregants. Some ministers in mixed churches switched to an impassioned delivery midway through the sermon with a higher pitch level and included shouts and singing. They might begin with intellectual preaching, then transition to emotional preaching with shouting and congregational responses.[93] These ministers presented an improvised type of sermon, rather than one written out, depending on the power of emotion and Bible stories to convey their messages. Again, Nix demonstrates that he is the exception to the rule, in that he was an educated minister but did not read from a script or typically use "eloquent" language in his sermons, but instead improvised his sermons from bullet points. He often spoke in a vernacular language with impassioned emotion and, in his earlier sermons, relayed Bible stories while simultaneously offering practical solutions to his congregants. Although he was formally educated, his homiletic techniques appealed to lower-class congregants and their preference for traditional vocalisms.

Upper-Class/Elite Churches

Some in the upper classes looked down upon those affiliated with storefront churches, which were usually in the poorer neighborhoods, and made assumptions about their members' educational status. The services in the lower-class churches were criticized as "jumping-jack religion," due to their physicalized emotional expressions. These assumptions are similar to Daniel Payne's admonishments against "heathenish" dancing and its associations with "primitive" religion. These upper-class church members associated storefront churches with "primitive" religion as well and considered their behavior the antithesis of uplift. One member of the Catholic Church stated, "No wonder white people laugh at colored people and their peculiar ways of worship. Just look at these storefronts. I don't believe in shouting and never did. I like a church that is quiet. I just can't appreciate clowning in a church."[94] The traditional Black churches, which focused on "sin and salvation,"[95] did not appeal to "sophisticated Negroes." As one high-status person remarked,

> I'm not in favor of these store-front churches. I think they give all churches a bad name. From what I know of them, the store-fronts are composed of people who have very little education, and their type of service is the kind that has made our people a laughing-stock for years. I may be too severe, but I think that everything people do ought to be done in an intelligent way.[96]

With the emergence of an educated and elite class in the late nineteenth century, some upper-class African Americans affiliated with churches historically attended by whites—Presbyterian, Methodist, Episcopal, Congregational, and Roman Catholic—that presented "sophisticated" services in contrast to the traditional Black folk church service.[97] Musically, many Black leaders, including clergy, advocated for assimilation by rejecting folk expressions linked to African Americans' past, instead opting for expressions linked to cultural sophistication and respectability, including listening to and performing classical music and choral renditions of standard hymns or anthems.[98] The adoption of classical music, in both public performance and in the private spheres of the Black church, was seen as a way to elevate African Americans through association with higher artistic merit. Instead of taking pride in folk heritage, many who adopted European musical values shut out any association with these folk forms, essentially demonstrating shame at these forms. Feelings of shame persisted in the Black churches as well. As James Weldon Johnson explained, "the Negroes themselves do not fully appreciate these old slave songs. The educated classes are rather ashamed of them, and prefer to sing hymns from books."[99] Johnson's comments reveal the disparaging attitude the elite took towards the spirituals and their preference for standardized, arranged hymns. In 1926, Langston Hughes, a staunch supporter of the Black folk, sarcastically commented on the emerging classist hierarchies and their effect on the arts: "many an upper-class Negro church, even now, would not dream of employing a spiritual in its services. The drab melodies in white folks' hymnbooks are much to be preferred. 'We want to worship the Lord correctly and quietly. We don't believe in "shouting." Let's be dull like the Nordics.'"[100] Hughes's comments reveal the conflicted beliefs within African American communities about the spiritual and spontaneous vocal expressivity, such as shouting, and their association with traditional folk voices. The upper class's assimilation to the dominant society's cultural aesthetics separated African Americans into hierarchal categories in both society and in their churches.

In a 1922 article, A. E. Perkins noted elite Black people's preference for classical music in the Black church and the gradual erasure of the folk spiritual:

> A growing sentiment for standard and classical music, both in church and social life, is tending to push the spirituals into the background. They must go, in fact. Many, many years will pass by, of course, before they will be forgotten and have fallen into complete disuse by the rural church, and in the church of the masses in the cities even; nevertheless they are passing away. They are almost entirely discarded to-day by the élite church of the race. They have no striking meaning for the spirit and life of the forward and intelligent groups of Negroes of to-day.[101]

Class standing therefore included musical preferences, with many of the "forward and intelligent groups" (i.e., the elite class) preferring classical music in the European tradition.

Genester Nix commented on the elite-class church members in her father's church, who she called the "Jack 'n Jills," as a "stand-offish" group who had their nose up to the lower classes. Elwood Nix claimed that his father chose the Baptist faith rather than one of the elite-class churches such as Episcopalian because "Episcopal is boring . . . they just talk. They quote the Bible, but they just talk, they don't act. They don't paint a picture of any sermons, it's like reading to you. . . . you just sit there and listen."[102] In other words, the elite church sermons did not express the emotionalism associated with the Black folk.

The assimilationist-type/upper-class churches typically did not include verbal responses from congregants, and the minister spoke in a natural tone of voice with texts considered practical. These ministers tended to associate demonstrative behavior and audible responses with the lower class. For example, one minister claimed, "If I were talking to a bunch of farmers who had been out in the field all day shouting to each other [read: lower class], I couldn't get their attention by a calm, quiet address. Yet for my congregation the best approach is the calm." Other "quiet" ministers associated shouting with irrational behavior: "Shouting is a form of emotional insanity. . . . People who shout the most are often the very devils afterwards. They go from heaven to hell in a short time."[103] Nix's congregation was an anomaly in that it *did* include verbal responses, and, instead of speaking in a natural tone of voice, he shouted, moaned, and included other vocal deliveries associated with folk traditions, despite the content of his sermons.

Categorizations such as these are difficult because, in the case of Nix, some do not fit comfortably into the three main categories of lower/working class, middle/mixed, or elite/upper class. Although Nix used vocal traditions typically associated with the lower-class storefront churches, such as shouting, moaning, and falling out, his congregation was composed of lower-, middle-, and elite-class congregants. Genester Nix confirmed, "in all his churches he did have the average as well as the elite. He had doctors and lawyers in his congregation."[104] However, while his musical and vocal tendencies would have appealed to the lower classes, his sermon texts would have appealed to the elite classes and their aspirations towards uplift and advancing the race. The most notable difference between Nix's church and the mixed type of church was in his musical choices. Nix and his congregants sang mostly folk spirituals and traditional hymns associated with the lower-class churches, while the typical elite-class or mixed church members sang anthems and classical music. Nix appealed to the middle- and elite-class sensibilities associated with self-help through his emphasis on uplift principles. Genester remembered, "Every church he went to he emphasized education,"[105] which was one of the goals of racial uplift. However, despite his sometimes patronizing attitude towards the lower classes, Elwood insisted that his father was a person with a big heart, who helped everyone he met. Reverend Nix's desire to help others was an inherent part of his good nature, not the result of an elitist attitude. Genester said she remembers the kindness her father showed to everyone, regardless of their status or class: "He did that all through his life because I can remember . . . he was sitting on the porch and a drunk came down the street, [and he said], 'Oh Professor, how you doing?' He would give them some self-worth. . . . Everyone was 'Professor' to him."[106]

Because Nix used traditional Black vocalisms in his preaching and singing but also spoke of the need for advancing the race through practical means, I consider his church and preaching style to be of a hybrid sort rather than one of the established old-line, mixed, middle-class churches of Chicago. Nix was an educated minister, yet he improvised his sermons and encouraged congregational responses, typical of the lower-class churches of the time. He utilized the chanted sermon, which had evolved from African American preachers in the late 1700s, and mostly sang folk spirituals or hymns rather than arranged spirituals or classical music. Nix privileged sound and utilized his voice as an instrument of power to communicate with his listeners and congregants, as had early, illiterate African American preachers. He also carried forth and preserved traditional Black vocalisms through the commodified medium of the phonograph, achieving celebrity status and making recordings that stood in competition with the secular music of the day.

CLASS DIVISIONS IN MUSICAL EXPRESSION

The modern era reflected a growing consciousness of the new, the progressive, the future, positivism, and realism.[107] The progress of science, technology, and industry was coupled with mass urbanization and rising literacy rates.[108] Industrialization and urbanization contributed to the transformation of economic life and a rise in capitalism and often included clashes of the old versus the "new" and of lowbrow versus highbrow musical expressions. Elements linked to traditional African American musical expressions, such as the spiritual, were creations aligned with the past, slavery, and the "Old Negro," conceptualized as lowbrow creations. For African American communities, those ideas and practices considered modern and new in the late nineteenth and early twentieth centuries presented two other options: highbrow expressions and modernized traditions.

Where highbrow artistic expressions blended African American musical idioms and folk music with Western classical music, the blending of traditional folk forms, or lowbrow expressions, with modern technology created what I call "modernized traditions." In this sense, there are two streams of musical modernity for African Americans: first, the efforts of groups like the Fisk Jubilee Singers and established African American congregations that sought to update and transform (modernize) selected African American musical traditions by adopting/adapting vocal techniques and other formal elements from the music of the dominant group; and second, the advent of commercial recordings of vernacular African American musical traditions—including the blues and recorded sermons—in the 1920s in which selected folk traditions were presented in more unvarnished, stylistic ways. I designate these two moments under the subheadings of "Creating Modern Black Voices" and "Modernized Tradition."

Creating Modern Black Voices

The idea that artistic sophistication through Western classical music could translate into equality was initiated with James M. Trotter's *Music and Some Highly Musical People* (1880). The purpose of Trotter's text was to bring attention to the public of the "highly musical" skills of African American musicians, which had been ignored due to racism from white people. Trotter praised the skills of African American classical musicians, not only to establish Black people as "highly musical," but also to demonstrate that white people were not the only race with sophisticated musical abilities. Trotter wrote of the musical skills of African American musicians, including Elizabeth Taylor Greenfield (the "Black Swan"), The Colored American Opera Company, and the Fisk Jubilee Singers, to name a few. Trotter's text is but one example of numerous claims of African Americans' musical excellence in the European classical tradition meant to improve the white majority's poor opinion of African Americans and thus inspire a more equitable relationship between the races. In addition, Trotter hoped to instill race pride into those who he believed were lacking in confidence and to inspire them to accomplish other feats of greatness. However, Trotter's denial that racism was the core issue revealed his own adherence to white people's assumptions of Black racial inferiority.[109]

This move toward European aesthetic values was part of the drive for African Americans to adopt the "sophisticated" and "cultured" vocal aesthetics of the dominant class, while simultaneously separating themselves from the vocalizations of the slave past.[110] As previously mentioned, vocal sophistication and exhibits of high culture were aspects of racial uplift, which Black elites believed could convince the dominant society of the humanity of African Americans.

Some elite African Americans adopted European classical vocal aesthetics as a means of expressing their own upper-class status. *The Negro Music Journal*, published only in 1902–1903, promoted classical music-making in the European tradition by African Americans. It featured columns on music performance,

African American and European classical music composers, music theory, and music history and frequently on African American vocalists and pedagogues. The purpose of the journal, as defined by its editor, was to

> endeavor to get the majority of our people interested in that class of music which will purify their minds, lighten their hearts, touch their souls and be a source of joy to them forever. It is the music of yesterday and today, or in other words, the music of the old masters like Bach, Handel, Haydn, Mozart and others . . . these names being only a few of the many great and good composers and musicians the world has given us.[111]

The journal frequently mentioned the "sweet" qualities of classical singers' voices as a marker of their vocal perfection and as a marker of class and respectability. The journal's sketch of Elizabeth Taylor Greenfield, a.k.a. the "Black Swan," described her "sweet clear voice" as the standard for vocal beauty.[112] In a column titled "The American Negro in Music," Clarence Cameron White discussed a soprano with "a remarkably strong and sweet voice" and another singer's aptly named rendition of "My Heart at Thy Sweet Voice," by Saint-Saëns, which he considered "grand."[113] Reviews of operatic singer Matilda Sissieretta Jones, a.k.a. "Black Patti," also focused on the "sweetness and smoothness of her tones, [and] her distinct enunciation" as proof of not only her "phenomenal voice" but also her higher-class status.[114] In Trotter's *Music and Some Highly Musical People*, a text of roughly 350 pages, ninety pages mentioned "sweet" or "sweetness" as a positive feature of an artist, either vocal or instrumental. Sweetness was described as an attribute of timbre, emotions, melody, harmony, sounds, or voice.

In *The Negro Music Journal*, the author of a column titled "Negroes as Singers" described the qualities of Black voices in essentialist terms as the result of biological differences between white and Black people:

> There is a peculiar vibrating quality in the Negro voice, due perhaps to a peculiar arrangement of the vocal chords [*sic*], which is not found in the white race. Its effect is absolutely unique and indescribable. In some degree this remarkable quality is lessened by cultivation although it is not entirely re-removed [*sic*], so that the most striking, even if less artistic, results are obtained from Negroes on the plantation. . . . Unquestionably some of this music is as old as the world, for it has been chanted in the wilds of Africa to the accompaniment of rude drum and punctured reed ever since human beings could articulate. It still retains music of its original savagery, and when sung with the peculiar timbre which is the especial attribute of the Negro's voice, it produces an effect which sets the nerves tingling with unwonted feeling.[115]

The author suggested that "cultivation" (i.e., voice training) can remedy some, but not all, of the "natural" resonances of Black voices. In the author's opinion, Black voices retain their "original savagery," regardless of vocal training; however, the implication is that "savagery" *with* training could result in an advantageous sound quality.

A vocal instruction manual from 1884 even claimed that race affected the tessitura of the voice: "The races which are still in the rear of civilisation ought . . . to have higher voices than the white races. This . . . is the case with the negroes and the Mongolians."[116] Essentialist narratives that focused on biological differences were not uncommon in general music and vocal pedagogy manuals of the early twentieth century, even from those published by highly esteemed institutions, such as the New England Conservatory of Music's *The Realm of Music*. Published in 1900, it discussed the varying vocal sounds produced by different ethnic groups, including African Americans:

> The voice of the American Negro is distinguishable from that of the white singer, and here, perhaps anatomy may afford a partial clue, for thick lips and a flat nose must influence the tone-production in a certain degree, and many, though by no means all, of our colored population have these anatomical peculiarities. Where these are absent however, the tone is more akin to the ordinary standard of the singing of other races.[117]

The white singer's sound was thus considered the standard by which other races were measured and was gauged as the norm in vocal pedagogy to which instructors should aspire. For example, vocal instructors Browne and Behnke claimed, "it is necessary in all training to make the student conscious of his possibilities, of nature's ideal intention regarding what is normal not only for the race but for himself."[118] Thus, ideals of a standard or "normal" tonal quality were measured by race. For these reasons, it is understandable why some elite African Americans sought to "prove" themselves as sophisticated artists to white America.

The New Negro

The new freedoms afforded to modern African Americans created shifts in perspectives and material gain and can be delineated in three specific changes that affected not only the bigger issues of life itself, but also musical and vocal expressions. First, the participatory elements of the traditional spirituals were transformed into an individualist approach with not only more solo performances, but also with the personalization of the subject matter in the lyrics, as in blues performance and blues lyrics, respectively.[119] Second, as more rural southerners migrated to the North to work in urban industries, they had, for the first time, expendable income, which they used partly for the pursuit of pleasure in entertainment, including phonographs and records.[120] Third, the idea of the Black body was reimagined from the minstrel trope of subjugation and ridicule to one that celebrated a sexualized Black body, as expressed and performed by both male and female blues singers.[121]

By the 1920s, African Americans who had migrated from the rural South to northern metropolises such as Chicago had gained access to many new forms of secular entertainment including jazz and blues, as well as new urban performance contexts where drinking, dancing, and gambling also occurred. However, these new options frequently conflicted with the goals espoused by some African American intellectuals who sought to reform the social and moral values of the folk. Booker T. Washington and other elites hoped to transform the negative image associated with the Black folk through the written arrangements of folk spirituals that conformed to the aesthetic principles derived from Western classical music.[122] Gaines explains,

> To Washington and many others, black culture was an admissible idea only within the context of elite culture. Washington . . . complained that "the Negro song is in too many minds associated with 'rag' music and the more reprehensible 'coon' song, that the most cultivated musician of his race, a man of the highest aesthetic ideals, should seek to give permanence to the folk-songs of his people by giving them a new interpretation and an added dignity."[123]

Although these elite leaders may have had the highest of intentions for the Black folk, both Du Bois and Washington accepted the "new interpretation" of the spirituals as a measure of advancement. These transformations were realized in the idea of the New Negro, who became the embodiment of Black sophistication and advancement in the modern age.

The term "New Negro" was in use as early as the late nineteenth century. As noted in the June 28, 1895, edition of the *Cleveland Gazette*: "A class of colored people, the 'New Negro,' . . . have arisen since the War, with education, refinement, and money."[124] In 1900, Booker T. Washington, along with Fannie Barrier Williams and Norman Barton Wood, published *A New Negro for a New Century* that had as its goal the reorientation of African Americans' image in society, positioning African Americans away from the stereotypes found in blackface minstrelsy, the plantation slave, and other racist propaganda, to a new attention to accomplishments of the "progressive" classes of the race. Washington and his coauthors provided discourses on African Americans and their achievements, including the formation of women's clubs and the accomplishments of artists. By 1908, S. Laing William in an essay titled "The New Negro" defined the differences between the Black man of the past and the present: "The ignorant, uncivilized and empty-handed man of 1865 has become a man of culture, a man of force and a man of independence. We shall have to look to this man to complete the great work of reconstruction."[125] Washington emphasized the necessity of vocal sophistication as a marker of the New Negro. New, sophisticated Black voices would eliminate the stereotypical voices associated with the Black "Sambo" or "coon songs." Along with education and refinement, "to *speak* properly was to *be* proper" and would ensure one's rights (italics in original).[126] Thus, the voice and vocal properties themselves became closely aligned with what was considered proper decorum.

The term "New Negro," as a "new racial self," most commonly refers to the experience of African Americans during the Jazz Age of the Harlem (or Negro) Renaissance. In the 1920s, Harlem became the center for a new Black intelligentsia, composed of writers, artists, and musicians. These New Negroes broke away from traditions of the past and chose a modern approach that celebrated Black life and culture.[127] The Harlem Renaissance was an "Afromodernist moment" during the mid-1920s in which African American literary, visual, and musical arts flowered prolifically, initially in New York's Harlem and later in Chicago and Philadelphia. The urban community of Harlem contrasted with the rural South.[128] It was a new age of sophistication for African Americans.[129] The hallmarks of the New Negro were recognition of education, financial prosperity, and refinement, as well as property rights. In addition, the "high art" of the New Negro included distinctly Black forms of expression, though in a "cultured" style.

The six primary leaders of the Harlem Renaissance, dubbed "The Six," included Alain Locke and James Weldon Johnson. The intellectuals at the helm of the movement believed that the development of "higher" forms of African American art would diminish racism and improve social relations, and positioned themselves in a self-imposed higher social order in league with the Talented Tenth and other uplift advocates, separating migrants from intellectuals in hierarchal class systems.[130] The divisions reflected two separate conceptual categories, with the New Negro, the Talented Tenth, members of the Harlem Renaissance, and high art in one court, and the Old Negro, folk, jazz, spirituals, the blues, and low art in the other, which created intracommunity tensions.

Despite these differences and the dualities that were created, they were ultimately unified through their shared goal for Black nationalism.[131] One purpose of the Harlem Renaissance was to negotiate the arts as leverage in the war for equality with white citizens. African Americans were often relegated to performances of minstrelsy, vaudeville, or other "primitive imagery" regardless of their talent or musical preferences and were often condemned for performing folk materials.[132] White people often ridiculed minstrelsy, blues, and jazz as "vulgar" and "primitive." Black classical singer Roland Hayes remarked, "My people have been very shy about singing their crude little songs before white folks. They thought they would be laughed at—and they were! And so they came to despise their own heritage."[133] The main reason for this shame, of course, was the history of white racism and prejudice toward African Americans.

Bringing Together Folk and Classical Forms

The leaders of the movement praised folk materials, including the spiritual, not for their intrinsic nature, but as source material that could be reformed into higher forms of artistic expression. On the one hand, many of the New Negro leaders lauded African American culture; but on the other, they emphasized the need for European form and technique.[134] Some of the sophisticated New Negroes looked down upon the existing values of tradition that were associated with the low art forms of the folk. Instead, they sought to replace folk musical forms with music that could demonstrate the worth and value of Black culture.[135] This suggests that elite African Americans, as a result of societal racism and discrimination, sought to reform Black folk culture as a possible solution to the race problem. With the flowering of the Harlem Renaissance, African American vernacular forms, such as spirituals, ragtime, and the blues, were transformed into the "high art" of operas and symphonic works, such as Dett's *The Chariot Jubilee* (1921) and Still's *Afro-American Symphony* (1930).

One of the New Negro leaders, Alain Locke, in his 1925 book, *The New Negro: Voices of the Harlem Renaissance*, espoused moving past the "old" ways, claiming that "the day of 'aunties,' 'uncles' and 'mammies' is . . . gone," and proposed instead a new self-determination by those who had "broken with the old epoch of philanthropic guidance, sentimental appeal and protest."[136] Locke hoped for a re-evaluation of African Americans based on their artistic achievements, "past and prospective," including the spirituals as a folk art, and new contributions, as "collaborator and participant in American civilization" by means of creative expression. In other words, creative expression was a key that could improve race relations, not by doing away with the old, but by appreciating the past and adding new contributions. However, despite his sentimental attitude towards the spiritual, Locke stressed, "we must be careful not to confine this wonderfully potential music to the narrow confines of 'simple versions' and musically primitive molds."[137] In other words, he believed the spirituals were a "primitive" source to be molded into modern, sophisticated versions. He emphasized this point by stating, "Only with the original Fisk Singers was their real simplicity and dignity maintained. . . . They will find their truest development then, in symphonic music or in the larger choral forms of the symphonic choir." In Locke's opinion, art music and folk music could be blended together to produce a "superior product."[138]

James Weldon Johnson was a lyricist, author, and educator and one of The Six. As a continuation of Locke's philosophy, Johnson commented on the importance of art and literature to the status of African Americans:

A people may become great through many means, but there is only one measure by which its greatness is recognized and acknowledged. The final measure of the greatness of all peoples is the amount and standard of the literature and art they have produced. The world does not know that a people is great until that people produces great literature and art. No people that has produced great literature and art has ever been looked upon by the world as distinctly inferior.[139]

In 1925, James Weldon Johnson and his brother, J. Rosamond Johnson, discussed how the spirituals had the influence to create a new prideful race consciousness through their raw power, replacing the previous shame and beginning the New Negro's association with classical music:

This reawakening of the Negro to the value and beauty of the Spirituals was the beginning of an entirely new phase of race consciousness. It marked a change in the attitude of the Negro himself toward his own art material; the turning of his gaze inward upon his own cultural resources. Neglect and ashamedness gave place to study and pride. All the other artistic activities of the Negro have been influenced.

There is also a change of attitude going on with regard to the Negro. The country may not yet be conscious of it, for it is only in the beginning. It is, nevertheless, momentous. America [read: white America] is beginning to see the Negro in a new light, or, rather, to see something new in the Negro. It is beginning to see in him the divine spark which may glow merely for the fanning. And so a colored man is soloist for the Boston Symphony Orchestra and the Philharmonic; a colored woman is soloist for the Philadelphia Symphony Orchestra and the Philharmonic; colored singers draw concert goers of the highest class; Negro poets and writers find entrée to all the most important magazines; Negro authors have their books accepted and put out by the leading publishers. And this change of attitude with regard to the Negro which is taking place is directly related to the Negro's change of attitude with regard to himself. It is new, and it is tremendously significant.[140]

While the Johnsons' comments reflect not only an introspective analysis of advancement and confidence from one's own "divine spark," they also reveal the brothers' belief that art music could create a new image for African Americans in the eyes of white America.

The blending of folk elements, such as those in the spirituals, with European classical techniques produced a hybrid product that created conflicts between those who believed in the "pure" forms of the spiritual and those who were interested in "elevating the music of their race."[141] While some of these New Negro musicians may have performed classical music for "art's sake," others, such as William Grant Still and Paul Robeson, believed that "Art is one form against which such [racist] barriers do not stand."[142] They essentially believed that high art could be used as propaganda, clothed as dignity.

In contrast with the New Negroes and their preference for European classical music and technique, some Black intellectuals, such as Langston Hughes, Zora Neale Hurston, and, as I suggest, Rev. A. W. Nix, looked to folk forms, not as low-class expressions unworthy of the sophistication of the concert hall, but as autonomous expressions that had artistic value in their own right. The now-famous statement by Langston Hughes stood up to the elitist stance of other Harlem Renaissance leaders:

> Let the blare of Negro jazz bands and the bellowing voice of Bessie Smith singing Blues penetrate the closed ears of the colored near-intellectuals until they listen and perhaps understand. . . . We younger Negro artists who create now intend to express our dark-skinned selves without fear or shame. If white people are pleased we are glad. If they are not, it doesn't matter. We know we are beautiful. And ugly too. The tom-tom cries and the tom-tom laughs. If colored people are pleased we are glad. If they are not, their displeasure doesn't matter either. We build temples for tomorrow, strong as we know how, and we stand on top of the mountain, free within ourselves.[143]

Hughes's statement evoked pride in the value of the folk, including the secular music of blues and jazz. He explicitly stated that he and other young artists were "without fear or shame." Although the Harlem Renaissance leaders and the Talented Tenth claimed to be taking charge of the image of the Black masses for the sake of uplifting the race and entering into white society as equals, race records, such as those recorded by Nix, contested elite hegemony on cultural expressions, granting ascendency to Black folk voices, creating "modernized tradition."

Modernized Tradition

Although many educated and elite African Americans aspired to modernity, advancement, and progress through the assimilation of Europeanized vocal aesthetics, a new modernized tradition developed that favored voices and sounds associated with the African American past. The sounds of Black vocal traditions, including recorded sermons—such as those by Nix—blues, and jazz, were recorded on phonographs and disseminated to African American mass audiences, becoming commercially successful in the 1920s. These new forms were hybrid expressions that combined Black vocal traditions with modern technology and emphasized oral traditions more so than written arrangements. The success of race records signals a second stage for African Americans in the modern era.[144]

The phonograph was invented in 1877 by Thomas Edison, and beginning in 1890, commercial recordings became available to the public through coin-operated phonograph machines.[145] "Talking machines," as they were called, were placed in arcades and other public places as novelties for white working-class audiences. Early recording industry professionals promoted music that appealed to the urban working class, especially music that centered on the New York region: Tin Pan Alley, Broadway tunes, and vaudeville numbers.[146]

Also beginning in 1890, record companies issued releases by African American artists performing early ragtime, minstrelsy, spirituals, quartets, "coon songs," comedy, classical music, poetry, and speeches. These recordings from the burgeoning record business were also considered novelties for the amusement of the white middle class.[147] For example, George W. Johnson sang "coon songs" and minstrel songs with such titles as "The Whistling Coon" and "The Laughing Coon," in 1895 and 1897, respectively, exemplifying the self-mimicry to which Black artists often had to subject themselves.[148] White-owned record companies were willing to record African Americans, but only as "product" for white consumers.[149]

In the early years of the twentieth century, the record industry shifted its emphasis from the phonograph as a novelty to one that promoted the education of the masses. Karl Hagstrom Miller calls this process a "campaign of cultural uplift," in which classical music was emphasized as a tool to promote the cultural heritage of the European tradition.[150] Phonograph cabinets and the records themselves also became symbols of middle-class respectability and sophistication. As William Howland Kenney explains,

> improvements to original design of the phonograph and to records were guided by the Victorian era's association of the home with "an oasis of calm" at which the wife/mother provided, among other things, refined and uplifting music with which to rejuvenate her hard-working husband and edify, enrapture, and improve the memories of her children, imparting a sense of proportion, good taste, high moral purpose, and brotherly and sisterly affection through inspiring music.[151]

The Victrola (a phonograph made and sold by the Victor Talking Machine Company) featured a "Victorian-style cabinet" that was "elegant and artistic in appearance," designed to lure the white middle class into purchasing a piece of furniture that would add to the elegance of their home parlor.[152]

Phonograph manufacturers also attempted to appeal to middle-class sensibilities by marketing their product's sweet and smooth tonal qualities. For example, in 1910, an advertisement for the Victrola claimed it had "the sweetest, most mellow tone ever known."[153] In a 1915 Aeolian-Vocalion product manual, the company repeatedly commented on the sweet and smooth tonal qualities produced by its phonographs: "How smooth, how wonderfully true are these tones . . . the bell-clear sweetness of the tenor voice . . . the sweet melody flows from a master's violin," and so on.[154] The Victrola ad compared the phonograph with a Stradivarius violin, but said it was "greater because it is all musical instruments and the perfect human voice."[155] Thus, apparently sweetness and smoothness—indices for vocal "whiteness"—were the desired goals of both the "perfect human voice" and the phonograph.

The emergence of the phonograph swept the market as new companies entered the playing field. In 1914, 1915, and 1916 the number of phonograph manufacturers rose from six, to eighteen, to forty-six, respectively.[156] The number of phonograph owners rose in accordance: from 540,000 in 1914 to 2,225,000 in 1919. The phonograph itself became a marker of modernity. Despite racial conflicts that prevailed during the early twentieth century, record companies produced recordings from a broad range of ethnic groups and their musical genres, which were sometimes recorded on field expeditions to various locations around the United States.[157] In the second decade of the 1900s, labels such as Odeon released recordings by ethnic groups to appeal to immigrant populations initially, with recordings by African Americans only coming into national prominence in the 1920s.[158]

As phonograph recordings became more popular, recording industry companies expanded past the boundaries of New York, spreading to Chicago and other large cities, as well as to remote locations to discover and record new talent where onsite field recordings were made by mobile recording units or field units.[159] The Brunswick-Balke-Collender Co. recorded many of these field recordings and became a major label in the 1920s, competing with the more-established companies of Victor and Columbia, becoming the third most successful record manufacturer in the United States by 1923.[160]

As early as 1913, an article in *Talking Machine World* addressed the potential for the widespread marketing of recordings by African Americans. In the article, a record executive was addressed by a Black jobber who stated, "the black man is greatly misunderstood. He is not nearly so ignorant and unappreciative as the world in general would have us believe," convincing the white executive that because "the colored man is exceedingly fond of music," a salesman could successfully sell music to Black patrons.[161] The typical attitude of the white-run record companies was that Black people would not support records from their own race,[162] and records by Black musicians and singers would not be of interest to the white majority except as novelty acts.[163] This began to change when, in October 1916, the *Chicago Defender* sent out a notice for Black phonograph owners to alert the *Defender* of their status of ownership, which would be passed on to the Victor company: "the record companies are seeking to find out how many victrolas are owned by members of the Race. When this is known, then records of the Race's great artists will be placed on the market."[164] In November 1916, the *Defender* encouraged its readers again to write to Victor Records to ask the company to record "noted artists" such as Anita Patti Brown, Roland Hayes, and other African American classical music celebrities.[165] Not until the 1920s when race records started to be distributed nationwide, did African American secular music and sacred sermons start to come to the attention of the general population of Black consumers.[166]

On February 14, 1920, OKeh Records recorded Mamie Smith, who was a vaudeville and blues artist, releasing "That Thing Called Love" and "You Can't Keep a Good Man Down," which sold 7,500 copies in the first week.[167] Because of the success of these first recordings, OKeh quickly recorded Smith again, accompanied by her Jazz Hounds, on August 10, 1920, and issued her first major hit, "Crazy Blues," making her the first female African American vocalist to record a popular record.[168] Smith's "Crazy Blues" (OKeh 4169) was such a huge hit—selling 75,000 copies in one month in 1920—that other labels began following suit, recording jazz and blues by Black artists.[169] Records were often sold by mail order or by Pullman porters, who sold copies on their routes to the South, which opened up the rural market. Not until Black newspapers, such as the *Chicago Defender*, began advertising for the record companies, partly for increased advertising revenues and partly to disseminate race pride, did the marketing to African American consumers begin.[170] After the success of Mamie Smith's 1920 release of "Crazy Blues," record companies realized that a viable market existed among African Americans.

On November 29, 1924, Brunswick acquired the Vocalion label and, in 1926, formed its race records division, which included artists such as King Oliver's Dixie Syncopators, Jelly Roll Morton, Alberta Hunter, Duke Ellington, and Rev. J. M. Gates.[171] Race records promulgated the sounds of popular music, jazz and blues, gospel, and recorded sermons, allowing for the widespread dissemination of the music and the voices of the Black folk, separate from Euro-centric art music. While record companies had previously marketed almost exclusively to middle-class whites, the advent of race records allowed Black consumers to purchase and listen to voices that historically had been ignored or dismissed,

Figure 2.1. OKeh Records advertisement, the *Chicago Defender (National Edition)*, January 7, 1922, 6.

including the voices of African American ministers. Although the term "race records" might be considered derogatory today, in the 1920s those records were a source of pride for African Americans, because the records allowed for music and spoken word to be recorded and distributed specifically to Black consumers. Between World Wars I and II, race consciousness was a positive but defensive reaction to racism. Race pride and advancing the race were emphasized for building morale, supporting Black businesses, political organization, and economic power. Thus, as a result of race pride, certain figures developed: the Race Hero, the Race Leader, the Race Man, and the Race Woman.[172] Therefore, race records can be thought of as expressions of race pride and group affinity. On January 7, 1922, OKeh placed an ad in the *Chicago Defender* stating, "All the greatest Race phonograph stars can be heard on OKeh Records" (Figure 2.1).[173]

Advertisements in the *Chicago Defender* often included photos and replications of blues artists for marketing purposes. The element of authenticity was used for marketing as well, as demonstrated in an advertisement for a new blues release: "Here They Are—Moanin', Whinin', Shoutin' Blues."[174] The use of the terminology of vocal characteristics associated with the religious traditions of the Black church clearly defined the blues as an authentic Black genre meant to appeal to Black musical tastes and was thus marketed as a commodity to African American audiences. Between 1920 and 1942, over six thousand blues and gospel recordings were issued by about twelve hundred artists.[175] Although record companies benefitted financially, African Americans also benefitted from race records by the dissemination of Black voices and by the entrance of African Americans into the consumer market. Phonograph records (and radio and sound films) thus influenced a hybrid blending as music, sound, and voices filtered from urban cities to rural communities and from the North to the South.

Although African American musicians were rarely featured on radio in the 1920s, phonograph recordings sold regularly to Black southerners. In the 1920s, 19 percent of African Americans owned a phonograph, and many of these were in sharecropper homes.[176] The November 1925 issue of *Phonograph & Talking Machine Weekly* stated that Vocalion records sold its records for seventy-five cents apiece.[177] African Americans were also frequent consumers of records and, according to one retailer, "outbought whites in record consumption 50 to 1."[178] Regardless of the economic hardships of many African Americans in the 1920s, phonographs and records were apparently important commodities and highly valued.

Despite the marketing of race records to African Americans, Black artists were paid nominally for their voices and talents. J. Mayo Williams, the African American talent scout and executive for Paramount Records, kept informal ledgers of the sessions and reportedly paid his artists between $25 and $50 per side.[179] Therefore, if a record sold ten thousand copies, as did Mamie Smith's "Crazy Blues," the label would net $7,500 before expenses, while the performer would earn a flat rate of $50 or less per side with no possibility for royalties. Despite these inequalities, recordings of African Americans flourished in the 1920s.

Phonograph recordings of sermons, the blues, and other folk voices functioned as more than just entertainment; they were "bearers and preservers" of folk traditions.[180] Phonograph recordings propelled previously silenced (or ignored) voices such as those of immigrants, African Americans, and rural Americans into the wider public arena. These recordings presented traditional material that resonated with the listener's "aural memory," creating emotional connections to the listener's past. Through the process of repetition, a listener can relive the emotional connections of these traditions.[181] African American vocal traditions had previously been perpetuated through the physical process of oral transmission, in which culture bearers passed a tradition on to the next generation. For example, singers would voice a song, which others learned by listening and repeating. In the same way, phonographs created new opportunities by functioning as a medium that allowed for the continuation of oral traditions through repetition.

Thus, phonographs were a modern technology put to the service of disseminating oral traditions. Rather than live physical voices repeating vocal sounds, these voices could now be reproduced and repeated via phonographs. Phonograph recordings allowed listeners to repeatedly listen to traditions, at will, by the simple process of playing a record. Phonographs also disseminated vocal traditions to a wider audience outside of one's immediate enclave. Traditions that had previously been isolated in the rural South, for example, were disseminated to northern metropolises and elsewhere. Also, phonographs displaced the written score of the arranged spiritual as a marker of advancement and modernity. As musicologist Guthrie Ramsey states,

> On the one hand, science in the form of recording technology served similar functions as notation did for instrumental Western European music and for the spirituals: it allowed a musical experience to be engaged outside of the circumstances of its original social and historical contexts. On the other hand, the orality of sound recordings, indeed their decidedly non-literary quality, undermines many modernist ideals that privilege the written as the sole signs of progress, history and consciousness.[182]

The recorded sermon, as a planned and rehearsed performance outside of its original context, thus was transformed from an "authentic" folk form into a modern, hybrid form that combined traditional elements with new technology and reflected the voices of the past in a commercially viable product that was planned, marketed, and sold to consumers. Recorded sermons diminished the element of spontaneity and improvisation (although Nix improvised as he recorded them) due to the fact that once they are recorded, they present exactly the same material and performance on subsequent listenings. Thus, they become a representation of the original presentation of traditional voices.

African American consumers, through their purchasing of recorded sermons, emphasized the values they placed on Black oral traditions. Recordings by Black ministers such as Nix even outsold the popular blues artists of the day, demonstrating the impact of these recorded sermons and the sacred vocal traditions they presented.[183] Recorded sermons offered urban Black communities a down-home alternative to the arranged spirituals and other European-influenced musical repertoires favored in some churches, with the vocal sounds of tradition functioning as important qualifiers of cultural autonomy.

Chapter 3

THE SERMONS

The Vocalion label recorded fifty-four sermons by A. W. Nix between 1927 and 1931 in Chicago. The Brunswick-Balke-Collender Company, which owned Vocalion, was formed in 1845 as a manufacturer of products including furniture and began production of phonograph cabinets and phonograph machines in 1913, becoming a producer of records by 1916.[1] Brunswick purchased the Vocalion label from Aeolian on November 29, 1924, and by 1925 began distributing its records through jobbers (i.e., wholesalers), achieving success that rivaled the larger labels such as Victor.[2] The Vocalion offices were initially located in the Brunswick headquarters on 799 Seventh Avenue in New York City.[3] Vocalion began its race record series in 1926 under the direction of Jack Kapp, a former Columbia Phonograph Co. sales executive. The May 1926 issue of *Talking Machine World* reported Brunswick/Vocalion's new race series:

> In issuing the race records the Brunswick company stated that the main purpose of its plan is to give the colored people records made by artists of their own race which are absolutely above reproach insofar as the theme and manner of presentation are concerned. . . . Jack Kapp, who heads the Vocalion race record division, is combing the country to secure the services of prominent colored artists and no effort will be spared to give the race the type of music that is most appealing.[4]

The records initially released under Kapp's supervision included jazz (King Oliver and His Dixie Syncopators, Duke Ellington), blues (Alberta Hunter, Ada Brown), and spirituals (The Cotton Belt Quartet).

Brunswick released its first electrical recordings on April 8, 1925, followed by Vocalion releases in May 1925. Thus, all of Reverend Nix's recordings were electrical.[5] Electrical recordings were themselves symbols of modernity and were frequently advertised, emphasizing the improved sound quality electrical recording provided.[6]

The Brunswick recording studios in Chicago were located on the twenty-first floor of the Furniture Mart Building at 666 N. Lake Shore Drive.[7] The Vocalion Record Department, as of 1928, was located at 623 S. Wabash Avenue.[8] Both of these locations were relatively close to Nix's Chicago address at 2075 Ogden Avenue, at 4.2 miles and 3.1 miles away, respectively.

Phonograph recordings by African American ministers such as Nix publicly disseminated sounds that had been segregated in the performances of the Black church, serving as a bridge that blurred the lines between the demarcation zones of race, class, and geography. Recorded sermons brought the vocal traditions associated with southern Black Baptist ministers such as Nix into the public sphere.

Record labels began recording sermons by African American ministers, beginning in February 1925, when Columbia released the first recorded sermon by Calvin Dixon, "As an Eagle Stirreth Up Her Nest." Dixon's recording was followed by Rev. J. M. Gates's "Death's Black Train Is Coming" and "I'm Gonna Die with the Staff in My Hand." Gates's two recordings, which essentially consisted of singing, not sermonizing, sold substantially better than anticipated. Gates's success led to the recording of other ministers, including "The Downfall of Nebuchadnezzar" by Rev. J. C. Burnett, which again stressed more singing than actual sermonizing and sold over 86,000 copies.[9] In Burnett's recording, a spiritual melody is hummed throughout once he begins his chanted and shouted sermon, which contains interjected shouts from the female congregants. Gates's and Burnett's recorded sermons differed from Dixon's in that they were more similar to the actual folk church experience, with chanted delivery, familiar Biblical themes, the singing of spirituals, and interjections by studio congregants, usually females. The vocal tendencies of Burnett were also more closely aligned with the traditions of the folk church, including strained and gravelly timbres executed in the speech-song style of the chanted sermon. On the other hand, Dixon employed carefully executed vocalisms on sermons that contain only preaching with no musical additions.[10]

Recorded sermons allowed their listeners to repeatedly relive the church experience in the privacy of their own homes and at their own leisure. Elwood and Genester Nix claimed that African Americans purchased recorded sermons "because they enjoyed what they heard" and because "they wanted to listen to [them] all the time." Elwood added, "People get down and they want to hear the word. Something the minister said [on the records] really struck them."[11]

By the end of the 1930s, recording companies, including Brunswick, had released over 750 sermons by seventy preachers.[12] The success of these recorded sermons catapulted Black preachers from relative obscurity to celebrity status, rivaling some of the era's biggest stars in Black secular music. As explained by religion and politics scholar Lerone A. Martin, recorded sermons on race records were popular for a number of reasons. First, they granted African Americans the ability to participate in the consumer market, which was considered an aspect of freedom. African Americans had expendable income, which they freely used to purchase material goods and entertainment, such as phonograph records. Second, recorded sermons and the dissemination of the spiritual message transferred the place of worship and sacred practices of the public church to the privacy of the home. Listening to recorded sermons in the home allowed for a one-on-one experience between an individual and the message on a recording. In addition, recorded sermons allowed Black ministers to enter into the consumer market, serving as competition to the popular entertainment of secular recordings. Black ministers served as the catalysts for progress in both the spiritual realm and the material world. On recordings, they functioned as performers, competing with secular performers and urban forms of entertainment. Urban amusements, such as dancing, live music, and movies in the theaters and dance halls, caused a decrease in church membership and de-centered the Black church as the center of social and religious life. As a result, Black ministers who recorded sermons "created another commercial commodity that helped to expand and sacralize black consumer culture." In response to secular forms of entertainment, as Martin suggests, "The rural preacher confronted his urban world by using contemporary technology to express his rural cultural and religious practices," essentially bringing tradition into the modern world.[13]

Newspaper articles that described the recording process detailed the importance of multiple rehearsals required to ensure the timing to be within the limit of approximately three minutes on 78 rpm recordings.[14] These rehearsals would naturally have some effect on the element of spontaneity and improvisation typical in recorded sermons. In the process of recording, it is likely that a minister could maintain this format if he adhered to a basic guideline and did not veer too far from his outline. He most likely instructed his female congregants on some of the specifics of what he expected from their participation. Nix provided a remedy for the time limitations of the recording medium by creating the multipart recording, as in his two-part "Black Diamond Express to Hell."[15]

Rev. Sutton Griggs also recorded sermons on race records. I previously mentioned that Reverend Nix served on the committee at the 1921 National Baptist Convention that distributed one of Griggs's books. Although Griggs and Nix appear to have known each other, Griggs delivered his vocals in a manner that may suggest his alignment with the Talented Tenth, vocal sophistication, and assimilation, in opposition to Nix's vocal aesthetics.

For too long, according to Griggs, Black people had depended upon oral traditions because they were prohibited from gaining education and thus literacy. Illiteracy also created roadblocks to Black leadership. He believed that, in order to succeed, "as a race we must move up out of the age of the voice."[16] Despite Griggs's contempt for the "age of the voice," he recorded six sermons for the Victor label, on September 18–19, 1928 (Table 3.1).

Table 3.1. Recordings of Rev. Sutton E. Griggs

Title	Label	Matrix Number	Date Recorded	Lyrical Theme	Musical Selection
"Saving the Day"	Victor V38516	BVE-47055-2	9/18/28	Black people use their bodies as human sandbags during a flood.	"Roll, Jordan, Roll"
"A Hero Closes a War"	Victor 21706	BVE-47056-1	9/18/28	Racial conflict between white and Black men, but a Black man ends the race war through his charity.	"Down by the Riverside"
"Self-Examination"	Victor 38516	BVE-47058-1	9/19/28	People must look at themselves before judging their neighbor.	"Standing in the Need of Prayer"
"Speaking the Truth"	Victor (unissued)	BVE-47059	9/19/28	Unknown	Unknown
"A Surprise Answer to Prayer"	Victor 21706	BVE-47060-1	9/19/28	Be careful what you pray for.	"Four and Twenty Elders"
"Keeping the Peace"	Victor (unissued)	BVE-47061	9/19/28	Unknown	Unknown

Source: Steven C. Tracy, "Saving the Day: The Recordings of the Reverend Sutton E. Griggs," *Phylon* 47, no. 2 (2nd Qtr., 1986): 159–66.

"A HERO CLOSES A WAR"

In Griggs's sermon "A Hero Closes a War," recorded September 18, 1928, he discusses a group of Black and white men who are thrown into the water of Chesapeake Bay, with each scrambling to return to the boat. The white men prevent the African Americans from re-entering the boat until a Black swimmer rescues the white men who are struggling to survive. The Black men are not allowed to be saved until the white men are rescued. Griggs's perspective may have been to "love all others as yourself"; however, this sermon clearly demonstrated Griggs's accommodationist stance. He claims that the "race war is over" *after* the Black swimmer graciously rescues the white men. Griggs says that the Black swimmer "was willing to bear the temporary implication of being a traitor to his race." In other words, Griggs suggests that by putting the needs and very survival of whites before themselves, African Americans could end racial strife. Griggs clearly believed that it was up to African Americans, not white people, to be the ones "to go forth helping the various races of mankind," despite the injustices that they had received at the hands of white people. No such demands are made upon the white men, who clearly do not care if the Black swimmers live or die.

The sermon begins with an introduction of the scriptural chapter (A), followed by the story of the boat and the swimmers (B), concluding with Griggs's advice to his congregants (C).

A

In the fourth chapter of Micah and the third verse
We have these words:
"They shall beat their swords into plowshares,
 And their spears into pruninghooks:
Nation shall not lift up sword against nation,
Neither shall they learn war anymore."

B (0:24)

It was in Chesapeake Bay
 One dark night during the World War.
 An open boat was carrying a crew composed of white and Negro men.
 The boat capsized,
 Throwing the entire crew into the water.
 There was now a scramble for the bottom of the upturned boat
 And some white men gained possession.

(0:48)

They sought to keep it for the sole use of the whites,
 Thinking that there would not be room enough for all.
 Feeling thus, they knocked back any Negro reaching the boat.
 Seeing the racial conflict, one Negro swam away,
 Secured a white man struggling in the water,
 And took him to the boat,
 Handing him to his white comrades.
 He did another white man the same way.
 Next he brought a Negro.
 Some of the men sought to deny asylum,

But they were made to desist by other white men,
And the Negro was taken aboard.

(1:24)

From that time on, the swimmer could bring white or colored
indiscriminately.
The race war was over.
That unknown Negro,
In the dark of the night in the water,
Menaced by death,
Was willing to bear the temporary implication of being a traitor to his
    race,
A thought that must have flashed through the minds
Of his fellows because of the war that was raging.
But he had their ultimate good in mind, and so persisted.

C (1:56)

With us,
It is day, not night.
We are safe ashore,
Not threatened with drowning.
Under these circumstances,
Far superior to those of this Negro hero,
Come what will or may,
Let us have the vision and the courage
To go forth helping the various races of mankind
To tolerate one another
On the bottom of the upturned boat
In the troubled, tempestuous sea of life.

Griggs's thematic approach contrasts with Nix's, in that Griggs emphasized the sacrifice of African Americans to "win" the race war, while Nix emphasized practical solutions to help his congregants.

Griggs's oratorical style and musical practices emphasized Victorian sound aesthetics and lacked the improvisatory and musical elements associated with the "emotionalism" of working-class Black church preachers such as Nix. Griggs's even and consistent rhythmic pace and tempo suggest that he was reading his text, rather than improvising from topic headings as did Nix and other folk preachers. In his delivery style, Griggs orated in a monotone voice with little differentiation in pitch and had a narrow range, consistent vocal timbre, and precise enunciation. Although he presented elements drawn from the folk vernacular in some of his novels, Griggs's recorded sermons present meticulous attention to Standard English.

All of Griggs's sermons were structured to cleanly separate speech from music. Hymns or spirituals are sung by themselves at the end of the recordings and lack the layered techniques common in African American traditions. The sung portions of the sermons are in a formally arranged style, without improvisation, presenting a rehearsed and well-prepared performance in four-part harmony, similar to the style of the Fisk Jubilee Singers' four-part arrangements. In the musical selections in Griggs's recordings, there are no emotional exuberances or interjections from the congregants, but instead they feature smooth vocal timbres and four-part arrangements of hymns, and the performances are relatively even-mannered. In addition, the solo soprano voice present on Griggs's recordings gives the impression of being a formally trained or semi-trained voice, consistent with Victorian ideals of a "good" singing tone. Griggs recorded only six sermons, two of them unissued, which suggests that their lack of popularity cost him any possibility for future recordings.[17] Possibly his adherence to Europeanized vocal values and his accommodationist themes diminished his chances for success as a recording preacher.

In contrast, Reverend Nix and his congregation continued the practices of traditional Black folk voices in his recorded sermons. The incorporation of these practices reflected Nix's conscious decision to highlight traditional vocal expressions that were familiar to his congregation while simultaneously integrating ideologies of uplift and modernity in his sermon texts. Nix used the music and sounds of the African American past to provide a place of familiarity for southern migrants who had moved to northern urban metropolises as he instructed them to confront the realities of modern urban life.

As Amanda Weidman asserts, the voice both operates as a physical part of the body with sonic qualities that can be adjusted to conform to cultural practices (and is thus malleable to an extent) and allows for "giving voice" as an opportunity to express opinion or agency to the vocalizer.[18] The actual physical and sonic qualities of Nix's voice, plus his use of particular vocal traits, recalled rural southern traditions that were perpetuated and propelled into the age of modernity by phonograph recordings. Nix's voice represents "modernized tradition," which was a hybrid of the old and the new, the traditional and the modern.

In the 1920s, recorded sermons and other race records served as agents of voice for African American musicians, ministers, and consumers who were still suffering under Jim Crow, frequent lynchings, and other forms of racial violence and discrimination. Nix's first recordings were contemporaneous with the continued ridicule embodied in blackface minstrelsy. The first "talkie," *The*

Jazz Singer, starring Al Jolson in blackface, was released on October 6, 1927, six months after Nix's first recording of his sermon "Black Diamond Express to Hell."[19] Recorded sermons allowed for Nix's voice to be disseminated nationwide in a country that continued to restrict the rights of African Americans.

THE RECORDED SERMON

Nix recorded a total of fifty-four sermons (plus two retakes and one that was not issued). Seven of these recordings have not been located. The analysis presented here focuses on the voices and vocal features of the remaining forty-seven recordings. Phonograph recordings made in the 1920s could hold only up to approximately three minutes of recorded material, requiring ministers to adjust their sermons to fit into this compact, time-limited space.[20] According to Genester Nix, her father's live sermons in the church setting were typically around forty minutes long.[21] Ten-inch 78 rpm recordings required ministers to condense their sermons into minisermons, sometimes called "sermonettes." Because of the condensed lengths, Nix arrived at the traditional climax portion of the sermon earlier than in the longer sermons given during a church service.

The vocal intensity of Nix's booming voice must have been spectacular for consumers who were only beginning to become familiar with sounds emanating from new phonograph technology. The three-minute limit of the recordings would require tight planning or rehearsals on the part of the minister and his studio congregants. The female congregants in the background of Nix's recordings often sound as if they are giving spontaneous and improvisatory reactions to his voice; however, he usually recorded two or three takes in an attempt to create the best recording. Some of his sermons were actually rerecorded at later dates, presumably to improve substandard initial releases. Because the recorded sermon could bring in substantial income to a minister, especially during the financial drought of the Great Depression, it is most likely that the minister would have taken the recording process very seriously to make sure that his sermon would not incur the excessive costs required for multiple takes.

Nix recorded primarily on Wednesdays and Saturdays, but also occasionally on Tuesdays, Thursdays, and Fridays. Because Sundays were a church day with five services, it is most likely that Mondays would have been a day of rest (Table 3.2).

Blues and Gospel Records: 1890–1943 and *Brunswick Records: A Discography of Recordings, 1916–1931, Vol. 3 (Chicago and Regional Sessions)* include the matrix numbers, record label name and number, recording dates, accompaniment information, and number of takes for each recording. The recordings

Table 3.2. Rev. A. W. Nix Recording Schedule			
Day of the Week	**Date**	**Year**	**Number of Recordings**
Saturday	April 23	1927	4
Wednesday	June 29	1927	4
Thursday	June 30	1927	2
Wednesday	October 12	1927	4
Wednesday	January 11	1928	2 (2 are unissued)
Wednesday	January 18	1928	9 (1 is unissued)
Friday	October 26	1928	4
Saturday	August 24	1929	4
Thursday	December 12	1929	4
Unknown	Mid-January	1930	4
c. Friday	c. February 18	1930	2
Tuesday	April 8	1930	2
c. Friday	c. June 20	1930	4
Saturday	November 1	1930	4
Saturday	March 28	1931	4

by Nix were usually completed in two or three takes, with an average of four recordings completed per session. Three sermons were recorded twice, thus totaling fifty-four titles. The recording notes mention that Nix typically brought either five or seven congregants with him to his recording sessions.[22] All of Nix's recordings were made in Chicago. The stock market crash in 1929 (October 24–29, 1929) does not seem to have impacted Vocalion's financial ability to record Nix during 1929 or 1930. The dates in Table 3.3 list the number of recordings by year.

Table 3.3. Rev. A. W. Nix Recordings by Year	
Year	**Number of Recordings**
1927	14
1928	15 (3 unissued)
1929	8
1930	16
1931	4

SERMON THEMES

A general comparison of Nix's forty-seven sermons reveals that the recordings averaged three minutes and the sermon texts averaged five hundred words. The recordings made between April 23, 1927, and October 26, 1928, typically begin with a quote from scripture, from either the Old or New Testament, followed by a biblical story or discussion. These themes are similar in nature and form to the chanted sermons by early folk preachers. However, after October 26, 1928, Nix eliminated scriptural and biblical references and shifted to themes associated with daily life of the common people.[23] Although there is no definitive explanation for Nix's shift, he apparently felt the need to address his congregants' daily lives directly. According to David Evans, dwindling sales may have encouraged the Vocalion record company to urge Nix to change his strategy in his sermons from biblical themes to themes of everyday life.[24] However, it is possible that this shift in consciousness from themes associated with the Old Negro to a more modern focus was the result of Nix's association with self-help and racial uplift.

Elwood Nix said that his father was gifted with his voice and his ability to preach. When Reverend Nix spoke, Elwood told me,

> you thought you was right there among all the Jews and Gentiles [people who lived at the time of Jesus]. You would walk out of the church, try to look at yourself and look at other people to see if there were Jews or Gentiles in the audience. I mean the man was superb. You just felt everything that he preached. . . . He was gifted and he felt it. Just like when he was preaching about Jesus on the cross. He would have a cross there. He would start from the pews carrying the cross to the pulpit. It was so beautiful. . . . You just thought you were right there. Some people would stand up to see what he was doing. He was like an actor too. But he felt it. The script was the story he was telling. . . . That made him famous. People clamored for him.[25]

Elwood added, "He didn't have anything false in his life as far as I am concerned. Everything was soulful, natural, and close to the truth."[26] Apparently Reverend Nix's natural abilities included his voice. In his sermons, Nix's texts often reflected the daily lives of his congregants and the issues that were relevant to them. He combined logical arguments with vocal devices to create an emotionally captivating sermon, rousing the sensibilities of his congregants. Nix's dynamic oratory abilities and booming voice, combined with dramatic effects, were his keys to success.

SERMONS' POPULARITY

Nix's first recording, "Black Diamond Express to Hell—Pts. I and II," was recorded on April 23, 1927, and released on the Vocalion, Melotone, and British Decca labels (Vo 1098, Me M12545, DeE F3850, F9720). The Black Diamond Express was a passenger train that ran between New York and Buffalo from 1896 to 1959.[27] Dixon and Godrich describe this sermon as "perhaps the best known sermon of any period."[28] Although no sales figures exist, the fact that Nix recorded six different "parts" of the sermon between 1927 and 1930 suggests that the sermon was popular enough to warrant follow-up recordings.[29] In 1927, an article in the *Pittsburgh Courier* stated that the recording was "one of the most popular phonograph records in years . . . [and] is literally taking the country by storm."[30] *Talking Machine World* reported that "both Brunswick and Vocalion record sales have been large [for June 1927], especially on the new Brunswick race series."[31] This report would most likely have been referring to sales after the April 1927 release of "Black Diamond Express to Hell—Pts. I and II." The *Pittsburgh Courier* article described Nix as a "widely known evangelist,"

Figure 3.1. "The Biggest Selling Record of Today" (advertisement), *The Chicago Defender (National Edition)*, October 1, 1927, 8.

Figure 3.2. "Death May Be Your Christmas Present" (advertisement), *The Chicago Defender (National Edition)*, December 10, 1927, 6.

adding, "Probably no race preacher has won as much national recognition as Rev. Nix. He is not only a powerful influence to the race as a whole, but he has won a host of white friends, who are helping the Reverend to further the cause of the race throughout the entire country."[32] Nix was portrayed as not only a nationally recognized minister, but also as a race leader, similar to Booker T. Washington, who had the support of white people. As previously noted, the sermon was also the inspiration for the preaching scene in the 1929 film *Hallelujah*. Newspapers frequently advertised "Black Diamond Express to Hell," which Vocalion claimed in one advertisement was "the Biggest selling record of today," describing Nix as a "Noted National Evangelist and Power in Jehovah's Quiver" (Figure 3.1).[33] The *Chicago Defender* advertised Nix's sermons a minimum of seventeen times between 1927 and 1929. The advertisements sometimes published the wrong titles of the recordings, such as "Death May Be Your Christmas Present" rather than the actual title of "Death Might Be Your Christmas Gift" (Figure 3.2).[34] Genester Nix claimed that the churches in which

Reverend Nix held revivals would distribute the newspaper advertisements in their churches.[35] Obviously, a nationally known minister could potentially attract large crowds to revival meetings.

Last, but of great importance, is James Weldon Johnson's mention of a Harlem preacher he had heard in the 1920s who called himself a "Son of Thunder"[36] and who "phrased his subject, 'The Black Diamond Express, running between here and hell, making thirteen stops and arriving in hell ahead of time.'"[37] Whether this preacher was definitively Nix is uncertain; however, it is likely, considering that Nix was indeed a Harlem preacher in the 1920s and created the sermon titled "Black Diamond Express to Hell." Johnson was so inspired by the "old-time preachers" that he wrote his own versions of folk sermons in his book *God's Trombones: Seven Negro Sermons in Verse*.

By 1933, an article in the *Spokesman* testified to Nix's popularity: "Rev. A. W. Nix of Cleveland, Ohio, pastor Mt. Calvary Baptist Church, was in our city this week. Rev. Nix is our record preacher, who has aroused the world to much consideration of the world to come."[38] Although Nix was no longer recording by this date, his legacy as a "record preacher" had apparently followed him.

SERMON FORM

The African American chanted sermon may have adopted some of its traits from Puritan sermons in New England. One standard form of the early sermons was to begin with a quotation from scripture (text) followed by an explanation of the text (context), thus called the text-and-content form.[39] The minister applied these concepts by speaking of everyday affairs within a simple structure that is orderly and easily understood. The chanted sermon arose out of the text-and-content form and, as we will see in Nix's sermons, this format was used consistently in his early sermons.

There are usually three main sections to the chanted sermon: the opening, the buildup, and the climax,[40] or sections A, B, and C. However, in the *recorded* chanted sermon, the A section usually consists of a brief introductory line, such as a line from scripture and the title of the sermon. In a standard (church-given) sermon, the opening section, A in this case, begins calmly and slowly, spoken in a conversational manner. The minister then becomes more dramatic and usually speaks at a faster pace (section B), until he reaches the climax (section C), which is the section in which the minister begins chanting. In the B section, the chanted sermon can be further divisible into independent units through the repetition of words, phrases, melody, rhythmic motives, or textual themes, creating individual strophes or verses.[41] Because of the three-minute time limitations of the recorded sermon, ministers such as Nix proceeded quickly between sections B and C, sometimes blurring the distinction of the two sections.[42]

A theme-and-variation type of form uses "bridge material," or the repetition of the primary theme or refrain line, to link and transition between the sermonic units.[43] For example, in Nix's "The Matchless King," he ends each strophe with the phrase "All have had a match" or "He finally met his match." These phrases serve as bridge material, separating the material preceding and following into independent verses or strophes.

It is in the climax section that the preacher's chanting evolves from being an individualistic expression to a group expression with participatory performance characteristics including the congregants' verbal interjections, shouting, singing, and clapping.[44] Typically in a live sermon, the preacher would also build up his vocal intensity, eventually switching to chanting, which would signal the arrival of the climax.[45] However, in the recorded sermon, the minister usually begins chanting almost immediately. Therefore, in Nix's recorded sermons, I have restructured the units as A (brief introduction), B (buildup and chanting), and C (brief conclusion).

My analysis of form is based on lyrical elements of the texts, not musical elements, except where interpolated songs function as verses or transitions (bridge material). I designate a section as a verse if the subject matter differs from that which precedes or follows it. For example, if the sermon begins with theme X, then proceeds to theme Y, I designate each section as a verse. If there are only slight variations in the verse material, I designate the sections with a superscript, as in B^1 and B^2, for example. If a song is inserted into the middle of a sermon and if it advances the message of the sermon, I also consider this either verse or bridge material, depending on its function.

Nix typically commented on biblical stories or characters and the issues that were relevant to his African American congregants in the 1920s, and he gave advice to his congregants. Therefore, the main sections that I have outlined are the following: an introduction to the sermon with a quote from scripture and the sermon title (for his earlier sermons through October 1928); a biblical story that centers on a scene or actors in the scene; issues of contemporary relevance (for the 1920s), often beginning with "many people . . ." or "some people . . ."; followed by Nix explaining how this particular issue was affecting a large number of people or giving advice in which he specifically addresses his congregants with "you," "sister," or "brother," such as "that bed is going to be too short for you" or "sister, watch that woman." The conclusion sections typically are a combination of advice from Nix and a general statement, followed by "Amen."

Nix utilized a simple ABC form in two of his early sermons: the first part of "Black Diamond Express to Hell" and "The Prayer Meeting in Hell," both recorded in 1927. Nix used many combinations of sections in his sermons, with no clear rule or template to the arrangement of the sections. While some of the sermons have simple forms of ABC or ABCD, other sermons have much more complex arrangements. For example, "Death Might Be Your Christmas Gift" has the form of ABCBCBCDCED, with the death theme in the C section recurring regularly, similar to a rondo form. An example of an ABCD form is in Nix's "After the Ball Is Over" (Table 3.4). Nix begins in Section A with a standard introduction, announcing the sermon text, theme, and title; Section B describes the biblical story; Section C gives examples of how these themes can happen in "real life," that is, the contemporary relevance of the theme; and Section D concludes with Nix pleading with sinners to change their ways and offering advice.

Table 3.4. Sections in "After the Ball Is Over"		
Section	**Subsection**	**Theme**
A		Introduction (quote from scripture and title).
B		Biblical story of Salome after the ball.
C		Examples of what happens after the ball.
	C¹	After the ball is when trouble starts.
	C²	Hell, which started on the ballroom floor, will come into the home.
	C³	Bad things can come after the ball, which can lead to death.
D		Pleads with "sons" and "daughters" to give up their frivolous ways before it's too late.

SERMON TRANSCRIPTIONS

In this section, I provide textual transcriptions of several of Nix's most popular sermons.[46] All audio files are taken from reissues on Document Records—*Rev. A. W. Nix, Vol. 1, 1927–1928* (DOCD-5328); *Rev. A. W. Nix & Rev. Emmett Dickinson, Vol. 2, 1928–1931* (DOCD-5490); and *Black Religious Music 1930–1956* (DOCD-5639)—and from the personal collection of Guido van Rijn. The sermon heading includes the date and place of the recording, the labels that recorded it, the Bible verse and chapter, the form, and the title of a spiritual or hymn, if applicable. The text to the left is Reverend Nix's (with his sung text in italics); the words to the right of Nix's and in italics are the congregational responses from the "prayer band," including spoken, shouted, or sung responses. I focus on sermons that were very popular, featured spoken roles, shared themes with bluesmen, demonstrated atypical themes compared with Nix's other sermons or demonstrated Nix's views on life in the 1920s. On the multipart sermons, I use the historical titles of the recordings, so there are minor stylistic inconsistencies among them.

"Black Diamond Express to Hell—Pt. I"

Nix's first recording, "Black Diamond Express to Hell," released on the Vocalion label (Vo 1098), was recorded in Chicago in two parts on April 23, 1927. Melotone (Me M12545) and British Decca (DeE F3850, F9720) also released the sermon.

Nix introduces the sermon with a scriptural verse from Matthew 7:13. The form of A, B, C is based on: (A) introduction of the Bible verse; (B) discussion of the Black Diamond Express Train; and (C) the train's various stops at "depots."

A

I take my text this morning in Matthew seventh chapter and thirteenth verse.
"Enter ye in at the straight gate.
For wide is the gate and broad is the way that leadeth to destruction
And many there be that go in thereat."   *Amen*

B[1] (0:14)

This train
Is known as the Black Diamond Express Train to Hell.   *Well, well*
Sin
Is the engineer,
Pleasure
Is the headlight,
And the Devil
Is the conductor.   [Spiritual melody]

B[2] (0:24)

I see the Black Diamond
As she starts off for hell.   [Spiritual melody]
The bell is ringing,
Hell-bound, hell-bound.

The Devil cries out,
"All aboard for hell."

C¹ (0:35)

First station
Is Drunkardsville.
Stop there and let all the drunkards get on board.   *Alright!*
I have a big crowd down there drinking jump steady,[47]
Some drinking Shinny,[48]
Some drinking moonshine,
Some drinking White Mule and Red Horse.   [Singing (single note)]
All you drunkards
You gotta go to hell on the Black Diamond Train.   *Preach!*

C² (0:52)

The Black Diamond starts off for hell now.
Next station is Liar's Avenue.   [Speaking]
Wait there,
And let all the liars get on board.
I have a big crowd of liars down there,
Have some smooth liars,
Some unreasonable liars,   [Spiritual melody]
Some professional liars,
Some bare-face liars,
Some un-Godly liars,   *Alright!*
Some big liars,
Some little liars,
Some go to bed lying,
Get up lying,   [Spiritual melody hummed]
Lie all day and lie on you and lie on me.   *Well, well, well*
A big crowd of liars,   [Spiritual melody]
You gotta go to hell on the Black Diamond Train.

C³ (1:24)

Next station
Is Deceiversville.
Wait there let all the deceivers get on board.   *Alright!*
Some of you been deceiving one another since you been in the world.

Friends deceiving friends,
Husbands deceiving wives,   [Spiritual melody hummed]
Wives deceiving husbands.
But they got to go to hell on the Black Diamond Train.

C⁴ (1:40)

Next station
Is Conjuration Station.
Wait there
And let all the conjurers get on board.   *Alright!*
I have a big crowd of Louisiana conjurers down there.
They got to go to hell on the Black Diamond Train.
They always taking brick dust and brass pins and matchheads
And making little hands[49] selling to one another.
But you got to go to hell on the Black Diamond Train.   *Alright!*

C⁵ (2:00)

Next station
Is Confusion Junction.
Wait there and let all the confusion-makers get on.
Some of you raise confusion in your home,
Confusion in the street,   [Speaking]
Confusion in the church, confusion everywhere you go.   [Singing]
But you got to go to hell on the Black Diamond Train.

C⁶ (2:15)

Next station
Is Fight's Town.   *Alright!*
Wait there,
And let all the church fighters get on board.   [Speaking]
I have a big crowd of church-fighters down there.
They never go to the prayer meeting,   [Speaking]
They never go to the Sunday school,   [Singing]
They never go to the morning service,
They always stay away from the morning church
Until they hear about the business meeting,
And they come running up out of Brazos Bottom[50]
To pull off a big fight in God's church.   [Spiritual melody]

Well, all you church fighters,
You gotta go to hell on the Black Diamond Train.

(2:45)

And now the Black Diamond Train will stop just a minute
To take on brimstone for hell.

"Black Diamond Express to Hell—Pt. II"

After a brief pause, the Black Diamond continues on its journey in section B.

B[3]

Black Diamond has taken on a fresh supply
Of brimstone
And now she's ready to pull out for hell.
Sin
Is the engineer
Pleasure is the headlight
And the devil
Is the conductor.   *Amen!*

C[7] (0:12)

Next station
Is Dancing Hall Depot.   *Well alright!*
Wait there.
I have a large crowd of church members to get on down
   there.   [Speaking]
Some of you think you can sing in the choir on Sunday
And Charleston on the ballroom floor on Monday.   *Well, well, well*
But you gotta go to hell on the Black Diamond Train.   [Speaking]
The Black Diamond pulls off now for hell.

C[8] (0:31)

Next station
Is Gambler's Tower.   [Speaking]
Wait there

And let all the gamblers get on board.   [Speaking]
I have a big crowd of gamblers and crap shooters and card
    players   [Singing]
And bootleggers got to ride
The Black Diamond Train to hell.   [Speaking]
They all gets on the Black Diamond Train, she starts off for hell now.
She's almost into hell.   [Singing]

C⁹ (0:51)

Next station
Is Stealin' Town.   *Alright!*
Wait there
And let all the church thieves get on board.   *Preach Elder!*
I have a big crowd of members in the church always been stealin'   *Well,*
    well, well
Ever since they been in the church.
Some always beggin' money for their church and never turn it in.
    [Speaking]
Always givin' church suppers
And then steal half the money.   *Oh my goodness!*
All you church thieves   *Alright!*
You got to go to hell on the Black Diamond Train.

C¹⁰ (1:15)

Next station
Is Plotter's Gap.
Stop there and let all the church plotters get on.   [Speaking]
Have a big crowd always plottin' against the church,   [Speaking]
Always plottin' against the preachem [preacher],   *Elder Preach!*
Always plottin' against the deacon,   [Speaking]
Out plottin' against the church program.   *Well, well*
Always be hid behind closed doors plottin' against me.
All you church fighters,   *Well, well*
You got to go to hell on the Black Diamond Train.   *Alright!*

C¹¹ (1:37)

Next station   *Well, well, well*
Is Little No Harm Park [?]   *Yeah!*

I got a big crowd
Always down at the park, parkin' all the time.   [Speaking]
They never can come to church on Sunday.   [Speaking]
Always parkin' all the time.

C^{12} (1:49)

And now,
The Devil sends a dispatch to the engineer   [Singing]
And tell him to pull his throttle wide open
And hit [the] damnation switch in the black shades of midnight   *Well,*
   well, well
And make a fast run for Hell.

D^1 (2:01)

Oh gambler   [Singing]
Get off the Black Diamond Train.   [Speaking]
Oh midnight rambler,   [Singing]
Get off the Black Diamond Train.
Oh, backslider,   [Singing]
Get off the Black Diamond Train.

D^2 (2:14)

Children aren't you glad,
You got off the Black Diamond Train   *Well, well, well*
A long time ago.   *Well, well, well*
I'm so glad I got off a long time ago.
Ever since I got off
My soul has been singing:

E (2:27)

All of my sins been taken away.
Well, all of my sins been taken away.
Well, all of my sins been taken away
Well glory hallelujah to his name.
All of my sins been taken away.

D³ (2:51)

Children aren't you glad
You got off a long time ago.   *Amen!*
I'm glad I got off a long time ago.   *Amen!*

Amen.

"The White Flyer to Heaven—Part 1"

"The White Flyer to Heaven" was recorded on June 29, 1927, in Chicago, just two months after the recording of "Black Diamond Express to Hell." It was released on the Vocalion (Vo 1170), Brunswick (Br 7020), and Supertone (St S2252) labels. The scriptural verse is from Matthew 7:14. The sermon includes a spiritual, "O the Blood," and a hymn, "Look for Me." Whereas the Black Diamond was loaded with sinners en route to hell, the White Flyer travels to heaven with those who have been saved.

The "White Flyer" is also a two-part sermon; thus, the second part is a continuation of the first. The form is based on the following parts: (A) introduction with a Bible verse, (B) description of the White Flyer, (C) train depots, (D) spiritual, (E) Nix speaks to the congregation, and a reprise of C. On the White Flyer, Jesus is riding on the train and directing its route. In "Black Diamond Express to Hell," the main theme centers around the stops at the various depots of sin. However, in "The White Flyer to Heaven," the focus is on Jesus, his trials, and what is required of those who want to be saved and ride on the train with him to heaven. In Part 1, the depots of the White Flyer are "Mount Calvary," the "first heaven," the "second heaven," the planets, and the "high rock of ages."

A¹

I take my text in Matthew seventh chapter and fourteenth verse.
"Straight is the gate and narrow is the way
Which leadeth into life
And few there be that find it."   *Amen*

B¹ (0:12)

This train
Is known as the White Flyer to heaven.
God is the engineer,

The Holy Ghost is the headlight,
And Jesus is the conductor.

B² (0:22)

I see the White Flyer
As she gets ready to start off for heaven.   *Well, well* [Sung]
The bell is ringing heaven-bound, heaven-bound.
Jesus cries out, "All aboard for heaven."   *Well*

B³ (0:34)

No liars   [Spiritual melody]
Can ride on this train.
No deceivers
Can ride on this train.
No murderers,
No gamblers can ride on this train.
Every man must purchase his ticket
At the station of Regeneration.

C¹ (0:49)

And as the White Flyer starts off for heaven,   *Well, well, well* [Sung]
Jesus will say,
"The first stop
Will be Mount Calvary.   *Alright*

(0:57)

I wants to show the saints of God
Where I died on the cross.   *Well* [Sung]
I want to see them   *Well, well* [Sung]
Where they put a crown of seventy-two thorns on my brow.
On the cross   [Singing]
Where they drove the nails in my hand.
On the cross,
Where they pierced me in my side.   [Singing]
On the cross, where I cried,   [Singing]
'It is finished.'   [Spiritual melody]
On the cross where

I signed every man's bond
With my own blood." *Preach!*

(1:27)

And as the train stops there a while. *Preach!*
I can hear some old battle-scarred child *Well, well, well* [Sung]
Of God look in the crowd and sing:

D¹ (1:35)

Oh the blood,
Oh the blood,
Oh the blood done signed my name
Oh the blood,
Oh the blood,
Oh the blood done signed my name
Oh the blood,
Oh the blood,
Well, the blood done signed my name
Oh the blood,
Done signed
My name[51]

E¹ (2:08)

Children,
Didn't He sign your name   [Shouting]
In His own blood?   [Shouting]
Have I got a witness here?   [Shouting]

C² (2:15)

And then when the train will leave Mount Calvary,
Will pass on through the first heaven. *Yes*
The heaven of the clouds, *Alright*
And through God's machine shop   [Humming]
Where he pick up his whirlwind in his storm.   [Spiritual]
And go higher and higher,
Higher and higher.

C^3 (2:31)

We'll pass on through the Second Heaven.   *Yes*
The starry big heaven   *Alright*
And view the flying stars
And dashing meteors,   *Well, well, well* [Sung]

C^4 (2:39)

And then pass on by Mars and Mercury
And Jupiter and Venus   [Spiritual]
And Saturn and Uranus and Neptune
With her four glittering moons.
But don't let me stop there.

C^5 (2:49)

Higher and higher,
Higher and higher,   *Preach!*
On up to
The high rocks of ages.   [Shouting]
And stop there in a shelter in a time of storm.   *Yes*
And rock our troubles away.   *Have mercy*

"The White Flyer to Heaven—Part II"

Part II begins with a repeat of section B, reintroducing the White Flyer. In section C, the train then travels up past the "rock of ages" and "beyond the sun, moon, and stars." While the train ascends, Nix refers to the lyrics of the hymn "Amazing Grace" in section D and sings the song "Look for Me." The White Flyer finally reaches heaven in section C.

B^4 (0:02)

And now the White Flyer
Will continue its trip to heaven.
God
Is the engineer,
The Holy Ghost is the headlight,
And Jesus is the conductor.   *Amen!* [Shouted]

C⁶ (0:12)

And as the White Flyer
Starts on
Up from the high rocks of ages,   *Yes*
On higher and higher,   *Amen* [Sung]
Up beyond the sun, moon, and stars,   *Amen* [Spoken]
Back behind God's eternal word,   *Yes*

D² (0:24)

Someone will cry out,
"Amazing Grace, how sweet the sound
That saved a wretch like me.   *Amen!* [Shouted]
I once was lost but now I'm found,   [Spiritual melody]
Was blind but now I see."   *Let the name of Jesus*
And then look back over the distance over which we have come
And then cry out:
"Through many dangers,
Toils and snares
I have already come.   *Amen*
T'was grace that brought me safe thus far,   *Let the name of Jesus*
And grace will lead me on home."

C⁷ (0:56)

And then go higher and higher,   *I really need*
Higher and higher,   *Your* [Indecipherable]
Until we
Will bid farewell to every tear   *Yes*
And wipe our weeping eyes.

C⁸ (1:05)

And then,
We'll go dashing through the pearly white gates   [Speaking]
On into God's eternal kingdom.   [Spiritual melody]
And when we get there,
I'm gonna sit down   *Yes*
And chatter with the Father   *Yes*
And chatter with the Son
And talk about the world I just come from.   *Yes*

(1:22)

And then someone will cry out,   [Spiritual melody]
"Trouble will be no more.
Home,
Home at last." [Sung single note]

(1:30)

And then when I get there,
Some mother's child will cry out:
"The reason why   [Speaking]
I've made up my mind   *Yes*
To go to heaven,   [Speaking]
I've
Got a mother up there.   *Well, well, well* [Sung]
I promised her
I'd meet her in glory.   *Amen!* [Shouted]
Yes,
I told her on her dying bed   [Speaking]
Before she left this world."   *Well, well* [Sung]

D⁴ (1:53)

Song: "Look for Me"⁵²
You may look for me but I'll be there, I'll be there   [Singers join in on "for
    me"]
I'll be there, I'll be there
You may look for me but I'll be there, I'll be there
Glory to His name

E² (2:20)

Children, are you going?   *Yes!* [Shouted & Spiritual melody]
Have you got the ticket?   *Yes!* [Shouted & Spiritual melody]
Well if you don't go,   [Spiritual melody]
I'm going on anyhow

(2:29)

And when I get there
I'm going to sit down
And meet my mother in heaven.
I'm gonna help her crown Jesus Lord of all,
When I get in glory.
Amen.

"The Black Diamond Express to Hell—Part 3"

Nix recorded the third and fourth parts of "The Black Diamond Express to Hell"
on August 24, 1929, in Chicago, and they were released on the Vocalion label
(Vo 1421). "The Black Diamond Express to Hell—Part 3" has a simple form of
ABC: (A) introduction of Black Diamond theme, (B) the devil, and (C) depots.

A

The second section
Of the Black Diamond Express Train is now pulling out for hell. *Alright*
Sin
Is the engineer. *Alright*
Pleasure is the headlight, *Yes*
The Devil is the conductor. *Alright*

B (0:10)

So many people are going to hell
Until the first section could not carry them all.   [Speaking]
The Devil has been busy day and night *Yes*
Getting his crowd ready
For the Black Diamond. *Alright*

(0:19)

He has a fine personality. *Yes*
He is a sheikh of sheikhs. *Yeah!*
The Black Diamond
Is now ready to pull out for hell. *Yes*
The devil cries out,
"All aboard for hell." *Alright*

THE SERMONS   129

C¹ (0:29)

First station
Is Murderer's Road.   *Yeah*
Got a big crowd of murderers down there.   [Speaking]
Old murderers and young murderers.
They'll murder your feelings   *Preach!*
And destroy your reputation.   *Yes*
But they got to go to hell on the Black Diamond.   [Speaking]

C² (0:41)

Next station
Is Immoral Switch.   [Speaking]
That's where young women
Lose their womanhood and virtue.   [Speaking]
Old girls   [Spiritual melody]
From good families
Are led astray by bad women
And no-'count men.
But they got to go to hell on the Black Diamond Train.

C³ (0:55)

Next station   [Spiritual melody]
Is Gossiping Town.   *Yes*
A big crowd of tattlers
And gossipers down there,   [Speaking]
Always going from door to door.   *Yes*
They're talking about everything and everybody.
Well, they got to go to hell on the Black Diamond Train.   *Alright*

C⁴ (1:06)

Next station
Is Knockersville.   [Speaking]
A big crowd of knockers down there.   [Spiritual melody]
Always knocking on the preacher,   *Preach!*
And knocking on the church
And knocking on the lodges.   [Speaking]
They're knocking on Heaven   [Spiritual melody]

And they're knocking on hell.
You may knock the Black Diamond,
But you got to go to hell on the Black Diamond Train.

C⁵ (1:22)

Next station
Is Cheating Town.   [Spiritual melody]
A big crowd down there
Are trying to get up in the world
By cheating everybody   *Yes*
At some of these grocery stores.
You can never get full weight   *No*
At some of these meat markets.
When the butcher weighs your meat,
He'll weigh his hands with it.   [Speaking and singing]
At some of these business stores,
When if you don't get a receipt when you pay your bill,
They'll make you pay it over again.   [Speaking]
And they got to go to hell on the Black Diamond Train.

C⁶ (1:45)

Next station
Is Dishonestville.   [Spiritual melody]
There's a big crowd down there   *Yeah*
That won't do right to save your life.   *Uh-huh*
They'll borrow money from you   [Speaking]
And never pay you back.   [Speaking]
They owe everybody in the neighborhood,
And if you ask them for it,
They'll get mad with ya'   [Speaking]
And stop speaking to you.
They always buying on credit
And never pay their bill.
They move every month.   [Spiritual melody]
To keep from paying their rent
But they got to go to hell on the Black Diamond Train.

C⁷ (2:10)

Next station
Is Hypocrite's Flag.   [Speaking]
A big crowd of hypocrites is at church down there.
They'll pray and shout all day Sunday   *That's right*
And raise hell all day Monday.   *Alright*
They claim to be your friend
But they're running with your enemies.   *Okay*
But they got to go to hell on the Black Diamond Train.

C⁸ (2:25)

And now the Black Diamond
Will stop just a minute
To see if there's anybody
That would like to get off.   [Speaking]

The "stations" at which the Black Diamond Train stops in Part 3 are a continuation of the stops from the first and second parts. As spoken by Nix, the train needs a "second section" to carry the large numbers of sinners to hell. The train pauses to give the sinners a chance to rethink their lives and get off the train before proceeding in Part 4.

"The Black Diamond Express to Hell—Part 4"

"The Black Diamond Express to Hell—Part 4" is a continuation of the Black Diamond Train's journey to hell. The form is as follows: (C) continuation of stations, (D) contemporary women, (E) the Black Diamond, (F) Nix's advice, (G) song, and a return to (F) Nix's advice. The stations are "Fussin' Town" and the twentieth-century style shop.

C⁸

A mother's girl
Who promised to meet her mother in Heaven
Has just stepped off the Black Diamond.   *That's right*
And now the Black Diamond
Will continue its trip on to Hell.   [Speaking]

C⁹ (0:08)

Next station
Is Fussin' Town. *Yeah*
A big crowd of women down there
Who'd rather fuss than to eat. *Yeah*
Some go to bed fussin'
Get up fussin' *Yes*
They go to work fussin' *Alright*
And come home fussin'. [Spiritual melody]
They'll raise a fuss anywhere. *Alright*
If it's possible,
They'd raise a fuss in Heaven. *Yes*
But they got to go to Hell on the Black Diamond Train. *Alright*

C¹⁰ (0:28)

Next station [Spiritual melody]
Is a twentieth-century style shop.
It's where the women
Get the latest styles
For the modern dress. *Alright*

D¹ (0:35)

The dresses the women are wearing these days *Yes*
Are almost a knock-out. *Yes*
Some are wearing Crêpe de chine and Georgette
That you can see clear through them. [Singing]
Some are wearing satin-beaded dresses *Yes*
With low necks and low backs. *Yes*
And all of them
Are wearing
Short, tight skirts cut off above the knees [Moaning] *Alright*
Through-peep shoes *Yes*
Window-pane stockings and socks *Alright*
And some no stockings at all *Alright*
With painted lips and powdered faces. [Spiritual melody]
They will charm you
And then talk to you with their eyes.

D² (1:02)

I tell you   [Singing]
This modern dress today
Is mighty hard on the men.
You can find
These women in large numbers   *Yes*
On Hastings Street in Detroit
And on Forty-Seventh
Street and South Parkway⁵³   [Singing]
In Chicago
Along Market Street in St. Louis   *Yes*
On Eighteenth Street in Kansas City   *Yes*
On Lennox Avenue in New York   *Alright*
On Beale Street in Memphis   *Yes*
On South Rampart in New Orleans
And on Decatur Street in Atlanta, Georgia.

D³ (1:29)

And when these women ride on the train
With their legs all crossed   [Singing]
The men will have to almost close their eyes.
And the thing that looks so bad now
Old women
Have cut off their dresses
Above their knees
Trying to look giddy and gay.

E¹ (1:42)

But the Black Diamond will give them
A fast ride on down to hell.
And when the Black Diamond
Will hit the main line   *Yes*
And make a fast run for Hell,   *That's right*
She'll land in Hell
While the Hell-fire's burning   *Yes*
And while the Hell-hounds are howling.   *Alright*
And when the Devil
Will pull out the linchpin of damnation   *Yes*

And a lake of fire and brimstone   *Yes*
The devil will unload in Hell.

F^1 (2:03)

Oh mother's son
Get off the Black Diamond Train.   *That's right*
Oh, midnight rambler   [Moaning]
Get off the Black Diamond Train.
Ever since I got off the Black Diamond Train
My soul has been singing:

G (2:15)

Well the awful sinner
When the world's on fire
Won't you want Christ's bosom
For to be your pillow
Oh hide me over
In the Rock of ages
Rock of ages
Cleft for me

F^2 (2:35)

Brothers!
If you don't get off
The Black Diamond Train
She'll land you in Hell
Just as sure as you're born.
Amen.

"The Black Diamond Express to Hell—Part 4" provides insight into Nix's views of the "modern woman." For over a minute, Nix discusses the "modern dress" of women in the 1920s, consisting of satin, beaded fabric, low-cut dresses, short skirts, and "peep toe" shoes popular with "flappers" of the era. Nix claims that the modern dress is "mighty hard on the men" who have to "close their eyes" in order not to be lured by women's sexy apparel. Nix does not give equal credit or responsibility to men, and according to him, women, their clothes, and their sinful behavior are the downfall of men. He also discusses women as the ones who are constantly "fussin,'" but again does not lay responsibility with men.

THE SERMONS   135

"A Country Man in Town"

Nix recorded "A Country Man in Town" on December 12, 1929, in Chicago. It
was released by the Vocalion label (Vo1448). The form is based on the following:
(A) introduction of the theme, (B) contemporary relevance, (C) Nix's advice,
with a return to (B) and (C).

A

I want to talk to you this morning from the subject:
A country man in town.   *Amen*

B¹ (0:04)

These country-fed and country-raised men   *Yes*
Who come to the big cities
They lose control of themselves.   [Shouts]
And they go crazy about
The city fast life   *Yes*
And the good-looking city women.   *Alright*

B² (0:16)

Let me tell you men
Some of these city women
Sure do know how to trim a country man.   [Shouts] *Well, well* [Sung]
They will feed him on a good promise   *Yes*
And make him believe
That everything is going to be peaches for him.   *Yes*
And that crazy fool will dump   *Well, well, well* [Sung]
His whole pocketbook   [Speaking]
And all his money
In that city woman's lap   *Amen*
Just on a good promise.   [Spiritual melody]
And all he gets
Is a lot of hot air   *Yes*
And a sweet promise.   *Oh yes*

B³ (0:40)

Some of these country men   [Spiritual melody]
Just from the backwoods

136 THE SERMONS

Of Mississippi, Georgia, and Alabama,
Texas, Arkansas, and Louisiana   *Amen*
Who have never
Been in the city life before   *Well, well* [Sung]
Will come up here
And forsake their own wives and children   *Well, well* [Sung]
And fall in love
And go crazy   [Spiritual melody]
About these butterfly,
Giddy and gay   *Yes*
Partnership
City women.

B⁴ (1:03)

And even long before
They are bumping
His head
And filling him up with a lot of hot air   [Speaking]
And sweet promises
Making him believe
That there will be
A big time for him   *Well, well, well* [Sung]
On Saturday night   *Yeah*
After he's paid off.   *Yes*

B⁵ (1:17)

And just as soon
As she gets all of his money   [Shouts]
She will call him sweet names   *Yes*
And hitch him with a sweet promise.
And while he is waiting,
She will go right out   [Shouts]
And give that money   *Lord have mercy*
To her whole regular city   *Yes he will* [Sung]
Sweetheart.   [Shouts]
And just . . . he's just a country man in town   *Yes*
Paying a big price   [Singing]
For the city life.   *Yeah*

B⁶ (1:35)

You young men,
They will
Take you out on this big crowd   *Yes*
And make you spend all the taxi fares,   [Singing]
Make you pay all
The midnight suppers   [Layers]
And all the midnight trains.   *Yes*
And all you get
Is a sweet name   [Humming]
And a sweet promise   [Humming]
And a lot of hot air.   [Humming]
"I will see you on Saturday night."   *Yeah*

C¹ (1:54)

Why don't you country men   [Humming]
Learn some sense   *Yes*
And ... be yourself   [Spiritual melody]
And have some sense?

(2:00)

Stay with your own wives   *Alright*
And your own children   *Yes*
Who love and care for you.   *Amen*
And uh, stop letting these city women   *Well, well, well* [Sung]
Make a big fool out of you.   *Alright*

B⁷ (2:09)

And the thing that looks so bad   [Spiritual melody]
Is to see an old man   [Layers]
Going crazy
About a young city girl   *Yes*
And, uh
She will told ...   *Well, well* [Sung]
And get what ...
Make him do everything she wants him to do.
And uh ...

138   THE SERMONS

This will be
An old man, when she gets through with him.   *Yes*
He'll look like
A lost tramp in a starving land.   *Well, well* [Sung]

B⁸ (2:28)

You   [Spiritual melody]
Ah, young men
And women.
These young women
Will . . . strip you   *Yes*
They'll make you go crazy about them
And carry you a cat's life.   *Amen*

(2:37)

She can do anything she wants to do.   *Yes*
She can stay
Out half the night   [Shouts]
And come home
And dare you to open your mouth.   [Spiritual melody]

B⁹ (2:44)

She can make
While her
Husband work every day
And on Sundays and holidays   *Alright*
And make him work overtime.
And while she run the streets
And have a big time.
And when she comes home at night,
All tired and broke down   *Yes*
And needs a little rubbing,
She's either sick,
Or feels bad,
Or sleepy.
It is a country man
All tired out   *Yes*
Living in hell   *Well* [Sung]
With the fast life.

C² (3:09)

Say old man,
You're going crazy   *Well, well* [Sung]
About your pig meat.   *Yes*
But before that pig meat gets through with you   [Singing]
You'll wish you had had
Hog meat.   *Alright*

C³ (3:17)

Let me tell you
You had better
Be yourself   [Singing]
Stay in your class!   [Layers]
Don't let your head run away with your feet!   [Layers]
That city fast life   [Layers]
Will soon carry [you to] your grave.   [Layers]
Amen.

While Nix's admonitions to new migrants to Chicago encouraged financial responsibility, they were also clearly class-based. For example, in "A Country Man in Town," he advises migrants from the "backwoods" of Mississippi, Georgia, Alabama, Texas, Arkansas, and Louisiana to "Stay in your class! Don't let your head run away with your feet! That city fast life will soon carry [you to] your grave." Nix used humor to get his point across in a language that his lower-class congregants could understand: "Say old man, you're going crazy about your pig meat [i.e., a young woman]. But before that pig meat gets through with you you'll wish you had had hog meat [i.e., an older woman]." The implication that male migrants were easily disillusioned with and taken advantage of by city women is almost identical to the portrayal in the film *Hallelujah*. In the film, a country man goes into the city and is swindled by a fast-living, loose, young city woman who then turns around and gives all of his money to her lover, a city man. "A Country Man in Town" was released just four months after *Hallelujah*'s release; thus, Nix may have taken his theme from the film. Regardless, it is apparent that Nix believed that rural southerners were different from and more vulnerable than their northern counterparts.

"Pay Your Honest Debts"

"Pay Your Honest Debts" was recorded in mid-January 1930 in Chicago and released by the Vocalion label (Vo 1470). In it, Nix uses the basic form of (A) introduction of the theme, (B) contemporary relevance, and (C) Nix's advice.

A

My dear friends
I'm to talk to you this morning from the subject:
Pay your honest debts.   *Well*

B¹ (0:06)

There are so many people in the world today
Who are trying to ride through on everybody.   *Well alright*
They will buy groceries on credit,
Eat them up and never pay for them.   *Hallelujah*
They'll buy furniture on credit and wear it out,   *Yes*
And never pay for it.

B² (0:21)

Some people even get married on credit   *Hm-hum*
And never pay the preacher.   *Yeah*
And I'm a good witness to that
Because a lot of all you here still owes me yet.   *Amen*
Brother,
Why don't you pay your honest debts?   *Well*

B³ (0:32)

Some of you all,
When you get sick you want the doctor to come on credit,
And you never pay your doctor's bill.   [Speaking]
And when you die,
The undertaker's going to get his pay   *Hm-hum*
If he has to take all your insurance.   *Hm-hum*
Brother why don't you be a man
And pay your honest debts?   *Well, well, well, well* [Sung]

THE SERMONS   141

B⁴ (0:47)

Some people even move every month
To keep from paying their room   *That's right*
And house rent.   *Preach!*
Some of you all dress so swell and fine.   *Preach Brother!*
You make a big show on the outside   [Speaking]
Just like you're going to do on Easter day
And you owe everybody in town.   *Hallelujah, have mercy*
And the collector
Is running you down every day.

C¹ (1:04)

Here's Sister Jane   *Well* [Sung]
Right here now   *Well, well, well, well* [Sung]
All dolled up
In her fine Easter outfit,   *Yeah*
And I bet she bought it on credit   [Shouts]
And has never paid for them.   *Hm-hum*

Female voice:

Brother pastor that's my business how I buy my clothes.
You just preach the gospel,
And stay off my clothes!
I always buy on credit.

Nix:

Well why won't you pay your honest debts then?

C² (1:23)

A lot of you all are here
Always borrowing money from your friends   [Humming]
And you never pay them back.
It's getting so these days
You hate to even meet your old friends.   *Yeah*
Just as soon as you meet them,   [Spiritual melody]
They're hard up

And want to borrow money
And if you let them have it,
They'll never pay you back.
They are just beating their way
Through the world.

C³ (1:43)

As fast
As some people work hard and save up a little money,
There's always someone coming along
Hard up and singing the blues
Who wants to borrow your money.
Brother!   *Well, well, well* [Sung]
You ought to pay your honest debts.

C⁴ (1:56)

Too many people are trying   [Shouts]
To live above their wants.   [Shouts]
You only get a small salary,
And why don't you live
According to your income?   *Alright*
You try to buy the finest cars   [Speaking]
And the finest clothes   *Have mercy*
And you never pay for any of them.   [Speaking]

C⁵ (2:09)

You're always
Up here in Chicago trying
To live in these high-   *Well* [Sung]
Priced flats.   *Well* [Sung]
You are doing   *Well, well, well* [Sung]
Towards everything to pay this high rent.   *Yes!*
Some of you are selling moonshine,   *Hm-hum*
Some of you playing the policy wheel,   [Shouts]
Some of you are giving house parties,   [Shouts]
Trying to live   [singing]
In these high-priced flats,   *Well, well*
And you know you're not able to pay for them.   [Singing]

C^6 (2:30)

You all
Are leaving your honest debts unpaid.   *Hm-hum*
Why don't
You live according to your income   *Well* [Sung]
And pay your honest debts?   *Well, well, well, well* [Sung]

C^7 (2:37)

Live so   [Singing]
You can look every man in the eye   [Speaking]
And tell him, shake his hand   [Singing]
And tell him where to go.   *Preach!*

C^8 (2:43)

Live so   *Preach!*
You can have . . .
You don't have to be running   *Well alright*
And dodging from everybody.   *Well, well, well, well* [Sung]
Whatever you buy,
Buy what you can pay for,   [Singing]
And pay for what you buy.

C^9 (2:53)

Brother this way,
Trying to rise through the world   *Well* [Sung]
On everybody
And borrowing money from everybody   [Blues riff]
And never paying your bill   [Shouts]
Has got to be stopped.   [Shouts]
Get you a job,   *Well, well, well, well* [Sung]
And go to work,
And pay your honest debts.   *Amen*
Amen.

Nix's advice to his congregants is honest work for honest pay, rather than illicit behavior and activities, such as gambling. He discourages conspicuous consumption and encourages his congregants to live within their means rather

144   THE SERMONS

than putting on "a big show on the outside." Nix is not afraid to confront his congregants, including those who owed him money, stating, "Some people even get married on credit and never pay the preacher. And I'm a good witness to that because a lot of you here still owes me yet." He encourages his congregants to not live above their means or become dependent on credit.

"It Was Tight like That"

Nix's sermons "It Was Tight like That" and "How Long—How Long," both recorded on the Vocalion label (Vo 1505) in Chicago in 1930, serve as reminders of two extremely popular blues songs that were recorded in 1928: the first, "It's Tight like That" (Vo 1216), was recorded by pianist and future gospel composer Georgia Tom (Thomas A. Dorsey) and guitarist Tampa Red; the second, "How Long, How Long Blues" (Vo 1191), was a hit by Leroy Carr and Scrapper Blackwell.[54] "It Was Tight like That" has a form of (A) introduction of the theme, (B) contemporary relevance, (C) Nix's advice, (D) contemporary women, and a recap of C.

A

My dear brothers and sisters
I'm going to speak to you this morning
From this famous subject:
It was tight like that.   *Well*

B[1] (0:07)

As we find ourselves standing upon the pathway of life,   *Yes*
And realize the many difficulties,
Through which we have come,   *Hm-hum*
And the many battles in which we have fought,   [Speaking]
Against our enemies and the devil himself,   *Yes*
We can all truthfully say,
It was tight like that.   *Well, well* [Sung]

B[2] (0:23)

This seems to be a hard and tight world we're living in these days,
It getting so nobody wants to be bothered with you,   [Spiritual melody]
Unless you got something to give them.   *Yes*
Old friends

THE SERMONS 145

Don't want to know you anymore.   *Alright*
And new friends
Don't want to meet you.
And strangers
Don't want to be bothered with you.   *Alright*
And you will find yourself
In the middle of a bad fix   *Yes*
When it's tight like that.   [Speaking]

B^3 (0:44)

Just think
When a man is cold,
Hungry and mad,
And ain't got no job   *Well, well, well* [Sung]
And you can't borrow any money,   *Yes*
And your credit is no good,   *Alright*
Your wife is fussin',   *Alright*
And the children are crying.
Brother,
You will feel like you in hell   *Well, alright!*
When it's tight like that.   *Yes*

B^4 (1:00)

Life ain't worth living   [Singing]
When you are broke.
Your appetite
Will call for everything
That's no joke.   *Yes*
There comes an opportunity   [Shouts]
That knocks on every man's door.   *Preach!*
There's no need of anybody being always broke,   *Well, well, well, well*
   [Sung]
Always out and down,
All the time.

C^1 (1:15)

I have been warning you men and women   [Unknown melody]
That these hard times would come,

When times would be tight,
Jobs would be hard to get, *Alright!*
And you couldn't get much money. *Yes*
You should have made preparations [Unknown melody]
For these hard times *Alright*
When it was tight like that. *Alright*

C² (1:28)

But now,
You've run through all your money [Unknown melody]
You've lost your job,
And starvation is at your door. *That's right*
Don't bring me your troubles now!
I can't use them. [Spiritual melody]
Bring me some money!
And bring along with you hams and chickens.
It's money I want,
And money I must have, *Yes*
And a-plenty of something to eat.
So I can satisfy
My gastronomical propensities
When it's tight like that.

C³ (1:51)

Get ready!
Starvation is coming!
Come down,
You high-minded men!
Live so you can have friends. *Well, well, well* [Sung]
Don't let your money and your job
Swell your head, [Shouts]
For the prodigal Son
Has plenty money.
But he lost all he had [Shouts]
When it was tight like that. *Alright*
Don't try to be what you are not. [Shouts]

D^1 (2:09)

There's Aunt Betsy sitting here now,   *Yes*
She's a member of our praying band.
She's too old to do anything else now but pray.
But I remember
When she was a wheel-horse in this town   [Singing]
Painting the town red.   [Shouts]
She had all you women's husbands running to her house,
And you were afraid to open your mouths.   [Shouts]
She would take any woman's husband,
When she was tight like that.

(2:29)

Female:
Yes Elder,
Praying is all I can do now.
But believe me,
When I think about the past,
This world don't owe me anything.
In my young days,
I had my time.
I was tight like that.

D^2 (2:41)

Nix:
Yes, sister,
But you ain't got nothing on me!
How can you feel so happy, Sister Lucy   *Well* [Sung]
When your house rent is due,   [Shouts]
And you're behind with your furniture bills,
And your lodge dues are not paid,   [Singing]
And you're behind in your pastor's salary,
And you haven't got no money and no friends,
Everything is tight like that,
What will you do?

(3:00)

Female voice:
Brother Pastor
When everything gets tight like that
I just let the bills go.
I ain't gonna let nothing send my soul to hell.
When I ain't got no money,
I got good religion.
Glory, Hallelujah!

C⁴ (3:12)

Nix:
Yes, religion is alright,
But I want to tell you all now,
When your bills are due and
Starvation's at your door,   *Yes*
And your friends are all gone,   [Shouts]
And everything is tight like that,   [Shouts]
You better have some money in your pocket   *Yes!*
To pay your bills   *Yes!*
When it's tight like that.   [Shouts]
Amen.

Nix describes the title "It Was Tight like That" as a "famous subject," implying that he had knowledge of both the song and its popularity.[55] The song title has an overt sexual reference, so it is surprising that Nix would have borrowed the title for his sermon. However, because the Dorsey-Tampa Red song was so well known, other preachers and artists obviously tried to capitalize on its popularity. Rev. J. M. Gates also recorded a sermon on the "Tight like That" theme, titled "These Hard Times Are Tight like That" (OK 8850) on December 12, 1930, ten months after Nix's recording.[56] "It Was Tight like That," released in February 1930, was not only a response to the Georgia Tom-Tampa Red song with the similar title, but also a response to the beginning of the Great Depression, which shook the world in 1929. Nix's version of "It Was Tight like That" comments on the hardships brought on by the Great Depression; however, some of Nix's lyrics imply sexual themes, similar to the original blues song:

But I remember
When she was a wheel-horse in this town

Painting the town red.
She had all you women's husbands running to her house,
And you were afraid to open your mouths.
She would take any woman's husband,
When she was tight like that.

Nix used the "tight like that" theme to refer to both economic hardships and risqué sexual behavior.

Nix's response to the female who says she "just lets the bills go" because she "got good religion" demonstrates his affinity for upward mobility, financial responsibility, and self-help. He insists that religion alone is not enough, that one must have faith plus action, referencing James 2:14–17, which states, "What does it profit, my brethren, if someone says he has faith but does not have works? Can faith save him? . . . Thus also faith by itself, if it does not have works, is dead."[57] In response to the female congregant, Nix claims, "religion is alright, but I want to tell you all now, when your bills are due, starvation's at your door, and your friends are all gone, and everything is tight like that, you better have some money in your pocket to pay your bills when it's tight like that." Nix reprimands his congregants, demanding that they take action in their lives—in essence, switching the emphasis from religion alone to practical solutions, demonstrating a shift from the slavery-era dependence on religion as the only way out to the modern uplift theme of self-help.

"How Long–How Long"

"How Long—How Long" is the B side to "It Was Tight like That" and has a form of (A) introduction of the theme, (B) contemporary relevance, (C) "how long" theme, (D) Nix confronts congregants, and (E) conclusion.

A

My dear brothers and sisters
I'm going to speak to you tonight
From the subject: How long, how long.   *Yeah*

B¹ (0:06)

This is a solemn question that comes to every man
Woman, boy, and girl.   *Yes*
It deals with your past and your future.   *Yes*
I have been preaching to you all these years,   *Yes*

Trying to get you to change your ways   *Yes*
And change your life,   *Yes*
And turn over a new leaf
And begin a new life.   [Speaking]
But you've been putting it off and making excuses   *Yes*
And I want to know,
How long, how long?   [Shouts]

C¹ (0:27)

How long will you women continue
To lie to your husbands   *Yes*
Like you've been doing?   *Yes*
When your husband is at home   [Spiritual melody]
You're always mad and fussing
And complaining that you are sick.   *Yes*
And just as soon
As he goes away,   [Shouts]
You are either in the streets running,   *Yes*
Or you got some man running to your house,
And all the time laying around.   [Speaking]

(0:47)

And sometimes,
When your husband comes home,
And knocks on the front door,   *Well, well, well* [Sung]
You are letting your old sweetheart
Out at the backdoor.   [Shouts]

C² (0:54)

You women
Are getting mighty sharp these days.   [Shouts]
You don't even want your husband to have a key   [Shouts]
To your front door
Of your house.   *No*
You want to keep all the keys   *I keep all my keys*
To yourself.
So when he comes home,   [Singing]
He can't get in

Until you let him in.   [Speaking]
That gives you a chance   [Shouts]
When he knocks on the front door,   [Shouts]
You can clear the house
Before he can get in.
How long, how long?   [Shouts]
How long   [Speaking]
Will you keep this up?   [Speaking]

C³ (1:18)

Say,
You all-night lodge men,   [Speaking]
You got so many lodge meetings
That keeps you at the lodge,
All night.
Two and three times a week.   [Singing]
You have been telling your wife
That same old lodge lie,
All these years.
How long, how long, how long?   *Well, well, well, well* [Sung]

C⁴ (1:34)

Some of you church members
Just make me sick.   [Shouts]
You're always   [Singing]
Full of religion one minute,   *Yes*
Then you're full of the devil next minute.
You're shouting one minute,   [Singing]
And cursing the next minute.
You laugh in my face one minute,   *Yes*
And shake my hand
And tell me that you love me,
And just as soon as I am through preaching,
Out the door you go,
You never pay your church dues,
How long, how long, how long?   [Shouts]
How long?   *Well, well* [Sung]

152   THE SERMONS

(1:56)

Do you expect to
Try to fool me
There is so much sham,   [Shouts]
In religion,   *Well, well* [Sung]
That these days,   *Yes*
Until you hardly know
Who is right.   [Singing]

C⁵ (2:04)

The deacon
Is always watching the preacher,   [Shouts]
And the preacher's jealous,
Of the good-looking choir members,   [Spiritual melody]
And the deacon.
The old women
Want the preacher
And the preacher want the young women.
Sisters,
Do you call that religion?   *No, no!*
How long, how long, how long
Will this last?   [Spiritual melody]

D¹ (2:21)

Miss Peaches,
What was the trouble with you
And old lady Ball this morning
In the choir back there?

Miss Peaches:
Brother Pastor, she got mad.
And was fussin' at me.
Because I showed her that sweet letter you wrote me.
She oughta know you don't want her,
Old jealous thing.

Female voice 2:
Yes, and you told me

You and the pastor went out driving last Saturday night.
And you didn't get home until two a.m.
You must-a have done some riding.[58]

Nix:
How long, how long, how long?
How long?

C7 (2:51)

Will you sisters continue to tell your
Trouble to one another?
That's what I say about women anyhow.   *Yes*
When you're doing well,
You won't let well enough do.   [Shouts]
When I go out to pray,
For the sick,
Whose business is it
Who I take with me
When I pray for the sick?
How long, how long, how long?   [Shouts]

E (3:07)

Will you people sit in judgement on your shepherd?   [Shouts]
Brother
And sister, Jesus said,   [Singing]
He that is without sin among you   *Yes*
Let him cast the first stone.   [Shouts]
Amen.

Ministers and blues artists commonly borrowed titles and themes from each other; for example, the "how long" theme was first heard in Alberta Hunter's 1921 song titled "How Long, Sweet Daddy, How Long" (BS 2008, Pm 12012).[59] The "How Long" theme may have also been taken from the spiritual "How Long, Brethren?"[60] or from a spiritual printed in *Slave Songs of the United States* titled "My Father, How Long?"[61] Nix's "How Long—How Long" may also have been inspired by the first words of Psalm 13:1, with its introductory words, "How long?" However, Nix usually announces a quote from scripture from which his sermon is taken at the beginning of each sermon. Not only does he not announce this text with scripture, but he uses the double-phrase format of "how long, how long," similar to the double phrase in the Carr-Blackwell blues song.[62] The blues song "How Long, How Long Blues" was so popular that six different versions of it were recorded.[63] Because of its popularity, it is quite plausible that Nix heard the song and used the title as his inspiration, also eventually recording his own six parts of "Black Diamond Express to Hell."[64] Possibly the multi-record format was a tactic by the record company to maximize its profits for well-received recordings.

In an interview, Genester Nix explained that enslaved African Americans cried to God, "How long!" for their suffering at the hand of white slave owners. In addition, ministers had also been expressing the "how long" theme prior to blues artists' recordings. An article in a 1902 edition of *Broad Ax* stated,

> How long! Oh, how long! will the Negro continue to erect costly and expensive temples unto the Gods, while his children are growing up in rags, and tatters and in ignorance, and while poverty and squalor surrounds him on every hand. How long! Oh, how long! will the Negro continue to prostrate himself before an imaginary God, who cannot nor will not harken unto him nor answer his prayers. How long! Oh, how long! will the Negro continue to sing that "old familiar song that others can have all the wealth of this world if they will only give me Jesus!"[65]

The article reprimanded African Americans for their belief in religion alone, without action against the obvious injustices of racism. William H. Pipes suggests that the Black minister was able to initiate release of the pent-up emotions of his congregants through use of the words "how long," which referred to the unending trials and tribulations faced by African Americans.[66] Congregants would shout in response to these words to release their frustration at having suffered for so long in the world.

"The Black Diamond Express to Hell—Part 5"

I am including a discussion of the fifth and sixth parts of "The Black Diamond Express to Hell" because of Nina Mae McKinney's spoken roles on both. Both were recorded on April 8, 1930, in Chicago on the Vocalion label (Vo 1486). As mentioned previously, McKinney plays the same role in the sermons as she does in *Hallelujah*: a hardened sinner who scoffs at religion. The form of the recording is (A) introduction of the theme, (B) the Black Diamond train, (C) dialogue with Nina Mae McKinney and others, (D) song, and recap of C.

A

My dear brothers and sisters,
The Black Diamond Express Train is going to make another trip to
hell.   *Uh-huh*

B¹ (0:05)

The first and second sections of the Black Diamond
Express Train
Carried a large crowd of high-class sinners   *Alright*
And professional liars of all kinds   *Yes*
And scientific gamblers.
Men and women of high society   *Yes*
Who had plenty of money to pay their way to hell   *Yes*
On high-class accommodations.   [Spiritual melody]

B² (0:23)

And now,
The Devil is running
A reduced rate excursion train to hell.   *Yes*
Come on here
All you cheap-skates,
You alley-rats,
You midnight-ramblers,   *Alright*
You little cheap street-walkers.
You all got to go to hell
On the Black Diamond reduced-rate excursion train,   [Singing]
Where you will burn in hell-fire
And brimstone,
Forever and forever.
In a lake of fire,   [Singing]
Where there'll be wailing
And gnashing of teeth.
Get on here
All you hell-bound sinners.

156   THE SERMONS

C¹ (0:50)

Nina Mae McKinney:
Ha, ha, ha!
Listen at that old preacher.
He's trying to scare somebody, talking about going to hell.
Say you can't scare me and make me cry
Like you done all those old people.
I ain't studyin' about that old hell-bound train.

Nix:

This train
Is leaving for eternal hell right now.   [Speaking]
All aboard for hell.

Female voice #2:
Mister Preacher, what can I do to keep from going to hell?

(1:11)

Nix:

You must come right up here now to the altar
And bow down
And repent of your sins.

(1:16)

Nina Mae McKinney:
Just look at those old crazy fools up there bowing down praying.
Say you can't make me pray.
Everybody calls me "Hard-Boiled."

(1:24)

Nix:

Yes
But you must give up the world   [Speaking]
And call on God

And be saved now.   *Alright*
Or else,
You will land in hell   [Speaking]
In the black shade of midnight.   [Speaking]
This is your last opportunity
To get off the Black Diamond Train.
I plead with you
To get off the Black Diamond.
I urge upon of you to get off the Black Diamond   [Speaking]
Before it'll be too late.

(1:44)

Female voice #3:
Elder I'll give up my sinful life and get off this hell-bound train.
Amen! Amen!

Male voice:
Glory, Glory!

Nix:

Will you give up sister?
Will you give up your heart to God right now?

Female voice #4:

Oh, Lord, have mercy upon my poor soul.
Yes, Elder, I'll give up, I'll give up, I'll get off this hell-bound train.

Nix:

Amen, glory hallelujah!   [Shouts]
Another soul born in the kingdom of God.

Let us all sing:

D¹ (2:08)

> *Free at last, free at last*
> *Thank God almighty, I'm free at last*

158   THE SERMONS

Free at last, free at last
Thank God almighty, I'm free at last[67]

C² (2:22)

Nina Mae McKinney:
Ha, ha, ha!
If that ain't a mess.
Say preacher, why don't you try to make me pray and cry.
You know better.
You know I won't fall for that kinda' stuff.
Say, you'll have to come after me some other way.
My name is Hard-Boiled
And believe me,
I'm a hard nut for you to crack.

(2:38)

Nix:
The downward road leads to eternal damnation   [Shouts]
And the upward road leads to eternal joy and happiness   *Well, well*
    [Sung]
And whosoever will can come now.
Choose you this day which road you will take.
The broad road leads to hell
And the narrow road leads to glory
And while the Black Diamond waits for a few minutes,
Make up your mind
Which road you gonna' take.

"The Black Diamond Express to Hell—Part 6"

In "The Black Diamond Express to Hell—Part 6," Nix convinces McKinney's
character, Miss Hard-Boiled, to get off the Black Diamond Train and be saved.
The form of this part is (B) Black Diamond, (C) dialogue with McKinney, (D)
song, and recap of C. The dialogue with McKinney returns every other verse,
similar to a rondo form. As with the first part of the sermon, a male voice
interjects "Glory, glory" in between Nix's dialogue. The train stops at "Farewell
Station" before proceeding on to hell.

B³

Nix:
This train will stop just a few minutes
At Farewell Station
Just long enough for everyone on board
To bid the world farewell.   *Farewell* [Sung]

(0:08)

It's where
The White Flyer
And the Black Diamond Train will separate.   *Yeah*
Mother
Will bid farewell to her children.   *Well* [Sung]
[Children] bid mother farewell.   *Alright*
Farewell. Farewell. Farewell.   *Farewell* [Sung]
Farewell you hard-boiled sinners.
The Black Diamond Express train   [Humming]
Will hit damnation switch
And make a fast run for hell.

B⁴ (0:27)

Every child of God
Will rise above the clouds
And bid farewell to every fear
And wipe their weeping eyes.
In hell
In the black shade of midnight,
In hell,
With all the demons crying,   *Well, well* [Sung]
In hell,
With all the hell-hounds howling,
The hobgobs of hell   [Singing]
Will be put upon your soul.   *Glory, glory*
You may not bow now,   [Speaking]
But you will bow in hell.
You may not cry now,
But you will cry in hell.
Listen,
I can hear some mother's daughter cryin'.

160 THE SERMONS

C³ (0:55)

Nina Mae McKinney:
Oh, Oh, Oh, Lord.

Nix:

All the stubborn-hearted men and women
Will be in hell.
All you hard-hearted sinners
Who turned down God *Well* [Sung]
And turned down the church
And turned down the Gospel, [Singing]
Will be in hell.
I bid you hard-boiled sinners
Farewell, goodbye. *Farewell* [Sung]
We never will see you no more.

Nina Mae McKinney:
Oh, don't leave me.
Please don't leave me.

Nix:
As we start out for heaven
And immortal glory,
I can hear the children of God singing,
As they goin' up higher. [Singing]

D² (1:28)

"Come and Go with Me to That Land"
 There is joy in that land
 There is joy in that land
 There is joy in that land
 Where I'm bound, where I'm bound.
 Well, there is joy in that land
 There is joy in that land
 There is joy in that land
 Where I'm bound.

C⁴ (1:52)

Nix:
Farewell. Goodbye.
We're leaving you now.

Nina Mae McKinney:
Ah, don't leave me.
Please don't leave me.
I don't wanna go to hell.
I will pray and be good.
Oh Lord, have mercy.

Nix:
Yes, my daughter.   [Singing]
I'm glad to see you come over on the Lord's side.

Nina Mae McKinney:
I will give my heart to the Lord
And serve Him as long as I live.

(2:15)

Nix:
God bless you my dear child.
God bless you.

Nina Mae McKinney:

Elder,
I'll do anything you want me to do.
Elder, will you please help me?

Nix:
Huh, what did you say?
Do you really mean that?
My dear, I will do anything you want me to do.   *Well, well* [Sung]
The Elder will comfort you now at this hour.

Nina Mae McKinney:
I will join the church and I will be baptized.

162   THE SERMONS

I will sing in the choir.
I'll lead prayer meetings.
I will do anything.
I wanna meet the Lord in peace.
Oh Lord, have mercy on my poor soul.

(2:44)

Nix:
This is the best step you ever did take my dear little child.   [Speaking]
The Lord is with you.
The Lord is in you.   *Well, well* [Sung]
You are one of the Lord's little lambs.

Nina Mae McKinney:
Oh I love the Lord.
And I love all of his people.
And Elder, above everything,
I sure love you.
You know I love you.

Nix:
My dear little one
You sure will meet the Lord in peace now.

Nina Mae McKinney:
I'm so happy.
Oh, I'm so happy.
I'm glad I got off that hell-bound train.

Nix:
Yes my dear little lamb.   [Singing]
Oh, you love everybody
And we all love you.
Amen.

"The Dirty Dozen—No. 1"

"The Dirty Dozen—No. 1" was recorded on June 20, 1930, in Chicago for
the Vocalion label (Vo 1526). Its form is (A) introduction of the theme, (B)

"lowdown" people, and (C) Nix interacts with congregants. In the first part of the sermon, Nix discusses the members of the Dirty Dozen: the drunkard, the gambler, the "sweetback," the wife-beater, the lazy scoundrel, and the selfish fool.

A

My dear friends
I come before you today with a very serious subject: *Amen*
The Lowdown Twelve.   *Yes*
Or in other words,
The Dirty Dozen.   *Alright*

B¹ (0:08)

We have so many lowdown men and women in the world today,   *Yes*
Until you hardly know what to do,   *Alright*
Or what to say or where to go for safety.   *Yes*
You will catch hell if you do,   *Yes*
And you'll catch hell if you don't.   *Alright*

B² (0:20)

The first lowdown person I bring before you today is: [Spiritual melody]
The drunkard.   *Yes*
Any man or woman who will drink
And get drunk off this mess
That is being made these days
Is bad off for a drink.   *Alright*
They are mighty lowdown.

(0:34)

A drunken man   [Spiritual melody]
Feels like
He owns the world.   *Yes*
And a drunken woman
Is a disgrace to the world.   *Alright*
And what they will do and say
Is mighty lowdown.

B³ (0:45)

We have another lowdown man: *Mm, hum*
A professional gambler.
A professional gambler
Will take a chance on losing anybody's money.   *Yes!*
He'll gamble away his wife's money.
He'll gamble the clothes off his back   *That's right!*
And gamble the shoes off his feet.
Gambling
Is a game of hit or miss.   *That's right*
And you will miss more than you will hit.   *Well*
And I can prove that by Sister Betty
Sitting here now.   *Well!*

C¹ (1:09)

Sister Betty,
Your husband is a gambler.   *Mm-hum*
Tell us,
Does he miss more than he hits?

Betty:
Well, Elder
I don't wanna do much talkin'.
But all I gotta say,
If I just show you all these scars on my head and my back
You would see that he has been hittin' more than he has been missin'.
And if you call that gamblin', he has almost ruined me.   *Well, alright*

Nix:
Yes, my sister
But you got a lowdown man.   *Yes*
And he belong
To the Dirty Dozen.   *Alright*

B⁴ (1:32)

We have another lowdown man: *Well, well, well*
A high-class sweetback.
This man

THE SERMONS   165

Is commonly known
As a jellybean.　*Yeah*
He is a sweetback.
This man is always dressed up.　*Yeah*
He never works.　*No*
If you talk to him about working,
You will hear him say, "My mother's named Work,　*Yeah*
And I promised not to hit her."
But he's a lowdown man.　*Lowdown!*

B⁵ (1:52)

We have another member of the Dirty Dozen:　*Yes*
A wife beater.
Any man who's always beating up his wife,
Is mighty lowdown.
Ain't that right Brother Ned?

C² (2:01)

Brother Ned:
But Elder some women are so mean and fussy, you just got to whoop 'em.
When they get to fussin' and quarrellin', well nothing'll do dem but a good
whoopin'.

Nix:
Well,
If you got to always whip your wife,　*Yeah*
And you can't get along without whipping her,
Send her home to her folks.　*Alright*
This fussin',
Fightin' like cats and dogs,　*Preach*
Is mighty lowdown.　*Yes*

B⁶ (2:20)

Another member
Of the Dirty Dozen　*Yes*
Is that man who says,
Let the women do the work.　*Alright*
That lazy scoundrel,

Always got some fool woman working for him.   *Yes*
While he walks the streets
Sitting around the pool room and barbershop telling lies,   *Alright*
While his w—wife is out doing the working.
He's mighty lowdown.   *Dirty!*

B⁷ (2:38)

We have another member
Of the Dirty Dozen: *Preach!*
A selfish fool.   [Singing]
Some folks are fooled and know it,   *Yeah*
And some are fooled and don't know it.
That man
Wants everything for himself.   *Yes*
He's full of greed, lust, and game.
He wants every woman he sees.   *Yes*
And he don't want his wife to look at another man.   *Well alright!*
He wants all the new clothes   *Yes*
And his wife to stay in rags.   *Yes*
He wants to do all the going
And his wife to stay at home.   *Alright*
He wants the world in a jug   *Yes*
And the stopper in his own hand.

(3:07)

And now we'll stop a few minutes   *Yes*
And then I will tell you about
A few lowdown women.
Amen.

Nix typically speaks disparagingly of women, often blaming them for the sins of men. However, in "The Dirty Dozen—No. 1," he discusses several men who are "lowdown." The "sweetback" is a man who lives off a woman, such as a pimp, and does not do work himself. The "jelly bean" is a man who dresses stylishly but has little else to show for himself. Nix takes an unexpected turn when he addresses Sister Betty, asking her, "Does he miss more than he hits?" She explains that she is beaten by her husband on a regular basis, leading Nix to add her husband to the list of the "Dirty Dozen." Surprisingly, Nix addresses "Brother Ned"—obviously spoken by a female—who argues that

THE SERMONS   167

women deserve to be beaten because "some women are so mean and fussy"
and beatings are the way to keep them in line. In this sermon, Nix sympathizes
with women who are beaten or taken advantage of.

"The Dirty Dozen—No. 2"

"The Dirty Dozen—No. 2" is a continuation of the Dirty Dozen theme; however,
whereas in No. 1 Nix focuses on "dirty" men, in part 2 he adds "dirty" women
to the list. He discusses men and women who live together, deceitful men and
women, the notorious thief, the heartbreaker, hypocrites, and Mr. and Mrs.
Lowdown. Because it is a continuation of No. 1, the form adds more "lowdown"
people in section B and advice from Nix in section D.

My dear friends,
We have just found a few more lowdown men and women.   *Yeah*

B[8] (0:04)

The double-life live-r
We have too many men and women living together
These days who are not married.   *Right*
A woman is lowdown   *Well alright*
Who will let a man live with her,   *Yes*
Load her down with children,   *Amen*
Wear her out   *Amen* [Loud]
Just as soon
As she begins to fade away,   [Spiritual melody]
And wrinkles come in her face.
He's ready to leave her
And get him a fresh woman.   [Speaking]

(0:25)

Some women
Don't know when they have enough of men on their strings.   [Speaking]
This double-life living
Is mighty lowdown.   [Speaking]

B[9] (0:33)

The next lowdown we have   [Spiritual melody]
Is deceitful men and women.   [Speaking]

Some men
Are going around deceiving women,   [Speaking]
Carrying a thick
Bank book in his pocket,   *Yes*
Marked up with several thousand dollars on it
To make believe he's got plenty of money.   [Speaking]
Because he knows   *Amen* [Loud]
Women these days
Are crazy about plenty money.   [Speaking]
A woman don't care so much about a man these days,
It's his money
She's crazy about.   [Speaking]
Some men and women
Will stoop to the lowest thing   [Speaking]
Of this world
To deceive one another.   [Spiritual melody]

B¹⁰ (1:02)

We have another member of the Dirty Dozen: [Spiritual melody]
The notorious thief.
This is a man
Who will steal bread out of a
Blind man's hand.   [Speaking]
He'll steal money
Out of a dead man's eyes.   *Yeah*
He will steal
Bread from a baby,   [Speaking]
Steal from his mother.   *Yeah*
He'll steal from the church,   *Well, well* [Sung]
And steal from the lodge.
He's so lowdown
He will steal from anybody.   [Spiritual melody]
He'd rather steal anything
Than ask for it.   *Alright*

B¹¹ (1:28)

The next
Lowdown member we have of the Dirty Dozen   *Yes*
Is a heart breaker.   *Well alright*

THE SERMONS 169

Some men and women
Will make love with every good-looking person they see.   [Speaking]
They are never satisfied with their own.   [Speaking]
They want what belong to somebody else.   [Speaking]
Some women
Will get a man dying crazy about her,   [Speaking]
Then see
Him fall hard to the ground.   [Speaking]
Any man or woman
Will steal your heart,
And then let you fall.
Is mighty lowdown.   *Alright*

B¹² (1:54)

We have another lowdown group: [Spiritual melody]
The hypocrites.
This world is full of hypocrites.
Men and women pretend to be what they are not.   [Speaking]
They will smile in your face   *Amen* [Loud]
And go behind your back   [Spiritual melody]
And bleed your heart.
They will wear a face for every occasion.
One while
They're like they're a saint from heaven.
And again
They're like a demon from hell.   [Spiritual melody]
They will listen what you say
And go out and tell it some other way.
And I tell you hypocrites
Are mighty lowdown.

B¹³ (2:20)

Last but not least,
We have the chairman of the Dirty Dozen,   [Spiritual melody]
Mister
And Mrs. Lowdown.   *Well alright*
This man or woman
Is the head of the lowdown crowd.   *Responses*
They stand at the head of the class.   *Yes*

They have no principles.   *No*
They have no self-respect.   *Alright*
They will do anything
When things
Are too low for anybody else to do.   [Spiritual singing]
It's just right for them.   *Amen* [Loud]
They are the ones
Who will do the dirty work.   [Speaking]
The lower the deed is,
The better they like it.   [Speaking]

D (2:49)

Brother!
These are the Lowdown Twelve   [Speaking]
Or the Dirty Dozen.
That you will find in this world today.   *Alright*
Clean out
The dirty dozen
And times will get better
For you and for me.
Amen.

"There's Something Rotten in Denmark"

Nix recorded "There's Something Rotten in Denmark"[68] on November 1, 1930, in Chicago on the Vocalion label (Vo 1578). It has a form of (A) introduction of the theme, (B) contemporary relevance, (C) Nix's advice, (D) interaction with congregant/humor, and a recap of C.

A

Dear brothers and sisters,
I want to talk to you tonight from the subject:
There's something rotten in Denmark.   *Yes*

B¹ (0:06)

There are so many unusual things
That are happening these days,   *Yes*

That keeps us always wondering and guessing what's next.   *My Lord*
  [Sung]
It seems that married life is almost soon to be a failure.   *My Lord* [Sung]
True love is almost run out.   [Shouts]
Nobody is taking life serious these days.   *No*
A lot of men and women are living together
These days not married to each other.   *No!*
And they want to be recognized and hold high places in the church,   *Yes*
And among the best society   [Shouts]
And they don't want the preacher to even say a word about
How they are living.   *Yes*
Brother, there's something wrong in Denmark!   [Shouts]

B² (0:38)

Just think of a man working hard
Every day   *Yes*
Making long hours and working overtime,   [Speaking]
Trying to keep his wife dressed up,   [Speaking]
Living in a swell flat   [Speaking]
With fine furniture and polished floors.   [Shouts]
She is too lazy
To have his meals on time   *Preach it brother!*
And fix his bath
When he comes home from work.   *Yeah!*
She wants ... uh, uh ... and when he wants to love her,   *Well, well, well,*
  well [Sung]
And put his arms around her,   *Yeah!*
She's always pushing him away   [Shouts]
And telling him,
"I don't want to be bothered,   *Yes*
I don't feel good."   *Yeah!*
Brother!
There's something
Rotten in Denmark.   [Shouts]

B³ (1:10)

Brother!
Her love for you has grown cold,   *Yeah!*
Because

172 THE SERMONS

There's another cat on your line.[69]   [Shouts]
Some men
Are always worrying and wondering   *Yeah!*
Why
All of his children don't favor him.   *Yeah!*
Brother when your wife is having children,
And some of them don't favor you,   *Yeah!*
You just put this down in your pipe and smoke it.   *Yeah!*
There's something
Rotten in Denmark.   [Shouts]

B⁴ (1:31)

B^4 (1:31)

Sister,
When your husband is working everyday
And drawing a good salary,   *Yes*
And every time pay day come,
He comes home,
To you and the children very late   [Speaking]
With a pitiful tale of woe,   *Yeah!*
Saying,   [Blues riff sung]
"I worked overtime,
And was robbed on the way home,
I lost my paycheck."   *Yeah!*
I just want
To say to you, don't believe that lie.   [Shouts]
Just remember,
There's something rotten in Denmark.   [Shouts]

C^1 (1:55)

Denmark,
May be in your home,   *Yeah*
Or it may be
On the other side of town.   *Yes*
You women
Must remember,
Men
Will pay off
Where they get the best treatment   [Blues riff sung]
And service.

And if they can't get it at home,
They will get it in Denmark.

D¹ (2:10)

Why, howdy do Sister Betty!
Is this your baby?
It hasn't been six months ago
Since I married you and Brother Joe.   *Well alright*
And you have a baby this quick?
This baby
Don't favor your husband.

Sister Betty:
Well, Brother Pastor,
I've been trying to explain to my husband
Why the baby was born so soon.
We've only been married five months, so I guess it must be a five-month
    baby.
And the reason why he don't favor my husband,
He takes after his great-great-great-grandfather!
But I can't get my husband believe it.   [Speaking]

Male Congregant:
My God, I don't believe it myself.

Nix:

Yes,
That may be alright sister.
But I want to tell you
You husbands
You . . . you . . . Your wife won't believe that tale.   [Speaking]
You husbands
Must recognize a [indecipherable].
There's something wrong in Denmark.   [Shouts]

C² (2:51)

Sister,
This way, trying to fool your husband   *Amen*

May work well sometimes,   *Yeah!*
But you gonna get caught.   [shouts]
Brother this way trying to fool your wife,   *Yeah!*
You can't get by
At it always.   *Yeah!*
Why don't you men and women
Be fair with and honest with your husbands and wives?   *Preach it Elder!*
Why don't you Christian men and women   [Singing]
Live true to God?   [Shouts]
Why do you have to always be making excuses,
Trying to explain
Why you do that,   *Yeah!*
And why you do that.
And why you're always getting caught?
Brother!
I want to tell you,   [Blues riff sung]
There's something rotten in Denmark.   [Shouts]
Amen.

Nix uses the abbreviated phrase "there's something rotten in Denmark" from Shakespeare's *Hamlet* as an analogy to the state of current affairs in one's own home. The sermon is one of the few sermons in which Nix uses humor to justify his point. His interaction with Sister Betty is obviously meant to be humorous, but Nix uses it to emphasize his point that people are having extramarital affairs and deceiving their spouses. The humorous section is used as a bridge to break up Nix's advice to his congregants and keep the dialogue entertaining. A striking difference in this sermon is the use of a male voice in the spoken dialogue. The majority of Nix's sermons have a female "prayer band," with his wife, Ida, as the lead. However, in "There's Something Rotten in Denmark," a male voice is heard talking with Nix and Sister Betty. Not only does the male interject spoken dialogue, but he also sings blues-style interjections at timepoints 1:43, 2:05, and 3:21.

The transcriptions of the words of Reverend Nix's sermons bring awareness of his concern for his congregants and the themes that mattered to him most. He focused consistently on themes associated with racial uplift. His congregants were of varying classes, yet Nix mostly reached into the vocal past to access the sounds of the folk to convey his powerful messages. I have explained how his sermons were caught between two worlds: the Old and the New, with Nix straddling the two by employing traditional sounds that were propelled into the modern age via the phonograph. Despite Nix's preference for traditional sounds, I must also stress that his formal education and broad learning, as well as his ability to condense his sermons into a coherent three-minute message, surely added to his success as a "performer" of recorded sermons.

TEXTUAL THEMES

Early Black preachers from the late nineteenth century were often criticized for "talking too much about how all God's children would surely get shoes in heaven, while doing almost nothing for the wretched poor who were left to go barefoot on earth."[70] Many Baptist ministers based their topics on fear—fear of what would happen if one did not give one's life to Jesus or continued living in sin. Many lower-class preachers took sin as the prevailing topic, which included "adultery, anger, atheism, cheating, 'acting stuck-up,' covetousness, 'being too critical,' deceit, dishonesty, disloyalty, gambling, hypocrisy, 'back-biting,' and 'spasmodic speaking to one another,' lack of personal cleanliness, fighting in the home, drunkenness, and 'sex immorality.'"[71] Emphasis on family life and the proper conduct in relations with the opposite sex were prevalent. However, some Black ministers shifted their focus to the dilemmas of daily life. The minister aided in not only spiritual education and support, but also moral, physical, and intellectual improvements as well, demonstrating the tenets of racial uplift.[72]

African American ministers believed that by proving their moral behavior was just, they could gain the same opportunities as white people. As Raboteau contends, "progress for the race and escape from poverty depended upon education, temperance (abstaining from the consumption of alcohol), thrift, and responsibility.... black ministers emphasized the importance of moral behavior and self-respect."[73] Many ministers believed that home ownership and savings were crucial goals of uplift and encouraged their congregants to lift themselves from poverty. In addition, African American ministers encouraged their congregants to better not only their economic conditions, but also their moral behaviors to disprove the common fallacies and prejudices of white people.

The ministers also promoted uplift through teachings that stressed education, Christian morals, and economic responsibility. Bishop Daniel A. Payne, who was an educator in addition to being a clergyman, was determined to promote racial uplift in the church through education, believing in an "educated ministry."[74] A.M.E. Zion bishop George W. Clinton explained, "the Negro pulpit became the pioneer in the first movements to better the condition of the race by lifting it from the degradation and disorganized state in which it was left by slavery."[75] In addition to education, Christian morality was a primary goal of nineteenth-century Black churches and ministers, including encouraging marriage as a goal for young people. Ministers believed that African Americans could achieve greatness if they could lift themselves through education and by being given the same opportunities offered to white people. African Americans, they argued, were not lacking in capabilities, only in opportunities. After the losses following the dissolution of Reconstruction, ministers realized that politics alone would not uplift the masses. Instead, they addressed social issues, such as temperance, as means to uplift the race, demonstrate self-responsibility with newly acquired freedom, and acquire favor from powerful (and hostile) white people.[76]

Although Black ministers were keenly aware of the challenges caused by racism and economic disparities, they encouraged their congregations to participate in the community and create a balanced family life. America was still considered the greatest country on earth, full of possibilities, and Black ministers wanted their congregants to achieve equality and be included in the opportunities that were available for them. Thus, they believed that a balance between "accommodation and possibility" was achievable through uplift.[77]

With the African American minister at the helm, the church community listened to his advice and was guided by his instructions. He interacted with members of his church congregation on a daily or weekly basis, knew of their needs, and heard their prayers. Although much has been written about Du Bois, Washington, Garvey, and other singular Black leaders of the day, less widely known individual ministers interacted with their congregants on a day-to-day basis, functioning not only as a minister but also as a leader and the center of community activities. The *Chicago Defender* noted that "The minister occupies the position of moral, spiritual and, in a sense, the social leadership of the Race. They have the ear of the people even more than a newspaper, for they reach a multitude of people who neither read nor think."[78] However, for the many who were illiterate, newspapers were out of reach, while the minister was close by and accessible. Thus, the minister had influence on the minds of his congregants and could encourage them to follow a certain path or philosophy.

While Nix's sermons may have offered practical solutions for the daily life of new migrants, he also discussed many themes that reflected uplift theories as a means for practical solutions and moral "improvement" to the problems they faced: chastity, the patriarchal family, thrift, temperance, personal responsibility, patriarchal authority, and education. He also frequently addressed the perceived evils that affected migrants' lives, including alcohol consumption, gambling, and "loose" women. As is evident from his condemnation of the modern woman, he evoked the patriarchal standard of the male as head of household with women as subordinate and chaste. Nix frequently admonished those who did not value (or seem to value) the sanctity of marriage. In addition, he stressed the need for personal and financial responsibility and offered practical solutions to his congregants through his sermons.

Nix's attention to uplift principles may have been influenced by his work with the General Association of Colored Baptists of Kentucky, State University's faculty and protocols, the *Chicago Defender*'s guidelines for recent migrants, and Sutton Griggs's Black nationalist literature, along with Nix's own ideals for the advancement of his congregants. While the spoken and sung nature of his sermons showed affinity for Black vocal traditions, his texts were meant to empower his listeners to take responsibility for their lives and to become prosperous, respectable, and moral people. For the most part, Nix preached about general Christian themes such as sin, repentance, and being saved. While he did preach on traditional themes, such as "old-time religion" and fire and brimstone, most of his sermons discussed uplift values, including chastity, the patriarchal family, temperance, and the dangers of gambling. These texts provide valuable insights into his ideology and complete the picture of Nix's life as a whole.

Other than the use of traditional spirituals and hymns, themes referencing traditional practices, such as old-time religion, were present in only five of the forty-seven extant sermons. For example, in "Robbing God," Nix condemned talent that is used in the service of the devil (i.e., in the realms of jazz and blues) and suggested old-time religion as the remedy for the ills affecting African Americans of the day. In the sermon he states, "Brother, what men and women need today is that old-time religion. That religion that will make you stay off the ballroom floor. That religion that will keep your feet off the gambling den."

Many lower-class preachers emphasized fire-and-brimstone themes, including the end of the world and atoning for one's sins in order to get to heaven. Fire-and-brimstone sermons typically used fear of God, God's wrath, or eternal damnation as themes. For example, Reverend Moses Hester (aka Uncle Mose) stated that "at de judgment all de sinners will be anni-hi-lated with fire."[79] Genester recalled that her father's congregation reacted to fire-and-brimstone sermons with themes of "if you don't do right, you go to Hell" with "crying and hollering and falling out."[80] While Nix did not typically use fire-and-brimstone themes to create fear in the minds of his congregants, some of his sermons such as "After the Ball Is Over," "Your Time Is Out," and "The Black Diamond Express to Hell—Part 5" contain imagery that is used to strike fear in the minds of the listeners. For example, in "After the Ball Is Over," Nix used the fear of illness to persuade his listeners: "After the ball is over, then you go out in the midnight air, you take bad cold, and then deep cough, and then pneumonia will set in, and then consumption, and end in an early grave." Evidence of this type of doomsday text is also present in the sermon "Your Time Is Out," in which Nix related the story of Noah and the Ark and referred to death and destruction as the outcome for nonbelievers. He warns, "Brother, before your time is out, God wants you to get right with Him. Seek Jesus now."[81] In "The

Black Diamond Express to Hell—Part 5," Nix warns sinners that "You got to go to hell on the Black Diamond reduced-rate excursion train, where you will burn in hell-fire and brimstone, forever and forever. . . . The downward road leads to eternal damnation." While Nix's version of fire-and-brimstone themes may be mild compared to those by other ministers, he did utilize the element of fear to encourage his congregants to change their ways.

Nix used biblical stories and characters frequently in his sermons. While Christian themes are expected for a Baptist minister, Nix often used the form typical of the chanted sermon, which begins with a quote from scripture, then tells the story from the Bible that relates to the scriptural quote, followed by an explanation of how the story applies to the common man. Christian themes and Bible stories are present in Nix's sermons recorded between April 23, 1927, and October 26, 1928. Many of the Christian-based sermons used exempla or anecdotes for "clinching a sermonly point."[82] For example, in "After the Ball," Nix related the story of Herod and Salome to make his point.

Nix occasionally offered practical advice to his listeners. While ministers are typically considered patriarchal figures responsible for their congregations, Nix mentioned topics that specifically applied to new migrants. In "Sleeping in a Dangerous Time," Nix advised his listeners to be alert because someone may be stealing one's belongings or significant other, suggesting that a roomer in one's house could be the source of bad intent. Renting rooms in one's home to roomers was common for many migrant families due to the shortage of livable homes in Chicago. Nix's advice served as a warning to new migrants, but also provides evidence that Nix himself was aware of the problems affecting migrants.

Nix also took the position of an elite citizen offering advice to new migrants who did not know the rules of urban life, similar to the twenty-seven points of advice given in the *Chicago Defender*. In "Who Dressed You Up for Easter," Nix advises his listeners to "clean up, shine up, and take a hot bath, and dress up and come out on Easter Sunday." As discussed previously, personal hygiene was a recommendation by both State University and the *Chicago Defender* for newly arrived migrants.

Nix reprimanded those of the lower class who adhered to traditional practices that were considered "backwards." For example, in "Black Diamond Express to Hell—Pt. I," Nix mentions "Louisiana conjurers" and their practices in a reference to hoodoo, which was deemed to be superstition, "black magic," and the like and antithetical and harmful to Baptist beliefs:

I have a big crowd of Louisiana conjurers down there.
They got to go to hell on the Black Diamond Train.
They always taking brick dust and brass pins and matchheads

And making little hands to sell to one another.[83]
But you got to go to hell on the Black Diamond Train.

The phrase "making little hands" refers to the "mojo hand" that Muddy Waters sings about in "I Got My Mojo Working." A "hand" is a small bag in which the hoodoo supplies or magical items were inserted. A mojo hand could be for good luck, as in Waters's case, but Nix was referring to sellable hands or bags that conjurers were using. Superstition was attributed to the storefront churches, and some upper-class Chicagoans looked down upon those who attended these churches and their preferences for superstition.[84]

Immoral Women

While members of the prayer band in Nix's recorded sermons were churchgoing women, he openly and repeatedly condemned the behavior of the modern woman. City women were, for him, closely associated with sin and being "of the world." Blues and jazz were part of city life, especially in Chicago in the 1920s, with classic blues singers such as Ma Rainey and Bessie Smith challenging the prevailing notions of ideal women as chaste and belonging only in the home. According to Angela Davis, "They [the classic female blues singers] . . . challenged the notion that women's 'place' was in the domestic sphere. Such notions were based on the social realities of middle-class white women's lives, but were incongruously applied to all women, regardless of race or class."[85] Nix adhered to old-fashioned sensibilities that stressed the home and family and asserted that the modern woman would be the downfall of marriage and the ruin of stability in the home.

Nix apparently believed in the domesticity of women and commented on the sinfulness of modern dress of the 1920s in several sermons. The majority of Nix's condemnation of the modern woman on record came on and after his October 26, 1928, recordings. In "Hang Out Your Sign," he describes "modern dress . . . [as] a disgrace to the society"—his first use of that theme. He adds, "you will see women, walking down the streets with the red-painted lips and powdered faces, or short tight skirts, window-pane stockings, walking on their shame." In Nix's opinion, women's modern apparel and makeup were the downfall of good men and women because of men's weakness to women's sexual appeal. In "The Black Diamond Express to Hell—Part 4," he says the twentieth-century style shop provides women with modern dresses that are so thin "you can see clear through them" and have "low necks and low backs . . . short, tight skirts . . . [and] peep shoes." Modern dresses, according to Nix, change women from demure and chaste to women who "will charm you and then talk to you with their eyes." Modern dress even corrupts the older, church-going women, as Nix describes in "Slow This Year for the Danger Signal": "a lot of these old women these days, that used to sing and pray and lead prayer meetings in the church, have cut their dresses off above their knees, and taken the sleeves out of their dresses, and painting and powdering up their lips and faces, trying to run with a young crowd and trying to flirt with the young men, while aches and pains are darting all through your old body."

Modern dresses, according to Nix in "The Black Diamond Express to Hell—Part 4," were worn by women in many major cities, such as Detroit, Chicago, St. Louis, Kansas City, New York, Memphis, New Orleans, and Atlanta. Nix made the point that modern, "sinful" women were from the city, not from rural communities. He made clear that city life was a bad influence on the thousands of migrants who left their rural communities. Nix referenced Forty-Seventh Street and South Parkway in Chicago—the hub of the Black entertainment district in Bronzeville—as the demoralizing place where loose women often socialized. Thus, it is apparent that Nix also associated immoral women and wearing the modern dress with jazz and blues and its social environment.

Women are said to be partially to blame for the decline in marriage, as Nix states in "The Dirty Dozen—No. 2," because "a woman don't care so much about a man these days, it's his money she's crazy about." This type of woman serves as a reminder of Nina Mae McKinney's character in the movie *Hallelujah*, who uses men and their money for her personal benefit. In *Hallelujah*, it is the city woman who takes advantage of the country man. Similarly, in the sermon "A Country Man in Town," released in 1929, just four months after the release of *Hallelujah*, Nix recounts the same theme, claiming that a city woman will take advantage of a country man, "filling him up with a lot of hot air and sweet promises, making him believe that there will be a big time for him on Saturday night after he's paid off. And just as soon as she gets all of his money, she will call him sweet names and hitch him with a sweet promise." Women of all colors, "chocolate brown, some high brown, some compromising brown, some tantalizing brown, some teasing brown," as Nix describes in "You Got the Wrong Man," have the ability to "almost make the preacher to lay his Bible down." Hence, in Nix's sermon, women of all ages and skin color become corrupt with the temptations of modernity and its sins. Infidelity, in Nix's mind, was primarily the fault of immoral women, not men. In "How Long—How Long," he says, "when your husband is at home, you're always mad and fussing and complaining that you are sick. And just as soon as he goes away, you are either in the streets running, or you got some man running to your house, and all the time laying around. And sometimes, when your husband comes home, and knocks on the front door, you are letting your old sweetheart out the back door." In Nix's sermon, this scene is played out exactly as in *Hallelujah*, in which

Nina Mae McKinney sneaks out the back window in order to run off with her former lover while her husband sleeps in the other room.

As mentioned previously, Nix sometimes used humor to get his point across. In "There's Something Rotten in Denmark," Nix asks a female congregant why her children do not favor her husband, to which she answers that the baby was a "five-month baby." Although stability in marriage was a serious topic for Nix, he used any means possible to get his message across.

Patriarchal Family

The home and the family were highly regarded as symbols of uplift, racial progress, and respectability.[86] Although Nix condemned loose women as the downfall of man, he contended that, in modern times, neither men nor women valued the sanctity of marriage or the value of home and family. In "Love Is a Thing of the Past," Nix remarks that marriage is not the outcome of a loving relationship, but is instead a tool that both men and women use on each other "just to get by easy . . . for convenience . . . for a meal ticket." The traditional family, for Nix, was a bygone thing that had been replaced with marriage in which love was not present. One problem identified by Nix, as he says in his sermon titled "Generosity," is that "too many men and women are living together without being married. You're living on the installment plan. You're trying them out by living by the week, trying to shun the real manly responsibility." In this sermon, Nix holds men responsible; however, in "You Got the Wrong Man," Nix remarks, "some of you husbands are going around here with your mouths all puffed out, wondering why all of your children don't favor you." Apparently, Nix did not hold men completely responsible for marital indiscretions. As Gaines explains, the importance and downright singular obsession with the patriarchal family became problematic as it

> came to displace a broader vision of uplift as group struggle for citizenship and material advancement. At worst, this misplaced equation of race progress with the status of the family blamed black men and women for "failing" to measure up to the dominant society's bourgeois gender morality, and seemed to forget that it was the state and constant threat of violence, not some innate racial trait, that prevented the realization of black homes and families.[87]

Gaines's analysis helps us to understand Nix's emphasis on the family. Rather than focus on racism as a cause for the downfall of African American family life, Nix chose to promote marriage and family stability. Although he may have had the best interest of his Christian congregants in mind, it is possible that Nix may have been trying to promote the patriarchal family as guidance to newly relocated migrants who were adjusting to the chaos and inequalities in post-riot Chicago.

Thrift and Financial Responsibility

Financial responsibility, as a tenet of racial uplift, included thrift and the accumulation of wealth as markers of advancement. Booker T. Washington, for example, supported property ownership as a means for economic self-sufficiency.[88] In "How Will You Spend Christmas?" (1930), Nix blames the men and women who "had good jobs but you wouldn't keep them. You were making good money, but you wouldn't save it. You spent it all on what you call a 'big time.' Don't blame anybody because you are broke. Just blame yourself. You should have saved up for these hard times." He did not offer sympathy, nor did he blame the larger society. Instead, he suggested personal and financial responsibility. The "big time" of which Nix spoke may be a reference to jazz and blues entertainment and their links with alcohol consumption and "loose women."

Nix encouraged African Americans, already with limited resources for financial advancement, to be thrifty with their money and admonished those who would waste it frivolously. In "You Have Played the Fool," he criticizes new migrants who became disillusioned with city life and were taken advantage of: "some of you men, when you come to this town, you had good money saved up in the bank. But you got with a fast crowd and you got played out when you got plenty money." He also encouraged financial responsibility in "Pay Your Honest Debts," by instructing his congregants to live within their means.

Conspicuous Consumption

During World War I, many in the African American lower classes were able to earn cash wages through regular employment, rather than through credit, which had been associated with the earlier system of sharecropping. Cash wages allowed earners extra money to spend on recreation rather than merely on survival needs.[89] Conspicuous consumption, as it was called, involved publicly spending money on extraneous activities or items for the appearance of seeming wealthier than one actually was. In the sermon "Pay Your Honest Debts," Nix admonishes congregants who spend above their means on dressing "swell and fine" to "make a big show on the outside." Even during the Depression years, the pursuit of worldly pleasure was an activity that many associated with the lower classes who spent their money on movies, music, alcohol, sports, and so on.[90]

Conversely and in opposition to conspicuous consumption, the middle class was linked to thrift and financial responsibility, as one aspect of racial uplift.

The public display of drinking, playing cards, and dancing was also seen as evidence of low-class lifestyles. Drake and Cayton explained that "they will 'dance on the dime' and 'grind' around the juke-box in taverns and joints, or 'cut a rug' at the larger public dance halls. . . . It is this *public* behavior that outrages the sensibilities of Bronzeville's 'dicties.' 'It gives The Race a bad name,' they are quick to announce [italics in original]."[91] In the sermon "Robbing God," Nix condemned people who spend their time and money at the theater, equating this with giving time and money to the devil. Such leisure activities, as Lerone A. Martin argues, were antithetical to the Black church's "notions of cultural propriety and morality."[92]

Class Associations

In addition to commenting on the general behavior of southern migrants, as he did in "A Country Man in Town," Nix also referred specifically to the behavior of those who attended the churches affiliated with the lower class. Spiritualist churches were typically storefront churches attended by lower-class congregants and offered what Nix calls "healing, advice, and 'good luck' for a prayer and the price of a candle or holy flower" with services conducted by preachers and mediums. Drake and Cayton suggested that "the Spiritualist church in Bronzeville [had] no unkind words for card-playing, dancing, policy [gambling], ward politics, or the 'sporting life.'"[93] The Works Progress Administration (WPA) study of Chicago stated, "The elder teacher one Sunday deplored the irregular practice of a majority of his colleagues: 'Ninety-eight percent of all spiritualists are making a regular gambling, voodoo, witchcraft, backbiting, policy number game of it. . . . All of these things are done under the name of spiritualism!'"[94] Nix addresses his listeners, in "Begin a New Life on Christmas Day—Parts I and II," who are known to play "policy wheels," host "moonshine parties," and be "backbiters," "conjurers," "trick-workers," "card-players," "dice-rollers," "whiskey-drinkers," and even "Sunday-school teachers" and "choir members," as people who have lost their way. Storefront churches included the Independent Church of God and Power Center, led by Father Morris, and the Church of All Nations, led by Elder Lucy Smith.[95] Smith's congregation consisted of "largely new arrivals from the South and those Negroes who have not and probably never will become urbanized. They are persons of little or no formal education, mostly day laborers, domestic servants, WPA workers, and relief clients."[96] Smith became so popular that she had a regularly broadcast radio program, despite the negative opinions of her by the higher class of the community. Probably the listeners of Nix's recorded sermons would have recognized the references.

Class affiliations were also evident in the Black churches of Chicago. In "Mind Your Own Business (A New Year's Sermon)," Nix mentions people who criticize the various denominations in Black Chicago, revealing the various viewpoints people had of 1920s churches in Chicago: "You can hear them say, 'the Presbyterians are too cold, the Methodists are too warm, the Episcopalians have too much ceremony, the Baptists are too tight, the Congregationalists too free, the Salvation Army's too noisy, and the Quakers are too quiet.'" Nix, in essence, gave voice to class stereotypes and divisions by describing the class dynamics between upper-class and lower-class Black churches.

Gambling

While Elder Smith's church may have turned a blind eye to illicit behavior such as gambling, Nix demonized it in his recorded sermons, making it one of his most frequent topics. Gambling by playing lottery numbers, known as "policy," was popular in Bronzeville as a chance opportunity to make extra money. But, as in all forms of gambling, some players chose playing policy over "real" work or became addicted to gambling. Drake and Cayton stated that there were some five hundred "policy stations" in Bronzeville at the time of their writing in the 1930s.[97]

Nix adds the gambler to his list of sinners in "The Dirty Dozen—No. 1," asserting that the gambler "will take a chance on losing anybody's money. He'll gamble away his wife's money. He'll gamble the clothes off his back. Gambling is a game of hit or miss." He encourages cardplayers, in "Begin a New Life on Christmas Day—Part II," to "throw away your cards. You dice-rollers, got to get off of your knees." However, he also realized that people were attempting to earn money by any means possible.

Temperance

Another of Nix's "hot topics" was the sin of alcohol consumption. Temperance was a goal for not only Victorian-era society, but also for leaders of uplift. In "The Dirty Dozen—No. 1," the "drunkard" is the first "lowdown person" that Nix admonishes. He claims, "A drunken man feels like he owns the world. And a drunken woman is a disgrace to the world. And what they will do and say is mighty lowdown." He mentions drunkenness as a "disgrace" in "How Will You Spend Christmas" and "That Little Thing May Kill You Yet (Christmas Sermon)." Genester Nix recalled that neither of her parents ever drank alcohol.

The Victorian quest for temperance created singing societies and choral singing groups as a means for moral uplift and dissuasion from alcohol consumption. The practice of choral singing as a means for uplift applied to African American choral groups as well. As stated in *The Negro Music Journal*, the Harry T. Burleigh Choral Society sought to "lift every member of the race in its community who will put himself under its protection. This society has at heart the real upbuilding of the race and believes that choral singing is one of the strongest means by which we may hope to do so."[98] Although Nix did not create social diversions such as singing clubs to dissuade congregants from consuming alcohol, he did preach about alcohol as a habit "that will kill you yet."

Personal Responsibility

Although Nix often blamed women as the cause of the downfall of men, he held both men and women personally responsible for their lives. In "You Got the Wrong Man," he states, "some of you girls are so lazy, you don't want to do anything but keep looking in the looking glass and a powder puff and a lipstick in your hand, primping all the time." However, women were not the only ones to blame. In "The Dirty Dozen—No. 1," Nix describes "a jellybean. He is a sweetback. This man is always dressed up. He never works." In the same sermon, he describes "another member of the Dirty Dozen," who is a man who says, "'Let the women do the work.' That man is countin' on always got some fool woman working for him. While he walks the streets, sitting around the pool room and barbershop telling lies, while his wife is out doing the working. He's mighty lowdown."

In "The Dirty Dozen—No. 2," Nix continues to accuse people whom he considers "dirty," including those who "have no principles. They have no self-respect. They will do anything when things are too low for anybody else to do. It's just right for them. They are the ones who will do the dirty work." The purpose of personal responsibility was, of course, to acquire dignity and a positive self-identity.

Patriarchal Authority

Women were often condemned in Nix's sermons as the source of immorality. However, as Evelyn Brooks Higginbotham contests, "women have traditionally constituted the majority of every black denomination"[99] and were the primary voices heard in the background on Nix's sermons. Attendance at lower-class churches was dominated by women, with less than one-third of the congregants comprised of men.[100] Elite Black women often focused their attention on raising funds for church, school, and social welfare services, believing that racial self-help would aid in fostering equality and respect from white society.[101] Despite their lofty goals and achievements, the women in Nix's church were treated as his "children," as he sometimes called them. The women in Nix's congregation treated him as the patriarchal head of the congregation and supported him as members of the prayer band, through the singing of spirituals on numerous recorded sermons and through their call-and-response-type interjections.

Nix acted as a father figure to not only his congregants, but to his larger community as well. Elwood Nix stated that his father would "sit out on the porch of our house and when people walked by—white, Black, drunkards—he would invite them in the house for breakfast"; Elwood said he "would come down a lot of times and see different people at the breakfast table."[102] Reverend Nix assumed the role of father to his congregants, the community, and even strangers. According to his children, he treated all people with kindness regardless of their gender, race, or religious affiliation.

Lodges and Clubs

Social clubs for African American elites were numerous in Chicago starting in the latter part of the nineteenth century. These clubs included church groups, adult and youth organizations, trade unions, and sororities and fraternities; and group activities of these groups included dances, picnics, and parties.[103] Social clubs were an important means for uplifting the race because they created opportunities for African Americans—who were otherwise not treated as equal members in white society—to serve important community roles such as holding positions as officers in these clubs. "These numerous organizations," as explained by Drake and Cayton, "express the middle-class standards of disciplined and ordered behavior as contrasted with the general disorganization at the lower-class level."[104] Social clubs included recreational activities, such as cardplaying and dancing, and were a substantial part of middle-class life in Bronzeville.

Genester Nix claimed that her father was a 33rd Degree Mason, although her brother Elwood disputed this.[105] Whether or not Nix was a member of this particular social order, he was obviously well aware of social organizations and spoke often of the "lodge." Social clubs, as well as women's groups, expressed middle-class ideals, which included "restrained" and "proper" behavior.[106]

Several of Nix's sermons mentioned affiliation with social organizations, such as the Masons, which required dutiful attendance and dues paid to the lodge. In his sermon, "How Long—How Long," Nix admonishes men who make excuses and lie to their wives, claiming that they spent time at the lodge, when in fact they were having extramarital affairs: "You all-night lodge men, you got so many lodge meetings that keeps you at the lodge all night. Two and three times a week. You have been telling your wife that same old lodge lie all these years." Nix expressed the same theme in "Your Bed Is Too Short and Your Cover Too Narrow." Not only did Nix claim that lodge meetings serve as a convenient alibi for wrongful affairs outside of marriage, but that the lodge takes money away from the church. In "It Was Tight like That," Nix states, "We have so many tight members of the church. They are liberal and generous in giving to the lodge, and giving to worldly pleasures and good-time sport, but they are tight when it comes, ah, to the church." Although social clubs and lodge meetings were beneficial for uplift principles, Nix called out his congregants who used the lodge as an escape from marital and financial responsibilities.

Education

During the Reconstruction era, education was one of the first aspirations of racial uplift and was regarded as "the key to liberation."[107] Nix, a college-educated man, never specifically mentioned education in his sermons or used his own education as a means for condescension to those of less educational achievement. As discussed previously, Nix adjusted his language to suit his listeners, often speaking in the vernacular. However, at times, he revealed his educated status through his use of certain words and topics. For example, in "The Prayer Meeting in Hell," Nix uses multisyllable words, such as "sumptuously" and "felicity," and in "It Was Tight like That," Nix mentions that he needs to satisfy his "gastronomical propensities." He also mentions Greek philosophers and authors in "The Matchless King."

In "There's Something Rotten in Denmark," Nix referenced Shakespeare's play *Hamlet*, in which the character Marcellus states, "Something is rotten in the state of Denmark."[108] Despite being a well-known line from one of Shakespeare's most famous plays, it is unknown whether his less-educated congregants would have understood its meaning.[109] Although Nix did not specifically encourage education for his congregants, he encouraged and supported his children to become highly educated and set an example for others by being educated himself.

In summary, the texts of Nix's sermons primarily reflected ideologies associated with uplifting the race. However, according to Wheeler, uplift meant more than accommodation to white society:

> Uplift entailed moral, social, economic and educational development. It included a sound family life and pride in ownership of property; it involved the adoption of moral standards and behavioral patterns that conformed to the norm in American civilization. The norm was correct not because it was American or white, but because any civilized society operated on such principles. . . . These ministers wanted

for themselves and their congregants to be included in American life, which they believed could be achieved through uplift. There was a balance between "accommodation and possibility" which ministers were in the role to achieve.[110]

Some ministers believed their uplift "was incomplete until they had uplifted others" as part of their view of "the Christian understanding of humanity and its relationship to God."[111] As previously mentioned, in his daily life Nix often invited strangers off the street to join his family for breakfast and called everyone he met "Professor." Even when dealing with issues of racism, he advised his children to treat everyone with respect. Therefore, Nix may have been operating primarily as a Christian (not merely as an uplift accommodationist) in trying his best to help his flock and tend to their salvation.

Whether he was consciously supporting uplift ideologies or merely operating as a Christian minister tending to his congregants is unclear. Possibly his background and exposure to uplift philosophies—instilled in him at an early part of his life and career—became second nature and remained unquestioned in his sermons. However, Nix's care and concern for his congregation may have also been affected by his own exposure to racism. He surely was aware of the racial inequalities taking place in 1920s Chicago and elsewhere and sought to protect his congregants, using any means possible. He must have been concerned for their basic survival in an era in which racial riots caused by discrimination and injustices led to the death and destruction of many in Chicago and in his hometown of Longview, Texas. The Great Depression also caused major suffering for thousands of people, but especially for African Americans who were already suffering economic injustices and limited opportunities due to racism. As a southern migrant himself, Nix noted the temptations of city life that other migrants pursued and saw too many become caught up in the lure of easy money, entertainment, and sexual activity. Nix's admonitions in his recorded sermons were possibly his way of dealing with these frustrations and working to protect his congregants from subjecting themselves to these temptations. But most important, his advice was meant as a tactic for surviving in a world that still subjected African Americans to ridicule, lynchings and other violence, economic and employment injustices, Black Codes, Jim Crow segregation, and many other injustices. He wanted his congregants not only to survive, but to thrive, and encouraged them to take responsibility for their lives, knowing full well the odds against them.

Chapter 4

VOCAL AND MUSICAL ANALYSIS

VOCAL ANALYSIS

African American vocal characteristics that were carried forth from the era of slavery were closely linked to notions of African American folk tradition and cultural identity. Through extensive research of primary historical and secondary source documents,[1] I have identified the characteristics that were mentioned most frequently and therefore likely assumed to have been commonplace during the eighteenth and nineteenth centuries. Correlations between concepts of traditional Black vocalisms extend from historical documents to contemporary secondary sources. In other words, many of the same vocal characteristics and performance practices that were mentioned in historical documents are still addressed and categorized in present-day writings. While not inclusive of every document, the following comprises a summary of the most frequently mentioned expressions and techniques that came to define traditional Black vocalisms, including singing, spoken, and chanted performance practices of sacred singing and preaching. While African American voices are frequently described in essentialist terms throughout the literature, my summary is not meant to essentialize all African Americans as naturally possessing the same vocal traits, but rather to identify a common set of vocal practices present in the rural areas of the southern states during the nineteenth century that were linked closely with the ideas (positive and negative) of an African American folk tradition. By the 1920s, many lower/working-class and middle-class African Americans brought these vocal practices with them as they moved to northern cities such as Chicago. Thus, for this study, I am focusing on the migration of traditional vocal sounds from one place and time (southern states in the nineteenth century) to another place and time (Reverend Nix and his congregations in Chicago in the 1920s).

As commented on by many writers, the vocalizations typically associated with African American traditions include shouts, moans, calls, cries, whoops, hollers, singing of folk spirituals, use of African American Vernacular English (AAVE), improvisation, call-and-response, use of the pentatonic or "gapped" scale, bent notes, "blue" notes, slides, melismas, loud vocal volume, vocal percussiveness, heterophonic textures, use of repetition, use of the entire gamut of the voice, gravelly, raspy, shrill, hard, strained, "dirty" or "throaty" vocal timbre, nasal vocal timbre, use of falsetto, and speech-song, also known as chanting or intoning.[2] While there *were* mentions of clear, beautiful voices, for the most part voices were noted as above.[3] To the ear of many white writers, these vocalizations would have been considered unusual, perhaps even jarring, in contrast with the softer, clearer, more uniform sounds with which they were familiar. African American aesthetics features a wide range of sounds rather than an idealized sound type, as in European aesthetics.

Nix employed traditional vocal features in his recorded sermons that were representations of rural southern religious vocal styles that resonated with the lower classes. The use of traditional forms of chanting and the chanted sermon not only ties Nix to tradition through the sermon's history as a sacred folk expression, but also through the traditional vocal elements present within its performance. Reverend Nix employed tradition in his recorded sermons using various vocal practices, musical expressions, and repertoire, including vernacular language; gravelly vocal timbres; shouts; moans; call-and-response/interjections; chanting with half-spoken, half-sung melodicized pitches; non-articulated sounds; loud vocal dynamics; "verses" created through the organization of lyrical themes; a build to a climax section through the use of moans, gravelly timbre, loud volume, and shouting; participatory performance with the congregation; folk hymns and spirituals; and repetition, improvisation, and vocal layering.

The overall melodic qualities of the chanted sermon and the formal arrangement of internal sections allow for analysis similar to that of other genres of music. Therefore, notated examples include melody, rhythm, and form to extract the data, vocal features, and musical features of the chanted sermon.

Shouts

Shouts are one of the traditions of the Black folk church that emerged during slavery and continued into the early twentieth century. Shouts and shouting have different definitions and functions depending on the circumstance. The ring shout, for example, was a religious dance with call-and-response singing and some percussive accompaniment, while shouting is an individualized activity in the Black church that involves not only vocal ejaculations, but also physical expression and movement. The shout I am referring to here is the shout as vocalization.

Early accounts referred to shouting as a vocal utterance with increased volume, as in Elizabeth Kilham 1870 description in which she stated, "In the pauses between the hymns, some brother or sister gives their 'experience,' always talking in a scream, and as if crying; a natural tone of voice not being considered suitable for such occasions; while the others slap their hands, stamp, and shout, 'yes, yes;' 'dat's so;' [and] 'praise de Lord.'"[4] An account by Mary Boykin Chesnut, who wrote from her South Carolina plantation during the Civil War, described the voices of enslaved worshippers during a praise-house church service: "The Negroes sobbed and shouted and swayed backward and forward, some with aprons to their eyes, most of them clapping their hands and responding in shrill tones: 'Yes, God!' 'Jesus!' 'Savior!' 'Bless de Lord, amen,' etc. It was a little too exciting for me. I would very much have liked to shout, too."[5] These accounts of shouting noted a "shrill tone," not in a "natural tone of voice," and a "screaming" voice, suggesting that the vocal production occurred in the upper register of the voice with higher pitches and was uttered with a loud volume. In this sense, the shout as vocalization suggests an accent or a quick expulsion of a loud sound with shrill timbre.

The vocalizations of the shout served not only as a release of emotions, but also as a spiritual process of salvation. An enslaved woman from a Louisiana plantation remarked about being rebuked for her vocalizations: "He didn't want us shoutin' and moanin' all day 'long, but you gotta shout and you gotta moan if you wants to be saved."[6] Religious conversion depended upon feeling and experience, and shouting contributed to the feelings of one's need to be saved.

Historical documents explain how shouting often began as a participatory activity. For example, during the slavery era, enslaved individuals would gather outdoors after the dinner hour to talk and sing. One reported that "Somebody would start humming an old hymn, and then the next-door neighbor would pick it up. In this way it would finally get around to every house, and then the music started. Soon everybody would be gathered together, and such singing! It wouldn't be long before some of the slaves got happy and started to shouting."[7] In Murphy's study of African American singing in the late nineteenth century, she explained, "suddenly they all began to sing and pat with me, and quickly adapted their different versions [of the song she was singing] to me. They lost no time in getting happy. They all jumped up and down in a perfect ecstasy of delight, and shouted, 'I feel like de Holy Spirit is right on my hade!'"[8] One of the criticisms from upper-class church members in the 1920s was that shouting and its associated physical activity were a throwback to slavery days.[9]

Shouting also refers to ecstatic behavior as a spontaneous expression of spirit.[10] Examples of ecstatic behavior include a report of a church service from 1926 that said, "there is one man who shouts by leaping from one bench to another over the heads of his fellow worshipers." Other shouters explained,

"I shout because there is a fire on the inside. When I witness the truth, the fire moves on the main altar of my heart, and I can't keep still." Another added, "Shouting is but the outward manifestation of an inward joy."[11] Shouting was specifically associated with "getting in the spirit" or feeling the spirit and expressing one's innermost feelings in physical actions. Shouts in the Black folk church service tended to go hand in hand with "getting happy" and "falling out." Getting happy was an expression of feeling the spirit and was physicalized through singing, dancing, shouting, and other physical movements. Elwood Nix recalled a memory of his mother getting happy when he was a baby: "When she started in church one time when Father was preaching and she got happy and she had me in her arms and next thing you know I am flying through the air and a deacon had to catch me."[12] Shouting and other physicalized emotional religious expressions were often looked down upon by those in the upper- and middle-class churches. One member of a large Baptist church in Chicago commented on the "frenzy" associated with the lower-class churches:

> They run up and down the aisles shaking and yelling, overcome as it were with emotion. I get happy to the point of wanting to cry and sometimes do, but I have known the sisters and brothers to become so happy that persons around them are in actual danger of getting knocked in the face. They might even get their glasses broken sometimes if the "nurses" didn't watch out for them.[13]

Emotional expression was, and is, one way to "escape from a wretched condition" of discrimination and injustice throughout the span of African American religious traditions: the experience of getting happy, said one participant, allowed one to forget one's troubles and feel the spirit of God, which "makes you cry . . . sometimes makes you pray; sometimes makes you moan."[14] My research informants explained that emotional expressivity is an essential quality in African American vocal performances, which they believe represents an authentic outpouring of emotion from deeply embedded pain, stemming from a long history of oppression. Soul, in Elwood Nix's opinion, is a result of long-term repression of African Americans that results in an "authentic" sound that "comes from within," which can only be acquired through "living it," by being exposed to oppression over a long period of time. Elwood contended that white people "can't make the sound like the Black people . . . [because] they just don't have the soul."[15]

Genester Nix's experience in her father's church was one that allowed for an articulation, either physically or vocally, of the pains of life. She said:

Emotion, and you know, when you have problems at home, regardless to whether they were financial or marital, or whatever the problem was, you come to church for relief. And for getting consolation. And when a preacher preaches, it has a certain effect on you. Black people are spiritually minded anyway. I mean, it's in our soul, it's in our blood; we feel the spirit easily. And it probably comes from our background—being treated so badly and so forth. And so, when we feel the spirit, we have to let it out, we have to give debt to it and whether it's falling out or whether it's getting happy or dancing or jumping, you do all of that. And they did that a lot in those days. You don't hear too much of it nowadays. People are more reserved. But back then, that's when you gave way to it. ... Black people love to give vent to their feelings. They don't hold back.[16]

Genester differentiated between merely talking back to the minister and shouting:

Shouting is getting up and jumping up and down, turning, twisting, crying, hollering, falling out, letting the spirit hit you, so much so that you are oblivious to your surroundings at times. People used to do a lot of this in past days, especially women. It seems as if they let their home life affect them to the extent that they let everything go in church. Most women back then were controlled by their husbands and felt relief in the church.[17]

Nix's church was an outlet for the pouring of emotions and was the place that allowed congregants to express themselves without judgment from the outside world. Although falling out was supposed to be an expression of spirit, which led one to physically collapse from the emotional intensity of the sermon, Genester admitted that some of the church women had a tendency to fall out into the arms of her handsome brother, Theophilus. However, for the most part, falling out was a result of the spiritual experience.

Shouting can create a participatory performance by the minister and the congregation together. As the minister builds tension in his sermon, the congregation shouts its enthusiasm with words such as "Amen!" and "Preach it!," creating an even higher level of excitement that often sends practitioners into the aisles for dancing and other physical movements. Elwood Nix remembered that, when he was a child in his father's church, "they really hollered and screamed and shouted,"[18] which was a tool Reverend Nix used to build up the emotional excitement and spiritual connection in his sermons. "In those days," Genester explained, "ministers preached differently than today's preachers. They preyed

Figure 4.1. Shouts in "The Black Diamond Express to Hell—Part 4" (1:56–2:05).

on the congregation's emotions a lot. This was to get them feeling the spirit to talk back to the preachers as well as to shout. In some churches, this kind of spirit lasted for hours, which prolonged the services."[19] The participatory aspect of shouting between preacher and congregants functions as call-and-response and a continuous flow of action and reaction through the sermon dialogue. It should be noted that call-and-response in Black expression is overlapping—that is, the response begins before or as the call ends with no break of pause.

Elwood Nix described his father's voice as a "preaching voice" that could change emphasis, "from real hoarse to a screaming voice . . . [to] make you think that you are right there."[20] The "screaming voice" was most likely the voice Nix used to shout. His changing inflections and timbres increased his ability to capture the mood of the sermon and to emotionally captivate the people to whom he was preaching. Elwood also claimed that the "prayer band"[21]—the female congregants who sat in the front two rows of the church called the "amen corner," most likely the female congregants heard on Nix's recordings—would express themselves in melody and sometimes would "get happy and start shouting."

In "The Black Diamond Express to Hell—Part 4," at 2:02–2:04 (Figure 4.1, marked with a thick line), Nix shouts and explodes on the word "Oh," stretching it out in a moan, while simultaneously using loud dynamics and a harsh vocal timbre.[22] The high pitch in combination with loud volume could produce the "screaming" quality that Elwood described.

Moans

The moan also has a dual purpose and function. It is not only a vocal inflection, but also serves as an index of African American musical tradition. I posit that the moan takes on different meanings according to its context, but is nonetheless a vocal practice closely associated with traditional Black vocalisms, regardless of the genre, due to its deep-seated history in both sacred and secular contexts. Moaning has been mentioned as one of the primary vocalizations used in the early Black folk church; the moan and moaning are also associated with the secular traditions of the blues; and the moan functions as an expressive device used by African American ministers and an integral part of the chanted sermon. The moan is thus an intertextual element used in multiple genres (sacred and secular) associated with Black vocal traditions. While the moan and moaning have been frequently addressed as a common feature in the music and preaching of African Americans, little commentary exists that reveals the actual properties of the moan.

Sacred Moans

Multiple accounts from white travelers and visitors to African American churches from the nineteenth to the early twentieth centuries noted the presence of the moan. Paul Svin'in, a Russian diplomat who visited an African American Methodist church in Philadelphia sometime between 1811 and 1813, described the Black voices he heard as "wild," and "piercing," in "loud, shrill monotone," with "howling and groaning," by "sad, heart-rending voices."[23] Ernest Abbott's report in 1901 described a prayer meeting in Atlanta in which the congregants' moaning "resembled nothing so much as the lowing of a great herd of cattle."[24] In *The Souls of Black Folk*, Du Bois described a Black church service: "The people moaned and fluttered, and then the gaunt-cheeked brown woman beside me suddenly leaped straight into the air and shrieked like a lost soul, while around about came wail and groan and outcry, and a scene of human passion such as I had never conceived before."[25] Natalie Curtis Burlin described the vocalizations she heard in an early twentieth-century Black church service in the South, stating "from the depths of some 'sinner's' remorse and imploring came a pitiful little plea, a real Negro 'moan,' sobbed in musical cadence."[26] The evidence from Svin'in, Abbott, Du Bois, and Burlin suggests the moan was a sort of intoned or pitched hum, cry, groan, or wail sounding in anguish as the result of spiritual passion and/or emotional pain. "For people with a certain background," as theologian Henry H. Mitchell explains, "it appears that a moaned message is more deeply spiritual than an unintoned one. Although this is not necessarily true, tone does signal a kind of affirmation of Black identity which is often used of the Holy Spirit as a catalyst for a deep religious experience."[27] The musical qualities of the moan demonstrate that resonance in the voice was preferred to the spoken word for the spiritual experience.

Folklorist and anthropologist Harold Courlander discusses the moan as a "noteworthy" part of the African American vocal tradition; however, his account contrasts with Svinin's and Burlin's statements, and he explains that "'Moaning' does not imply grief or anguish; on the contrary, it is a blissful or ecstatic rendition of a song, characterized by full and free exploitation of melodic variation and improvisation, sometimes with an open threat [throat], sometimes with closed lips to create a humming effect."[28] Burlin's description of the moan as "tortured" conflicts with Courlander's explanation of it as "blissful."

Possibly it was both, depending on the circumstance, and also an expression of deep emotion, such as that described by Du Bois.

Gospel music composer and bluesman Thomas A. Dorsey, aka "Georgia Tom," reflected on the moan, stating that it "is just about known only to the black folk."[29] Dorsey's comment suggests cultural "ownership" of the moan and its deep alignment with Black folk vocal traditions. From the comments provided, we can speculate that the moan was a hummed or otherwise nonverbal sound with extended or augmented rhythmic and melodic embellishments, which extend the linear space from the worded version of a song.

Elwood Nix described the preacher's moan, such as his father's, as a melodicized utterance, but not necessarily a sung utterance. Rather, in the style of the speech-song vocalizations of the chanted sermon, Elwood claimed, "They hold the syllables longer and hum, like a hum, like when he says 'How long.... How long...' [he holds the vowel out for an extended amount of time]. Do you hear the humming in my voice?"[30] Elwood remembered the moan as having a humming quality, rather than being sung full-voiced. A moan is a vocal technique used to create emphasis, either for the meaning of the word or simply for dramatic effect. Thus, in Nix's case, a moan is a word, syllable, or hum that is extended in length on the same pitch.

In a metered score, the moan could be analyzed as an augmentation of a word or syllable. Courlander concurs with Elwood's description of the moan as a "humming effect," sometimes with closed lips.[31] In Jeannette Robinson Murphy's 1899 study of African American singing, she emphasized vocal characteristics and stylistic traits that were necessary for one to sing "negro melodies." She mentioned the necessity that a singer "must also intersperse his singing with peculiar humming sounds—'hum-m-m-m.'"[32] These sounds were apparently moans. Drake and Cayton explained the moan as used by a lower-class minister in a Chicago church: "It is possible to find preachers who merely repeat phrases over and over with a rising and falling inflection of the voice, or who take one word such as 'Oh-h-h-h' and sing it as a chant, with the congregation shouting all the while."[33] The extension of "Oh-h-h-h" implies a moan. Both Murphy's and Drake and Cayton's examples provide evidence of the augmentation of the word or syllable to produce a moan.

Secular Moans

The moan in the secular setting of the blues also presents two differing qualities: one associated with meaning, and the other a vocalization with a distinct sound quality. Meaning in the blues moan often referred to sexualized themes or broken-hearted, unrequited love, while the sound of the blues moan was consistent with the sound of the sacred moan. Moaning is a device in blues and not a special subcategory of blues. Some of the songs with "moan" in the title contain no actual moaning. Clara Smith's "Awful Moanin' Blues" (1923) was a big hit, and she became known as the "World's Champion Moaner." This record perhaps launched the "moaning" fad in commercial blues titles.

My survey of Dixon, Godrich, and Rye's *Blues and Gospel Records: 1890–1943* reveals over eighty titles recorded between 1923 and 1941, mostly blues, which include "moan" or "moaning" in the title. Of those titles, there are forty-seven recorded between April 1927 and March 1931, the same years that Nix recorded his sermons. The fact that the word "moan" was prevalent in recordings during the years of Nix's recording career provides evidence that the moan was a well-known vocal feature in both African American sacred and secular recordings. Representative recordings of blues from the 1920s with the word "moan" in the title are listed in Table 4.1.

Table 4.1. Blues Songs with "Moan" in Title			
Artist	**Title**	**Label**	**Date**
Blind Lemon Jefferson	"That Black Snake Moan"	OK 8455; JCl 511; JSo AA513	March 14, 1927
Furry Lewis	"Sweet Papa Moan"	Vo 1116	April 20, 1927
Kid Cole	"Sixth Street Moan"	Vo 1186	May 28, 1928
Ma Rainey	"Deep Moaning Blues"	Pm 12706, 14011; JC L1	June 12, 1928
Tampa Red and Georgia Tom	"Chicago Moan Blues"	Vo 1244	January 9, 1929
Tampa Red	"Moanin' Heart Blues"	Vo 1484; Spt S2230	February 7, 1930
Tampa Red	"Chicago Moan Blues"	Vo 1484	February 7, 1930
Tampa Red and Georgia Tom	"I. C. Moan Blues"	Vo 1538; ARC 7-03-73; Cq 8860	Mid-June 1930
Note: In the Label column, abbreviations of record labels are as follows: OK (OKeh), JCl (Jazz Classic), JSo (Jazz Society), Vo (Vocalion), Pm (Paramount), JC (Jazz Collector (British), Spt (Supertone), ARC (American Record Company), and Cq (Conqueror).			

The lyrics to Blind Lemon Jefferson's "That Black Snake Moan" link the vocal technique to sexual physicality:

I ain't got no mama now.
I ain't got no mama now.
She told me late last night, "You don't need no mama no how."

Mmm, black snake crawlin' in my room.
Mmm, black snake crawlin' in my room.
And some pretty mama had better come an' get this black snake soon.

While Jefferson's moan refers to sexual ecstasy or sexual desires, Ma Rainey's "Deep Moaning Blues" on the Paramount label (Pm 12706), recorded June 12, 1928, links the moan to feelings of being "down-hearted," typical in blues lyrics associated with lost or unrequited love. Rainey's song not only demonstrates the meaning of the moan associated with heartbreak, but also the vocalized traits of the moan. The entire chorus section of Rainey's song is moaned through her use of hums on "hmmm" and slides in the melody. Rainey's moan is also hummed but vocalized with distinct pitches.

Hmmm, hmmm (Moaning)
Hmmm, hmmm (Moaning)
Hmmm, hmmm (Moaning)
Hmmm, hmmm (Moaning)

My bell rang this morning, didn't know which way to go.
My bell rang this morning, didn't know which way to go.
I had the blues so bad, I sit right down on my floor.

I felt like going on the mountain, jumping over in the sea.
I felt like going on the mountain, jumping over in the sea.
When my Daddy stay out late, he don't care a thing for me.

The transcription of Ma Rainey's "Deep Moaning Blues" (Musical Example 4.1) illustrates the singer's use of hums, slides between notes (using the glissando figure), scoops up to a note, also called a "bent note" (using the bent arrow symbol), and blue notes, in this case the Ab in the fourth measure of the treble clef. The lyrical focus of Rainey's song centers on love lost or a love that "treats me mean," causing pain and heartache, with the moan functioning as an index of emotional, romantic pain. Thomas A. Dorsey mentions that he wrote "the low moaning type" of blues, which was typically associated with romantic heartbreak.[34] The blues singers of the 1920s were most likely familiar with the sacred context and sound of the moan, and employed similar vocal features

Musical Example 4.1. Ma Rainey, "Deep Moaning Blues," YouTube, accessed July 17, 2018.

in their blues repertoire, such as Rainey's moans, to emulate the sad, forlorn feeling associated with the moan in the early Black church services.

Though Blind Willie Johnson's "Dark Was the Night—Cold Was the Ground," recorded on the Columbia label (Co 14303-D) (Musical Example 4.2) on December 3, 1927, does not use the word "moan" in the title, the entirety of the piece consists of moaning. The transcription of Johnson's moans demonstrates a similarity with Rainey's moans, in that the blues moans consist of hums, slides between notes, and scoops up to notes (bent notes). Johnson's piece is a stylized instrumental interpretation of a lined-out hymn. After the verses of such a hymn are lined out and sung, the performance often continues with

Musical Example 4.2. Blind Willie Johnson, "Dark Was the Night—Cold Was the Ground," YouTube, accessed July 17, 2018, https://www.youtube.com/watch?v=BNj2BXW852g.

moaning of the melody. This is the portion that Johnson sings (i.e., the moan rather than the preceding lyrics).

The distinctions between the secular broken-hearted moan and the sacred spiritual-ecstasy moan were sometimes blurred through the close relation of musical characteristics in the blues, the folk spiritual, and the chanted sermon. Advertisements for race records in the 1920s, placed by white-owned record labels, frequently mentioned the secular blues and sacred sermons together in the same ad, despite objections to the blues as the "devil's music" by the Black religious folk. For example, an advertisement in the *Chicago Defender* (Figure 4.2) placed blues singer Furry Lewis's "Sweet Papa Moan" and Reverend Nix's "Black Diamond Express to Hell," parts I and II, in the same advertisement, linking African American secular and sacred genres in the same context.[35]

Moans, along with other vocal characteristics associated with African American voices, were also used for marketing purposes as a means to demonstrate authenticity of Black vocal traditions. An advertisement for one new blues release emphasized several vocal gestures: "Here They Are—Moanin', Whinin', Shoutin' Blues."[36] The association of specific vocal gestures with the religious traditions of the Black church clearly helped establish the blues as an authentic African American genre meant to appeal to the sensibilities of the Black masses and marketed as a commodity to Black audiences. While ministers in the Baptist tradition demonized the blues and jazz for their association with worldly matters, using the word "moan" in advertisements for both religious and secular music functioned to conceptually link these two arenas of African

Figure 4.2. "Sweet Papa Moan" (advertisement), the *Chicago Defender*, November 19, 1927, 3.

American music in the 1920s as it simultaneously pointed to the vernacular vocal traditions associated with the "down-home" folk of the South.

In "The Matchless King" (Vo 1158), recorded January 18, 1928, Nix incorporated moans. Words that are moaned are of a longer value than naturally spoken words. As Nix builds up the sermon's intensity by incorporating moans, his phrases increase in length, not as a result of more or longer pauses or breaths between the phrases, but as a result of an increase in word length. In the phrase "He came all the way from glory" (Figure 4.3), the word "all" is extended 7/10ths of a second, representing a moan. Nix stretches out the vowel ("a-a-a-h") part of "all" to create a forward momentum. The phrase "And said, He's my well of water in a dry place" consists of all one-syllable words except for "water," so we could expect all of the words except "water" to be of similar length and value

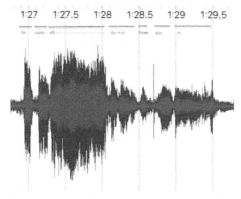

Figure 4.3. Moans on "He came all the way from glory" in "The Matchless King" (1:27–1:29).

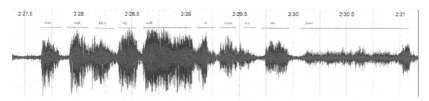

Figure 4.4. Moans on "And said, He's my well of water in a dry place" in section D of "The Matchless King" (2:27–2:31).

(Figure 4.4). In fact, most of the words are approximately 2/10ths of a second in length, but the word "well" is 5/10ths of a second, and "place" is 9/10ths of a second in length. Nix utilized moans through the stretching of words to create greater emphasis and build momentum in the sermon. Often the moans are accompanied by an increase in both volume and gravelly timbres. Not only did Nix use moans to emphasize words and create dramatic effect; he continued a tradition frequently addressed in historical documents as a common feature of African American ministers.

Loudness

Several individuals who witnessed singing by African Americans in the nineteenth and early twentieth centuries identified loudness as a common feature of Black vocalists. George Pinckard, on his journeys to the West Indies in 1816, remarked on the singing of enslaved Africans he encountered on a slave ship: "Their song was a wild yell, devoid of all softness and harmony, and loudly chanted in harsh monotony."[37] The qualities of songs being "loudly chanted" in "harsh monotony" are similar to the chanted sermon's predilection toward loud enunciations around a somewhat static pitch center, thus suggesting the possible historical connections between the monotoned chants of enslaved persons and the chanted sermon. The preference for loud church services was noted by a nineteenth-century Baptist preacher, "Uncle Jack" of Nottaway County, Virginia, who expressed his disdain for "black noise," stating, "You noisy Christians remind me of the little branches (of streams) after a heavy rain. They are soon full, then noisy, and as soon empty. I would much rather see you like the broad, deep river, which is quiet, because it is broad and deep."[38] Jack's "proper" decorum was noted by a white Presbyterian minister, William White, who in 1859 wrote admiringly of Jack's "silence" as a symbol of his stature. In the same year, a letter written from Rev. R. Q. Mallard to Mrs. Mary S. Mallard described the vocal tendencies at a revival meeting of enslaved individuals: "The whole congregation kept up one loud monotonous strain, interrupted by various sounds: groans and screams and clapping hands. . . . one woman specially under the influence of the excitement . . . accompanying the whole by a series of short, sharp shrieks."[39] In the first book of Negro spirituals, *Slave Songs of the United States*, published in 1867, its authors described the Black stevedores who loaded West Indian vessels and sang "with a volume of voice that reached a square or two away."[40] In 1870 at a church service in Richmond, an anonymous writer, presumably white, described how the service began with a hymn followed by foot-stomping, "until the noise was deafening; and as the excitement increased, one and another would spring from their seats, and jump up and down, uttering shriek after shriek; while from all parts of the house came cries of, 'Hallelujah;' 'Glory to God;' 'Jes' now Lord, come jes' now;' 'Amen;' and occasionally a prolonged, shrill whoop, like nothing earthly, unless it be some savage war-cry."[41] W. E. B. Du Bois commented on a church service he attended in the late nineteenth century, in which

> the Frenzy or "Shouting" . . . was the last essential of Negro religion and the one more devoutly believed in than all the rest. It varied in expression from the silent rapt countenance or the low murmur and moan to the mad abandon of physical fervor,—the stamping, shrieking, and shouting, the rushing to and fro and wild waving of arms, the weeping and laughing, the vision and the trance. . . . These were the characteristics of Negro religious life as developed up to the time of Emancipation.[42]

Du Bois's comments imply contrasting dynamics that ranged from "silent" to the "mad abandon" of noise and physical activity. E. A. McIlhenny, who attended Black church services during Reconstruction in Louisiana as a child with his "Mammy," described the "great volumes of voices when the hymns were sung, and the activity of both men and women in jumping up and down when in the frenzy of 'getting religion' and the jumping about of those who had been baptized when the 'spirit' struck them as they came up from the water."[43] The consistent descriptions of loud singing or "shrieking" in these discourses suggest that both Black and white observers interpreted loud volume as an important characteristic of Black vocal traditions.

One sister in the early Black folk church, represented as speaking in AAVE, discussed the necessity of loudness as a harbinger of the spiritual experience and a prerequisite for the release of pent-up emotions:

> I goes ter some churches, an' I sees all de folks settin' quiet an' still, like dey dunno what de Holy Sperit am. But I fin's in my Bible, that when a man or a 'ooman gets full ob de Holy Sperit, ef dey should hol' dar peace, de stones would cry out; an' ef de power ob God can make de stones cry out, how can it help makin' us poor creaturs cry out, who feels ter praise Him fer His mercy. Not make a noise! Why we makes a noise 'bout ebery ting else; but dey tells us we mustn't make no noise ter praise de Lord. I don't want no sich 'ligion as dat ar.[44]

The need for "making a noise" was necessary, at least for this woman, for praising God. She contended that "we makes a noise 'bout ebery ting else," suggesting that loudness was commonplace in both sacred and secular African American vocalizations in the post-Civil War era.

Loudness was a vocal characteristic that also became an index for class affiliation. In the early twentieth century, new migrants from the South who moved to Chicago during the Great Migration were instructed by the *Chicago Defender* to "Keep Your Mouth Shut, Please!," noting, "There is entirely too much loud talking on the street cars among our newcomers."[45] Southern migrants were associated with "low breeding," and their loud vocal tendencies often brought embarrassment and shame to middle-class Chicagoans. One Chicagoan commented, "When I first came to Chicago I was a member of the Baptist Church. But I never joined a church here because I did not like the way people exhibited their emotions. At home, in the church I belonged to, people were very quiet; but here in the Baptist churches I found people rather noisy."[46] Instruction for new migrants to Chicago was given by the Urban League on how to behave in public, which included "*I will refrain* from loud talking and objectionable deportment on street cars and in public places" (italics in original).[47] In the 1920s in Chicago, southern migrants sometimes conducted themselves in accordance with what they believed whites expected of them. This included boisterous behavior, creating the image of the happy-go-lucky and loud African American, who was tolerated by white people "as long as his dialect, his wit, and his manner are amusing enough."[48] Loudness thus became

Figure 4.5. Increase in volume in sections A and C² in "Black Diamond Express to Hell—Pt. I."

an index for southern migrants and lower-class status, with some in the upper class feeling that "Lower-class people are those who give free rein to their emotions, whether worshiping or fighting, who 'don't know how to act.'"[49] Although Nix's congregation was diverse in terms of class, his loud booming voice and the interactive chatter by the sisters would probably have been condemned by many Black elite Chicagoans.

Elwood Nix said he believes timbral and dynamic differences in voices can grant power (or not) to the orator. He stated, "if you notice a high voice, it shakes, it trills, [you're] not sure what's coming out of the mouth. A somber voice sounds more authentic, and a loud voice is, I would say, boisterous voices have more truth to it. . . . A high voice sounds weak."[50] Elwood's comments implied that he believes loud and full voices are more commanding. As previously discussed, loudness was not only a means to draw listeners in, but also was a standard performance practice in traditional Black vocalisms, aligning Nix with these practices. The chanted sermon utilizes an increase in the volume of the dynamics to emotionally draw in the listeners.

In "Black Diamond Express to Hell—Pt. I," there is a clear increase in volume between section A (0:00–0:23) and section C² (0:52–1:24), from which a consistent volume is maintained to the end of the sermon. In other words, Nix implements an increase in dynamics to emotionally draw in the listeners. The sound file demonstrates more depth and height in section C², exemplifying the amplitude or increase in volume. Regardless of the recording levels, comparison of the two sections reveals an overall increase in dynamics within the sermon itself (Figure 4.5).

Call-and-Response

Call-and-response is a musical feature in which one singer or group of singers sings a line of text, which is then answered with a response from another singer or group. Call-and-response is thus a participatory performance, as it is necessary for multiple voices to interact, functioning as question-answer, antecedent-consequence, or leader-group. Call-and-response has been well documented as a feature of both African song forms and African American slave song forms. "Lining out," a related practice that is also common in Black worship services, involves group repetition of a spoken or chanted line and was used for instructional purposes. Lining out dates back to the colonial period and differs from call-and-response in that in lining out the response to the leader is much longer and more elaborate than the original chant of the leader.[51] In contrast to lining out, call-and-response is not used for instructional purposes; the response line is different from the call line and usually vocalizes a line that functions as a refrain. Often the same response line is reiterated throughout the performance. While both practices are responsorial, the voices in call-and-response serve as part of the melody of the song, functioning within the rhythmical structure as established by the call, with both the call and the response lines equal in importance.

An example of call-and-response is found in the spiritual "Swing Low, Sweet Chariot," in which the solo singer sings the call, which is then answered by the refrain line of "Comin' for to carry me home."

Call: *Swing low sweet chariot,*
Response: *Comin' for to carry me home*
Call: *Swing low sweet chariot,*
Response: *Comin' for to carry me home*

Call: *I look'd over Jordan, an' what did I see,*
Response: *Comin' for to carry me home*
Call: *A band of angels comin' after me,*
Response: *Comin' for to carry me home*[52]

In Nix's chanted sermon, the interjection of words and phrases by the congregation serves as the "response" to his "call." Although the interjections of congregation members do not repeat Nix's "call" with a repeating responsorial line, they *function* as call-and-response and are an integral part of the overall performance of the sermon. However, in two of the songs Nix and his congregation sang on his recorded sermons—"All o' My Sins Done Taken Away," from "Black Diamond Express to Hell—Pt. II," and "Nowhere to Hide" from "Hiding Behind the Stuff"—call-and-response is used. For example, in "All o' My Sins Done Taken Away," Nix sings the "call" line, answered by the congregation in the "response" line:

Nix: *All of my sins*
Congregation: *All of my sins*
Nix: *Been taken away*
Congregation: *Been taken away.*

Timbre

Historical documents describe Black voices as having similar vocal timbre and often refer to vocal timbre to bring attention to racial difference and the supposed inferiority of African Americans. For example, Natalie Curtis Burlin wrote that the "rough sons and daughters of toil, ragged and unkempt" (implying field workers and poor rural Black people) were exempt from the "smooth influence of 'refined white environment.'"[53] In another example, which appeared in 1855, a collector of slave songs commented on the "rich, unctuous, guttural" sounds of the southern African American minstrel singer. [54] Consistently, Black voices were described as hoarse or guttural, while white voices were considered smooth or sweet. Smooth and sweet sounds were usually associated with the European tradition and were not the desired timbres for traditional Black voices. The voices associated with the Black folk church typically featured raspy, throaty, noisy, or gravelly timbres. As folklorist Harold Courlander claimed, "Apparently valued in Negro folk music is the 'throaty' quality that has 'body' to it," adding, "Sermons preached in this type of voice appear to create a special emotional tension."[55] Ernest Hamlin Abbott's report of a Black church service, in the 1901 *Outlook*, described a minister who "was as wrought up as his audience" and declaimed his sermon with a "hoarse and screaming voice."[56] While there *were* smooth and sweet vocal timbres used by some African American vocalists, these timbres were often ignored in the writings because they did not fit the idea of racial "difference." African and African American aesthetics features a full range of vocal and instrumental sounds rather than an idealized sound, as in the Euro-American classical music tradition. For example, harsh and guttural voices were disparaged in white musical aesthetics and confirmed stereotypes of cultural inferiority.

As Samuel A. Floyd Jr. explains, early blues singers such as Charley Patton, Blind Lemon Jefferson, and Leadbelly (Huddie Ledbetter) had in common the vocal quality and variations in timbre that make the blues a distinctive genre: the "nasal, foggy, hoarse texture that delivered the elisions, hums, growls, blue notes, and falsetto, and the percussive oral effects of their ancestors,"[57] attributing timbral distortions to African traditions. Specific timbres *can* also be associated with specific musical genres. For example, Floyd associates a "nasal, foggy, hoarse" vocal timbre with the blues, similar to the association of the distorted tone of an electric guitar to heavy metal music. These generalizations do not imply a homogeneous sound ideal that cannot be changed, but a sound ideal that typifies common performance practices of the genre.

Although raspy, hoarse, and guttural timbres have often been associated with racial categories, associations with class standing were also common. For example, a 1906 account of a service at Little St. John's Church described the singing of a Black male whose voice was "not of the rasping, guttural variety common among mountain whites [read: lower-class whites], but deep and suave as an organ-pipe."[58] Guttural vocal timbres have typically been associated with the voices of African Americans, yet this example clearly designates vocal timbre by class. My purpose for mentioning the common vocal characteristics of Black and white singers is not only to challenge the common essentialist notions that Black and white voices sounded different based on biological differences, but also to call attention to the fact that voices, whether Black or white, were often distinguished by class.

Reverend Nix's voice had a gravelly timbre, and according to Genester Nix, it was his "regular voice." She claimed he was never hoarse and that he did not need a microphone to carry his voice at revivals: "His voice was so different than anybody else's. His voice was so powerful yet magnetic. It drew people, and every time he had the revivals, it was full, packed and he was all over the United States preaching. . . . People loved to hear him preach. I mean, people gathered there, everywhere he went."[59] Elwood Nix claimed his father consciously changed his timbre to reflect the text that he was speaking and to connect with his audience, consciously using timbre as a means of communication.

Genester's and Elwood's comments provide evidence that Reverend Nix's voice was naturally gravelly in timbre and that he was able to change his voice to suit his audience. Thus, there are two distinct voices or uses of the voice: the voice one is born with and its inherent timbre, and a second voice that can be adjusted to suit whatever situation or condition one chooses.[60] In voices in general and Nix's voice specifically, this could mean timbral adjustments to suit cultural expectations. The gravelly timbre of Nix's voice was apparently one key source of his success and one he used frequently and consciously.

The spectrogram graph gives some indication of timbre and shows frequency in the vertical axis, with loudness represented by color.[61] The fundamental pitch is shown as the lowest frequency (sounding pitch) with partials or overtones above. The fundamental and lower harmonics give "warmth" and richness to the sound, while harmonics higher up in frequency sound "bright" or shrill.[62] Thus, the more compact the lower harmonics, the "warmer" the sound; harmonics that "stretch" into the higher regions sound more shrill. However, a "noisy," "dirty," or "gravelly" timbre will be displayed as a "snowstorm," reaching into the higher frequencies.

In addition, vocal timbre can be distinguished between "dark" and "bright" tones depending on the shape of the mouth. According to the CHARM tutorial for Sonic Visualizer,

> Acoustically, vowels and consonants are patterns of relative loudness among the sounding frequencies across the spectrum. Vowels are made

by changing the shape of one's vocal cavity, and the effect of that is to change the balance of harmonics in the sound. That balance will remain the same whatever the pitches one may be singing. When singers want to change the colour of their voice they shift the vowels up and forward (brighter) or down and back (darker) in the mouth, and the spectrum changes as a result.[63]

Therefore, it is possible to change one's vocal timbre by altering the shape of the mouth. It is possible that Nix focused his tone (probably unconsciously) in the back of his mouth to extract a darker timbre.

The differences between bright and dark timbres are readily apparent when we compare Nix's dark and gravelly timbre with the prayer band's bright and nasal timbre as heard in the traditional spiritual "My Sins Been Taken Away" found in "Black Diamond Express to Hell—Pt. II." The lines "Well glory hallelujah to His name, all of my sins are taken away" are sung by Nix in a gravelly timbre, and contrast with the sisters' clean and nasal timbre in their response, "taken away," marked in a black box in both the spectrogram and the sound file (Figure 4.6). The sisters sing "taken away" without Nix, and although there are multiple female voices, together their clean timbre does not compare to the gravelly timbre of Nix, as evidenced by the snowstorm effect when he is

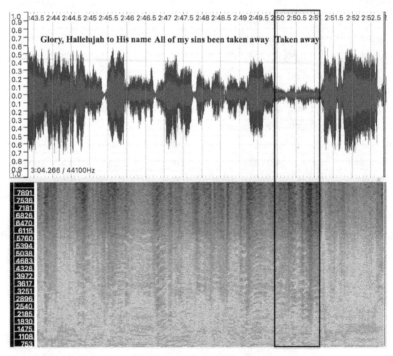

Figure 4.6. Timbral differences in "My Sins Been Taken Away" (2:41–2:52).

singing. The overtones in Nix's gravelly voice carry up into the higher parts of the graph as evidenced by the snowstorm effect, while the spectrogram demonstrates the lighter and brighter quality of the voices of the sisters. Thus, the timbres of Nix and the female congregants were noticeably different. Both timbres would have been considered undesirable by those who chose assimilation to Western art standards.[64]

Sound was important, even essential, to the folk preacher in emotionally communicating with and drawing in his congregants. Nix's voice was probably shocking to hear on early phonograph machines because his voice, as Paul Oliver states, "roared in leonine tones."[65] The gravelly timbre of Nix's voice was most likely not only part of his physical vocal makeup, but also a tool he consciously employed to excite and entice his listeners.

Heterophony

In many of Nix's sermons, the female congregants, or "prayer band," sing a spiritual melody simultaneously, but not in unison. Each of the singers contributes in her own individual way, some entering with slight rhythmic alterations and some with melodic alterations. This type of group singing is called heterophony, which is defined as "an improvisational type of polyphony, namely, the simultaneous use of slightly or elaborately modified versions of the same melody by two (or more) performers, e.g., a singer and an instrumentalist, the latter adding a few extra tones or ornaments to the singer's melody."[66] Although the group members sing together, their performance is not "strict," as in European choral music, which depends upon vocal blend. In Nix's recordings, each of the female singers stands out individually despite the group nature of the performance.

Chanting

Preaching traditions in the folk church include the chanting of sermons, sometimes called "whooping, intoning, chanting, moaning, and tuning."[67] The use of chanting itself is a tradition that extends back possibly to the eighteenth century and involves a combination of speaking and singing. It emphasizes the words through the use of a half-spoken, half-sung quality of delivering the text to create heightened emotion among members of the congregation. Historically, Black preachers intoned their sermons. Oral traditions were passed from African chants to African American hollers, moans, and the intoning and chanting of preachers. Historical documents provide evidence of some of the features of the chanted sermon. For example, a chanted sermon performed at a camp meeting in Nashville, Tennessee, in 1928 was reported as beginning with a "warming up" section, in which the preacher presents sound argument, making practical applications to everyday life. ... He is feeling his way until the spirit strikes him. With the coming of the spirit ... the speaker's entire demeanor changes. He now launches into a type of discourse that borders on hysteria. His voice, changed in pitch, takes on a mournful, singing quality, and words flow from his lips in such a manner as to make an understanding of them almost impossible.[68]

A Black preacher in former slave quarters near Fort Motte, South Carolina, was featured in a report from 1926, which described the words of the sermon as "short, staccato drum-beats," emphasizing their rhythmic qualities.[69] As early as 1847, Peter Randolph, an enslaved individual in Virginia, noted the qualities of the chanted sermon as demonstrated in prayer meetings: "The speaker usually commences by calling himself unworthy, and talks very slowly, until feeling the spirit, he grows excited."[70] The chanted sermon and the folk spiritual share many common features, as is evident from John Mason Brown's 1868 "Songs of the Slave," in which he stated: "Many years ago there originated a negro ballad. ... It was generally sung in chanting style, with marked emphasis and the prolongation of the concluding syllable of each line."[71] Reports such as these provide evidence of the preacher's use of pitch, dramatic delivery in his performance, use of nonarticulated sound, and rhythmic declamation.

One of the most prominent features of the folk minister is his use of pitch, a definitive characteristic in the chanted sermon and the very element that makes the chanted sermon *chanted*. Some describe the chanting feature as melody or as being intoned and the speech-like quality attained through the use of "dirty" timbre, growling, or vocal straining.[72] The transition from speech to speech-like song can be sudden or gradual to heighten the emotional content of a piece. Once the pitch center, or "tuning pitch," is established, both the minister and the congregants respond via this pitch, singing in the same "key."

In *The Science of English Verse* (1911), Sidney Lanier analyzed what he called "speech-tune," or speech-like song, of the African American chanted sermon:

One who has ever heard a typical negro sermon will have observed how the preacher begins, in the ordinary tones of voice, announcing his text and gradually clearing the way to the personal appeal of the sermon: here he rises into a true poetic height, and always falls into what is an approach to musical recitative: "Yes, my bretherin and sisterin," (he will say) "ef you don' make haste and repent of all your sins and wash yourself clean in de river of life, de Lord will fling de las' man of you down into everlasting perdition."[73]

Musical Example 4.3. Lanier's transcription of a chanted sermon. From Lanier, *The Science of English Verse*, 276–77.

Lanier, as was typical for the time, showed his own bias against the African American chanted style, comparing the "crude approach to the speech-tune made in the half-chanted sermon of the negro ... [with] the highest delicacy of the cultivated speech-tune," such as is present in a sonnet.[74] Despite his bias, Lanier provided evidence of the sermon moving from "ordinary tones" to "musical recitative," or chanting. Lanier transcribed the preacher's text and chanting, as shown in Musical Example 4.3. From his transcription, it is evident that he heard clear pitches, meter, and rhythm. He notated the melodic back-and-forth pattern between the tonic and third-scale degree, as well as rhythmic declamations and accents.

Through his chanting, the minister builds up the excitement and emotional intensity until the "Spirit of God is most noticeable."[75] The chanted sermon is the medium through which he performs. Albert J. Raboteau confirms the importance of not only oral traditions, but also the performative qualities and style associated with the preacher:

> Because the oral rather than the written word has been the primary bearer of black culture, verbal skill is valued highly in the black community.... Style of delivery determines the success of the oral performer

whether bluesman, gospel singer, or preacher. It is not, then, merely the word as spoken—much less read—but the word as *performed* that must be taken into account if the sermon is to be adequately understood. In this case, more than in most, style is content [italics in original].[76]

The performative qualities of chanting equate it with performed song rather than mere spoken words. Whereas spoken words are often read, singing and chanting are performative expressions, with chanting most often being improvised. However, whereas in song the emphasis is on melody, in chanting the emphasis is on the text or words, with few pitches. Thus, chanting embraces both the melodic and rhythmic qualities of the spoken voice, as well as the regularized intonation of the sung voice, but reduced to a recitative type of utterance. In his recorded sermons, Nix easily transitions or style-switches between speaking, chanting, and singing, without hesitation, delivering a wide range of performative qualities through his voice and providing a continuum between speech and song. Spoken words alone are not of the same importance as chanted words, which produce additional layers of meaning. Performed language in the form of chanting, rather than spoken language, allows for enhanced emotional nuances to be communicated.

In addition to words and verbal skill, Gerald L. Davis discusses the importance of non-articulated sound to the African American sermon:

> "Sound" manifested during an African-American sermon is not "noise." Community-determined ideas and values are communicated in the coded sound channels of the sermon event. And the concurrent coding and decoding processes which characterize preacher and congregational oral-aural interaction during sermon segments have philosophical and aesthetic dimensions. This nonarticulated but full voice is as significant to a congregation's interpretation of the preached sermon as the articulated word.[77]

Preacher-produced sound/semantic units, which Davis calls "sermonphones," take precedence over the words or text and carry "semantic affect" in the context of the performance. Sound units can include verbal units (in the form of a single word or phrase) or nonverbal units, which are non-articulated sounds that are the stylistic feature of chanting in preaching. Davis claims that non-articulated sounds "are used at that point in the sermon performance when articulated words are inappropriate to the quality of the affect requiring expression and may consist of highly stylized, and easily recognized, grunts, groans, and hums."[78] For example, Thomas A. Dorsey credited the "cry" in the voice as powerful enough to evoke an emotional response from both secular and sacred music listeners, inspiring listeners to shout, creating a participatory response.[79] Nonverbal sounds convey meaning and often outweigh the importance of words in the oral transmission of the sermon. The preacher and congregation generate sound intentionally with full knowledge of its historical precedents and appropriateness.

Participatory Performance Elements

Participatory performance, as defined by ethnomusicologist Thomas Turino, is "a special type of artistic practice in which there are no artist-audience distinctions, only participants and potential participants performing different roles."[80] In a participatory performance, the attention is centered on the *doing* of the performance, resulting in a heightened social interaction. It is the social interaction that creates a communal experience, in which participants engage with each other but focus on their inward feelings. Through heightened concentration, the performer creates a feeling of "flow," in which thoughts and distractions fade from awareness, leaving only feelings of transcendence.[81] The level of feeling becomes the gauge for the quality of the performance.[82] As previously discussed, feeling is imperative in the conversion experience and for spiritual awareness. The interaction of congregants, inspired by the minister and his chanted sermon, creates heightened emotions leading to the spiritual experience.

The interaction between preacher and congregation—a form of participatory performance—is similar to singing in that rhythmic patterns become established and, if the minister chants, pitches are established as well.[83] The responses from the congregation to the minister are cues that the congregation approves and wants the speaker to continue.[84] The preacher and congregation work in tandem, feeding off and influencing each other's responses and emotional energy. The congregation, through its interjections, ultimately influences the preacher's timing and delivery of his sermon.[85]

In "The Black Diamond Express to Hell—Part 3," the sisters interject verbal and sung responses throughout most of the sermon and create the sonic illusion of a live church congregation with numerous voices overlaying one another, only pausing when Nix is shouting. They interject after Nix has spoken, often responding directly to his text. In "The Prayer Meeting in Hell," the female congregants' responses (shown in italics) appear after Nix's phrases:

And the rich man opened up a prayer meetin' in hell   *Alright, Yes*
And cried out,
"Oh Abraham,   *Yes*
Oh Abraham,   *Have mercy on us*

Figure 4.7. "The Prayer Meeting in Hell" (advertisement), the *Chicago Defender (National Edition)*, October. 22, 1927, 3.

    Have mercy on my soul!
    And if I am tormented in these flames   *Yes!*
    Send the angels down here   *Have mercy*
    That he might dip his finger in cool water   *Hallelujah*
    And cool my scorching tongue
    Because I'm tormented in the flame."   *Alright*

As is apparent in the text, the female congregants interject on nearly every phrase after Nix has spoken, creating a continual flow of participatory energy in the sermon. The advertisement for "The Prayer Meeting in Hell" (Figure 4.7) provided a visual representation of Nix's fire and brimstone theme.

Vernacular Language

Early Black preachers such as John Jasper were criticized for their use of African American Vernacular English (AAVE), previously called dialect. For example, William E. Hatcher's 1908 description of Jasper's use of AAVE stated, "Did mortal lips ever gush with such torrents of horrible English? Hardly a word came out clothed in its right mind."[86] Jasper spoke in a manner that his audience could understand and appreciate and that was thus appropriate for them. Old-time preachers used biblical English and simple, short words in a familiar idiom.[87] However, the use of simple words colored with AAVE created sermons that were powerful and captured "the ethos of their people."[88] AAVE is spoken by many working-class African Americans, creating what Walter F. Pitts claims is a sense of "home, familiarity, racial identity, and group loyalty."[89] For these reasons alone, use of AAVE reflected group values, identity, and class standing. Shifts from Standard English (SE) to AAVE are apropos in African American religious rituals, and use of AAVE was significant for both Jasper and Nix to identify with their congregants. If Jasper had spoken in SE, his congregants would have thought his language was "horrible."[90]

Howard W. Odum, in his study of African American folk songs, declared that "In giving the dialect no attempt is made at consistency; for the negro of the present generation has no consistency of speech. He uses 'the' and 'de,' 'them' and 'dem,' 'gwine' and 'goin',' 'and' and 'an',' together with many other varied forms."[91] Mary Allen Grissom's 1930 account of the singing of freedmen in Kentucky also noted the inconsistency of not only speech, but pronunciation. For example, she explained, "one word may have three pronunciations in the same song, as for example, *my, mah,* or *muh* according to what precedes or follows it,—*my,* if much emphasized" (italics in original).[92]

Thomas Wentworth Higginson, in his memoir published in 1869 as *Army Life in a Black Regiment*, described a "marching song" that was sung by his Black regiment in which the singers used AAVE with words such as "gwine," "de," and "ob":

> *All true children gwine in de wilderness,*
> *Gwine in de wilderness, gwine in de wilderness,*
> *True believers gwine in de wilderness,*
> *To take away de sins ob de world*[93]

The word "gwine" was also used consistently in the spirituals, with titles such as "Gwine Up,"[94] "Dry Bones Gwine Er Rise Ergin,"[95] "I'm Gwine Up to Heab'n Anyhow," and "Gwinter Sing All Along de Way," arranged by J. Rosamond Johnson.

Nix used the word "gwine" on several occasions, in an example of style switching,[96] in which he chose to speak in AAVE for emphasis although he could have just as easily spoken in SE. The use of "gwine" ("going to") evokes the vernacular speech of the uneducated and/or enslaved individual. In "Hiding Behind the Stuff," Nix states,

And then we have another class of people always
Living in the future tense.
Talking about "what I'm gwine to be,
What I'm gwine to do,
How I'm going to give and serve,"
And never do anything.

Another use of AAVE is the predominance of the last syllable to be changed, resulting in a hum or moan effect. This kind of "softening" of the ultimate consonant is a typical feature in Black folk songs, especially religious songs.[97] In "Hiding Behind the Stuff," Nix substitutes the final consonant with an "M" sound, resulting in "shim" for ship, "Jonam" for Jonah, and so on. This feature was possibly a type of effect meant to elongate the words, similar to the moan.

I saw the four-way wind:
One got on the right side of the shim [ship],
Another got on the left side of the shim [ship],
One got in the front of the ship,
And another got on
A-behind the shim [ship]

Ministers of the mixed type of church in Chicago, associated with the middle classes, used language shifts between AAVE and SE to develop rapport with their lower-class members.[98] However, Genester Nix claimed her father used AAVE "so that his congregation could understand. That was in the beginning of his preaching, but as time moved on and people became more educated, he continued to preach the same way for emphasis."[99] Despite the class level of his congregants, Nix's use of AAVE was "within the experience" of his listeners who were familiar with it as an expression of traditional Black vocalisms.

Elwood Nix said he believes that his father's frequent travels, in which he was introduced to a multitude of different people and language uses, allowed him to "paint a picture" through the use of his voice and to appeal to people of varying classes in different regions. This may account for Nix's ability to style-switch to appeal to the particular demographic of people to whom he was preaching. Elwood remarked that "wherever he [Nix] went [and] he heard people talk, he kind of related that to his voice when he preached to them. . . . so they could understand him more. Like if it was down South, he would preach, you know, the blues."[100] In other words, Reverend Nix consciously altered his voice to "speak in the language" of his audience. Nix's inclusion of the vernacular implies the use of a "common" language, learned by aural practice, by those of "common" class status rather than the elite.

Beginning in January 1930, Nix started incorporating speaking roles by his congregants into his recordings. "How Long—How Long" is one of the first of Nix's recorded sermons that includes spoken word by voices other than Nix's. The female voices that are incorporated into the dialogue demonstrate contrasting characteristics of lower-class and middle-class cultural standards. In "How Long—How Long," the first female speaker, "Miss Peaches," uses slang expressions, such as "fussin'," while the second speaks more slowly, enunciating her words clearly, demonstrating a more nuanced approach. The dialogue sets up Miss Peaches as a petty woman who has lied about her relationship with the pastor, insinuating a more intimate relationship. She also accuses the second woman of being jealous of the imagined relationship. The second speaker, the "old jealous thing," is revealed to be not only older, but more mature and sophisticated. She has caught Miss Peaches in a lie and emphasizes the word "riding." All of her words except "riding" are pronounced clearly and within the same pitch range, but "riding" is almost grunted and in a much lower range. The word itself, which presumably demonstrates the disgust of the second speaker at the first, takes on an entirely different timbre and pitch. Miss Peaches, who speaks in AAVE, is set up as being backward, dishonest, and petty, while the second woman appears mature, honest, and trustworthy. Nix used the voices of the two women to create a strong analogy between the lower class, associated with folk traditions and vernacular language, and the middle class, associated with sophistication and SE. The juxtaposition of AAVE and SE and the actual texts spoken by the two women clearly showed class differences. Nix established Miss Peaches as being associated with unsavory habits, such as gossip and lying, while the second woman demonstrates higher moral standards.

Miss Peaches:
Brother Pastor, she got mad.
And was fussin' at me.
Because I showed her that sweet letter you wrote me.
She oughta know you don't want her,
Old jealous thing.

Female Voice 2:
Yes, and you told me

You and the pastor went out driving last Saturday night.
And you didn't get home until two a.m.
You must-a have done some riding.[101]

Nix:
How long, how long, how long?
How long?

Vernacular language was used by Nix on other occasions, presumably to identify with his lower-class congregants. In "It Was Tight like That," recorded in the midst of the Great Depression, he initially references the problems associated with the economic crisis in the line "This seems to be a hard and tight world we're living in these days" and continues to describe the troubles many downtrodden, unemployed Americans faced at the time, such as being "cold, hungry, and mad." Nix clearly changes language style and introduces many vernacular words and phrases, possibly to relate to his working-class listeners who were suffering from the economic crisis. For example, "And ain't got no job," "Your wife is fussin'," and "You will feel like you in hell" display Nix's ability to style-switch to identify with a particular group or class of listeners.

The female congregants also speak in the vernacular. One female congregant exclaims, "When I ain't got no money, I got good religion." As a commentary on the congregant's justification of religion, as if having religion were enough to survive, Nix admonishes her and preaches the necessity of being fiscally responsible and taking precautions in preparation for disasters such as the Great Depression.

His message spoke of practical solutions to impoverished African Americans. In this sense, we can notice a shift in Nix's sermon themes from religion as the end-all to practical advice for his working-class congregants. Self-help and fiscal responsibility were themes associated with the "New Negro" and racial uplift. Through the use of AAVE on the recordings, Nix clearly identified with the lower class and separated himself from educated ministers such as Rev. Sutton Griggs, who tried to separate themselves from the lower classes through their use of SE.

Rhythm

Rhythmic declamation of text, accented by shouts, moans, and other vocal inflections, creates the foundation of the sermon and is perhaps the most important element in the sermon.[102] The use of accents, higher pitch, and percussive declamation further enhances the rhythmic intensity. Vocal percussiveness, sometimes called "hitting-a-lick," which Jon Michael Spencer notes as having historical reference as early as 1855,[103] is utilized through accented and verbalized consonants, such as Ps.

A regular rhythmic pulse underlies the minister's declamation, with the words spoken in the vernacular at a moderate pace. He then adds intensity to his words, which are delivered with much gusto and fervor, increasing in intensity, dynamics, and tempo, eventually reaching the climax section. It is in the climax that congregants get happy, inspiring them to shout, dance, and so on.[104] Increased word count causes the preacher to speak or shout faster, so that the tempo of the "measure" remains relatively constant. He speeds up or slows down his rhythmic timing to match the meter of the beat.[105] The minister also can add time through the augmentation or stretching of notes and words, the repetition of words and phrases, or the addition of vocal embellishments.[106]

James Kennard Jr. claimed in an 1845 article in *The Knickerbocker* that consistency in metrical feet or measures had been practiced since the slavery era. He described the singing by Black oarsmen on an expedition down the St. Johns River in Florida: "Little regard was paid to rhyme, and hardly any to the number of syllables in a line: they condensed four or five into one foot or stretched out one to occupy the space that should have been filled with four or five; yet they never spoiled the tune. This elasticity of form is peculiar to the negro song."[107] The practice of elongating and condensing phrases to adapt to the rhythm of the sermon is a common feature in African American preaching traditions.[108] As Walter F. Pitts Jr. writes, "The sense of recurring meter is probably a result of squeezing and elongating syllables into the durational restrictions of a breath group. Although not metrical, poetic expression in West African and Afro-Baptist traditions of declaiming share rhythmicity [*sic*], based on the breath group, which distinguishes declamation from normal, conversational speech."[109] Bruce A. Rosenberg also claims that "when a phrase is too short . . . [the preacher] lengthens it, and when the line is too long, he squeezes it musically to fit, or nearly fit, his meter."[110]

The following is a report of the climax of a sermon by a minister who pastored a United Primitive Baptist church in Chicago in the 1920s:

> By this time he had found his gait and maintained it for the next thirty minutes. Words came so fast that an effort to discover any coherence was futile. One could only hear a hurried jumble of syllables. The marvel of it all was the preacher's endurance. Long after one would suppose him utterly exhausted he forged onward never lessening the time of the rhythm. Even his body followed a regular cycle of motions. . . . His breathing became more and more difficult. Every gasp was loud and made with a jerky contraction of the chest.

The encouragement from the crowd was a stimulus to his efforts—
"Preach on! Preach on!" "Well! Well!" "Now he's Preaching!" "That's real
preaching!" "Glory be to God!" "Sho 'nuf Oh, sho 'nuf!" "Yes indeed! The
whole truth!" Finally words failed to come. He paused for a few breaths.
An elder seated near by solicitously remarked, "There now, take it easy.
Don't hurry." But in an instant he was off again for another lap. After two
more such pauses and fresh starts he stopped abruptly, exhausted, and
probably convinced that he had done well enough.[111]

The climax portion of this sermon included a regular rhythmic gait and a fast
delivery of the text, so much so that the syllables became slurred and the pastor
gasped for breath to keep the timing regular. It is in the climax section that a
minister will intone or sustain pitch, with congregational responses interjected
to inspire him to continue. The minister responds to their enthusiasm, building to an even higher climax, with his voice rising in pitch and emphasis. A
preacher may also create rhythmic motives or textual motives, which are either
repeated throughout the sermon or are part of the congregation's response.
Motivic devices such as these help to alleviate the possibility of a static, monotone, or dull sermon.

The temporal lengths of the phrases of the sermons are contained within
units of similar lengths but not with the same stresses or number of syllables as
in the metric "feet" of poetry.[112] I have considered each phrase of text between
pauses (breaths) to be a measure. Although Nix does not employ the same metric feet or syllables in each measure, the units of time in each phrase are similar
enough to consider them measures. Nix builds intensity from the beginning
of the sermon by increasing the number of words per measure, and regardless
of the number of words he employs in each phrase, his measure lengths are
relatively consistent.

Using the Sonic Visualizer's tempo feature, I mapped out the tempo according to each measure in the beginning and ending of "Black Diamond Express to
Hell—Pt. I" in Sections B^1 (Table 4.2) and C^6 (Table 4.3). The columns in both
tables (left to right) represent the measure numbers, the corresponding text,
the time marking (at the end of the phrase), and the tempo marking in beats
per minute (bpm). In Section B^1, except for the second line, there are only one
to three words per measure; however, in Section C^6, there are five to ten words
per measure. In Section B^1, Nix takes his time, speeding up and slowing down
his delivery, varying between 21 and 71 bmp per measure, averaging 50 bpm.
In Section C^6, the measures are more condensed, with not only more words
per phrase, but also less time between measures, varying between 23 and 34
bpm, demonstrating a relatively steady tempo. The average tempo for section
C^6 is 27 bmp, almost half of that in section B^1. Thus, the tempo slows down to

VOCAL AND MUSICAL ANALYSIS

Table 4.2. Tempo Markings in "Black Diamond Express to Hell—Pt. I," Section B[1]

Measure Number	Text	Time Marking	Tempo Marking in bpm
5	This train	0:14	43
6	Is known as the Black Diamond Express train to hell	0:18	21
7	Sin	0:19	57
8	Is the engineer	0:20	48
9	Pleasure	0:21	71
10	Is the headlight	0:22	58
11	And the devil	0:23	49
12	Is the conductor	0:24	49

Table 4.3. Tempo Markings in "Black Diamond Express to Hell—Pt. I," Section C6

Measure Number	Text	Time Marking	Tempo Marking in bpm
71	I have a big crowd of church-fighters down there	2:25	24
72	They never go to a prayer meeting	2:27	34
73	They never go to Sunday school	2:29	32
74	They never go to morning service	2:31	29
75	They always stay away from the morning church	2:33	29
76	Until they hear about the business meeting	2:35	28
77	And they come running out of Brazos Bottom	2:37	25
78	To put up a big fight in God's church	2:40	23
79	Well, all you church fighters	2:42	24
80	You gotta go to hell on the Black Diamond Train	2:45	26

accommodate the increase in word count; however, the increased word count dramatically increases the intensity in this last section of the sermon. In a sense, Nix goes into half time, doubling the word count to stimulate the emotional intensity of his text. As the evidence shows, Nix maintains consistency in the metrical tempo. Nix stretches and condenses syllables to fit within the space of a measure, demonstrating his adherence to this traditional practice.

Reverend Nix's Chanted Sermon

Because of the three-minute limitation of the recorded sermon, Nix segues into the chant almost immediately at the beginning of his recordings. In "Black Diamond Express to Hell—Pt. I," Nix begins intoning in the sermon's third phrase (0:06) centering around pitch E^3, establishing the tonic pitch. In Musical Example 4.4, the third phrase (0:07) centers around the pitches of E, B, and C#. The rhythms displayed are an approximation, showing relative long and short durations, except for the word "broad," in which Nix extends the rhythm slightly into a moan. Beginning with the fifth phrase (0:14) on "This train," Nix begins intoning with scale pitches E and G, implying a minor pentatonic scale. He continues fluctuating between these two pitches as notated in the transcription in Musical Example 4.5. This fluctuation between thirds (pendular thirds) is typical in African American musical genres.[113] Within the first twenty-two seconds of the sermon, Nix has already established the pitches for his chant.

In "The White Flyer to Heaven—Part II," the chant is represented by the repetition of the tonic pitch (Musical Example 4.6). The rhythms displayed are an approximation, showing relative long and short durations, and rests represent pauses between phrases. The arrows show Nix's pitch bends upwards. Again in this recording, Nix implies a minor pentatonic scale.

In "After the Ball Is Over," Nix slowly builds to his climax through the use of chanting on pitches, shouts on a pitch an octave above the starting pitch, moans, loud dynamics, and a gravelly timbre. The building to the climax includes chanting at 0:04 on "when Herod's birthday was kept"; moans on "all" at 0:29; shouts on a loud volume and chants an octave above the starting pitch on "turn

Musical Example 4.4. Chanting in "Black Diamond Express to Hell—Pt. I" (0:07–0:11), recorded April 23, 1927, on Vocalion (Vo 1098), reissued on Document Records (DOCD-5328).

Musical Example 4.5. Implied minor pentatonic scale in "Black Diamond Express to Hell—Pt. I" (0:14–0:19), recorded April 23, 1927, on Vocalion (Vo 1098), reissued on Document Records (DOCD-5328).

Musical Example 4.6. Vocal gestures in "The White Flyer to Heaven—Part II."

on more lights!" at 0:39; and at 0:45 a combination of all of these techniques—a gravelly timbre, an octave higher pitch, moans, and shouts on a loud volume on the single word "call." At 1:49, Nix uses shouts, gravelly timbre, moans, and an octave-higher pitch on the entire phrase "Brother, just after the ball is over," followed by a descending minor pentatonic scale on "so many bad promises are made." This climactic "formula" is repeated at 2:13, in which Nix states, "After the ball is over, then you go into the midnight air." Nix then uses moans, a gravelly timbre, loud volume, and shouting—which climaxes at 2:30 on "Oh, mother's son"—continuing at 2:36 on "Oh, father's daughter" and at 2:40 on "If you don't come off the ballroom floor, hell will be your home." Nix's use of vocal elements, including chanting, octave shouts, moans, loud dynamics, and gravelly timbre, increases as the sermon proceeds, shown in Figure 4.8. Because the recorded sermon had to be compacted into a three-minute time frame, Nix utilizes multiple vocal tools to build to the climax. As in any type of performance or oratory when faced with the challenges of limited delivery time, the preacher or performer must use all of his or her abilities to have an impact quickly. In the case of Nix, he built up the intensity throughout the sermon by using his voice to the utmost, exploiting the booming dynamics of his voice, his gravelly timbre, moans, and shouts in the upper registers of his voice.

Similarities of the Chanted Sermon and the Blues

The chanted sermon of the folk preacher has often been compared to the blues due to the extensive use of improvisation, gravelly vocal timbres, and the pentatonic or gapped scale in both. However, as just noted, both the sermon and the blues are rooted in the folk church and the rural fields of the South, with the chanted sermon undoubtedly emerging prior to the blues. Blues scholar David Evans supports the influence of the folk church on the blues by claiming that "it seems very likely that prayers, along with field hollers and perhaps preaching, helped to shape blues singing."[114] While Nix may have employed numerous vocal characteristics as heard in the blues, his roots were in the field and the church and, as confirmed by his daughter, he did not listen to the blues.

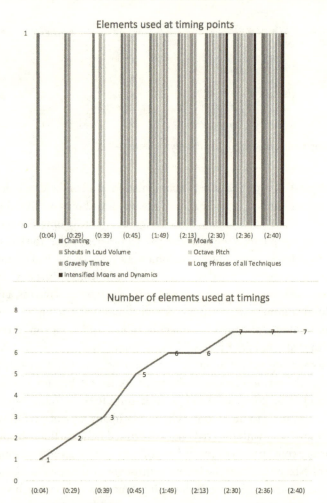

Figure 4.8. Increase in vocal gestures to build to a climax in "After the Ball Is Over."

Scholars have expressed the opinion that some similar features link the chanted sermon with the blues.[115] After the abolition of slavery, music that had previously been a communal, participatory experience of the group and a collective experience expressed "*by* the group" became an individualized performative expression "*to* the group," such as in the blues. Harris contends that the folk preacher also communicated "to the group," thus concluding that "the bluesman and the preacher, beyond surface distinctions, were cultural analogues of one another . . . [and shared a] homologous development."[116] However, in Nix's recorded sermons, the folk sermon was both a group, participatory performance and a performative individual expression with the minister "performing" to his congregation.

MUSICAL ANALYSIS OF TRADITIONAL SPIRITUALS AND HYMNS IN NIX'S SERMONS

African American singing traditions also included the singing of folk spirituals, which differed from the arranged spirituals in that the folk spirituals were orally transmitted,[117] while the arranged spirituals were concertized versions published in written arrangements. Because no recordings exist of performances of the spiritual from the slavery era, we must rely on historical descriptions of the singing. For example, McIlhenny described the unique qualities of the spirituals, which included "oft repeated words, which if read seem monotonous, but when properly sung causes [sic], through voice inflections and by the monotony of repetition, a hypnotic effect and spirit exaltation on both singers and listeners quite beyond the power of other music."[118] He discussed the heterophony present in the spirituals as multiple voices sang: "each one will be singing the same song, only differently, but the whole is a delightful and thrilling blend of harmony in which the words mean almost nothing." In the 1867 classic *Slave Songs of the United States*, the authors described the singing of folk spirituals. They noted the presence of interjections between phrases such as "I say now" and "God say you must" and also the use of the vernacular, improvisation, blue notes, slides, and melismas. In addition, they commented on the layering effects created by numerous voices interjecting simultaneously: "The rests, by the way, do not indicate a cessation in the music, but only in part of the singers. They over-lap in singing, as already described, in such a degree that at no time is there any complete pause."[119] These commentaries provide evidence of the correlation between the folk spiritual and the folk sermon. The monotonous repetition of words and pitches, interjections between phrases by congregation members, and use of the vernacular, improvisation, guttural timbre, layering, and heterophony show many similarities with the chanted sermon.

Recordings by African American ministers such as Reverend Nix often included the singing of folk spirituals as part of their recorded sermons. However, these traditional spirituals were often disparaged in middle-class northern Black churches of the 1920s. James Weldon Johnson and J. Rosamond Johnson wrote that "Immediately following Emancipation those ranks revolted against everything connected with slavery, and among those things were the Spirituals."[120] Recorded sermons thus are significant for their inclusion of folk spirituals, allowing researchers not only to listen to and transcribe audio recordings of actual voices singing these songs, but also to contest the shunning of the spiritual.

Andrew Nix probably experienced both the folk spiritual and chanted sermon from a young age, influenced by his father's experience with slavery in the

Deep South and his preaching history in Texas.[121] In addition, the qualities of Andrew's voice were probably influenced more by the singing of folk spirituals than the blues, for the reason that blues and jazz were deemed "of the world" and were not allowed in the Nix household. Andrew's familiarity with the folk spiritual is evidenced by his inclusion of several spirituals on his recordings. Apparently, he made little or no effort to assimilate to white-influenced singing styles or repertoires, but instead incorporated Black oral traditions including folk spirituals into the modern recordings of his sermons.

Repertoire Choice

Andrew Nix chose to incorporate folk spirituals into his recorded sermons, but chose not to use arrangements from "modern" hymnals such as *Gospel Pearls* and *The Baptist Standard Hymnal*. Andrew's brother, William, was not only a committee member of the Sunday School Publishing Board that published *Gospel Pearls* and *The Baptist Standard Hymnal* in 1921 and 1924, respectively, but was also a renowned singer who marketed the songs of *Gospel Pearls* at the 1921 National Baptist Convention. However, Andrew did not use songs from either of these hymnals on his recorded sermons.

Of the forty-seven extant sermons recorded by Nix, fourteen (29.7 percent) include folk spirituals or hymns that have been identified in repertory and hymn books published in the first decades of the twentieth century, which clearly establishes the early history of these melodies. Knowing that Nix made a conscious decision of the songs he chose and understanding the correlation of these songs to folk traditions help us to understand the sense of pride he must have felt, his passion for the music, and his musical heritage. Of the fourteen songs, five are included in the *National Jubilee Melody Song Book*, published in 1923.[122] Because of the similarity in Nix's recorded versions and the printed versions in the songbook, it appears that this is one of the main songbooks that Nix used in his church and his recordings. The publisher describes the songbook as a "collection of old plantation songs[,] the words and music of which were composed and sung by the African slaves of the United States of American during the days of slavery." The publisher lists five reasons why these particular songs were added to the collection:

> FIRST: It is and should be the idea of the present generation to keep alive the great religious achievements of our ancestors and hand them down to posterity as a legacy of noble sires to their sons.

> SECOND: It is known throughout the length and breadth of this country that every people, from the early Jews, or Hebrews, down to the present

day, have expressed their peculiar religious emotions, thoughts and deep meditations in proverbs, poetry and rhythm.

THIRD: It is the belief of the Publishing Board that these melodies express the emotion of the soul of the Negro race as no other collection of music—classically or grammatically constructed could possibly do.

FOURTH: It is the purpose of the Publishing Board in publishing this collection in book form to build a monument to the memory of our Negro ancestry and show the rising generation who may not yet become a great and educated people that they sprang from a deep and prayerful religious race, whose religious convictions and faith in their God towered above any other race in a like condition.

FIFTH: In publishing this collection of melodies the Board wishes to give due credit to Mr. K. D. Reddick, of Americus, Ga., and Mr. Phil V. S. Lindsley, of Nashville, Tenn., for their faithful and painstaking work in collecting these songs['] rhythms and melodies from the various rice, cane and cotton plantations of the South—just as they were handed down by the tradition on the old plantations and kept alive by the offsprings of these old slaves.

While the words and sentences may not have the grammatical construction and classical musical rhythms of the present day, yet they express the deep emotion and religious convictions of a true people and in such a way will be compelled to keep alive the clear pictures and bright metaphors of conditions as they existed or appeared to exist to these people in those dark ante-bellum days.[123]

Thus, it becomes clear that the songs in the *National Jubilee Melody Song Book* were considered to be songs of enslaved persons, not modern musical expressions or classical music. Although that songbook contained four-part a cappella arrangements as in other hymnals, the songs chosen by Nix from it were based on slave songs considered part of the tradition. Although *Gospel Pearls* and the *Baptist Standard Hymnal* both contain spirituals, the *National Jubilee Melody Song Book* was clearly devoted to only including songs from the era of slavery.

Most of the other songs were written or arranged by revered specialists in the field of African American folk music, such as John W. Work, J. Rosamond Johnson, and James Weldon Johnson, had been collected by noted collectors during or just after the slavery era, or were included in songbooks from the early twentieth century.[124] I have also included songs from *Songs of Zion*, edited by J. Jefferson Cleveland and Verolga Nix, Reverend Nix's younger daughter, because of her first-hand experience with his choice of songs.[125] Reverend Nix also included songs of unknown origin. On the recordings, Nix's studio congregants typically sing with him in unison rather than in the four-part harmony of the written arrangements. Such arrangements would have suppressed the spontaneity that was a fundamental part of the folk tradition that Nix preferred.

Nix incorporated hymns or spirituals consistently on his first recordings in 1927 (seven out of the first eight), then only sporadically in recordings from the end of 1927 to 1930. Almost 30 percent of his extant sermons have either a spiritual or hymn, but most are in his first year of recording. After October 26, 1928, when Nix stopped using scriptural references and started giving practical advice, he included musical selections on only five more sermons, and those were in his themed sermons, such as his Christmas message or the Black Diamond train themes. Four of the six parts of "Black Diamond Express to Hell" include either a spiritual or hymn:

"Black Diamond Express to Hell—Pt. II": "All o' My Sins Done Taken Away"

"The Black Diamond Express to Hell—Part 4": "Hide Me Over in the Rock of Ages"

"The Black Diamond Express to Hell—Part 5": "Free at Last"

"The Black Diamond Express to Hell—Part 6": "Come and Go with Me to That Land"[126]

"All o' My Sins Done Taken Away," "Hide Me Over in the Rock of Ages," and "Free at Last" are included in collections of spirituals and folk songs by noted collectors and arrangers, such as James Weldon Johnson, J. Rosamond Johnson, and John W. Work, and in others such as E. A. McIlhenny's *Befo' de War Spirituals* (1933). All of the spirituals or hymns are in printed sources or on audio recordings except "Nowhere to Hide"[127] and "Deep Down in My Heart," which I could not locate in either. A brief discussion of each song follows.

"All o' My Sins Done Taken Away"
The spiritual "All o' My Sins Done Taken Away," recorded in the sermon "Black Diamond Express to Hell—Pt. II," is mentioned in several sources, thus documenting its extended history in African American vocal traditions.[128] Howard W. Odum, in 1909, eighteen years prior to Nix's recording, described it as a "very popular song," confirming its longevity in the folk repertory.[129] In the *National Jubilee Melody Song Book*, there are two versions of the song—one

titled "My Sins Are Taken Away," and the other titled "All o' My Sins Done Taken Away," the version used by Nix with the word "done" substituted with "been."[130] In the sermon, Nix exclaims, "aren't you glad you got off the Black Diamond Express train a long time ago," which he follows by leading the group in singing "All o' My Sins Done Taken Away." The spiritual's lyrical message is one of living a life without sin, which is exemplified in the stops of the train.

"I Got Mah Swoad in Mah Han'"

In the sermon "Goin' to Hell and Who Cares," Nix incorporated the spiritual "I Got Mah Swoad in Mah Han," also found in Mary Allen Grissom's *The Negro Sings a New Heaven*.[131] Grissom claimed, "Many of the tunes are led by the older Negroes who are able to add modern verses to the old tunes, making them fit present-day needs, yet losing none of their former setting of dignity and beauty. Herein, lies much of their charm. Others are left just as they were sung years ago. The wonder is that they are handed down from generation to generation with such accuracy." She explained, "Most of the songs included in this volume have been taken directly from the Negroes in their present-day worship, and have been selected from those sung in the neighborhood of Louisville, Kentucky, and certain rural sections in Adair County."[132] Her book was published in 1930, but she probably collected the songs for many years prior to this date. As described previously, Reverend Nix was a student at State University in Louisville, graduating in 1915, and served as a minister in Georgetown, Kentucky (seventy miles east of Louisville) from 1914 to 1918, presumably living there until his first position took him elsewhere in 1919. It is thus possible that he was exposed to the same songs as Grissom collected and may have heard this particular version of "I Got Mah Swoad in Mah Han."

The lyrics of the spiritual in this sermon speak from the perspective of the enslaved individual: "My mother's in one place an' I in another; Jedgmun' Day's a-gonna bring us all together." It goes through the cycle of identifying all of the loved ones kept apart—"my mother," "my sister," "my father," and "my friends"—who would all be joined together in the afterlife on "Jedgmun' Day." The connection to slavery is explicit. Nix presented the spiritual as an introduction to his sermon, which encourages sinners to "get in touch with Jesus."

"Nowhere to Hide"

In the sermon "Hiding Behind the Stuff," Nix and his congregants sing "Nowhere to Hide" using call-and-response in a participatory performance. I could not find this song in any printed or audio source. Nix begins the recording singing this song before introducing his sermon. The text reflects Nix's theme of "hiding from God," using the story of Jonah as his reference. In the sermon, Jonah hides on the ship but is discovered, thrown into the sea, and eaten by the whale.

"O the Blood"

Howard W. Odum claimed that "the negro singers have exhibited a characteristic specimen of their *word combinations, concrete pictures,* and *theological principles*" (italics in original) in this spiritual.[133] The song lyrics present visual images of where sins have been "washed in the blood of the Lamb," including "in de Kingdom," "in de Lamb's book," "on de mountain," and "in the valley." The song confirms that the blood will sign "my name" because "Jesus said so" and "God he tole me." Nix recounts Jesus' time on the cross where he "signed every man's bond with my own blood." Nix and his female congregants sing the spiritual in unison and place it in the middle of the sermon.

"Look for Me!"

The gospel song "Look for Me!" (also titled "You May Look for Me for I'll Be There") was arranged in 1905 by Charles Austin Miles, and its first known publication was in the 1906 *New Songs of the Gospel No. 2: For Use in Religious Meetings.*[134] The lyrics in the first verse state, "When you get to Heaven, as you surely will, if the Savior's name you own, after you have greeted those you love the best, who are standing round the throne." Nix describes the White Flyer's journey to heaven and only includes the chorus of the song, which states, "You may look for me, for I'll be there." In other words, the song focuses on the life-after-death experience of heaven. This is one instance of Nix including a song written by a well-known white composer.[135]

"When the Saints Go Marching In"

This hymn is well known in both white and African American churches. In Nix's sermon "The Seven Rs," Nix and the congregants sing "When the Saints Go Marching In" as a response to those who are "calling with their robe washed in the blood of the Lamb." Nix leads the hymn in call-and-response, with some of the female congregants singing along with Nix.

"I'm So Glad I Got My Religion in Time"

In Nix's sermon "It Is a Strange Thing to Me," he begins with "I'm So Glad I Got My Religion in Time."[136] In the sermon, Nix describes the "strange" and amazing miracles of Jesus and how one must be born again to understand these miracles. Nix shouts the word "born" with a gravelly timbre, but is able to immediately transition into singing the spiritual, demonstrating the flexibility of his voice. Throughout the spiritual, he continues singing with a gravelly timbre. The transcription in Musical Example 1.1 (in Chapter 1) provides evidence that Nix only sang the basic melody and included minimal melismas or other vocal embellishments in his singing. His lack of melismas could be due to the inability of his heavy, gravelly voice to sing fast-moving passages. Also, because he is singing with his congregants, the group would probably favor singing the basic melody without extensive embellishments. Prior to Nix's recording, the song was recorded by the Wiseman Sextette in July 1923[137] and later by Sandhills Sixteen on July 21, 1927 (Vi 20904)[138] and the Mississippi Juvenile Quartette on February 26, 1928 (OK unissued).[139]

"Deep Down in My Heart"

Although I could not find any written or oral record of "Deep Down in My Heart" and thus have no knowledge of its origins, I wanted to include the song in this discussion because of its stylistic qualities that contrast with the other traditional songs used by Nix in his recorded sermons. It is one of only two songs that includes piano accompaniment (the other being "Done Found My Lost Sheep") and includes an unnamed solo soprano.[140] Her voice is clear; she uses Standard English, vibrato, and strict rhythm; and she rolls her Rs on certain words, clearly demonstrating an affinity for trained, Western classical aesthetics. At times, the chorus sings in harmony, which is rare for Nix's singers.

However, regardless of the elements indexing "sophistication" in this rendering, the traditional Black folk elements are also present. For example, the solo singer alternates with the chorus, creating a call-and-response effect; the chorus is in a heterophonic texture, with certain voices entering at slightly different rhythmic increments; and Nix's gravelly voice contrasts with the soprano's clear timbre. In this regard, Nix was emulating the Fisks' straddling of the Western classical world and the folk world, keeping some semblance of "Blackness" while experimenting with modernity. This example demonstrates the gray area in which Nix included both traditional and Western classical aesthetics and that he did not restrict himself within strict boundaries of style.

In the sermon, Nix explains that "religion is a love deep down in your heart." This sermon consists of only two verses of sermonizing and the song sung in its entirety by the solo female singer—a rarity for Nix. For unknown reasons, the original recording, recorded on October 12, 1927, was rerecorded on January 18, 1928, and was probably meant to be substituted for the original recording. Possibly Nix was not satisfied with the original recording and sought to perfect it in this later recording. However, the second recording of "Deep Down in My Heart" was not issued.

"Done Found My Lost Sheep"

"Done Found My Lost Sheep" is featured in the sermon with the same name.[141] Nix used J. Rosamond Johnson's arrangement of the song, which Johnson published in 1925 with his brother James Weldon Johnson in the anthology titled *The Book of American Negro Spirituals*. Nix's version was released in January 1928, just three years after the published anthology. Possibly Nix or the pianist on the recording purchased the anthology, knew the Johnson brothers and received the arrangement directly from them, or knew this version from tradition. "Done Found My Lost Sheep" is unique for two reasons: it is the only song in which Nix sings the verses entirely by himself (the congregants sing with him in unison only on the choruses), and it is one of only two songs that includes piano accompaniment (the other is "Deep Down in My Heart").[142] Again, Nix only sermonizes for two verses, and the spiritual is sung in its entirety for the majority of the sermon. Although Nix may have used the Johnsons' arrangement, the pianist alters and develops the chords somewhat, creating a descending chromatic line in the verses.

"Great Change Since I Been Born"

In "Begin a New Life on Christmas Day—Part II," Nix encourages his listeners to change from their ways of sin and "turn over a new leaf" as they begin a new year. This allows for a "great change" and the singing of the song. I could not find this song in any source. Nix leads his congregants in four verses of the song in which the female congregants sing with a particularly nasal timbre. Although I could not find this song in any source that predated Nix's recording in 1928, the song is named and discussed in Wyatt Tee Walker's *Spirits That Dwell in Deep Woods: The Prayer and Praise Hymns of the Black Religious Experience.* Walker mentions that while the songs are reminiscent of the early hymnbook era (c. 1885–1925), they can also be described as "folk-music of the Black religious experience," due to the unknown authors of the songs, similar to the spirituals; and he claims that "Great Change Since I Been Born" originated in South Carolina's low country, south of Columbia, although this cannot be verified.[143] There are also several recordings of the song from the late 1920s and 1930s, including those by the Virginia Four (1929)[144] and the Norfolk Jubilee Quartet Singers (1938).[145]

"Hide Me Over in the Rock of Ages"

In "The Black Diamond Express to Hell—Part 4," Nix sings the hymn "Hide Me Over in the Rock of Ages."[146] His version is different from the well-known "Rock of Ages, Cleft for Me," which is considered a standard in the white hymn tradition. I include both songs for the sake of comparison (Musical Example 4.7).[147] The version of "Rock of Ages, Cleft for Me" presented in the Baptist hymnal (on the left) has a different melody and different lyrics from Nix's version (on the right). The version Nix used is identical to the version printed in the *Jubilee Melody Songbook* except for the line of the lyrics in which Nix substitutes "loving sinner" with "awful sinner." Also, Nix and his congregation sing the hymn in unison rather than in four-part harmony, showing his affinity for folk practices rather than arranged hymns. In Nix's sermon, he describes

Musical Example 4.7. "Rock of Ages, Cleft for Me" and "Hide Me Over in the Rock of Ages."

more "stations" on the Black Diamond Express to Hell and exclaims, "Ever since I got off the Black Diamond Train, my soul has been singing"—a line leading directly into the singing of "Hide Me Over in the Rock of Ages."

"Free at Last"

"The Black Diamond Express to Hell—Part 5" includes a spoken word segment by the famous African American actress Nina Mae McKinney, who played the leading role in *Hallelujah*. McKinney was already a well-known actress by the time of the recording in Chicago in April 1930; thus, the inclusion of her voice on Nix's recordings could have garnered substantial sales of the two sermons on which she recorded. Nix set this sermon as the first of a two-part story that is continued in "The Black Diamond Express to Hell—Part 6." Because McKinney's character, "Miz Hard-Boiled," has not been converted by the end of "The Black Diamond Express to Hell—Part 5," listeners are enticed to listen to Part 6, in which she finally converts.

Upon the conversion of one anonymous female congregant, Nix exclaims, "another soul born in the kingdom of God," which leads to the singing of the spiritual "Free at Last," which was included in John W. Work's *American Negro Songs* and other sources.[148] As mentioned previously, the Work brothers, along with Andrew's brother, William (W. M.) Nix, all served as committee members of the Sunday School Publishing Board for the National Baptist Convention, which published *Gospel Pearls*. James Weldon Johnson and J. Rosamond Johnson also released a version of the same spiritual in their anthology.[149] The Work version is titled "Free at Last," while the Johnson version is titled "I Thank God I'm Free at Las." Nix may have included this spiritual, whose lyrics repeat the theme of being "free at last," as part of his audio "movie" used as incentive to convince Miz Hard-Boiled to join the expedition to heaven.

"Come and Go with Me to That Land"

In "The Black Diamond Express to Hell—Part 6," Miz Hard-Boiled is a stubborn sinner who won't convert until she realizes she is about to be left behind. The dialogue between Nix and McKinney at times sounds overly dramatic and could easily be confused with the expression of carnal desires. However, Nix, who was fifty years of age at the time of the recording, was evidently playing the father figure to McKinney, who was only sixteen at the time. In a sense, McKinney was playing the same character she played in *Hallelujah*: the hardened sinner who becomes converted after witnessing a church service and hearing the minister preach. In the recording, Nix states that sinners will encounter "hell-hounds howling [and] the hobgobs of hell" and other horrors. In contrast, those who get off the train and go to heaven will find joy, emphasized by singing the spiritual "Come and Go with Me to That Land."[150]

> *There is a joy in that land*
> *There is a joy in that land*
> *There is a joy in that land*
> *Where I'm bound, where I'm bound.*
>
> *Well, there is a joy in that land*
> *There is a joy in that land*
> *There is a joy in that land*
> *Where I'm bound.*[151]

By the end of the sermon, Miz Hard-Boiled has indeed converted and joined Nix on the heavenly journey. The song was recorded prior to Nix's 1930 recording by the Gospel Camp Meeting Singers on May 11, 1929, on the Vocalion label (1283). Dixon, Godrich, and Rye state that the Gospel Camp Meeting Singers may have included Thomas Dorsey and Tampa Red as members, and the song was also recorded by the Belt Sacred Quartet on October 21, 1929, on the Victor label (23398).[152]

"I Want Jesus to Walk with Me"

This song was included in the anthology *Songs of Zion*, coedited by Nix's daughter Verolga Nix.[153] In the recorded sermon "Too Much Religion," Reverend Nix describes hypocritical people who talk about religion but don't actually practice it. He claims, "A real child of God is humble and submissive as they go through this world, amid howling wolves and tempting devils." The spiritual "I Want

Jesus to Walk with Me" allows a "real child of God" to call on Jesus in times of trouble, including "all along my pilgrim journey," "when my heart is almost breaking," and "when my head is bowed in sorrow." The spiritual is in a minor key and is plaintive both musically and lyrically.

Lyrical References

In addition to sung spirituals and hymns, Nix used Bible themes present in the spirituals. For example, "The Matchless King" was partly based on Song of Solomon 2:1, which is also present in the spiritual "He's the Lily of the Valley."[154] The spiritual includes the lyrics "He's the lily of the valley . . . He's the white Rose of Sharon . . . He's the Great Physician." "The Matchless King" includes the following text, which shows the possible influence of these sources:

> The doctor said,
> "He's my Balm in Gilead."
> The botanist said,
> "He's my Rose of Sharon
> And my lily of the valley."

The theme in "Your Bed Is Too Short and Your Cover Too Narrow" is shared with the spiritual "Oh Sinner," and both Nix's sermon and the spiritual take their theme from Isaiah 28:20.

> Nix's text:

> I take my text in Isaiah twentieth-eighth chapter and twentieth verse.
> For the bed is short and the man
> Can't place himself on it.
> And the cover is narrow
> And he can't wrap himself up in it.

> Spiritual "Oh Sinner"[155]:

> *Oh sinnuh*
> *Yo' bed's too short*
> *Oh sinnuh*
> *Yo' bed's too short*
> *Oh sinnuh*
> *Yo' bed's too short*
> *Um, my Lawd.*

Nix clearly referred to songs that are in the repertoire of the African American folk tradition, either in use of the actual songs or through his texts.

Mystery Spiritual

On forty-one of his forty-seven extant sermons, Nix included a spiritual melody that I have not located in any anthology of spirituals or in any hymnbook; hence, I am calling the melody the "mystery spiritual."[156] Nix included performances of the same spiritual on multiple recordings for almost the entirety of his recording history.

The female congregants, in the background of Nix's preaching, sing the spiritual melody. The transcription in Musical Example 4.8 reveals its use of the minor pentatonic scale, slides between notes (notated with the glissando symbol), and bends up to notes (notated with the up-arrow symbol). The lyrics for this particular performance of the mystery spiritual are based on Psalm 23.[157] Throughout multiple recordings, this spiritual melody functions as an obbligato, providing a contrapuntal response to Nix's preaching, creating a layering effect. It is not harmonized and is sung a cappella. The lyrics of each rendering of the spiritual are based either on Psalm 23, as in the above rendering, or are not articulated clearly enough to understand thoroughly.

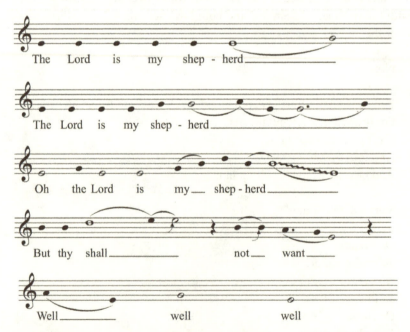

Musical Example 4.8. Mystery spiritual in "Begin a New Life on Christmas Day—Part I," recorded October 26, 1928, on Vocalion (Vo 1217), reissued on Document Records (DOCD-5328).

The mournful quality of the melody adheres to historical descriptions of spirituals from the era of slavery. For example, an account from 1863 described the qualities of a folk song, presumably a spiritual, in the Black church: "It was a strange song, with seemingly very little rhythm, and was what is termed in music a minor; it was not a psalm, nor a real song, as we understand these words; for there was nothing that approached the jubilant in it. It seemed more like a wail, a mournful, dirge-like expression of sorrow."[158] In another example from 1870, Elizabeth Kilham stated, "The most beautiful melody the negroes have ... [is] a chant, carried by full, deep bass voices; the liquid soprano of the melody wandering through and above it, now rising in triumphant swell, now falling in softened cadence."[159] Kilham's description of a male voice with a soprano "wandering" melody is similar to the mystery spiritual, which is contrapuntal in texture, with the female-sung melody weaving above the chant of Nix's voice. More than sixty years after the 1863 article, the same qualities are present in the mystery spiritual on Nix's recordings. In addition, the song presents qualities that have been identified with those of the folk spiritual: slow, sustained melodic lines; use of the pentatonic scale; a clear tonal center; a monophonic performance (of the spiritual melody itself, not including Nix's voice); performances featuring the human voice as the primary instrument; inclusion of slides and bends; use of improvisation (from one rendering to the next); and texts taken from the Bible, such as Psalm 23. Except for the accompaniment of body movement, which of course is not discernible from a sound recording, the characteristics all correspond with those of the folk spiritual. All of the renderings of the mystery spiritual are based on the same melodic content, regardless of the text or improvisatory words. In other words, despite the reliance on the text of Psalm 23 in the above example, the melody corresponds to the same melody as in all of the other examples of the mystery spiritual.

In addition, in several of the recorded performances, the female voices repeat the melody sometimes several times within a single sermon. Their entrances often appear spontaneous and impromptu, creating an element of unpredictability and excitement, despite the numerous repetitions of the melody. Because different voices sing the melody, either alone or as a group, the melody is never repeated identically. Based on the characteristics formulated from historical documents and by respected scholars in the field of Black music, I have concluded that the mystery spiritual is most likely a folk spiritual.

Nix's daughter Genester and another (anonymous) family member said they remember hearing the female congregants sing this particular melody during Reverend Nix's church services. Unfortunately, they were not able to definitively identify it. During Nix's recorded sermons, the prayer band sings the melody as part of its improvisational responses to his sermons, which provide opportunities to express feelings through song by making up words or

Musical Example 4.9. "The White Flyer to Heaven—Part II" (0:36–1:02), mystery spiritual melody, recorded June 29, 1927, on Vocalion (Vo 1170), reissued on Document Records (DOCD-5328).

humming spontaneously. Through repetitive renderings, the melody serves as an overarching, binding factor that ties together the sermons into one cohesive unit, revealing the theme of intertextuality between his sermons.

The rendering of the mystery spiritual in "The White Flyer to Heaven—Part II" (Musical Example 4.9) reveals different lyrics (some indecipherable) and a looser rhythmic structure than the rendering in "Begin a New Life on Christmas Day—Part I."[160] A comparison with the mystery spiritual in Musical Example 4.8 reveals similarities in the melody but with slight variations.

Nix's recording sessions featured female members of his congregation, including his wife, Ida, whom he brought to the recording sessions in Chicago. Certainly, he was familiar with their musical repertoire and either allowed them to choose their pieces or instructed the singers on what to sing. The repeated singing of the mystery spiritual on 87 percent of Nix's recorded sermons demonstrates his affinity for not only the melody itself, but also the performance of it by the sisters. The presence of the spiritual on Nix's recordings also highlights his preference for including oral traditions of the folk on the recordings. Despite the climate of the emerging middle class who aspired to uplift the race, Nix and his congregants clearly resisted the proposition that they needed to change their traditions and adopt "civilized" vocal aesthetics and repertoire to conform to uplift ideologies.

In Reverend Nix's era, the ability to preach, sing, and record Black folk songs and melodies must have been empowering in the face of discrimination, oppression, and cultural pressures. In the midst of segregated society and in an era in which lynchings were still prevalent, recordings that could be played in the privacy of one's home allowed for a re-enactment of the Black working-class church experience without the threat of persecution or judgment by either members of the dominant white society or by members of the Black middle and elite classes. Black consumers consciously purchased recorded sermons on which they heard distinctly Black oral traditions, despite the pressure from Black elites to uplift the race via Europeanized vocal sounds.

Tropes

Nix used the practice of intertextuality quite often, borrowing lines and subject themes from other sources, including blues songs and sermons by other ministers. According to David Evans, Nix recorded several other titles based on existing popular song titles: Bert Williams's (aka Elder Eatmore) "Generosity" and "Throwing Stones"; Reverend Gates's "Death Might Be Your Santa Claus"; Speckled Red's "The Dirty Dozen"; and the Tin Pan Alley song "After the Ball" by Charles K. Harris, published in 1892.[161]

The practice of borrowing and recirculating melodies and texts was common in the era of the folk spirituals, and lyrics and melodies were interchanged freely among sources.[162] Historian Lawrence Levine explains, "Identical or slightly varied stanzas appear in song after song; identical tunes are made to accommodate completely different sets of lyrics; the same song appears in different collections in widely varied forms."[163] Some songs common in hymnals, such as "All o' My Sins Done Taken Away," have multiple titles and different lyrics from version to version. This re-creation process from genre to genre or song to song is essential and integral to Black music.[164] In other words, the traditions of Black music are continually perpetuated, albeit in different forms through continuous revisions. The following discussion focuses on lyrical tropes and figurative tropes used by Nix on his recordings.

Lyrical Tropes

In his sermon "Watch Your Close Friend," Nix borrowed the theme of distrust as expressed in a song recorded by evangelist Rev. Edward W. Clayborn (The Guitar Evangelist) titled "Your Enemy Cannot Harm You (But Watch Your Close Friend)" on December 8, 1926. Nix's sermon "Watch Your Close Friend," recorded on October 28, 1927, was based on the same theme.[165] A comparison of the lyrics used by Clayborn and Nix in their two versions is given here.

Clayborn's "Your Enemy Cannot Harm You (But Watch Your Close Friend)":

Your close friend,
Your close friend,
Your enemies cannot harm you
But watch your close friend.

Nix's "Watch Your Close Friend":

> Your enemy
> Cannot harm you,
> But you must watch your friend.

Nix borrowed the lyrics of Clayborn's song almost word for word. Because the song was quite popular, Nix must have come across either the title or the complete recording of Clayborn's song, suggesting that Nix paid attention to what was popular in the field of race records and capitalized on popular themes. The popularity of some songs led many early recording artists to rerecord cover versions of songs made popular by other artists. For example, Blind Willie Davis, a guitar evangelist, also recorded "Your Enemy Cannot Harm You" for the Paramount label (12726, ca. December 1928) as a cover version of Clayborn's original song.

Also in his sermon "Watch Your Close Friend," Nix uses the personal pronoun (I) in the text to establish a personal relationship with Jesus, stating, "I thank God that there are some true friends in the world today," such as Jesus. The personalization of the vocalist's relationship with Jesus in the here and now was a departure from the lyrics of slavery-era spirituals in which heaven was in the hereafter, not in the present. Michael Harris opines that Thomas A. Dorsey borrowed Nix's personal-relationship-with-Jesus theme, although earlier hymns also used this theme.[166] Dorsey in his song "If You See My Savior" wrote, "If you see my Savior tell Him that you saw me." In this way, both Nix and Dorsey described Jesus as a friend or close acquaintance, which differed from the earlier emphasis on the hereafter. The commonality between Nix's chanted sermons and Dorsey's gospel song led Harris to claim, "As did Nix, Dorsey went to a well of shared experiences to find a message for his listener—but while Nix drew from the Bible, Dorsey dipped from everyday life." Although Harris apparently believed that Nix influenced some of Dorsey's choice of themes, it is unlikely that Nix alone deserves the credit, as the personal-relationship-with-Jesus theme was widespread in gospel songs and Black religious thought from the late nineteenth and early twentieth centuries onward.[167]

As discussed earlier, Nix also borrowed the titles of famous blues songs for his sermons "It Was Tight like That," "How Long—How Long," and "The Dirty Dozen."

Figurative Tropes

The "Black Diamond Express to Hell—Pt. I" recounts the various "stops" the "train" makes on its way to hell, carrying all kinds of sinners: drunkards, liars, deceivers, conjurers, confusion-makers, and fighters. The train theme functions as a trope, which is a continuation of the "chariot" theme in the spirituals, with both representing vehicles of freedom. The chariot theme in the spirituals and the train theme in the blues have been repeated, revised, and recirculated in numerous African American musical genres, and thus exemplify the intertextual interplay common in these genres. Nix may have gotten the idea for the train theme from either Rev. J. M. Gates's July 1926 recording of "Death's Black Train Is Coming" (CO 14145D) on the Columbia label or an earlier Christian hymn. An article published in 1898 mentioned the train theme as being associated with a hymn written by an enslaved man:

> There was current, not many years since, a hymn in which the Christian was likened to a traveler on a railway train. The conductor was the Lord Jesus, the brakemen were eminent servants of the Church, and stoppages were made at Gospel depôts to take up waiting converts or replenish the engine with the water of life or the fuel of holy zeal. The allegory was developed with as much accuracy and verisimilitude as though the author of the hymn had carefully studied the *Pilgrim's Progress*; yet it was imagined and composed by Oscar Buckner, an illiterate and ignorant negro slave.[168]

The train stops in this early Christian hymn are reminiscent of the White Flyer's stops en route to heaven. Regardless of the source of Nix's inspiration, his use demonstrates the train-as-trope theme and how it applied to not only hymns, spirituals, and the blues, but to recorded sermons. As Samuel A. Floyd Jr. explains, "in the African-American musical tradition, intergenre and cross-genre troping is widespread, with lines and phrases of songs being borrowed and used as needs and desires arise. Such troping, as momentary as it sometimes is, is nevertheless frequent."[169] The variations of parts three through six of "Black Diamond Express to Hell" not only repeated the main train theme, but also varied the details in each individual sermon, creating a trope within the extended parts of the sermon.

The "White Flyer to Heaven" sermons provide another version of the train-as-trope theme, but rather than descending to hell as the Black Diamond does, the White Flyer ascends to heaven. The theme of traveling to the upper stratosphere to reach heaven was fully explicated in Nix's sermon "The White Flyer to Heaven—Part 1," in which he describes:

The starry big heaven
And view the flying stars
And dashing meteors,
And then pass on by Mars and Mercury

And Jupiter and Venus
And Saturn and Uranus and Neptune
With her full-glittering moons.

In 1912, James Weldon Johnson discussed a minister's sermon in which "the preacher described the beauties of that celestial body . . . [which reached] the evening star . . . past the sun and the moon—the intensity of religious emotion all the time increasing—along the milky way, on up to the gates of heaven."[170] The similarity of the themes of Johnson's heard sermon and Nix's spoken sermon is close enough to assume an intertextual relationship.

Repetition

As discussed previously, repetition is a common feature in African American music and sermons. Nix's use of repetitive phrases presented material that was altered with each iteration and increased the dramatic tension with each passing.

In Nix's sermon "How Long—How Long," he uses the title phrase as a repeating phrase, creating an AAAB-type form in which the B line functions as a refrain that concludes each stanza, very similar to the Leroy Carr-Scrapper Blackwell blues song form of "How Long, How Long Blues" (Musical Example 4.10).[171] Each of Nix's hook lines increases in intensity as the sermon progresses, including the addition of extra "how long" phrases to the text, along with an increase in vocal range. He melodicizes the words to the pitches of $\hat{1}$, $b\hat{3}$, $\hat{5}$, and $b\hat{7}$ implying a minor-pentatonic scale. The transcription of the chorus statements shows the progression of intensity through the increased range of Nix's vocal line. Not only does Nix repeat the "how long" phrase throughout the sermon, but he alters each rendering melodically. He also builds momentum by increasing the range, climaxing in the fifth phrase (2:47–2:51), extending the high B$^\flat$ pitch into a moan in a gravelly timbre on "How." His underlying rhythmic structure is a pattern of sixteenth notes and dotted eighths (Musical Example 4.11). The repetition of this pattern, the repetition of the words "how long," the use of improvisation to alter each repetition, the melodic expansion climbing to the high B$^\flat$, and the use of moans and gravelly timbre effectively build the tension in the sermon.

In addition to the repetition of phrases such as "how long," the repetition of individual musical "cells" unites Nix's sermons together as a larger, cohesive group, functioning as a motive figure. David Brackett, in his analysis of James Brown's vocals in "Superbad," explains that musical cells are "bits of text, [or] a syllable" and that "recycling many vocal cells at identical pitch levels from song to song" is another form of intertextuality.[172] For example, the words "well, well, well" are the last words sung in the mystery spiritual that itself functions

Musical Example 4.10. "How Long—How Long," recorded c. February 18, 1930, on Vocalion (Vo 1505), reissued on Document Records (DOCD-5490).

Musical Example 4.11. Rhythmic structure of "How Long—How Long," recorded c. February 18, 1930, on Vocalion (Vo 1505), reissued on Document Records (DOCD-5490).

as an ostinato that links most of Nix's sermons together. The "well, well, well" phrase is also present as a stand-alone interjection to Nix's preaching in various sermons as the response to his call (Musical Example 4.12). "Well, well, well" is often used as a melodic and lyrical cell, with or without the full rendering of the mystery spiritual melody. The cell is often used to anticipate the singing of the spiritual melody, functioning as a precursor to its onset, as in "Black Diamond

Musical Example 4.12. Repetitive cells in "Black Diamond Express to Hell—Pt. II" (1:02–1:04), recorded on April 23, 1927, on Vocalion (Vo 1098), reissued on Document Records (DOCD-5328).

Express to Hell—Pt. I" (Section A). However, in "Black Diamond Express to Hell—Pt. II" the cell is random, neither preceding nor following the spiritual melody. In this case, it serves as a reminder of the spiritual. "Black Diamond Express to Hell—Pt. II" is one of the few sermons in which the melody I have identified as the mystery spiritual is not sung. However, the repetition of the "well, well, well" cell—eight times within the sermon—reminds the listener of the mystery spiritual. Brackett explains that "the repetition of fragments with discrete variations . . . alternately create expectations and thwart them." Similarly, the musical cell in Nix's sermons creates expectations of the singing of the mystery spiritual, which is sometimes fulfilled and other times not. The repetition of the cells also provides contrast to Nix's rap-like, rhythmic declamations, creating balance between his fast-paced utterances on the one hand and the melodic and rhythmic regularity of the musical cell on the other.

Improvisation

One of Nix's most important sermons, which was not recorded, was his "Baseball Sermon." Nix was an avid baseball fan, even naming his son Elwood after a Chicago Cubs baseball player, Elwood English. Genester and Elwood claimed that the baseball sermon was one of Nix's most popular, and he used it frequently at revivals and would preach it every Friday at church during baseball season.[173] Nix would "act out" the parts and could draw a large crowd due to his descriptive abilities, keeping his audience in suspense. Part of his success was his ability to paint a vivid picture in his sermons and captivate the audience with his emphasis. Elwood emphasized that other ministers would try to imitate his father.

Genester remembered her father preparing for his sermons with typed notes that consisted of bullet points rather than a fully written narrative. Loosely structuring his sermons around an outline allowed Nix to improvise and make adjustments as he proceeded. Genester explained, "When he preached, he didn't write them out like that. He just outlined them. And when he would get to certain [words] . . . he would write little notes, 'Watch out,' or 'end here,' or things like that."[174] The typed text, which Nix typed himself (one finger at a time), demonstrates his preference for general headings, rather than a fully scripted

VOCAL AND MUSICAL ANALYSIS   245

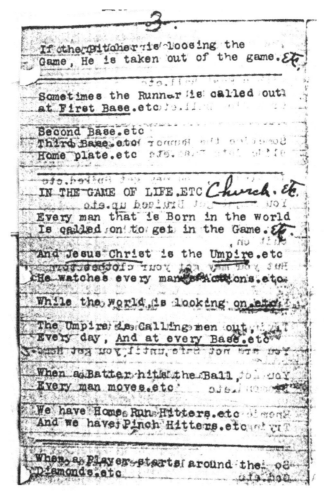

Figure 4.9. Nix's original "Baseball Sermon." Used by permission of Genester Nix.

sermon.[175] Ministers who improvised their talks were considered more "spiritual" than the ministers of the educated class who merely read from scripts.[176] The manuscript for the baseball sermon (Figure 4.9) demonstrates Nix's use of an outline from which he would improvise. The handwriting and typed words are Nix's own. While we have evidence that Nix used typed bullet points for his church sermons, it is unknown if he read from scripts or from outlines for his recorded sermons. The three-minute time limit of recordings would most likely necessitate a rehearsal in advance of the recording to ensure its ability to fit within these time constraints. Based on Genester's comments, Nix most likely typed a guide to the main points in outline form, which allowed for improvisation during the recordings.

Vocal Layering

The female congregants who sing on the recordings not only give the impression of a live sermon in the church, but they also keep up the excitement and energy of the sermon performance, interjecting regularly after Nix's phrases. Despite Nix's raw vocal power, the vocal interjections keep up the intensity throughout the sermon by never allowing for a silent moment. For example, when Nix pauses to breathe between phrases, the female voices fill the silence by interjecting their responses, serving as call-and-response throughout the sermon. If call-and-response works as a horizontal or linear pattern, moving in a forward trajectory, it can also function as a vertically stacked or layered pattern. The process of layering is one in which different patterns, riffs, or statements are uttered simultaneously with the primary statement. As some congregants shout, another congregant sings the mystery spiritual, while Nix chants. In this case, the spoken, shouted, and sung words of the congregants serve the function of providing layering to the sermon, creating a cohesive whole (Musical Example 4.13). In "The White Flyer to Heaven—Part II," Nix chants and shouts, the solo singer sings the spiritual melody, and the females interject with speaking, singing, and shouts. This layering effect creates a sense of flow, allowing for the multiple voices to function as a single voice, creating a sense of spiritual harmony and unity with all of the voices in tune with each other, literally and figuratively.

Nix's use of traditional folk spirituals and hymns, as well as tropes, repetition, improvisation, and vocal layering, again demonstrate his alignment with traditional African American vocal practices and repertoires. In this sense, he

Musical Example 4.13. Layering in "The White Flyer to Heaven—Part II" (0:59–1:05), recorded June 29, 1927, on Vocalion (Vo 1170), reissued on Document Records (DOCD-5328).

was highlighting his affiliation with the Black folk, rather than the elite class. Despite pressure from many African American elites to reform or neglect the folk spiritual and adopt the vocal aesthetics and repertoire of the dominant culture, Nix held his ground, continuing the traditions of the folk. But this was not an absolute rejection of reformist or uplift tendencies. While Nix presented numerous examples of his preference for folk vocal traditions, in his sermon texts he revealed middle-class ideologies in alignment with racial uplift theories.

Musical Transcription of "The White Flyer to Heaven—Part II"

I have transcribed the entirety of "The White Flyer to Heaven—Part II" (Musical Example 4.14), so that the reader may see Nix's use of various vocal techniques throughout one sermon. An arrow follows the symbol for the length the technique is extended. Because I am focusing on the vocal gestures, the notes are stemless and do not denote rhythm. I have notated shouts and loud dynamics separately because, as mentioned previously, in historical documents, shouts were not only uttered in a loud volume, but were accompanied by a "shrill tone" and a "screaming" voice in the upper register of the voice with higher pitches. Thus, the shout is a combination of loud vocal volume, "shrill tone," and higher pitches and requires a symbol separate from dynamics. I have notated the dynamics as *mf* and *ff* due to the fact that the exact dynamic level is impossible to discern from a recording. However, I am able to discern differences, including increases and decreases of volume, within the recording.

Nix begins in a natural speaking voice without gravelly timbres or loud dynamics. The interjections by the congregants begin within the first eleven seconds of the sermon. Nix begins speaking with a gravelly timbre at 0:24 and continues thereafter. His first shout, moan, and loud dynamic occur on the word "I" at 0:31, after which he returns to his original volume level. The female congregant begins singing the mystery spiritual at 0:36. At 0:42, Nix again reaches a climax but returns to a moderate volume at 0:52 through the end of this section.

At 1:05, Nix's shouts, loud dynamics, and high pitches fluctuate between moderate volume and lower pitches. In other words, between 1:05 and 1:34, Nix fluctuates between highs and lows as he builds tension to keep the attention of his listeners. At 1:34, the climax section begins, which includes high pitches, shouts, loud dynamics, and interjections from the congregants. The climax continues to 1:53, when "Look for Me" is sung by the group. As mentioned previously, the spiritual functions as a bridge between the climax and its recap. The second climax (at 2:19) includes moans, shouts, high pitches, loud dynamics, interjections from the congregants, and the mystery spiritual. The energy

Symbols for Vocal Gestures	
Vocal Gesture	**Symbol**
Gravelly timbre	
Shout	▲
Moan	➤
Scoop up	
Scoop down	
Slide	
Mystery spiritual	✛
Interjections from congregants	✖

Musical Example 4.14. Transcription of "The White Flyer to Heaven—Part II," recorded June 29, 1927, on Vocalion (Vo 1170), reissued on Document Records (DOCD-5328).

VOCAL AND MUSICAL ANALYSIS 249

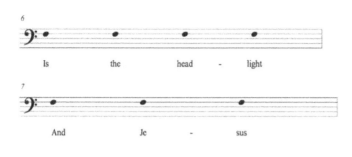

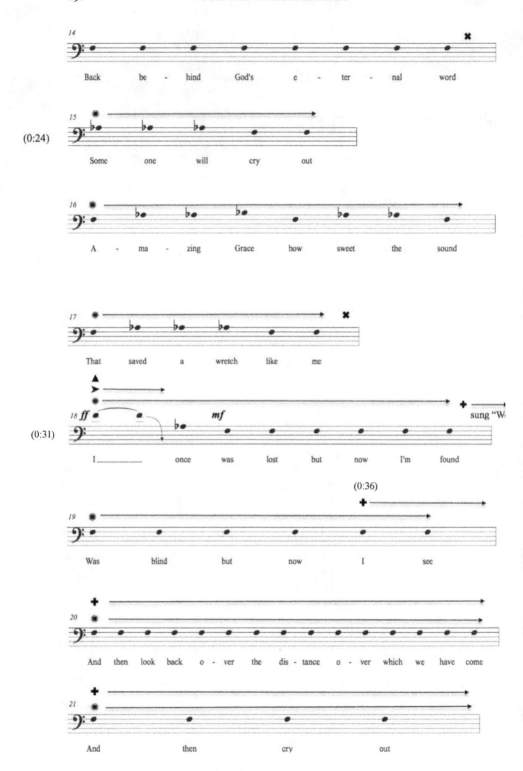

251

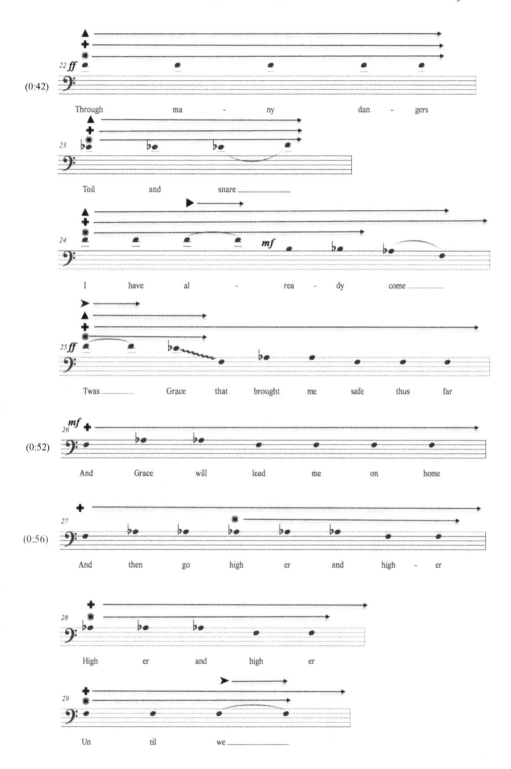

252 VOCAL AND MUSICAL ANALYSIS

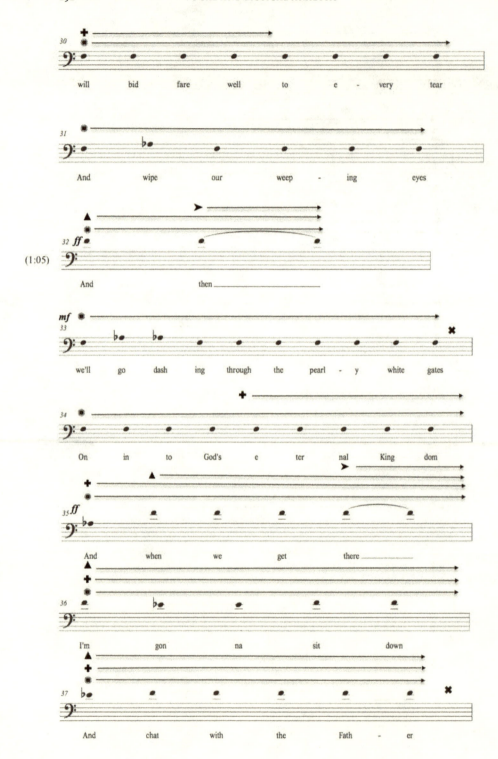

VOCAL AND MUSICAL ANALYSIS

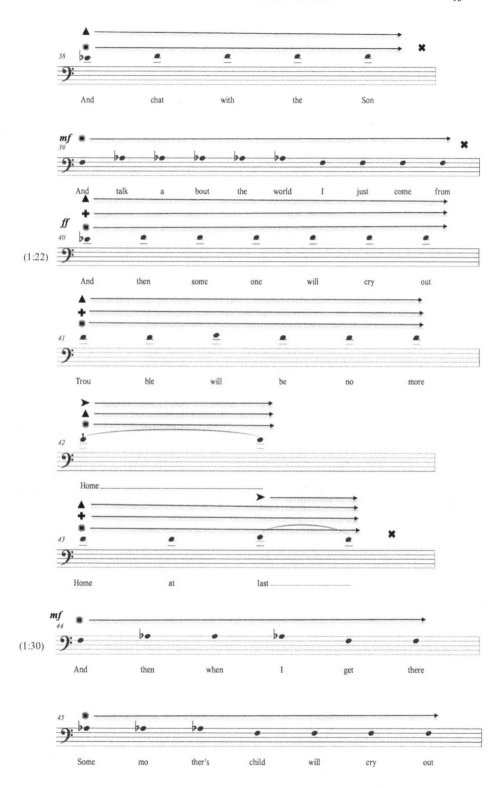

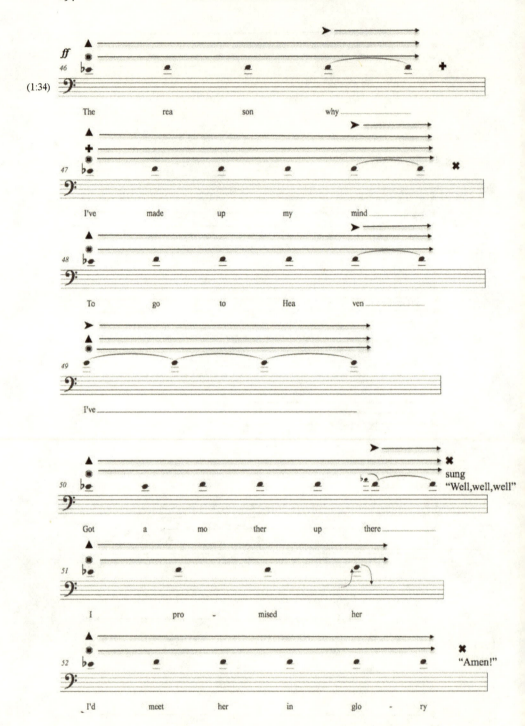

VOCAL AND MUSICAL ANALYSIS

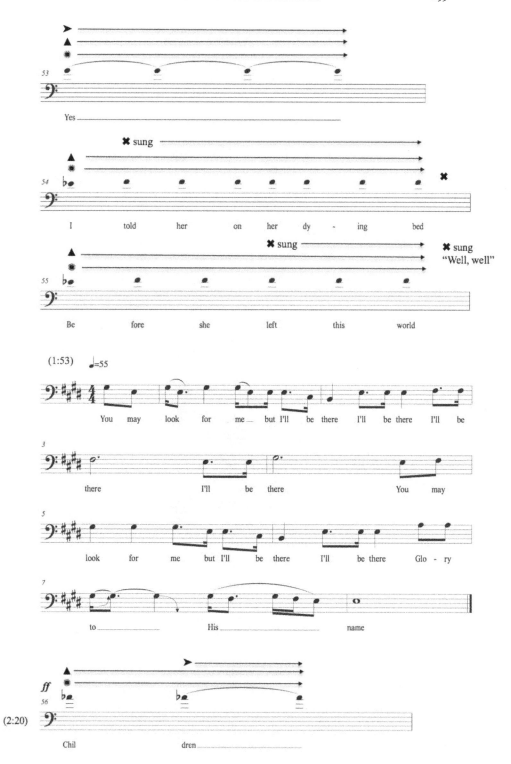

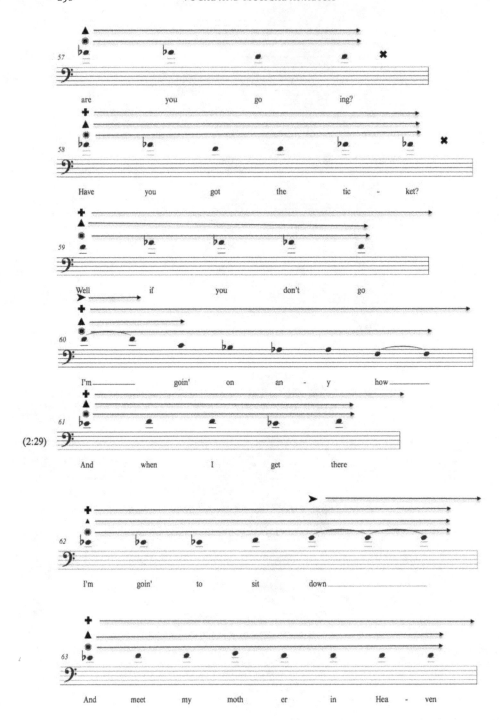

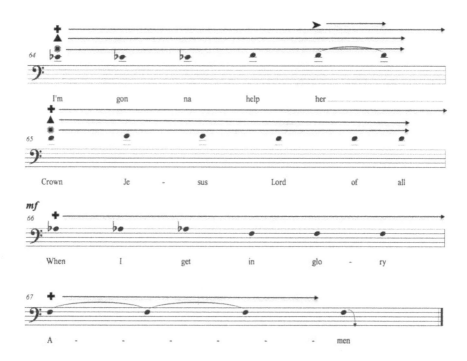

continues until 2:41, when the last two phrases return to a moderate dynamic on "When I get in glory, Amen."

I have notated the number of occurrences of the elements that contribute to a heightened intensity: gravelly timbre, shouts, loud dynamics, moans, high pitches, inclusion of the mystery spiritual, and interjections by the congregants. A linear graph (Figure 4.10) shows the tension within the sermon and provides a view of the number of vocal gestures in each time occurrence. The highs and lows of the graph provide evidence of Nix's use of gestures for dramatic effect. He consistently alters his use of gestures to provide tension and release throughout the sermon. However, before and after the singing of the spiritual (at 1:53–2:19), Nix climaxes in the sermon. Although Nix has six climaxes within the sermon, at 1:34–1:53 his phrases are much longer than earlier in the sermon. Thus, he keeps up the intensity for a longer period in this section and in the recap after the spiritual is sung. For example, the first climax (at 0:42–0:52) lasts ten seconds, while the fifth climax (1:34–1:53) lasts twenty-one seconds, and the recap (at 2:19–2:41) lasts twenty-two seconds. Plus, Nix sings the highest notes of the sermon in these two sections with the most intensity.

Through Nix's use of shouts, moans, loud vocal dynamics, gravelly timbre, and high pitches, as well as vernacular language, words and phrases directly associated with folk spirituals, and moan-type adjustments to words, he demonstrated his attention to both sound and African American folk vocal traditions.

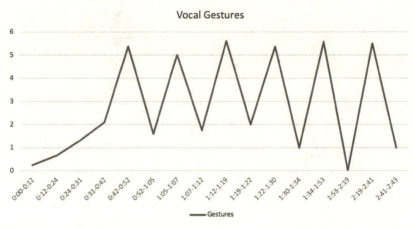

Figure 4.10. Linear graph of "The White Flyer to Heaven—Part II."

In addition, Nix employed traditional hymns and folk spirituals, discussed earlier. Identity is closely linked to sound, more so than appearance, and communication through sound is highly regarded for Black ministers.[177] Therefore, the evidence demonstrates that Nix utilized sound through vocal gestures to communicate with and draw in his listeners.

VOCALISMS IN CONTEMPORARY PREACHING

As I have shown, Nix used a variety of vocal techniques to draw in and inspire his congregation. But the question remains: how have vocalisms and preaching practices changed or stayed the same in the church of today? I asked this question of Genester Nix, Elwood Nix, and Genester's son, Dr. John Wilson. Wilson is also a Baptist minister and has served on ministerial staffs but is currently working in higher education. I also consulted the writings of contemporary scholars who have written about practices in the modern African American church.

Genester Nix explained to me that the preachers in her father's day did not have the education of a seminary and thus concentrated on preaching about

> getting into heaven by loving your neighbors, being good, not drinking alcohol, lying, stealing, cheating on your spouse, prostitution, etc. . . . Preachers would use a moaning sound during and near the end to get the congregation to shout and get happy. This is what they called "having church." If the preacher didn't holler or moan or jump around or preach about getting to heaven, then he was considered as having failed to reach the people.

Now, our churches require a pastor to have graduated from a seminary and be able to teach the Bible. So in their preaching they should include some background, you know, the whys, when, where, etc. They use intonation of voice for emphasis of points in the sermon. The preachers teach more and try to connect it to what's happening in our world today.

Most of the people [in the congregation] are educated. In fact, I would say all [of] the congregation have finished high school and most college. So the people require more of the pastors. The information in the sermon must be on their level and must show preparation and research. Their English must be correct as different [from] in my father's time.[178]

While Genester explained that modern-day preachers must be educated and try to teach more than exhort, Elwood Nix complained that this is the very reason he considers modern-day preachers to be "boring":

Preachers are different today—they try to teach the Bible. They don't really do a good job because they can't paint the picture for you to understand what was going on. It's different, life was different than it is now. Life was simple. Today preachers don't really understand the Bible to explain it to different people. The preachers before . . . they understood the Bible and could read a story and decipher it whereas the preachers today can't do that.

They [preachers] don't get emotional now like the preachers did back then. They try to teach [but] the words don't come out. It's like they're lecturing. They don't inspire [the congregation]. That's what makes it really boring.

Preachers today try to be too sophisticated. If they pranced around and jumped around, it would make them feel uneducated. Down South they still do it. They shout and they feel everything. Up North they don't paint the pictures no more.[179]

Reverend Nix's grandson and Genester's son, John Wilson, commented on Elwood's statements and explained why he understood Elwood's position:

You have to consider who his father was and what he saw. My grandfather, Reverend Nix, understood something that a lot of preachers do not understand: getting people to listen to you and getting people to listen to God is an art. It is an art. It is an artform. And you are trying, with a sermon, to win ears and minds and spirits. You are trying to get people's attention, and the attention span in 2021 is not what it used to be a hundred years ago when my grandfather was coming through. Now there's all kinds of competition for mental and spiritual bandwidth. And unless you capture the attention of the listener, then they are unlikely to hear you. So I translate what Elwood Nix is saying into this: it is unacceptable to merely stand up there and speak the English language and think that you are communicating. Effective communication requires a deeper combination of inspiration and information, and it is an art and a gift to illustrate a point. If reaching people requires you to move around, then move around. If it requires you to reach into popular culture or into movie scenes or into popular music for comparisons and metaphors and ironies, then you do so. You will reach people a lot better. So, in my view, Elwood Nix is simply advising that the preachers of today ought to tap the same artistry of preaching that Reverend Nix tapped.[180]

As mentioned previously, Elwood Nix remarked that if his father had not been a Baptist, he most assuredly would have been Pentecostal due to his use of shouting, whooping, and other elements typically associated with Pentecostalism. Similar to how the upper- and middle-class church members in 1920s Black Chicago ridiculed the practices of the lower-class churches, Pentecostals have received derision from other African American denominations. According to Ashon T. Crawley, Pentecostal practices "were and are considered to be excessive performances, unnecessary because of their purported lack of refinement, discardable because of their seeming lack of intellectual rationality and rigor."[181] As a result, Pentecostals often feel as though they are pushed out and banished from mainline religions, such as Baptist, Methodist, and AME traditions.[182] However, while current-day Pentecostals may feel exiled as a result of their practices, Nix did not seem to care what others thought about his preaching practices, and as I have mentioned, he took pride in voicing African American traditions in the midst of condemnation from those who shunned these practices as "backwards." Therefore, while Nix may have used some practices associated with modern Pentecostalism, he proudly shouted, moaned, and sang spirituals despite the condemnation from others.

John Wilson, Genester's son, also spoke with me about some of the practices of modern-day preaching. Having grown up in the Baptist church and having been ordained as a Baptist minister himself, he is well aware of not only the history of his grandfather's style of preaching, but also the transitions preachers have made in the twenty-first century. Wilson described his grandfather as a "trailblazer" for his ability to popularize the sermon through the use of his voice. Wilson contended that there are some modern-day preachers, such as Rev. Dr. Marcus D. Cosby and Rev. Dr. Frederick Douglass Haynes III, both from Texas, who have an approach that is similar to that of Nix. Wilson claimed that both of these ministers use multiple pitches and build to a crescendo in their sermons. He also mentioned, with great admiration, the preaching of Howard-John Wesley in Alexandria, Virginia. There are many examples of African American preachers who chant, shout, and use loud vocal volume and a gravelly vocal timbre, such as Nix did.[183] Wilson claimed that these vocalisms are common and "what you find in most African American churches."

Regarding the practice of call-and-response, Wilson explained the deeper meaning attached to this practice:

> The call-and-response . . . is the most common because most preachers today need to know "are you hearing me and feeling me? Am I making sense? Are you hearing what I am saying as truth? And if you believe what you are hearing, say 'amen!'" There is this need of affirmation. For some it tends to be egocentric—they need to determine, are you hearing *me*? [italics mine]. But on a deeper level, there is a need to understand, "are you hearing from God in what I'm saying?" And that is what a call-and-response is more about. That is what it's supposed to be more about than it is anything else because a preacher is a vessel. And as a vessel, they are an instrument of God. So the ego is not supposed to be in it and yet there is the need for any speaker to get confirmation that what is being communicated is being received.
>
> In my view, the vocal techniques in the Black church have always been about that. There has always been this sensibility to the peculiar experiences of African American congregations. For centuries, the American environment has been dominated by a struggle against racism and hate. That has provoked a need, a heavy need, for the congregants to be faithful that "this too shall pass," that "everything is gonna be alright!" So the call-and-response and the whole style of the Black church is to get confirmation that you are believing in the truth that is being conveyed. And *that's* what the speaker-hearer interplay is all about [italics mine].[184]

I asked Wilson if modern-day preachers also style-switch as Nix did. He explained:

> Style-switching is often used to appeal to different congregations. Different people in the church are in different walks of life. Some are very successful; some are not so successful. Some are going through a personal life storm; others may be cruising. At any given time, they may have two different sets of needs. So, the person who was cruising last week, last month or last year, could be in a difficult spot now and vice versa. So, sometimes you come to church with more of an emotional need, and sometimes you come to church with more of an intellectual need.

And again, preaching has always been—at least preaching in the Black church and I would say preaching in general—it has always been about comforting the afflicted, and afflicting the comfortable. You can't get too comfortable in life. If you are cruising, the preacher may urge you to be very aware that it will not always be that way. The preacher may urge you to listen very well and gain strength because your storm is coming. The preacher may also charge you with the responsibility of taking care of others who are in need. That is what it means to afflict or disrupt your comfort by making you aware of a set of obligations, or imperatives. But if you are already discomforted or uncomfortable or afflicted in some way, then I want to comfort you. So, there are two different kinds of messages.

Style-switching is used to impart both messages. It is very important to recognize that some who enter the service are broken and some are whole. You want to charge each, according to their needs.

Moreover, you want to address the needs of congregants at different levels of education. Some need more substance than others. Some need to get the sense that you have prepared and you have been thoughtful about the morning message. They may want something a little more robust in information and perhaps not as much inspiration. And then there are people who are not as credentialed and may not be looking for you to share all the background of the scripture and the history. They may not have an appetite or interest in knowing what was going on in the twentieth year of the life of Jesus in Rome. They may say, "I just need the inspiration part of this." They may not hold the pastor to the information part as much as some others may. So that is what code-switching is about too: you have to meet those two main audiences where they are.[185]

Therefore, Nix used style-switching to appeal to congregants of different classes, while Wilson describes style-switching as a need to appeal to the needs of congregants on different emotional and intellectual levels.

Musically, some African American churchgoers feel that the music in the church has strayed too far from its spiritual roots and thus does not represent their religious identities. For example, in some Pentecostal churches, the music now resembles hip-hop genres, also known as "holy hip-hop" or "hip-hop gospel," which Melvin L. Butler describes as "too worldly" for conservative Pentecostals.[186] However, Kirk Franklin, a contemporary minister-musician and sixteen-time Grammy winner, uses contemporary music to spread his message.[187] His gospel-music is fused with jazz, hip-hop, and R&B and features his rap style of ministering woven into a mélange of vocalists and choirs in catchy, singable melodies. According to Butler, Franklin uses a speech-song type of oration in his music,[188] similar to Reverend Nix's, demonstrating a continuity in preaching vocalisms despite a change in musical styles. John Wilson claimed that

> Music has always been the twin sister of the sermon. There are two real highlight moments in a service: one is the music and the other is the spoken word—usually it's the sermon but it's also the prayer. So the spoken word and the word that comes through music—it's an interplay. Music is essential and it always has been. And I'll remind you and you know well my grandfather's history. He and his brother were a team. His brother provided the music. I like to say that my grandfather was at the ground floor of some of the most popular and noteworthy Black preaching in the African American tradition and his brother was at the ground floor of African American music because his brother inspired Thomas Dorsey, who is widely recognized as the founder of gospel music. So you have in one family the roots of so much of what is essential in the Black church experience, to this day.[189]

As a preacher-singer, Nix did not hold back his voice, and his voice alone may have been his strongest asset, leading to his success. In gospel music performance in the modern African American Christian church, the performer—as separate from the minister—is expected to have charisma and to be flamboyant, thus sometimes drawing attention to himself or herself rather than to the message.[190] Whereas there is now sometimes a separation between preacher and musical leader, Nix embraced both simultaneously, which strengthened his message rather than detracting from it. As Wilson claimed, and I agree, "Rev. Andrew W. Nix was one of the greatest artists who ever stood in the pulpit—full stop."[191]

CONCLUSION

Rev. A. W. Nix was an educated African American Baptist minister from Texas who received a formal education and moved to Chicago in the 1920s, where he experienced a modern urban environment that was markedly different from that of his upbringing in the South. As a minister, he utilized the new medium of phonograph recordings to present sermons with messages urging his listeners to avoid the worldly lures of city life and lift themselves up. But he chose to present these messages on recordings that incorporated the rich and distinctive vocal traditions of preaching and singing that had been closely associated with African Americans in the rural South since the days of slavery.

The evolution of technology, specifically phonographs and sound film, provided opportunities for Black ministers such as Nix to (re)present traditional folk voices and vocalisms as modern twentieth-century options for African American consumers.[1] The popularity of recorded sermons on phonograph records demonstrated the values that African Americans continued to place on these traditions. In addition, recorded sermons injected the vocal styles of traditional Black church services into the public sphere, creating a modern sonic space for African American oral practices. The process of learning vocal traditions through live oral and aural repetition was replaced by the phonograph, which allowed for multiple repetitions at the listener's leisure. Similarly, the recordings of blues and jazz by African American musicians also transformed important secular traditions. In addition, recorded sermons presented new leisure options for African American communities as they struggled to find a place of equality in a rapidly changing world. Recorded sermons by Nix and other preachers created places for new, modern Black voices, which were hybrid fusions of African American folk vocal traditions and modern technology.

Perhaps Nix's decision to include on his recordings vocal traditions linked to the African American past gives evidence of his pride in his race's history. Perhaps his decision was a protest statement against assimilation to European cultural aesthetics. Perhaps it was a sign of his love of Black traditional musical expressions. Perhaps it was all of the above. Likewise, his audiences may

CONCLUSION

have identified with his sermons because they heard themselves and their experiences in the moans and timbres of Nix's voice and the voices of his church members and showed that they valued these traditions by purchasing his recordings. By doing so, African Americans in the 1920s, many of whom were financially strapped, made a conscious decision to use their financial resources to support and own that which they considered of value. Although many churches chose to assimilate to the dominant culture's aesthetic values, the popularity of Nix's recorded sermons provides evidence of the cultural values of many African Americans in the 1920s.

The success of recorded sermons attests that African Americans of diverse class standings valued the sermons and their accompanying voices and music as modern incarnations of cultural heritage. In contrast to Rev. Sutton Griggs's restrained and "proper" vocalisms and the New Negro's affinity for classical music, the marketing of race records of sermons by Black ministers demonstrated that the "rougher" folk vocalisms disseminated via the phonograph were popular among African American mass audiences. These recordings thus established traditional vocalisms as counter to or a replacement for the New Negro's vision for advancement and uplift.

Additionally, I suggest that Nix's use of voice transformed notions of respectability and spoke of pride for traditions that arose from the rural South and may have resisted the pressure by elite African Americans to assimilate to white vocal aesthetic values. As Lawrence Schenbeck has argued,

> Popular genres are more apt to be engaged for expressing community pride, confronting social issues, calling for justice. For one thing, they are more deeply rooted in the communities that create them. For another . . . they do not as often seek to harmonize with the songs of the oppressor. Neither musically nor lyrically are they born asking to be let in, begging to become one with the great homogenizing forces of this "one nation, indivisible."[2]

Due to the community's affiliation with the Black church and its ministers and the popularity of recorded sermons, I argue that these recordings did not depend on being transformed or "lifted" into "high art" or more "sophisticated" expressions.

One of the main purposes of this study has been to interrogate the strict binary modalities typically used to understand African American experiences in the twentieth century. Many scholars describe the early twentieth century as a period of strict duality for African Americans with oppositions like Black/ white, the "Old Negro"/"New Negro," South/North, rural/urban, working class/ middle class, primitivism/progress, Du Bois/Washington, and so on. Du Bois himself coined the term "double consciousness" to signify the life of duality that many African Americans lived in the early part of the century. While these dualistic representations still exist, African American culture is much more complex and diverse than these binaries suggest. While some intellectuals, such as Alain Locke, clearly distinguished between the noisy oral traditions of the "Old Negro" and the sophisticated art of the "New Negro," in this study I have presented evidence that these two spheres were not mutually exclusive and interacted in complex ways. Some leaders like Nix adhered to both. Nix employed vocal traditions associated with the rural South and the Old Negro, yet aspired to uplift his congregation through his sermon texts, reflecting New Negro ideologies. In this way, Reverend Nix stood as a bridge between the conceptualized worlds of the Old Negro and the New Negro. His voice and vocal style suggest that he believed in a continuation of tradition, an expansion, an awareness, of something not to be shunned, hidden in shame, or expressed with self-loathing but rather to be embraced as the past while looking to the future. Nix chose to express his own racial pride through these traditions while presenting them via technologies linked to scientific progress and modernity. He stood with one foot in each world.

Some may argue that Nix was indeed the perfect representation of double consciousness because of his alignment with tradition, on the one hand, and uplift and modernity, on the other. However, Nix's position is more nuanced than this. Du Bois's original explanation of double consciousness as "two warring ideals in one dark body"[3] does not, I suggest, characterize Nix. Rather, he was being true to himself, his ideals, and beliefs, which were layered and multiple and certainly influenced by his environment and the time in which he lived. There are usually gray areas in the responses people have to real-life situations, and they do not always fit in neat little packages. Nix, for the most part, adhered to southern rural traditions, but on occasion included music or vocals that were outside of these traditions and were considered by some to be more sophisticated. Similarly, in his texts, he mostly adhered to subjects and themes that were intended to uplift African Americans through practical means. He occasionally would address his congregants by using sophisticated words and subjects, demonstrating his own alignment with the educated upper classes. At times though, Nix demonstrated his own conservatism and southern rural past through his opinions about women and their dress and his use of vernacular language. However, Nix was motivated as a Christian minister to help and care for his congregants and may not have been consciously advocating simple accommodation to the dominant society.

Another purpose of this study has been to contest the simple alignment of vocal expressions along class lines. As I have shown, in the 1920s, the lower-class members of the African American community were frequently associated with

CONCLUSION 267

more boisterous forms of vocal worship, and the preachers who ministered to them were known to shout, moan, and chant during their services. Those African Americans with higher social standing in the community were associated with more restrained forms of worship, with many completely disavowing their cultural heritage in favor of assimilation to white modes of expression. However, Nix broke these strict categories and rules. He shouted and chanted despite his formal education, his middle-class economic standing, and his knowledge of racial uplift and advancement as intellectual ideas.

In addition, essentialist myths of a timeless and homogeneous Black musical culture have all too often characterized African American music and voices as singular expressions. Essentialist narratives have filtered through every aspect of musical and vocal Blackness from the beginning of the enslavement of Africans to the present era. Certainly, common musical and vocal features exist in African American communities, and it is these common features that I have focused on as a way to understand the enduring sameness of expressing cultural values. It is understood that cultural groups express common practices and traits. However, there must also be an understanding of a middle ground or gray area—that not *everyone* in that group expresses himself or herself in exactly the same manner. Black voices are not homogeneous expressions, but instead are multivalent expressions, and this diversity has existed throughout history. While class hierarchies evolved in the aftermath of the Civil War, there are and were varying degrees of expression associated with classist and racial identities, creating, as Paul Gilroy claims, a "changing same."[4] The recorded sermons demonstrate how notions of tradition changed from one associated with slavery and the old ways to one associated with technology, modernity, and advancement. In addition, notions of musical modernity and advancement expanded from those associated with Europeanized written forms and vocalisms to the recorded sermons that presented African American folk oralities via modern technology.

It is important to remember that tradition itself is a cultural construct and is often reified as something that has always existed. However, tradition signifies choice in terms of what is valued and what best represents one's or a community's identity. Based on my analysis of historical writings and the frequency with which they reported certain Black vocal practices, I assert that those specific sounds became highly valued by members of African American communities and repeated enough to forge a path that came to be associated with racial identity. These sounds were the sounds with which many chose to identify at a particular time in history, eventually becoming associated with an ongoing tradition.

Nix took pride in these traditions. He did not shy away from his southern roots; he shouted with a voice that had more power than any other Black minister of the era; he employed spirituals and hymns favored by the Black church; and he did not adopt white aesthetic standards, such as vocal smoothness or sweetness. Despite the pressure from African American leaders and criticism from within 1920s Black society, Nix did what he always did: he chanted, shouted, and sang—full of life and without restraint. While there were others who also supported Black folk traditions, such as Zora Neale Hurston, Langston Hughes, and W. C. Handy, many Black leaders from the 1920s eschewed these vocal traditions.

I introduced Sutton Griggs as a vocal example epitomizing the idea of the New Negro. Griggs's sermons did not achieve the same commercial success as Nix's, demonstrating that many African Americans valued Black vocal traditions more than assimilated voices such as that of Griggs. And while elite Black leaders toiled to determine what the people "should" do according to their doctrines to assimilate into dominant society, many African Americans instead supported the traditions of the past that were disseminated by Black ministers such as Nix. Thus, in a sense, the African American folk minister, who had previously been largely restricted to preaching in the confines of the church, now was able to reach listeners via phonograph recordings (and radio), essentially displacing the hegemony of many elite leaders such as Griggs and becoming a public voice of the people. And while Griggs eschewed oral traditions and sought to move into the world of written words through literacy, the modern phonograph reinforced the "old ways" of oral traditions.

Although Nix was not particularly vocal about his political beliefs, he supported the advancement of his fellow African Americans, both individually and as a congregation, and even supported many of Griggs's literary endeavors. Nix wanted to help his people become the best they could, despite his patriarchal standards about women. We must remember the times and environment in which Nix preached: men were the unquestioned heads of households, "good" church women dressed modestly and behaved accordingly, and racism was rampant in the South and the North. Despite these facts, Nix never focused on being a victim of racism, although he apparently was, but chose to be a giving and loving person to his family and to his congregation. He never turned his back on anyone and always reached out a hand to help. Nothing was false about Nix, a point that his son Elwood expressed to me.

Finally, but most importantly, this study gives voice to a man described by his relatives as a "great man." Everyone with whom I communicated spoke of Nix positively, even majestically. He created a legacy within his own family, yet his name has often been clouded with erroneous information. He has been portrayed in numerous discourses incorrectly, with scholars misidentifying Andrew (A. W.) Nix or failing to distinguish him from his brother, William

CONCLUSION   269

(W. M.) Nix. I hope I have fully and indelibly explained the differences between the two brothers and each's distinctive contributions.

Although Nix did espouse racial pride, he also affiliated himself with uplift theories and continuously urged his listeners to improve their lives economically, physically, and spiritually. He disapproved of alcohol consumption, gambling, "loose women," laziness, lying, and deceit; however, aren't those many of the same things we fret about today? He may have been aligned with Victorian modes of conduct, but these moral views are alive and well in today's so-called post-postmodern society. Thus, his own life and the choices he made reflect another aspect of the changing same.

Nix's success in the recording and film industries may have established him as one of the first, along with Rev. J. M. Gates, to broadcast religious thought via modern media.[5] Lerone A. Martin contends that Gates modernized Black Protestant religion through recorded phonograph sermons, which became established as sites of Black emancipation and progress.[6] Simultaneously, Black ministers such as Nix used the modern phonograph, which allowed listeners to stay connected to their southern rural traditions.

FUTURE RESEARCH

The qualities associated with Black traditional voices have often been described in generalized terms, but few transcriptions of these sounds and qualities exist. Although notation software is evolving, it is still difficult if not impossible to notate the subtleties of vocal timbre and other aspects of vocal interpretation. While the Sonic Visualizer software is able to visually project many of the features associated with these sounds, I doubt that many could simply "hear" a timbre merely by looking at its overtones on paper. More research is needed in this area.

Sales and distribution data for Nix's records are not available. Many of the records from the past are simply disappearing due to modern record companies' lack of storage space, their belief that these works are no longer of importance, and/or the destruction of archival materials.[7] While more research is needed, some sources are simply no longer available. Thus, I was not able to provide detailed data to quantify the sales figures for Nix's recorded sermons or to characterize more specifically who purchased his records. My hope is that someday these data will be found.

While much of the historical scholarship on Black music has focused on folk spirituals, blues, jazz, Black gospel music, and rhythm and blues, little has been published about the importance of late nineteenth- to early twentieth-century

African American ministers and their voices. Their long-standing history as pioneers in legitimizing the rough gravelly voice—along with contemporaries such as Bessie Smith, Louis Armstrong, Blind Willie Johnson, and Bessie Johnson—deserves attention. More research needs to be conducted that investigates the connections between the minister's voice and the development of Black vocal styles, such as those utilized by James Brown, who admitted to being influenced by his childhood preacher. Is it possible that the early Black minister's voice influenced not only the creation of the spirituals, but also much of our popular American music, from blues to jazz to soul to funk to R&B to rap? Obviously, preachers had a huge influence on gospel singing. A number of famous gospel singers are or were preachers or became preachers. A number of blues singers also became preachers, and a few went the opposite way.

CONTEMPORARY INFLUENCES

Nix's recorded sermons were not only influences on subsequent forms of modern media, such as the sound film *Hallelujah,* but also on today's music and musicians. Reverend Nix's sermon "Black Diamond Express to Hell" was such an influence on an eight-piece rock band from Leith, Edinburgh, that its members named their band after the sermon.[8] Nix's sermons have been on the playlist of Ketch Secor, a member of Old Crow Medicine Show.[9] Bob Dylan's spiritual-soaked 1997 release *Time Out of Mind* includes references to the themes in old sermons, including Nix's.[10] Some scholars claim that rap music is also influenced by early preachers such as Nix.[11] More research is needed on the influence of the voices of Black ministers on subsequent music styles.

FINAL THOUGHTS

Black leaders of the 1920s attempted to alleviate and reduce racism by whatever means possible. They truly wanted to help their people and were up against incredible odds. Racism was a huge wall that just would not (and has not) come down. Although racism and discrimination against African Americans have definitely declined in the last hundred years, there is still more work to be done. Rev. A. W. Nix was an exemplar in expressing pride for Black folk traditions, in resisting the pressure to assimilate, and in aiding his congregation to live fruitful lives.

Although focusing on the differences between racialized groups is often frowned upon for falling into an essentialist trap, Radano argues that the sound of Black voices operated as a powerful agency for African Americans during the slavery era.[12] By emphasizing vocal difference, they established layered identities, distinguishing themselves from their oppressors. And in the 1920s while racism raged on, the sound of traditional Black voices possibly served as a measure of resistance to assimilation to the dominant society's values.

It is understandable that, in the 1920s, African Americans were frustrated, tired, angry, sad, and a host of other emotions. After the Civil War, they had been promised the hope of a new future, freedom, equality, and a new beginning; instead, they were the victims of violence and murder and were discriminated against, publicly scorned, humiliated, and ridiculed. Unfortunately, although there have been many advances in race relations since the 1920s, we still struggle with racism in the United States today. In addition, Black music and the sound of Black voices have been continually appropriated, disparaged, celebrated, demonized, and idealized. It is my belief that the more historical ethnomusicologists such as myself research the past, the more it will influence the present and bring light to cultural inequalities that continue to exist. Music resonates close to our hearts and can often express that which words cannot, including our deepest values. For groups that have been the most silenced or ignored, musical voices can reveal what matters most.

NOTES

ACKNOWLEDGMENTS

1. St. Clair Drake and Horace R. Cayton, *Black Metropolis: A Study of Negro Life in a Northern City* (Chicago: University of Chicago Press, 1970); The Chicago Commission on Race Relations, *The Negro in Chicago: A Study of Race Relations and a Race Riot* (Chicago: University of Chicago Press, 1922); and Brian Dolinar, ed., *The Negro in Illinois: The WPA Papers* (Urbana: University of Illinois Press, 2013).

2. Sonic Visualizer, accessed August 15, 2018, https://www.sonicvisualiser.org.

INTRODUCTION

1. W. E. B. Du Bois, *The Souls of Black Folk* (1903; New York: Dover Publications, 1994), 116.

2. An example of the "frenzy" can be found in the film *Hallelujah*, which will be discussed later in this chapter: https://youtu.be/GGyR_34_Ibg.

3. David Levering Lewis, *W. E. B. Du Bois: A Biography, 1868–1936* (New York: Holt Paperbacks, 2009), 49, 57, 60. Du Bois attended Fisk University in Nashville, Tennessee, between 1885 and 1888, and for two summers after his sophomore year, he taught public school attended by African American students in Wilson County, Tennessee. It was during this time that he encountered religious services of the Black folk.

4. Thomas Brothers, "Ideology and Aurality in the Vernacular Traditions of African-American Music (ca. 1890–1950)," *Black Music Research Journal* 17, no. 2 (Autumn 1997): 179.

5. Drake and Cayton, *Black Metropolis*, 636–46.

6. Nina Sun Eidsheim, "Voice as a Technology of Selfhood: Towards an Analysis of Racialized Timbre and Vocal Performance" (PhD diss., University of California, 2008), 42, 64, 69, 116.

7. Drake and Cayton, *Black Metropolis*, 526–715.

8. Based on interviews I conducted with University of Florida Gospel Choir singers in 2014.

9. Samuel A. Floyd Jr., "Black American Music and Aesthetic Communication," *Black Music Research Journal* 1 (1980): 3.

10. William Howland Kenney, *Recorded Music in American Life: The Phonograph and Popular Memory, 1890–1945* (New York: Oxford University Press, 1999), xvii–xviii.

NOTES   273

11. Kenneth R. Durham Jr., "The Longview Race Riot of 1919," *East Texas Historical Journal* 18, no. 2 (1980): 13–24.

12. Drake and Cayton, *Black Metropolis*, 65–76.

13. Du Bois, *Souls of Black Folk*; Allan H. Spear, *Black Chicago: The Making of a Negro Ghetto, 1890–1920* (Chicago: University of Chicago Press, 1967); Drake and Cayton, *Black Metropolis*; E. Franklin Frazier, *Black Bourgeoisie* (New York: Simon & Schuster, 1957); E. Franklin Frazier, *The Negro Church in America* (New York: Schocken Books, 1974); Lawrence W. Levine, *The Unpredictable Past: Explorations in American Cultural History* (New York: Oxford University Press, 1993); Lawrence W. Levine, *Black Culture and Black Consciousness: Afro-American Folk Thought from Slavery to Freedom* (Oxford: Oxford University Press, 2007); and Hortense Powdermaker, *After Freedom: A Cultural Study in the Deep South* (Madison: University of Wisconsin Press, 1993).

14. Brackette F. Williams and Drexel G. Woodson, introduction to Powdermaker, *After Freedom*, xxi–xxii, xxvii–xxviii. Powdermaker explains that class was based not only on economic standing but on patterns of behavior and conduct.

15. See Drake and Cayton, *Black Metropolis*, 673. Drake and Cayton explained that Black churches in Chicago in the 1920s included "mixed" churches that adhered to both formal, ritualistic patterns and traditional patterns of emotional demonstrativeness.

16. Drake and Cayton, *Black Metropolis*, 521.

17. Du Bois publicly denounced Washington in "Of Mr. Booker T. Washington and Others," in *Souls of Black Folk*.

18. Kevin K. Gaines, *Uplifting the Race: Black Leadership, Politics, and Culture in the Twentieth Century* (Chapel Hill: University of North Carolina Press, 1996), xiv–xv.

19. Gaines, *Uplifting the Race*, 74.

20. However, there may have been some Black singers who were attracted to the vocal styles of the dominant society and practiced these styles independent of cultural pressures.

21. Gaines, *Uplifting the Race*, 2–3.

22. Gaines, *Uplifting the Race*, 6.

23. Spear, *Black Chicago*, 51.

24. Spear, *Black Chicago*, 53. The Black church as an independent entity has long been the subject of scholarly debates. For clarity and consistency, I have chosen to identify with Southern, Raboteau, Frazier, and others who recognize the church in this framework.

25. Booker T. Washington, "My View of Segregation Laws," in *Let Nobody Turn Us Around: An African American Anthology*, ed. Manning Marable and Leith Mullings (Lanham, MD: Rowman & Littlefield, 2009), 179.

26. Gaines, *Uplifting the Race*, 3.

27. Robert T. Kerlin, *The Voice of the Negro: 1919* (New York: Arno Press, 1968), 1.

28. Kerlin, *Voice of the Negro*, ix.

29. *Memphis Times*, quoted in Kerlin, *Voice of the Negro*, 11.

30. George C. Anderson (The Wayfarer), "The Negro and the Stage," in Kerlin, *Voice of the Negro*, 166.

31. James M. Trotter, *Music and Some Highly Musical People* (Boston: Lee and Shepard Publishers, 1880), 94, 96, 347.

32. See Trotter, *Music and Some Highly Musical People*, 1878; and *The Negro Music Journal* 1–2 (1902–1903).

274 NOTES

33. Alain Locke, ed., *The New Negro: Voices of the Harlem Renaissance* (1925; New York: Touchstone, 1992), 10.

34. Gaines, *Uplifting the Race*, xv.

35. Lawrence Schenbeck, *Racial Uplift and American Music: 1878–1943* (Jackson: University Press of Mississippi, 2012), 7.

36. Ronald Radano, "Soul Texts and the Blackness of Folk," *Modernism/Modernity* 2, no. 1 (January 1995): 74.

37. See numerous examples in Dena J. Epstein, *Sinful Tunes and Spirituals: Black Folk Music to the Civil War* (Urbana: University of Illinois Press, 2003); and Daniel Alexander Payne, *Recollections of Seventy Years* (Nashville: Publishing House of the A.M.E. Sunday School Union, 1888), 254–55.

38. Evelyn Brooks Higginbotham, "Rethinking Vernacular Culture: Black Religion and Race Records in the 1920s and 1930s," in *The House That Race Built*, ed. Wahneema Lubiano (New York: Pantheon Books, 1997), 164.

39. Citations of historical material will employ the terms used in the original.

CHAPTER 1: REV. A. W. NIX HISTORICAL BACKGROUND

1. United States Bureau of the Census, Tenth Census of the United States, 1880, Rusk County, Texas, Enumeration District No. 75, sheet 89. The Rusk County census does not specify if William Nix owned land.

2. United States Bureau of the Census, Twelfth Census of the United States, 1900, Gregg County, Texas, sheet 3. The 1900 Gregg County census specifies that William Nix was a landowner in Justice Precinct No. 2, Supervisor's District 7, Enumeration District 33. The 1910 Gregg County, Texas, Population Census, 1910, sheet 10, reports William and Ida as residing on The Airline Road in Justice Precinct No. 2, Enumeration District 4.

3. United States Bureau of the Census, Census of the United States 1870, Barnwell County, South Carolina, sheet 7.

4. "Negro Preacher Dead," *Longview News-Journal*, January 25, 1927, 1.

5. Gregg County Record of Deeds, Book Q, 125–27.

6. Thad Sitton, "Freemen's Settlements," in *Handbook of Texas Online*, accessed August 18, 2017, http://www.tshaonline.org/handbook/online/articles/uef20.

7. Christopher Long, "The Ridge, TX," in *Handbook of Texas Online*, accessed August 18, 2017, http://www.tshaonline.org/handbook/online/articles/hrtfg.

8. Van Craddock, *Longview* (Charleston, SC: Arcadia, 2010), 7, 9.

9. Craddock, *Longview*, 28.

10. Craddock, *Longview*, 30.

11. Genester Nix, interview by author, Philadelphia, May 23, 2017.

12. Genester mentioned to me that her brother had told her that Ida was Native American. Thus, she based her assumptions on his comments and Ida's physical features. Genester Nix, telephone interview by author, June 1, 2020.

13. Genester Nix, interview by author, Philadelphia, May 24, 2017. I found no newspaper articles that mentioned Emma's name, so it is possible that she only sang in local churches.

14. "William Nix, Jr.," *New York Age*, September 27, 1919, 7.

NOTES 275

15. *Baptist Rival* (Ardmore, Oklahoma), August 18, 1909, 1.

16. "William Nix, Jr.," 7.

17. United States Bureau of the Census, Fourteenth Census of the United States, 1920, Cook County, Illinois, District 5.

18. There were three Emma Nixes in the Nix family: the daughter of William Sr. and Ida; the wife of William Jr.; and the daughter of William Jr.

19. This performance will be discussed in more detail at the end of this chapter.

20. "Notice to Music Lovers," *Longview News-Journal*, June 29, 1926, 4.

21. The 1930 census lists William as being forty-eight years of age and Pauline as being thirty-seven. The 1940 census lists William as being sixty-two years of age and Pauline as being forty-three. Thus, she was either eleven or nineteen years his junior.

22. *Monrovia New-Post*, January 13, 1934, 2.

23. Genester Nix, personal biography. Twelve is a typical age for young boys in the country to be taken to a revival and be "saved" for baptism.

24. Levine, *Black Culture and Black Consciousness*, 240.

25. "Rev. Adrew [*sic*] Nix Death a Shock," *Christian Review* 35, no. 23 (January 13, 1949): 1.

26. Elizabeth Dowling Taylor, *The Original Black Elite: Daniel Murray and the Story of a Forgotten Era* (New York: HarperCollins, 2017), 129.

27. *Horton Headlight-Commercial*, April 23, 1908, 5.

28. Thomas C. Cox, *Blacks in Topeka, Kansas, 1865–1915: A Social History* (Baton Rouge: Louisiana State University Press, 1982), 180.

29. No information has been located about Reverend Nix's first wife.

30. *Topeka Plaindealer*, September 10, 1909.

31. Elwood Nix, interview by author, Philadelphia, May 24, 2017. This is a traditional folktale and may not be fact as it relates to Nix.

32. Elwood Nix and Genester Nix, interview by author, Philadelphia, May 24, 2017.

33. Tabernacle Baptist Church, anniversary book, 1936.

34. "Rev. Adrew [*sic*] Nix Death a Shock," 1.

35. Lawrence H. Williams, *A History of Simmons University: "Ole State University," 1873–1930* (Earlington, KY: General Association of Kentucky Baptists, 1977), 13.

36. General Association of Colored Baptists in Kentucky, *Minutes of the Forty-Third Annual Session of the General Association of Colored Baptists in Kentucky*, 1911, 4, Simmons College of Kentucky Collection, University of Louisville, http://digital.library.louisville.edu/cdm/landingpage/collection/simmons.

37. Catalogue of State University (1908–1909), 9, Simmons College of Kentucky Collection, University of Louisville, http://digital.library.louisville.edu/cdm/landingpage/collection/simmons.

38. General Association of Colored Baptists in Kentucky, *Minutes of the Forty-Sixth Annual Session of the General Association of Colored Baptists in Kentucky*, 1914, 51, Simmons College of Kentucky Collection, University of Louisville, http://digital.library.louisville.edu/cdm/landingpage/collection/simmons.

39. General Association, *Minutes of the Forty-Sixth Annual Session*, 54.

40. General Association, *Minutes of the Forty-Third Annual Session*, 11–12.

41. General Association, *Minutes of the Forty-Third Annual Session*, 12.

42. Donna Loftus, "The Rise of the Victorian Middle Class," BBC, accessed October 16, 2016, http://www.bbc.co.uk/history/british/victorians/middle_classes_01.shtml.

43. General Association, *Minutes of the Forty-Sixth Annual Session*, 54.

44. Eileen Southern, *The Music of Black Americans: A History*, 3rd ed. (New York: W. W. Norton, 1997), 453–54.

45. Payne, *Recollections of Seventy Years*, 254–55.

46. Part of this section on Griggs is taken from my paper presented at the 2015 Society for Ethnomusicology conference.

47. "Rev. Sutton E. Griggs, A.M., B.D.," *Alexander's Magazine* 2, no. 4 (August 15, 1906): 8.

48. Wilson J. Moses, "Literary Garveyism: The Novels of Reverend Sutton E. Griggs," *Phylon* 40, no. 3 (3rd Qtr., 1979): 204.

49. W. E. B. Du Bois, "The Negro in Literature and Art," *The Annals of the American Academy of Political and Social Science* 49, The Negro's Progress in Fifty Years (September 1913): 236.

50. Moses, "Literary Garveyism," 203n.

51. Sutton E. Griggs, *Imperium in Imperio* (Cincinnati: The Editor Publishing Co., 1899), 62.

52. Fleetwood Ball, "Southern Baptist Convention," *Baptist and Reflector* 25, no. 40 (May 20, 1915): 9.

53. David M. Tucker, *Black Pastors and Leaders: Memphis, 1819–1972* (Memphis: Memphis State University Press, 1975), 79.

54. Tucker, *Black Pastors and Leaders*, 81.

55. Tucker, *Black Pastors and Leaders*, 72.

56. Thomas Oscar Fuller, *History of the Negro Baptists of Tennessee* (Memphis, 1936), 76–77, quoted in Steven C. Tracy, "Saving the Day: The Recordings of the Reverend Sutton E. Griggs," *Phylon* 47, no. 2 (2nd Qtr., 1986): 159.

57. Discography of American Historical Recordings, accessed October 2, 2015, http://adp.library.ucsb.edu/index.php/talent/detail/25186/Griggs_Sutton_E._Rev._author.

58. Paul Oliver, *Songsters & Saints: Vocal Traditions on Race Records* (Cambridge, UK: Cambridge University Press, 1984), 146.

59. Rev. C. H. Parrish, ed., *Golden Jubilee of the General Association of Colored Baptists in Kentucky: The Story of 50 Years' Work From 1865–1915* (Louisville: Mayes Printing Company, 1915), 164.

60. State University, founded in 1879, was originally named the Kentucky Normal and Theological Institute in Louisville. Its current name is Simmons College of Kentucky.

61. Catalogue to State University (1908–1909), 1.

62. Booker T. Washington, "Atlanta Exposition Address," in *Let Nobody Turn Us Around: An African American Anthology*, ed. Manning Marable and Leith Mullings (Lanham, MD: Rowman & Littlefield, 2009), 175.

63. Manning Marable and Leith Mullings, "Booker T. Washington and the Politics of Accommodation," in Marable and Mullings, *Let Nobody Turn Us Around: An African American Anthology*, 119.

64. Catalogue to State University (1908–1909), 23.

65. Catalogue to State University (1908–1909), 35.

66. Catalogue to State University (1914–1915), 29–30.

67. Catalogue to State University (1913–1914), 25.

68. Catalogue to State University (1908–1909), 23.

69. General Association, *Minutes of the Forty-Sixth Annual Session*, 42, 44.

NOTES

70. Parrish, *Golden Jubilee*, 102. This photo attributes Nix with a D.D. degree (Doctor of Divinity); however, in actuality he graduated with a Bachelor of Divinity degree (B.D.), and no evidence has been found of an honorary Doctor of Divinity degree.

71. First Baptist Church Georgetown, accessed June 2, 2017, http://www.fbcgeorgetown-ky.org/about-us.html.

72. General Association of Colored Baptists in Kentucky, *Minutes of the Forty-Fourth Annual Session of the General Association of Colored Baptists in Kentucky*, 1912, 71.

73. Parrish, *Golden Jubilee*, 218.

74. Parrish, *Golden Jubilee*, 32, 36–37, 50, 52.

75. Genester Nix, interview by author, Philadelphia, May 23, 2017.

76. 1240 Buena Vista Street, N.S., Pittsburgh, PA.

77. Andrew's mother and wife were both named Ida.

78. "Keep Your Mouth Shut, Please!," *Chicago Defender (Big Weekend Edition)*, March 24, 1917, 10.

79. "Some Don'ts," *Chicago Defender (Big Weekend Edition)*, May 17, 1919, 20.

80. Spear, *Black Chicago*, 139.

81. Marable and Mullings, *Let Nobody Turn Us Around*, 118.

82. Spear, *Black Chicago*, 132, 140.

83. "Freezing to Death in the South," *Chicago Defender (Big Weekend Edition)*, February 24, 1917, 1.

84. Robert Lee Sutherland, "An Analysis of Negro Churches in Chicago" (PhD diss., University of Chicago, 1930), 16.

85. Durham, "Longview Race Riot of 1919," 1.

86. "Police Work to Keep Lynching a Secret," *Chicago Defender*, July 5, 1919, 2.

87. Durham, "Longview Race Riot of 1919," 10.

88. Spear, *Black Chicago*, 11, 184, 201.

89. Chicago Commission, *Negro in Chicago*, 140, 93.

90. Spear, *Black Chicago*, 211.

91. Sutherland, "Analysis of Negro Churches," 16.

92. Spear, *Black Chicago*, 221–22.

93. I concluded that Nix remained in New York at Mt. Moriah until 1923 based on evidence from newspaper articles. In an article in the *New York Age* on December 2, 1922, Rev. A. W. Nix was named as "state evangelist," which confirms that he was living in the New York area at this time. By June 1923, his first child was born in Chicago. Thus, he and Ida probably moved from New York to Chicago between December 1922 and June 1923.

94. 1920 Census Map, accessed August 25, 2017, www.alookatcook.com.

95. United States Bureau of the Census, Fifteenth Census of the United States, 1930, Cook County, Illinois, 13th Precinct, Enumeration District 16–901, Supervisor's District 6, sheet 9A. The Nix family rented their portion of the house for $30 per month.

96. United States Bureau of the Census, Fourteenth Census, 1920, Cook County, Illinois, District 5.

97. "Rambling about Chicago: Items of Interest All around Town," *Chicago Defender (Big Weekend Edition)*, June 18, 1910, 1.

98. Drake and Cayton, *Black Metropolis*, 12.

99. James N. Gregory, *The Southern Diaspora: How the Great Migrations of Black and White Southerners Transformed America* (Chapel Hill: University of North Carolina Press, 2005), 115.

100. Ace, "On the Stroll by Ace," *Chicago Defender*, December 7, 1929, 7.

101. Gregory, *Southern Diaspora*, 137–38.

102. I have not been able to locate information about Mt. Olive Baptist Church in Chicago.

103. "A Brief History of the Life of Our Pastor, Rev. A. W. Nix," Anniversary Book, Tabernacle Baptist Church, Pittsburgh, Pennsylvania, 1936.

104. "Brief History of the Life of Our Pastor."

105. *Chicago Defender*, May 24, 1924, 14.

106. Genester Nix, interview by author, Philadelphia, May 23, 2017.

107. The negative economic effects of the Great Depression are obvious when one considers the reduction in price of Vocalion records from the initial price of seventy-five cents in 1925 to thirty-five cents by 1934. This lower price was maintained until the end of the 1930s. See Steven Lasker, "What Price Records? The U.S. Record Industry and the Retail Price of Popular Records, 1925–1950," accessed June 2, 2017, http://www.vjm.biz/new_page_11.htm. In 1934, Brunswick Radio Corporation sold its three offices and factories in New York and Chicago to the Decca label "as is" for $60,000. See Ross Laird, *Brunswick Records: A Discography of Recordings, 1916–1926* (Westport, CT: Greenwood Press, 2001), vol. 1, 13. The sale of Vocalion to Warner Bros. and then ARC, followed by a substantial reduction in the cost of the records, and the sale of their physical holdings in New York and Chicago demonstrate the possible effects of the Great Depression on the Vocalion label.

108. Trinity Home Services: Olivet Institutional Baptist Church, accessed June 2, 2017, http://www.trinityhomeservices.com.

109. Anniversary Book, Tabernacle Baptist Church.

110. Genester Nix, interview by author, Philadelphia, May 23, 2017.

111. "Rev. Verolga Nix Allen, 81, World-Class Pianist, Chorale Director," *Philadelphia Tribune*, December 19, 2014, accessed June 19, 2017, http://www.phillytrib.com/obituaries/rev-verolga-nix-allen-world-class-pianist-chorale-director/article_e1c1d8b4–30d1–59c0–97d9–3400b798ca0d.html.

112. Eileen Southern, "Hymnals of the Black Church," *The Black Perspective in Music* 17, no. 1–2 (1989): 163.

113. Genester Nix, interview by author, Philadelphia, May 23, 2017.

114. Genester Nix, interview by author, Philadelphia, May 23, 2017.

115. Genester Nix, interview by author, Philadelphia, May 23, 2017.

116. Genester Nix, personal biography.

117. Genester Nix, interview by author, Philadelphia, May 23, 2017.

118. Genester Nix, email message to author, October 25, 2017.

119. Spear, *Black Chicago*, 140, 142–50.

120. Genester stated that her father earned $40 per week ($2080 per year) when she was in college in the 1940s.

121. Sutherland reports that the average two-income family earned approximately $150 per month ($1800 per year). See Sutherland, "Analysis of Negro Churches," 104.

122. Most new migrants to Chicago accepted employment in the manufacturing sector as laborers, earning on average $25 per week, or $1,300 per year. See Spear, *Black Chicago*, 157.

123. Genester Nix, personal biography.

NOTES

124. *Christian Review* 35, no. 23 (January 13, 1949): 1.

125. Genester Nix claimed that Lincoln University intended to grant Reverend Nix an honorary doctorate; however, he died before this took place.

126. Genester Nix, interview by author, Philadelphia, May 23, 2017.

127. Elwood Nix, interview by author, Philadelphia, May 24, 2017.

128. "Rev. Adrew [*sic*] Nix Death a Shock," 1.

129. Sources that either misidentify Andrew as the singer at the convention or provide erroneous information about him include Southern, *Music of Black Americans*, 460; Oliver, *Songsters and Saints*, 150–51; Michael W. Harris, *The Rise of Gospel Blues: The Music of Thomas Andrew Dorsey in the Urban Church* (New York: Oxford University Press, 1992), 156; and Jonathan L. Walton, "The Preachers' Blues: Religious Race Records and Claims of Authority on Wax," *Religion and American Culture: A Journal of Interpretation* 20, no. 2 (Summer 2010): 207–8.

130. Jim O'Neal and Amy O'Neal, "Georgia Tom Dorsey," *Living Blues* 20 (March/April 1975): 29.

131. Harris, *Rise of Gospel Blues*, 156.

132. Oliver, *Songsters and Saints*, 150–51.

133. Robert Dixon, John Godrich, and Howard Rye, *Blues and Gospel Records: 1890–1943*, 4th ed. (Oxford, UK: Clarendon Press, 1997), 881–82.

134. Genester Nix, interview with author, April 30, 2017. Genester claimed that it was the song "I Know a Great Savior," sung by her father at the National Baptist Convention, that inspired Dorsey to write gospel music.

135. "Hear Rev. Nix," *Chicago Defender (Big Weekend Edition)*, February 21, 1920, 13.

136. William (W. M.) Nix Jr. also served on the Sunday School Publishing Board that published *The Baptist Standard Hymnal with Responsive Readings: A New Book for All Services* (Nashville: Sunday School Publishing Board, 1924).

137. Music Committee of the Sunday School Publishing Board, *Gospel Pearls* (Nashville: Sunday School Publishing Board, National Baptist Convention, 1921).

138. Southern, "Hymnals of the Black Church," 162.

139. Southern, *Music of Black Americans*, 281–82.

140. National Baptist Convention of the United States of America, *Proceedings of the Forty-First Annual Session of the National Baptist Convention: Held with the Baptist Churches, 1921*, 136, 211, 217, 332.

141. National Baptist Convention, *Proceedings*, 136.

142. Music Committee, Preface, *Gospel Pearls*.

143. Harris, *Rise of Gospel Blues*, 68.

144. Harris, *Rise of Gospel Blues*, 69.

145. Dorsey, quoted in Harris, *Rise of Gospel Blues*, 68–70.

146. O'Neal and O'Neal, "Georgia Tom Dorsey," 23.

147. Harris, *Rise of Gospel Blues*, 70–71.

148. Harris, *Rise of Gospel Blues*, 214–15, 219–20.

149. It is unclear if this was Dorsey's model for a singer or Harris's interpretation.

150. Harris, *Rise of Gospel Blues*, 152–53.

151. O'Neal and O'Neal, "Georgia Tom Dorsey," 30.

152. Harris, *Rise of Gospel Blues*, 163. Harris describes "gospel blues" as Dorsey's religious compositions fused with blues idioms; see 76, 96.

153. Elwood Nix, interview by author, Philadelphia, May 24, 2017.

154. Genester Nix, interview by author, Philadelphia, May 27, 2017.

155. O'Neal and O'Neal, "Georgia Tom Dorsey," 19.

156. Thomas A. Dorsey lived at 27th and Dearborn Streets. See O'Neal and O'Neal, "Georgia Tom Dorsey," 21.

157. Rev. D. C. Rice also recorded during this time period; however, Rice was a Sanctified preacher and minister of the Church of the Living God, Pentecostal on the East Side. See Oliver, *Songsters and Saints*, 180.

158. Georgia Tom (with Kansas City Kitty) and Rev. A. W. Nix both recorded in Chicago in November 1930. The masters are sequential, implying that they could have been recorded on the same date: Rev. A. W. Nix (C6468–6471), Kansas City Kitty & Georgia Tom (C6472–6473). The recordings prior to these were on October 30, 1930; the recordings after are dated November 2, 1930—thus, the Georgia Tom and Nix recordings probably took place on either October 31, 1930, or November 1, 1930. However, the date is listed as "November, 1930," thus most likely specifying November 1, 1930. See Ross Laird, *Brunswick Records: A Discography of Recordings, 1916–1931*, Vol. 3: Chicago and Regional Sessions (Westport, CT: Greenwood Press, 2001), 1170.

159. Oliver argues, "For the devout church member it was probably extremely difficult to bring himself to sing blues or blues-songs." Oliver, *Songsters and Saints*, 206.

160. Likely there was a friendship between Nix and Dorsey; however, novelty sermon topics were common and became popular in the very late 1920s and early 1930s.

161. Dorsey, quoted in Harris, *Rise of Gospel Blues*, 153.

162. Dorsey, quoted in Harris, *Rise of Gospel Blues*, 134.

163. Dorsey met Hall around 1930. Harris, *Rise of Gospel Blues*, 153, 171.

164. Harris, *Rise of Gospel Blues*, 171, 178.

165. "Nina Mae McKinney," American Film Institute, accessed June 11, 2018, http://catalog.afi.com/Catalog/PersonDetails/117815.

166. Donald Bogle, commentary on *Hallelujah*, directed by King Vidor (Metro-Goldwyn-Mayer, 1929), DVD (Warner Brothers Entertainment, 2013).

167. Bogle, commentary on *Hallelujah*.

168. Judith Weisenfeld, *Hollywood Be Thy Name: African American Religion in American Film, 1929–1949* (Berkeley: University of California Press, 2007), 23–24.

169. Earl A. Ballard, "N. Y. Critics See Race Insult in 'Hallelujah,'" *Afro-American Baltimore*, August 31, 1929, 8.

170. Ballard, "N. Y. Critics," 8.

171. Ballard, "N. Y. Critics," 8.

172. Eva Jessye, "The Truth about 'Hallelujah,'" *Afro-American, Baltimore*, July 26, 1930.

173. Jessye, "Truth about 'Hallelujah.'"

174. An example of the "frenzy" can be found in *Hallelujah*, https://youtu.be/GGyR_34_Ibg .https://youtu.be/GGyR_34_Ibg.

175. Bogle, commentary on *Hallelujah*.

176. Du Bois, quoted in Arthur Knight, *Disintegrating the Musical: Black Performance and American Musical Film* (Durham, NC: Duke University Press, 2002), 141.

177. "Movie Star Makes Record," *California Eagle*, May 18, 1930, 10.

178. Bogle, commentary on *Hallelujah*.

NOTES 281

179. King Vidor, "Another Negro Film: King Vidor Realizes Ambition by Making 'Hallelujah,' an Audible Picture," *New York Times*, June 2, 1929.

180. "Finding Screen Negroes: The Outstanding Role. A Happy Accident. Finding the Villain," *New York Times*, August 25, 1929, X6.

181. "Finding Screen Negroes."

182. *Plaindealer* 32, no. 11 (March 15, 1930): 5.

183. George D. Tyler, "All in a Week," *Chicago World* 11, no. 19 (June 29, 1929): 8. A "sweetback" is a man who exploits and/or lives off women, such as a pimp.

184. Ace, "'Hallelujah' Discloses Talents of Race Actors," *Chicago Defender (National Edition)*, February 1, 1930, 6.

185. Ace, "Dixie's Attitude Toward 'Hallelujah' May Affect Future of Race in Films," *Chicago Defender (National Edition)*, January 11, 1930, 6.

CHAPTER 2: CLASS DIVISIONS DURING THE MODERN ERA

1. Henry Louis Gates Jr. states that the largest percentage of racist images of African Americans occurred between 1880 and 1920. See Gates, "The Trope of a New Negro and the Reconstruction of the Image of the Black," *Representations* 24, Special Issue: America Reconstructed, 1840–1940 (Autumn 1988): 149–50.

2. "The 'New Crowd Negro' Making America Safe for Himself," *The Messenger* 2, no. 9 (September 1919): 17.

3. Philip V. Bohlman, *Music, Nationalism, and the Making of the New Europe*, 2nd ed. (New York: Routledge, 2011), 29.

4. Bohlman, *Music, Nationalism*, 29.

5. Throughout this study I refer to these vocal practices as "Black oral traditions," "traditional Black vocalisms," "vernacular," "Black vocalisms," and "Black folk traditions."

6. Gerald L. Davis, *I Got the Word in Me and I Can Sing It, You Know: A Study of the Performed African-American Sermon* (Philadelphia: University of Pennsylvania Press, 1985), 26.

7. Davis, *I Got the Word in Me*, 27, 30.

8. Brothers, "Ideology and Aurality," 180.

9. Levine, *Black Culture and Black Consciousness*, 158.

10. "Waist-Deep in Death," in *God Struck Me Dead: Voices of Ex-Slaves*, ed. Clifton H. Johnson (Cleveland, OH: Pilgrim Press, 1969), 165.

11. "More Than Conqueror," in *God Struck Me Dead: Voices of Ex-Slaves*, 171.

12. Albert J. Raboteau, *Canaan Land: A Religious History of African Americans* (Oxford, UK: Oxford University Press, 2001), 46.

13. Henry H. Mitchell, "African-American Preaching," *Interpretation* 51, no. 4 (October 1997): 371.

14. Ronald Radano, *Lying Up a Nation: Race and Black Music* (Chicago: University of Chicago Press, 2003), 118.

15. Raboteau, *Canaan Land*, 17.

16. Walter F. Pitts Jr., *Old Ship of Zion: The Afro-Baptist Ritual in the African Diaspora* (New York: Oxford University Press, 1993), 47.

17. Pitts, *Old Ship of Zion*, 64–65.

18. Albert J. Raboteau, *Slave Religion: The "Invisible Institution" in the Antebellum South* (Oxford, UK: Oxford University Press, 2004), 132–33, 178.

19. Raboteau, *Canaan Land*, 19, 21–22.

20. Dolan Hubbard, *The Sermon and the African American Literary Imagination* (Columbia: University of Missouri Press, 1994), 14.

21. Johnson, *God Struck Me Dead*, xxi.

22. Raboteau, *Canaan Land*, 235.

23. Albert J. Raboteau, *A Fire in the Bones: Reflections on African-American Religious History* (Boston: Beacon Press, 1995), 150.

24. Raboteau, *Slave Religion*, 236–37.

25. Alice Mabel Bacon, "Work and Methods of the Hampton Folklore Society," *The Black Perspective in Music* 4, no. 2, Bicentennial Number (July 1976): 153.

26. Powdermaker, *After Freedom*, 223.

27. Elizabeth Kilham, "Sketches in Color: Fourth," *Putnam's Magazine: Original Papers on Literature, Science, Art and National Interests* (1868–1870) 5, no. 27 (March 1870): 308.

28. Robert Russa Moton, quoted in Levine, *Black Culture and Black Consciousness*, 162.

29. Harriet Beecher Stowe, quoted in Levine, *Black Culture and Black Consciousness*, 163.

30. Payne, *Recollections of Seventy Years*, 254–55.

31. Albert J. Raboteau, Introduction, *God Struck Me Dead*, xxii.

32. Raboteau, *Canaan Land*, 103.

33. Ernest Hamlin Abbott, "Religious Life in America: IV. Religious Tendencies of the Negro," *Outlook* 69, no. 17 (December 1901): 1072.

34. Abbott, "Religious Life in America," 1071.

35. Abbott, "Religious Life in America," 1073.

36. Harris, *Rise of Gospel Blues*, 155.

37. Abbott, "Religious Life in America," 1071.

38. Drake and Cayton, *Black Metropolis*, 613.

39. Rev. L. K. Williams, "The Urbanization of Negroes: Effect on Their Religious Life," *Chicago Daily Tribune* (1923–1963), January 13, 1929, 12.

40. Sutherland, "Analysis of Negro Churches," 47.

41. Williams, "Urbanization of Negroes," 12.

42. Quoted in Dolinar, *Negro in Illinois*, 172–73.

43. Dolinar, *Negro in Illinois*, 77.

44. Frazier, *Negro Church in America*, 54, 57.

45. Williams and Woodson, introduction to Powdermaker, *After Freedom*, xxi–xxii, xxvii–xxviii.

46. Powdermaker, *After Freedom*, 67–68.

47. Spear, *Black Chicago*, 91.

48. Chicago Commission, *Negro in Chicago*, 144–45.

49. Chicago Commission, *Negro in Chicago*, 488.

50. "Some 'Don'ts,'" *Chicago Defender (Big Weekend Edition)*, May 17, 1919, 20.

51. Sutherland, "Analysis of Negro Churches," 4–7.

52. Dolinar, *Negro in Illinois*, 214.

53. Drake and Cayton, *Black Metropolis*, 530, 537–40, 611–52, 673–78.

54. Chicago Commission, *Negro in Chicago*, 475.

55. Chicago Commission, *Negro in Chicago*, 486.

56. I am referring to the "working class" as the "lower class" in keeping with Drake and Cayton's terminology of the time.

57. Drake and Cayton, *Black Metropolis*, 600.

58. Sutherland, "Analysis of Negro Churches," 57, 65.

59. Spear, *Black Chicago*, 96.

60. The Black Pentecostal movement, including the proliferation of storefront churches, really gathered steam following the Azusa Street Revival of 1907.

61. Drake and Cayton, *Black Metropolis*, 634.

62. Johnson, *God Struck Me Dead*, 2n.

63. Chicago Commission, *Negro in Chicago*, 146.

64. Bruce A. Rosenberg, *The Art of the American Folk Preacher* (New York: Oxford University Press, 1970), 30.

65. Genester Nix, email message to author, November 16, 2020.

66. Sutherland, "Analysis of Negro Churches," 71.

67. Levine, *Black Culture and Black Consciousness*, 179–80.

68. Drake and Cayton, *Black Metropolis*, 620–21.

69. Paul Oliver, Max Harrison, and William Bolcom, *The New Grove Gospel, Blues and Jazz with Spirituals and Ragtime* (New York: W. W. Norton, 1986), 196.

70. The quote is drawn from "Ellis" in Zora Neale Hurston, *Mules and Men* (1935; New York: HarperCollins, 1990), 22.]

71. Drake and Cayton, *Black Metropolis*, 653.

72. Drake and Cayton, *Black Metropolis*, 652.

73. Lucy Smith, quoted in American Folklife Center at the Library of Congress, *A Report on the Chicago Ethnic Arts Project* (Washington, DC: Library of Congress, 1978), 51.

74. Drake and Cayton, *Black Metropolis*, 650.

75. Drake and Cayton, *Black Metropolis*, 630.

76. Drake and Cayton, *Black Metropolis*, 672.

77. Gaines, *Uplifting the Race*, 90.

78. Elwood Nix, interview by author, Philadelphia, May 24, 2017.

79. Elwood Nix's comment is a generalized statement. Many jack-leg preachers were sincere and felt a calling to preach.

80. Drake and Cayton, *Black Metropolis*, 583.

81. Oliver, *Songsters and Saints*, 199–228.

82. Drake and Cayton, *Black Metropolis*, 630–31.

83. Drake and Cayton, *Black Metropolis*, 662, 663, 668.

84. Drake and Cayton, *Black Metropolis*, 689.

85. Drake and Cayton, *Black Metropolis*, 620.

86. Drake and Cayton, *Black Metropolis*, 674.

87. Frazier, *Negro Church in America*, 81.

88. Anthem spirituals are choral arrangements of the spirituals. See Harris, *Rise of Gospel Blues*, 106, 113–15, 188.

89. "Mt. Olive Baptist Church," *Pittsburgh Courier*, September 3, 1927, 9.

90. Genester Nix, email message to author, July 15–16, 2020.

91. Nix included some of this "intelligent" rhetoric with his references to Shakespeare and Greek philosophers and authors.

92. Drake and Cayton, *Black Metropolis*, 678, 682.

93. Traditional sermons also began in a calm (though not necessarily "intellectual") manner and transitioned to an emotional delivery.

94. Drake and Cayton, *Black Metropolis*, 671.

95. Spear, *Black Chicago*, 96.

96. Drake and Cayton, *Black Metropolis*, 671.

97. Spear, *Black Chicago*, 94. Drake and Cayton claim the upper classes were Congregationalists, Episcopalians, or Presbyterians; see *Black Metropolis*, 530.

98. Levine, *Black Culture and Black Consciousness*, 188.

99. James Weldon Johnson, *The Autobiography of an Ex-Colored Man* (1912; New York: Dover Publications, 1995), 86.

100. Langston Hughes, "The Negro Artist and the Racial Mountain," in Marable and Mullings, *Let Nobody Turn Us Around*, 255.

101. A. E. Perkins, "Negro Spirituals from the Far South," *Journal of American Folklore* 35, no. 137 (July–September 1922): 223–24.

102. Elwood Nix, interview by author, Philadelphia, May 24, 2017.

103. Sutherland, "Analysis of Negro Churches," 126.

104. Genester Nix, interview by author, Philadelphia, May 27, 2017.

105. Genester Nix, interview by author, Philadelphia, May 27, 2017.

106. Genester Nix, interview by author, Philadelphia, May 27, 2017.

107. David Beard and Kenneth Gloag, *Musicology: The Key Concepts* (London: Routledge, 2005), 109–10.

108. Leon Botstein, "Modernism," *Grove Music Online*, accessed May 3, 2018, https://doi-org .lp.hscl.ufl.edu/10.1093/gmo/9781561592630.article.40625.

109. Schenbeck, *Racial Uplift*, 56–61.

110. See Schenbeck, *Racial Uplift*; Samuel A. Floyd Jr., ed., *Black Music in the Harlem Renaissance: A Collection of Essays* (Knoxville: University of Tennessee Press, 1990); and Trotter, *Music and Some Highly Musical People*.

111. J. Hillary Taylor, "Music in the Home," *The Negro Music Journal* 1, no. 1 (September 1902): 10.

112. A. C., "Elizabeth Taylor Greenfield: A Sketch," *The Negro Music Journal* 1, no. 2 (October 1902): 18.

113. Clarence Cameron White, "The American Negro in Music," *The Negro Music Journal* 1, no. 5 (January 1903): 76.

114. *Daily Saratogian*, August 16, 1892, quoted in John Graziano, "The Early Life and Career of the 'Black Patti': The Odyssey of an African American Singer in the Late Nineteenth Century," *Journal of the American Musicological Society* 53, no. 3 (Autumn 2000): 571–72.

115. "Negroes as Singers," *The Negro Music Journal* 1, no. 9 (May 1903): 173.

116. Lennox Browne and Emil Behnke, *Voice, Song, and Speech: A Practical Guide for Singers and Speakers from the Combined View of Vocal Surgeon and Voice Trainer*, 2nd ed. (London: Sampson Low, Marston, Searle, and Rivington, 1884), 97.

117. Louis C. Elson, "Race Peculiarities in Singing," in *The Realm of Music: A Series of Musical Essays, Chiefly Historical and Educational*, 4th ed. (Boston: New England Conservatory of Music, 1900), 275.

118. S. S. Curry, *Mind and Voice: Principles and Methods in Vocal Training* (Boston: Expression Company, 1910), 149.

119. Harris, *Rise of Gospel Blues*, 154.

120. Lerone A. Martin, "Selling to the Souls of Black Folk: Atlanta, Reverend J. M. Gates, the Phonograph, and the Transformation of African American Protestantism and Culture, 1910–1945" (PhD diss., Emory University, 2005), 13, 30, 85, 92.

121. Angela Y. Davis, *Blues Legacies and Black Feminism: Gertrude "Ma" Rainey, Bessie Smith, and Billie Holiday* (New York: Vintage Books, 1998), 21–22.

122. Historically Black colleges, such as Fisk, Tuskegee, and Hampton, were often leading advocates of the spirituals—although in arranged form.

123. Gaines, *Uplifting the Race*, 77.

124. *Cleveland Gazette*, quoted in Gates, "Trope of a New Negro," 129.

125. S. Laing William, "The New Negro," quoted in Gates, "Trope of a New Negro," 148.

126. Gates, "Trope of a New Negro," 136.

127. Manning Marable and Leith Mullings, introduction to "Langston Hughes and the Harlem Renaissance," in *Let Nobody Turn Us Around*, 253.

128. Stephen Calt, "The Anatomy of a 'Race' Label, Part II," *78 Quarterly* 1, no. 4 (1989): 10.

129. Nathan Irving Huggins, *Harlem Renaissance* (New York: Oxford University Press, 1971), 14, quoted in Guthrie P. Ramsey Jr., *Race Music: Black Cultures from Bebop to Hip-Hop* (Berkeley: University of California Press, 2003), 112.

130. Ramsey, *Race Music*, 111.

131. Samuel A. Floyd Jr., *The Power of Black Music: Interpreting Its History from Africa to the United States* (New York: Oxford University Press, 1995), 134.

132. Rawn Spearman, "Vocal Concert Music in the Harlem Renaissance," in *Black Music in the Harlem Renaissance*, ed. Samuel A. Floyd Jr. (Knoxville: University of Tennessee Press, 1993), 44, 48.

133. Roland Hayes, quoted in Southern, *Music of Black Americans*, 411.

134. Jennifer Hildebrand, "'Two Souls, Two Thoughts, Two Unreconciled Strivings': The Sound of Double Consciousness in Roland Hayes's Early Career," *Black Music Research Journal* 30, no. 2 (Fall 2010): 292.

135. Floyd, *Black Music in the Harlem Renaissance*, 5.

136. Locke, *New Negro*, 5, 7.

137. Locke, *New Negro*, 15, 208.

138. Alain Locke, *The Negro and His Music* (Washington, DC: The Associates in Negro Folk Education, 1936), 130.

139. James Weldon Johnson, preface to *The Book of American Negro Poetry* (New York: Harcourt, Brace, and Company, 1922), vii.

140. James Weldon Johnson and J. Rosamond Johnson, *The Books of American Negro Spirituals* (1925; New York: Da Capo Press, 1969), 49–50.

141. Floyd, *Black Music in the Harlem Renaissance*, 13.

142. Paul Robeson, quoted in Floyd, *Black Music in the Harlem Renaissance*, 13.

143. Hughes, "Negro Artist," 257.

144. Race records were on the same labels as white artists' records and sold for the same prices.

145. Sarah Filzen, "The Rise and Fall of Paramount Records," *The Wisconsin Magazine of History* 82, no. 2 (Winter 1998–1999): 107.

146. Karl Hagstrom Miller, *Segregating Sound: Inventing Folk and Pop Music in the Age of Jim Crow* (Durham: Duke University Press, 2010), 159–60.

147. Tim Brooks, liner notes to *Lost Sounds: Blacks and the Birth of the Recording Industry, 1891–1922*, CD-ROM (Champaign, IL: Archeophone Records, 2011), 6–7.

148. Tim Brooks, *Lost Sounds: Blacks and the Birth of the Recording Industry, 1890–1919* (Urbana: University of Illinois Press, 2004), 40, 43.

149. Brooks, *Lost Sounds*, 7.

150. Miller, *Segregating Sound*, 159–60.

151. Kenney, *Recorded Music in American Life*, 46.

152. Kenney, *Recorded Music in American Life*, 51.

153. *Atlanta Constitution* (1881–1945), January 20, 1910, 5.

154. The Aeolian Company, *The Aeolian-Vocalion*, n.p.

155. *Atlanta Constitution*, 5.

156. Filzen, "Rise and Fall of Paramount Records," 108–9.

157. Kenney states that American companies issued at least 30,000 different 78 rpm records between 1900 and 1950—all marketed to foreign-born communities. Kenney, *Recorded Music in American Life*, 67.

158. Kenney, *Recorded Music in American Life*, 78, 114.

159. Expansion to Chicago took place in the 1920s. See Laird, *Brunswick Records*, vol. 3, ix, xiii.

160. Laird, *Brunswick Records*, vol. 3, ix, xiii.

161. Howard Taylor Middleton, "Concerning the Black Race and Blue Records," *Talking Machine World* 9, no. 9 (September 15, 1913): 26.

162. Middleton, "Concerning the Black Race and Blue Records," 26.

163. Brooks, liner notes to *Lost Sounds*, 7–8.

164. "Victor Records Made by Race Artists in Sight," *Chicago Defender (Big Weekend Edition)*, October 21, 1916, 5.

165. "Demands Records of Our Artists," *Chicago Defender*, November 11, 1916, 4.

166. Oliver, *Songsters & Saints*, 8.

167. Filzen, "Rise and Fall of Paramount Records," 110.

168. Kenney, *Recorded Music in American Life*, 114.

169. Locke, *New Negro*, xx.

170. Kenney, *Recorded Music in American Life*, 118.

171. Laird, *Brunswick Records*, vol. 3, xiv.

172. Drake and Cayton, *Black Metropolis*, 390–92.

173. "Famous Race Records" (advertisement), *Chicago Defender (National Edition)*, January 7, 1922, 6.

174. Filzen, "Rise and Fall of Paramount Records," 116.

175. Kenney, *Recorded Music in American Life*, 110.

176. Kenney, *Recorded Music in American Life*, 129.

177. *Phonograph and Talking Machine Weekly*, November 4, 1925, 1.

178. Kenney, *Recorded Music in American Life*, 129.

179. Calt, "Anatomy of a 'Race' Label," 17, 28.

180. Levine, *Black Culture and Black Consciousness*, 231.

181. Kenney, *Recorded Music in American Life*, xvi–xvii.

NOTES 287

182. Guthrie P. Ramsey Jr., "Secrets, Lies and Transcriptions: Revisions on Race, Black Music and Culture," in *Western Music and Race*, ed. Julie Brown (Cambridge, UK: Cambridge University Press, 2007), 35.

183. Alain Locke claims that Mamie Smith's "Crazy Blues" sold 75,000 in one month in 1920, while Rev. J. C. Burnett, as reported by Paul Oliver, sold 86,750 copies of "The Downfall of Nebuchadnezzar." See Locke, *New Negro*, xx; and Oliver, *Songsters & Saints*, 140.

CHAPTER 3: THE SERMONS

1. Laird, *Brunswick Records*, vol. 1, 2.

2. Laird, introduction to *Brunswick Records*, vol 3.

3. Laird, *Brunswick Records*, vol. 1, 7.

4. *Talking Machine World* (May 1926), quoted in Laird, *Brunswick Records*, vol. 1, 9.

5. Laird, *Brunswick Records*, vol. 1, 18.

6. Electrical recordings were made with a microphone rather than through a horn.

7. Ross Laird, email message to author, June 9, 2017.

8. "These Jobbers Have Been Appointed to Distribute the New Vocalion Records," *Talking Machine World* (June 1928): 13.

9. Oliver, *Songsters and Saints*, 140.

10. Dixon's records sold fairly well. Although sales figures are not available, the records are somewhat common among collectors. Rev. C. D. Montgomery also recorded in 1925, but his sermon was inexplicably released in the Columbia hillbilly series. Also, Rev. W. A. White's sermon was released on Paramount in 1925. All of these sermon records of 1925 (the first year of electrical recordings) sold fairly well, indicating a good reception by Black consumers, even though they didn't include spontaneous congregational responses. They were novelties, and there were few of them, so there was not much competition. Before 1925, the only records featuring Black performers were of comic sermons and parodies by popular artists (e.g., Bert Williams).

11. Genester Nix and Elwood Nix, interview by author, Philadelphia, May 24, 2017.

12. Oliver, *Songsters and Saints*, 145.

13. Martin, "Selling to the Souls of Black Folk," 2–3, 34, 90–92, 106, 212. Very few of the recorded Black preachers were actually living in rural locations, though they may have come from rural backgrounds or used a style with origins in the rural South.

14. Laird, *Brunswick Records*, vol. 1, 22.

15. Vocalion, among record labels, seems to have been especially prone to issue two-part and follow-up recordings, such as Tampa Red and Georgia Tom's "It's Tight like That," Leroy Carr and Scrapper Blackwell's "How Long–How Long Blues," and Speckled Red's "The Dirty Dozen."

16. Sutton E. Griggs, *Life's Demands or According to Law* (Memphis: National Public Welfare League, 1916), 51.

17. According to the Discography of American Historical Recordings, Griggs's sermons "Saving the Day" and "Self Examination" (Victor V-38516) sold 2,328 copies, while "A Hero Closes a War" and "A Surprise Answer to Prayer" (Victor 21706) sold 2,989 copies. See Discography of American Historical Recordings, s.v. "Victor V-38516 (10-in. double-faced "Race" series)," accessed June 8, 2020, https://adp.library.ucsb.edu/index.php/object/detail/31726/Victor_V-38516; and Discography of American Historical Recordings, s.v. "Victor 21706 (Black label (popular)

18-in. double-faced)," accessed June 8, 2020, https://adp.library.ucsb.edu/index.php/object/detail/19253/Victor_21706.

18. Amanda Weidman, "Gender and the Politics of Voice: Colonial Modernity and Classical Music in South India," *Cultural Anthropology* 18, no. 2 (May 2003): 194–232.

19. In *The Jazz Singer*, released in 1927, Al Jolson sang (or belted) in black face. Jolson attempted "authentic" renderings of Blackness through his burnt-cork makeup. This presents even more dilemmas when we consider that some middle-class Black people were assimilating to white culture, and here Jolson was appropriating Black culture.

20. Alan Young, *Woke Me Up This Morning: Black Gospel Singers and the Gospel Life* (Jackson: University Press of Mississippi, 1997), 190. A handful of recorded sermons were made on 12" discs of five minutes in length.

21. Most live sermons were typically around twenty minutes in length.

22. The following sermons included a congregation of five women: Vo 1170, Vo 1125, Vo 1156, Vo 1157, Vo 1158, and Vo 1159. The unissued recordings of "Generosity" and "Throwing Stones" included "four women and three guitars." The following sermons included a congregation of seven women: Vo 1421 and Vo 1431. The only sermons that included a male voice as part of the congregation were Vo 1486 (with Nina Mae McKinney), Vo 1553, and Vo 1578. It is unknown if the missing tracks included a male voice in the congregation.

23. Paul Oliver mentions that, in the fall of 1927, Rev. J. M. Gates's preaching format also changed from those that utilized Biblical texts to an "increasing directness to issues and the examples of the day" (*Songsters and Saints*, 160–62). Possibly Nix was influenced by Gates, or perhaps both men made the decision to change their formats based on current events of the day. Alain Locke's *The New Negro* was published in 1925, and possibly his theories were taking hold by 1927–1928. Also, topical blues about current events began to occur more frequently beginning in 1927 with the release of Bessie Smith's "Back-Water Blues" that year. It's possible that most of the traditional themes had already been recorded and the record companies encouraged new novelty topics.

24. David Evans, liner notes to *Rev. A. W. Nix and Rev. Emmett Dickinson*, Vol. 2, 1928–1931, Document Records, DOCD-5490, 2000.

25. Elwood Nix, interview by author, Philadelphia, May 24, 2017.

26. Elwood Nix, interview by author, Philadelphia, May 24, 2017.

27. "Black Diamond (train)," Wikipedia, accessed August 7, 2018, https://en.wikipedia.org/wiki/Black_Diamond_(train).

28. Robert Dixon and John Godrich, *Recording the Blues* (New York: Stein and Day, 1970), 56–57.

29. If we include the parts of "The White Flyer to Heaven" as an "answer" or response to "Black Diamond," then there would be a total of eight parts.

30. "'The Black Diamond Express to Hell' Is a Popular Record," *Pittsburgh Courier*, July 2, 1927, 2.

31. *The Talking Machine World* (July 1927): 90.

32. "'The Black Diamond Express to Hell' Is a Popular Record."

33. "The Biggest Selling Record of Today" (advertisement), *Chicago Defender (National Edition)*, October 1, 1927, 8.

34. "Display Ad 18," *Chicago Defender (National Edition)*, December 10, 1927, 6.

35. Genester Nix, interview by author, Philadelphia, May 25, 2017.

NOTES
289

36. Reverend Johnnie Blakey, who recorded on the Paramount label in the 1920s, was also known as a "Son of Thunder."

37. James Weldon Johnson, *God's Trombones: Seven Negro Sermons in Verse* (1927; New York: Viking Press, 1955), 2.

38. G. W. Harts, "Church News," *The Spokeman* 1, no. 8 (January 21, 1933): 8.

39. Rosenberg, *Art of the American Folk Preacher*, 14.

40. Pitts, *Old Ship of Zion*, 160.

41. Rosenberg, *Art of the American Folk Preacher*, 10.

42. There were a handful of five-minute sermon recordings by other ministers.

43. Davis, *I Got the Word in Me*, 56.

44. Raboteau, *Fire in the Bones*, 144.

45. Pitts, *Old Ship of Zion*, 140.

46. Regarding the text transcriptions: each sermon has been transcribed with separate lines designating the places in which Nix pauses or breathes between phrases. I have also placed letters (A, B, C, . . .) to represent separate "verses." For the musical selections within the sermons, I designated these as "songs," as a generalized term for sung music rather than the specifics of genre. The words to the right in italics are the responses by the "sisters." If the responses are discernible, I transcribed them literally; if not, I wrote "[speaking]" to demonstrate that multiple voices are speaking simultaneously and "[indecipherable]" if the words are not discernible at all. If one or more voices are singing, I designated it as "[singing]." However, if the "mystery spiritual" is being sung, I designated it as "[spiritual melody]." Singing may continue for multiple lines. Nix recorded a total of fifty-four records; however, two were retakes ("Generosity" and "Throwing Stones"), and one was unissued ("Deep Down in My Heart").

47. See Kathleen Morgan Drowne, *Spirits of Defiance: National Prohibition and Jazz Age Literature, 1920–1933* (Columbus: Ohio State University Press, 2005), 28.

48. Shinny is a type of moonshine. It is mentioned in Harper Lee's *To Kill a Mockingbird*: "Maycomb welcomed her. Miss Maudie Atkinson baked a Lane cake so loaded with shinny it made me tight." See Michael Bagnulo, "Loaded with Shinny: Lane Cakes & *To Kill a Mockingbird*," *Forbes*, June 29, 2010, https://www.forbes.com/sites/booze/2010/06/29/loaded -with-shinny-lane-cakes-to-kill-a-mockingbird/#62b9525c7fd9.

49. As in "mojo hand." See "Mojo: African-American Culture," Wikipedia, accessed February 10, 2018, https://en.wikipedia.org/wiki/Mojo_(African-American_culture).

50. See John Mason Brewer, *The Word on the Brazos: Negro Preacher Tales from the Brazos Bottoms of Texas* (Austin: University of Texas Press, 1953), 3–4. Brewer's informants claimed that the formerly enslaved persons who resided in the Brazos River Bottom area were considered by those residing in other parts of Texas to be "the most illiterate, humble, and mistreated Negroes in the state" and were commonly referred to as ignorant with comments such as "You mus' be from de Brazos Bottoms" or "You ack jes' lack a Brazos Bottom Nigguh."

51. "The Blood Done Signed My Name," Hymnary, accessed May 5, 2017, http://hymnary .org/hymn/HFS1939/d40.

52. Hymn written by Charles Austin Miles, c. 1905. This song is quoted in Sutherland, "Analysis of Negro Churches," 90.

53. The intersection of 47th and South Parkway was the theater district in Bronzeville, where the Metropolitan Theater, Regal Theater, and Savoy Ballroom all were located. See "47th Street/South Parkway District," JazzAgeChicago, accessed April 15, 2018, https://jazzagechicago

.files.wordpress.com/2015/12/47street_1945.pdf. South Parkway was changed to Martin Luther King Drive in 1940. See "Chicago Street Names," Chicagology, accessed April 15, 2018, https://chicagology.com/chicagostreets/streetnamechanges/.

54. Jeff Todd Titon, "Ethnomusicology of Downhome Blues Phonograph Records, 1926–1930" (PhD diss., University of Minnesota, 1970), 14.

55. The original song "It's Tight like That" by Georgia Tom and Tampa Red was so popular that it inspired many cover versions by other artists: Tampa Red's Hokum Jug Band, (October/November 1928); Tampa Red (as a solo artist) (January 16, 1929); Clara Smith (January 26, 1929); Southern Blues Singers (April 1, 1929); Slim Barton (c. May 1929); and Huddie Ledbetter (Leadbelly)'s version titled "Tight like That" (February 1935 and August 23, 1940). By the time of Nix's recording of his sermon in February 1930, there had already been released the original version plus five other versions. Nix stated that the song's subject was "famous" by beginning his recorded sermon "It Was Tight like That" with the verse: "My dear brothers and sisters, I'm going to speak to you this morning from this famous subject: It was tight like that."

56. OK is the abbreviation for OKeh Records (sometimes spelled Okeh).

57. James 2:14–17 (New King James Version).

58. "Riding" can be slang for sexual activity, as in the term "rider" meaning a lover.

59. BS and Pm are the abbreviations for Black Swan and Paramount Records, respectively. The words "How long" are also present in spirituals, such as "Before This Time Another Year (How Long Oh Lord, How Long?)" included in the hymnal *National Jubilee Melody Song Book* (Nashville: National Baptist Publishing Board, 1923) and recorded by Odette and Ethel (1926). *Slave Songs of the United States* contains a spiritual titled "My Father, How Long?" A multitude of blues songs with the "how long" theme were recorded prior to Nix's recording, including "How Long, How Long" by Blind Lemon Jefferson (1928), "How Long, Daddy, How Long" by Ida Cox (1925), and "How Long? How Long? (Absent Blues)" by Daisy Martin (1921).

60. Robert Darden, *Nothing But Love in God's Water: Black Sacred Music from the Civil War to the Civil Rights Movement*, vol. 1 (University Park: Pennsylvania State University Press, 2014), 149n40.

61. William Francis Allen, Charles Pickard Ware, and Lucy McKim Garrison, *Slave Songs of the United States* (1867; New York: P. Smith, 1951), 93.

62. Titon, "Ethnomusicology of Downhome Blues Phonograph Records," 14. The recording of "How Long, How Long Blues," consisting of only piano and acoustic guitar as accompaniment, led to the development of other recorded piano and guitar duos.

63. Samuel B. Charters, *The Country Blues* (New York: Rinehart & Company, 1959), 141.

64. Nix's first two parts of "Black Diamond Express to Hell" were recorded on April 23, 1927; Leroy Carr recorded his six parts on June 19, 1928, December 19, 1928 (two recordings), August 12, 1929 ("The New How Long, How Long Blues), January 16, 1931 ("The New How Long, How Long Blues—Part 2"), and March 15, 1932 ("How Long Has That Evening Train Been Gone"). Nix's "Black Diamond Express to Hell" records were each a two-part production, that is, a single sermon in two parts (sides). In a few cases, a single part could possibly stand alone as a sermon, but the records really should be conceived as one sermon in two parts. The second and third records were attempts to exploit the success of the first by introducing some original lyrics into a familiar format.

65. *Broad Ax* 7, no. 14 (January 25, 1902): 1.

66. William H. Pipes, *Say Amen, Brother! Old-Time Negro Preaching: A Study in American Frustration* (Detroit: Wayne State University Press, 1992), 118.

67. John W. Work, *American Negro Songs: 230 Folk Songs and Spirituals, Religious and Secular* (Mineola, NY: Dover Publications, 1998), 197.

68. This line is taken from Shakespeare's *Hamlet*, in which he states, "Something is rotten in the state of Denmark."

69. "Cat on the line" references Reverend Gates's sermon "Dead Cat on the Line" (3/18/1929 and 4/23/1930) and that by Rev. F. W. McGee (1/28/1930). There are also songs with this title in prewar blues, such as Tampa Red/Georgia Tom's "Dead Cats on the Line" (2/4/1932), and in postwar gospel recordings, such as those by Elder Charles Beck (1949) and Sister Lillie Mae Littlejohn (1947).

70. Tucker, *Black Pastors and Leaders*, 102.

71. Drake and Cayton, *Black Metropolis*, 613.

72. Edward L. Wheeler, *Uplifting the Race: The Black Minister in the New South, 1865–1930* (Lanham, MD: University Press of America, 1986), xiii.

73. Raboteau, *Canaan Land*, 25–26.

74. Payne, *Recollections of Seventy Years*, 5, 46, 76, 137, 169.

75. George W. Clinton, "To What Extent Is the Negro Pulpil [*sic*] Uplifting the Race?" in Culp, *Twentieth Century Negro Literature*, 115–6, quoted in Wheeler, *Uplifting the Race*, 23.

76. Wheeler, *Uplifting the Race*, 82.

77. Wheeler, *Uplifting the Race*, 30.

78. Kerlin, *Voice of the Negro*, 176.

79. Jerome Dowd, "Sermon of an Ante-Bellum Negro Preacher," *The Southern Workman* 30, no. 11 (November 1901): 657.

80. Genester Nix, interview by author, Philadelphia, May 23, 2017.

81. Rev. A. W. Nix, "Your Time Is Out," Document Records, DOCD 5328, 1995, CD.

82. J. Mason Brewer, *The Word on the Brazos: Negro Preacher Tales from the Brazos Bottoms of Texas* (Austin: University of Texas Press, 1953), 2.

83. As in "mojo hand." See note 46 in chapter 3.

84. Drake and Cayton, *Black Metropolis*, 561. See also Raboteau, *Slave Religion*, 276.

85. Davis, *Blues Legacies and Black Feminism*, 11.

86. Gaines, *Uplifting the Race*, 45.

87. Gaines, *Uplifting the Race*, 6.

88. Gaines, *Uplifting the Race*, 21.

89. Martin, "Selling to the Souls of Black Folk," 30.

90. Drake and Cayton, *Black Metropolis,* 608.

91. Drake and Cayton, *Black Metropolis,* 610.

92. Martin, "Selling to the Souls of Black Folk," 31.

93. Drake and Cayton, *Black Metropolis*, 642.

94. Dolinar, *Negro in Illinois*, 212.

95. Drake and Cayton, *Black Metropolis*, 643–44.

96. Dolinar, *Negro in Illinois*, 213.

97. Drake and Cayton, *Black Metropolis*, 470.

98. *The Negro Music Journal* 1, no. 12 (August 1903): 251.

292   NOTES

99. Evelyn Brooks Higginbotham, "The Black Church: A Gender Perspective," in *African American Religious Thought: An Anthology*, ed. Cornel West and Eddie S. Glaude Jr. (Louisville: Westminster John Knox Press, 2003), 188.

100. Drake and Cayton, *Black Metropolis*, 612.

101. Higginbotham, "The Black Church," 193, 199.

102. Elwood Nix, interview by author, Philadelphia, May 24, 2017.

103. Dolinar, *Negro in Illinois*, 176.

104. Drake and Cayton, *Black Metropolis*, 669.

105. Genester Nix, interview by author, Philadelphia, May 24, 2017.

106. Drake and Cayton, *Black Metropolis*, 689.

107. Gaines, *Uplifting the Race*, 1–2.

108. William Shakespeare, *Hamlet*, act 1, scene 4.

109. "There's Something Rotten in Denmark" also references Rev. F. W. McGee's recording "Dead Cat on the Line," Victor (V-38579-A), 1930.

110. Wheeler, *Uplifting the Race*, 28–30.

111. Wheeler, *Uplifting the Race*, 30, 37.

CHAPTER 4: VOCAL AND MUSICAL ANALYSIS

1. Some of the texts I reviewed are the following: E. A. McIlhenny, *Befo' de War Spirituals: Words and Melodies* (Boston: The Christopher Publishing House, 1933), 21; William Arms Fisher, ed., *Seventy Negro Spirituals* (Bryn Mawr, PA: Oliver Ditson Company, 1926), viii; Mary Allen Grissom, foreward to *The Negro Sings a New Heaven* (Chapel Hill: University of North Carolina Press, 1930), [ii]; Jon Michael Spencer, *Sacred Symphony: The Chanted Sermon of the Black Preacher* (New York: Greenwood Press, 1987), 1–5; Southern, *Music of Black Americans*, 454–55; Pipes, *Say Amen, Brother!*, 152; Harold Courlander, *Negro Folk Music, U.S.A.* (New York: Columbia University Press, 1963), 23; Brothers, "Ideology and Aurality," 173; Sandra Jean Graham, "Spiritual," Grove Music Online, accessed September 14, 2017, http://www.oxfordmu siconline.com.lp.hscl.ufl.edu/subscriber/article/grove/music/A2225625; Epstein, *Sinful Tunes and Spirituals*; Howard W. Odum, "Religious Folk-Songs of the Southern Negroes," *American Journal of Religious Psychology and Education* 3, no. 3 (July 1909); and James Weldon Johnson and J. Rosamond Johnson, *The Books of American Negro Spirituals* (1925; Cambridge, MA: Da Capo Press, 1969).

2. Graham, "Spiritual"; McIlhenny, *Befo' de War Spirituals*, 21; Fisher, *Seventy Negro Spirituals*, viii; Grissom, foreward to *Negro Sings a New Heaven*, [ii]; Spencer, *Sacred Symphony*, 1–5; Southern, *Music of Black Americans*, 454–55; Pipes, *Say Amen, Brother!*, 152; Courlander, *Negro Folk Music*, 23; Brothers, "Ideology and Aurality," 173; and Epstein, *Sinful Tunes and Spirituals*.

3. A survey of vocal characteristics and performance style in Epstein's *Sinful Tunes and Spirituals* reveals the predominance of certain features. I focused on the oral sounds of sing-ing, rather than the overall performance practices. For example, while the ring shout typically included singing, I did not include it in my survey as it was primarily a physical dance. I also did not include whether the singing was done in a major or minor key, but I did include men-tions of whether the singing was "joyous" or "plaintive," as these are performative qualities not necessarily based on key signature. The number of instances of singing practices totaled two

hundred. Based on these figures, I concluded that the most frequent mentions were monotone singing or chanting (15 percent), loudness (14 percent), melancholy or plaintive singing style (6 percent), the use of improvisation (6 percent), shouting or yelling (5.5 percent), and call-and-response (5.5 percent). Vocal timbres included shrill (3.5 percent), beautiful/pure/clear (3.5 percent), rough/strained/cracked/hard/heavy/hoarse (3 percent), sweet (1 percent), and nasal (1 percent). The timbres and vocal sounds considered unsatisfactory according to Western European standards—shrill, rough/strained/cracked/hard/heavy/hoarse, and nasal—together total 7.5 percent. Satisfactory timbres and vocal sounds—beautiful/pure/clear and sweet—together total 4.5 percent. Therefore, unsatisfactory vocal sounds were mentioned almost twice as often as those of satisfactory sounds.

4. Kilham, "Sketches in Color," 305.

5. Mary Boykin Chesnut, quoted in Levine, *Black Culture and Black Consciousness*, 28.

6. Elizabeth Ross Hite, quoted in Levine, *Black Culture and Black Consciousness*, 41.

7. Johnson, *God Struck Me Dead*, 88.

8. Jeannette Robinson Murphy, "The Survival of African Music in America," *Appletons' Popular Science Monthly* (September 1899): 664.

9. Drake and Cayton, *Black Metropolis*, 674.

10. The "ring shout" was also a known as the "holy dance" and is not the same as shouts or shouting. The ring shout was a dance in which participants formed a circle and moved in a counterclockwise manner while shuffling their feet. See Levine, *Black Culture and Black Consciousness*, 38.

11. Johnson, *God Struck Me Dead*, 11.

12. Elwood Nix, interview by author, Philadelphia, May 24, 2017.

13. Drake and Cayton, *Black Metropolis*, 672.

14. Pipes, *Say Amen, Brother!*, 77, 85.

15. Elwood Nix, interview by author, Philadelphia, May 24, 2017

16. Genester Nix, interview by author, Philadelphia, May 23, 2017.

17. Genester Nix, email message to author, March 25, 2018.

18. Elwood Nix, interview by author, Philadelphia, May 24, 2017.

19. Genester Nix, email message to author, February 24, 2018.

20. Elwood Nix and Genester Nix, interview by author, Philadelphia, May 24, 2017.

21. Elwood and Genester claimed the prayer band was composed of women only, who sat in the first two pews and always sang along. They met every Wednesday to "pray, hum, and sing, and have a good time." Another term for the prayer band is the "Amen Corner." According to David Evans, the "Amen Corner" is on the right front as one faces the preacher; opposite them, on the left, are the deacons. See Mellonee V. Burnim and Portia K. Maultsby, *African American Music: An Introduction*, 2nd ed. (New York: Routledge, 2015), 197.

22. "The Black Diamond Express to Hell—Part 4," *Rev. A. W. Nix & Rev. Emmett Dickinson*, Document Records, DOCD-5490, 2000.

23. Pavel Petrovich Svin'in, *Picturesque United States of America, 1811, 1812, 1813, Being a Memoir on Paul Svin'in, Russian Diplomatic Officer, Artist, and Author, Containing Copious Excerpts from His Account of His Travels in America with Fifty-Two Reproductions of Water Colors in His Own Sketch-Book* (New York: W. E. Rudge, 1930), 20.

24. Abbott, "Religious Life in America," 1070.

25. Du Bois, *Souls of Black Folk*, 116.

26. Natalie Curtis Burlin, "Negro Music at Birth," *The Musical Quarterly* 5, no. 1 (January 1919): 88.

27. Henry H. Mitchell, *Black Preaching: The Recovery of a Powerful Art* (Nashville: Abingdon Press, 1990), 90.

28. Courlander, *Negro Folk Music*, 25.

29. Quoted in Harris, *Rise of Gospel Blues*, 22.

30. Elwood Nix, interview by author, Philadelphia, May 24, 2017.

31. Courlander, *Negro Folk Music*, 25. While Nix typically extended his moans on the same pitch, some modern ministers include melismatic passages while chanting. See Pastor Nathan Simmons (https://youtu.be/oYGGMnnOdKg), who chants, shouts, and uses melismas and a gravelly vocal timbre.

32. Murphy, "Survival of African Music in America," 665.

33. Drake and Cayton, *Black Metropolis*, 625.

34. O'Neal and O'Neal, "Georgia Tom Dorsey," 24.

35. "Display Ad 10" (advertisement), *Chicago Defender (National Edition)*, November 19, 1927, ProQuest Historical Newspapers: Chicago Defender, 3. The blues songs "Friday Moan Blues" and "Wailing Blues" were also advertised by Brunswick/Vocalion alongside Reverend Nix's sermons.

36. Filzen, "Rise and Fall of Paramount Records," 116.

37. George Pinckard, *Notes on the West Indies, Including Observations Relative to the Creoles and Slaves of the Western Colonies and the Indians of South America; Interspersed with Remarks upon the Seasoning or Yellow Fever of Hot Climates*, 2nd ed., vol. 1 (London: Baldwin, Cradock, and Joy, 1816), 103.

38. Mechal Sobel, *Trabelin' On: The Slave Journey to an Afro-Baptist Faith* (Princeton, NJ: Princeton University Press, 1988), 195.

39. Letter from Rev. R. Q. Mallard to Mrs. Mary S. Mallard, Chattanooga, May 18, 1958, in *The Children of Pride*, ed. Robert Manson Myers (New Haven, CT: Yale University Press, 1972), 483, quoted in Portia K. Maultsby, "Africanisms in American Music," in *The African Presence in Black America*, ed. Jacob U. Gordon (Trenton, NJ: Africa World Press, 2004), 47–48.

40. Allen, Ware, and Garrison, *Slave Songs of the United States*, viii.

41. Kilham, "Sketches in Color," 306.

42. Du Bois, *Souls of Black Folk*, 116.

43. McIlhenny, *Befo' de War Spirituals*, 15.

44. Kilham, "Sketches in Color," 306.

45. "Keep Your Mouth Shut, Please!," 10.

46. Drake and Cayton, *Black Metropolis*, 538.

47. Chicago Commission, *Negro in Chicago*, 193.

48. Chicago Commission, *Negro in Chicago*, 302.

49. Drake and Cayton, *Black Metropolis*, 563.

50. Elwood Nix, interview by author, Philadelphia, May 24, 2017.

51. Jeff Todd Titon, "'Tuned Up with the Grace of God': Music and Experience among Old Regular Baptists," in *Music in American Religious Experience*, ed. Philip V. Bohlman, Edith L. Blumhofer, and Maria M. Chow (Oxford, UK: Oxford University Press, 2006), 319.

52. Johnson and Johnson, *Books of American Negro Spirituals*, 62–63.

53. Burlin, "Negro Music at Birth," 89.

54. "Negro Minstrelsy—Ancient and Modern," *Putnam's Monthly Magazine of American Literature, Science, and Art* (1853–1857) 5, no. 25 (January 1855): 78.

55. Courlander, *Negro Folk Music*, 23.

56. Abbott, "Religious Life in America," 1070.

57. Floyd, *Power of Black Music*, 80.

58. John Bennett, "A Revival Sermon at Little St. John's," *Atlantic Monthly* 98 (1906): 257.

59. Genester Nix, interview by author, Philadelphia, May 24, 2017.

60. John Laver, *The Phonetic Description of Voice Quality* (Cambridge, UK: Cambridge University Press, 1980), 9–10.

61. Spectrogram settings: Scale dBV^2; Window 2048, 75%.

62. Nicholas Cook and Daniel Leech-Wilkinson, "A Musicologist's Guide to Sonic Visualiser," CHARM, accessed December 19, 2017, http://charm.cch.kcl.ac.uk/redist/pdf/analysing_recordings.pdf, 14–15.

63. Cook and Leech-Wilkinson, "Musicologist's Guide to Sonic Visualiser," 16.

64. Scott A. Carter, "Forging a Sound Citizenry: Voice Culture and the Embodiment of the Nation, 1880–1920," *American Music Research Center Journal* 22 (2013): 21, 23.

65. Oliver, *Songsters and Saints*, 151.

66. *Harvard Concise Dictionary of Music*, s.v. "heterophony."

67. Spencer, *Sacred Symphony*, 1.

68. Andrew P. Watson, "Negro Primitive Religious Services," in Johnson, *God Struck Me Dead*, 5. Reportedly witnessed at a camp meeting in Nashville, in the summer of 1928; see page 3.

69. Clifton Joseph Furness, "Communal Music among Arabians and Negroes," *The Musical Quarterly* 16, no. 1 (January 1930): 49.

70. Peter Randolph, quoted in Raboteau, *Slave Religion*, 217.

71. John Mason Brown, "Songs of the Slave," *Lippincott's Magazine of Literature, Science, and Education* 2 (1868): 622.

72. Brothers, "Ideology and Aurality," 173.

73. Sidney Lanier, *The Science of English Verse* (New York: Charles Scribner's Sons, 1911), 276.

74. Lanier, *Science of English Verse*, 277.

75. Hubbard, *Sermon and the African American Literary Imagination*, 36.

76. Raboteau, *Fire in the Bones*, 142.

77. Davis, *I Got the Word in Me*, 95.

78. Davis, *I Got the Word in Me*, 7, 98–100.

79. Harris, *Rise of Gospel Blues*, 181.

80. Thomas Turino, *Music as Social Life: The Politics of Participation* (Chicago: University of Chicago Press, 2008), 26.

81. Turino, *Music as Social Life*, 4.

82. Turino, *Music as Social Life*, 26, 28–29.

83. Courlander, *Negro Folk Music*, 27.

84. Pitts, *Old Ship of Zion*, 160.

85. Hubbard, *Sermon and the African American Literary Imagination*, 35.

86. William E. Hatcher, quoted in Pipes, *Say Amen, Brother!*, 133.

87. Pipes, *Say Amen, Brother!*, 136.

88. Houston A. Baker Jr., "Completely Well: One View of Black American Culture," in *Key Issues in the Afro-American Experience*, ed. Nathan I. Huggins, Martin Kilson, and Daniel M. Fox (San Diego: Harcourt Brace Jovanovich, 1971), 30.

89. Pitts, *Old Ship of Zion*, 136.

90. Pipes, *Say Amen, Brother!*, 141, 133.

91. Odum, "Religious Folk-Songs," 301.

92. Grissom, foreward to *Negro Sings a New Heaven*, [ii].

93. Thomas Wentworth Higginson, *Army Life in a Black Regiment* (1869; Boston: Beacon Press, 1962), 133.

94. Thomas P. Fenner, *Cabin and Plantation Songs as Sung by the Hampton Students* (New York: G. P. Putnam's Sons, 1876), 216.

95. Perkins, "Negro Spirituals," 242.

96. Style-switching is also known as code switching.

97. Courlander, *Negro Folk Music*, 26.

98. Drake and Cayton, *Black Metropolis*, 675.

99. Genester Nix, email message to author, February 24, 2018.

100. Elwood Nix, interview by author, Philadelphia, May 24, 2017.

101. "Riding" can be slang for sexual activity, as in the term "rider" meaning a lover.

102. Rosenberg, *Art of the American Folk Preacher*, 42.

103. Spencer, *Sacred Symphony*, 5.

104. Pipes, *Say Amen, Brother!*, 74.

105. Raboteau, *Fire in the Bones*, 144.

106. Maultsby, "Africanisms in African American Music," 52.

107. James Kennard Jr. [aka Salt-Fish Dinner Correspondent], "Who Are Our National Poets?," *The Knickerbocker* 26, no. 4 (October 1845): 338.

108. Rosenberg, *Art of the American Folk Preacher*, 39.

109. Pitts, *Old Ship of Zion*, 61.

110. Rosenberg, *Art of the American Folk Preacher*, 39.

111. Sutherland, "Analysis of Negro Churches," 93.

112. According to the University of Pennsylvania, a "foot" of poetry is a "unit of rhythm" based on stresses and syllables. See "Rhythm and Meter in English Poetry," accessed November 8, 2018, http://www.writing.upenn.edu/~afilreis/88/meter.html.

113. Floyd, *Power of Black Music*, 6.

114. David Evans, liner notes to *Goodbye Babylon*, Dust-to-Digital, B0000DBOCB, October 27, 2003, 11.

115. The bluesman-preacher similarity was first suggested in 1966 by Charles Keil in *Urban Blues* (Chicago: University of Chicago Press, 1966), 143–48.

116. Harris, *Rise of Gospel Blues*, 154.

117. Scholars offer various explanations for the creation of the spirituals. For example, Mellonee Burnim writes that the spirituals were "music created and transmitted via the oral tradition" ("Spirituals," 51); Eileen Southern claims that they were created "by nonprofessional musicians, altered by other singers and passed along from one generation to the next by oral transmission" (*Music of Black Americans*, 184); and Lawrence Levine states that they were the result of "spontaneity" and "instantaneous community" (*Black Culture and Black Consciousness*, 25).

118. McIlhenny, *Befo' de War Spirituals*, 21–22.

119. Allen, Ware, and Garrison, *Slave Songs of the United States*, ii–xxxii.

120. Johnson and Johnson, *Books of American Negro Spirituals*, 49.

121. I retrieved genealogical evidence from the Rusk County, Texas, county clerk's office in which William Nix is listed as officiating at a wedding in 1890.

NOTES 297

122. I have concluded that Nix used the *National Jubilee Melody Song Book* for the following songs: "Free at Last," "I'm So Glad I Got My Religion in Time," "My Sins Are Taken Away," "O the Blood," and "Hide Me Over in the Rock of Ages."

123. *National Jubilee Melody Song Book*, 160.

124. Sources include the following: Odum, "Religious Folk-Songs"; Work, *American Negro Songs*; Johnson and Johnson, *Books of American Negro Spirituals*; Grissom, *Negro Sings a New Heaven*; A. E. Perkins, "Negro Spirituals from the Far South," *Journal of American Folklore* 35, no. 137 (July–September 1922): 223–49; McIlhenny, *Befo' de War Spirituals*; J. Jefferson Cleveland and Verolga Nix, eds., *Songs of Zion* (Nashville: Abingdon Press, 1981); Herbert J. Lacey, C. Austin Miles, and Maurice A. Clifton, eds., *New Songs of the Gospel No. 2: For Use in Religious Meetings* (New York: Hall-Mack Company, 1905); *National Jubilee Melody Song Book*; and Mrs. A. M. Townsend, ed., *The Baptist Standard Hymnal with Responsive Readings: A New Book for All Services* (Nashville: Sunday School Publishing Board, 1924). I also searched through the following historical songbooks: D. E. Dortch, *National Tidings of Joy* (Nashville: National Baptist Publishing Board, 1899); William Rosborough, *Celestial Showers, No. 1* (Nashville: National Baptist Publishing Board, 1895); D. E. Dortch and W. G. Cooper, *Pearls of Paradise: Part One: A Collection of the Song-Gems of the Ages, Containing Hymns and Music Suited for Every Service of the Christian Church* (Nashville: National Baptist Publishing Board, 1901); William Rosborough, *National Anthem Series: Prepared Especially for the Church Choirs and Young People's Meetings* (Nashville: National Baptist Publishing Board, 1906); Emmett S. Dean, *New Victory: For Christian Work and Worship* (Nashville: National Baptist Publishing Board, 1918); and D. E. Dortch, *Dortch's Gospel Voices: For Sunday Schools, Church Services, Gospel and Evangelistic Meetings, Young People's Societies, etc.* (Nashville: Southwestern Co., 1900). The National Baptist Publishing Board also published other songbooks directed towards the African American community that I could not locate; those included *Choice Songs, No. 1*; *National Harp of Zion*; *Celestial Showers, No. 2*; and *Golden Gems*. All of these songbooks are discussed in Duncan Eric Jackson, "A Survey of Hymnody Usage in Selected African American Baptist Churches in the State of Florida," PhD diss., Florida State University, 2009.

125. Cleveland and Nix, *Songs of Zion*.

126. The Black Diamond recordings were titled differently on the Vocalion label. The first two use Roman numerals and abbreviate the word "part," for example, "Black Diamond Express to Hell—Pt. I." Parts two through six use Arabic numerals, include the word "The," and write out the word "part," for example, "The Black Diamond Express to Hell—Part 3."

127. I have assigned the title "Nowhere to Hide" to this song because it is not included in any written source I have seen.

128. See Odum, "Religious Folk-Songs"; Work, *American Negro Songs*, 158; Perkins, "Negro Spirituals," 233–34; and McIlhenny, *Befo' de War Spirituals*, 67–69. John Lomax recorded a version of the song in 1939. See Library of Congress recording, accessed May 3, 2017, https://www.loc .gov/item/lomaxbib000409/. Other references to the song are posted at Fresno State, accessed May 3, 2017, http://www.fresnostate.edu/folklore/ballads/Ch085.html.

129. Odum, "Religious Folk-Songs," 302. Odum remarks on the multiple titles and chorus lines for this song, including "All My Sins Done Taken Away" and "All My Sins Taken Away."

130. *National Jubilee Melody Song Book*, 14, 37.

131. Grissom, *Negro Sings a New Heaven*, 64.

132. Grissom, foreword to *Negro Sings a New Heaven*, n.p.

133. Odum, "Religious Folk-Songs," 345.

134. Lacey, Miles, and Clifton, *New Songs of the Gospel*, 44. According to Hymnary.org, the hymn is available in thirty other hymnals. See Hymnary.org, accessed October 28, 2018, https://hymnary.org/text/when_you_get_to_heaven_as_you_surely_wil.

135. Hymnary.org, accessed October 28, 2018, https://hymnary.org/person/Miles_CAustin.

136. "I'm So Glad I Got My Religion in Time" in *National Jubilee Melody Song Book*, 25. The song sung by Nix is the same as the fourth verse of the song titled "Hush, Hush, Somebody's Callin' Mah Name" in Cleveland and Nix, *Songs of Zion*, 100, and *African-American Heritage Hymnal* (Chicago: GIA Publications, 2001), 556. The melodies and lyrics are the same in both songs; however, the song "Hush, Hush, Somebody's Callin' Mah Name" contains a refrain.

137. Dixon, Godrich, and Rye, *Blues and Gospel Records: 1890–1943*, 1058–59.

138. *Discography of American Historical Recordings*, s.v. "Victor matrix BVE-38994. Hush! Hush! Somebody's calling my name / Sandhills Sixteen," accessed November 27, 2020, https://adp.library.ucsb.edu/index.php/matrix/detail/800013256/BVE-38994-Hush_Hush_Somebodys_calling_my_name. This recording has the same title as the printed version in Cleveland and Nix, *Songs of Zion*.

139. *Discography of American Historical Recordings*, s.v. "OKeh matrix W400351. Hush! Somebody's calling my name / Mississippi Juvenile Quartette," accessed November 27, 2020, https://adp.library.ucsb.edu/index.php/matrix/detail/2000209120/W400351-Hush_Somebodys_calling_my_name. This recording has the same title as the printed version in Cleveland and Nix, *Songs of Zion*.

140. The recording notes state that Nix was "assisted by Sister Ida W. [*sic*] Nix." However, Genester Nix confirmed that the singer was not Ida Nix but a soloist from the choir. Genester Nix, email message to author, June 29, 2020.

141. Johnson and Johnson, *Books of American Negro Spirituals*, i, 167–69.

142. In his live preaching, Reverend Nix used singing as an introduction to his sermons. As Genester Nix explained, "my dad would sing before every sermon.... Just the part of one song. He wouldn't sing a whole song or anything like that. Something that pertained to the sermon." These songs were not part of the sermon, although there might have been a smooth transition from one genre to the other.

143. Wyatt Tee Walker, *Spirits That Dwell in Deep Woods: The Prayer and Praise Hymns of the Black Religious Experience* (New York: Martin Luther King Fellows Press, 1987), 1–2, 14–15, 17.

144. *Discography of American Historical Recordings*, s.v. "Victor matrix BVE-57730. Since I been born / Virginia Four," accessed November 27, 2020, https://adp.library.ucsb.edu/index.php/matrix/detail/800028613/BVE-57730-Since_I_been_born.

145. *Discography of American Historical Recordings*, s.v. "Decca matrix 64034. Great change / Norfolk Jubilee Quartet Singers," accessed November 27, 2020, https://adp.library.ucsb.edu/index.php/matrix/detail/2000292147/64034-Great_change.

146. Work, *American Negro Songs*, 60.

147. "Rock of Ages, Cleft for Me," taken from *Baptist Hymnal*, #463 (Nashville: LifeWay Worship, 2008), 637, accessed July 17, 2018, https://hymnary.org/hymn/BH2008/page/637. "Hide Me Over in the Rock of Ages" taken from *National Jubilee Melody Song Book*, 62.

148. See Work, *American Negro Songs*, 197; Johnson and Johnson, *Books of American Negro Spirituals*, ii, 158; and McIlhenny, *Befo' de War Spirituals*, 95–97.

NOTES

149. Johnson and Johnson, *Books of American Negro Spirituals*, ii, 158.

150. A version of the song was recorded by Blind Willie Johnson on April 20, 1930, titled "Come and Go with Me to That Land" (Columbia 14556-D), accessed July 27, 2018, https://www.youtube.com/watch?v=ZnTN1ev84yU. Nix recorded his version on April 8, 1930, two weeks prior to Blind Willie Johnson's version. Blind Willie Johnson was from Marlin, Texas.

151. Lyrics in the later verses refer to the experience of slavery: "There'll be no slavery in that land, I'll throw my shackles to the ground, and lay my burdens all around, waiting for my Lord to set me free." I cannot guarantee if these lyrics were in the original version or later added by the arranger. See J. W. Pepper, "Come and Go with Me to That Land," accessed July 27, 2018, https://www.jwpepper.com/Come-and-Go-with-Me-to-That-Land/10514617.item#/submit.

152. Dixon, Godrich, and Rye, *Blues and Gospel Records: 1890–1943*, 52.

153. Cleveland and Nix, *Songs of Zion*, 95.

154. Grissom, *Negro Sings a New Heaven*, 96.

155. Grissom, *Negro Sings a New Heaven*, 44.

156. Parts of this section are taken from my unpublished paper presented at the Society for Ethnomusicology conference in 2016.

157. I used "Begin a New Life on Christmas Day—Part I" (0:21–0:44) for the example because the female vocal is clear and prominent and the lyrics are discernible.

158. George H. Hepworth, *The Whip, Hoe and Sword; or, The Gulf Department in '63*, (Boston: Walker, Wise, 1864): 163–65, quoted in Epstein, *Sinful Tunes and Spirituals*, 291.

159. Kilham, "Sketches in Color," 304.

160. Example 4.17 was transposed to start on the same pitch as 4.16.

161. See David Evans, liner notes to *Rev. A. W. Nix*, Vol. 1, 1927–1928, Document Records, DOCD-5328, 2000; and liner notes to *Rev. A. W. Nix and Rev. Emmett Dickinson*, Vol. 2, 1928–1931, Document Records, DOCD-5490, 2000.

162. This kind of intertextuality was also characteristic of folk blues. See David Evans, *Big Road Blues: Tradition and Creativity in the Folk Blues* (Cambridge, MA: Da Capo Press, 1987) and the sources referenced in it.

163. Levine, *Black Culture and Black Consciousness*, 29.

164. Samuel A. Floyd Jr., "Ring Shout! Literary Studies, Historical Studies, and Black Music Inquiry," *Black Music Research Journal* 11, no. 2 (Autumn 1991): 272–73.

165. Clayborn's record was a hit and was on Vocalion, Nix's label. Nix often played on big hits from the Vocalion catalog, or perhaps the company encouraged him to. For example, Nix recorded his version of "The Dirty Dozen," "How Long, How Long," "Jack the Ripper," and "It Was Tight like That."

166. Harris, *Rise of Gospel Blues*, 168–70. The "personal-relationship-with-Jesus" theme was common in the late nineteenth and early twentieth centuries in hymns such as "In the Garden" by C. Austin Miles. See https://hymnary.org/text/i_come_to_the_garden_alone.

167. For example, in *Gospel Pearls*, several songs mention the Jesus-as-friend theme: "Jesus Is All the World to Me" (1904) states "Jesus is all the world to me. . . . He's my friend"; "'Tis So Sweet to Trust in Jesus" (1882) states "I'm so glad I learn'd to trust Thee, Precious Jesus, Savior, Friend"; "I Must Tell Jesus" (1898) states "I need a great Savior, One who can help my passionate Friend; If I but ask Him, He will deliver"; "Close to Thee" states "Thou my everlasting portion, more than friend or life to me"; and "When Our Story Has Been Told" states "In the palace

of the King who now befriends us." See Music Committee of the Sunday School Publishing Board, *Gospel Pearls*.

168. Brown, "Songs of the Slave," 619.

169. Samuel A. Floyd Jr., "Troping the Blues: From Spirituals to the Concert Hall," *Black Music Research Journal* 13, no. 1 (Spring 1993): 36.

170. Johnson, *Autobiography of an Ex-Colored Man*, 83.

171. Other recordings of "How Long, How Long" include the following: Leroy Carr, "How Long, How Long Blues" (November 6, 1928); Tampa Red's Hokum Jug Band, "How Long, How Long Blues" (November 9, 1928); Tampa Red (The Guitar Wizard), "How Long, How Long Blues" (January 16, 1929), Vocalion (VO 1258, VO 1228); Leroy Carr & Scrapper Blackwell, "The New How Long, How Long Blues" (August 12, 1929), Vocalion (VO 1435); and Leroy Carr & Scrapper Blackwell, "How Long, How Long Blues, No. 2" (January 16, 1931), Vocalion (VO 1585).

172. David Brackett, "James Brown's 'Superbad' and the Double-Voiced Utterance," *Popular Music* 11, no. 3 (October 1992): 318.

173. Elwood Nix and Genester Nix, interview by author, Philadelphia, May 24, 2017. Nix may have been inspired to write his "Baseball Sermon" by Rev. J. M. Gates's sermon "The Ball Game of Life" (OKeh 8562), released in 1928.

174. Genester Nix, interview by author, Philadelphia, May 23, 2017.

175. Genester Nix confirmed to me that her father did not write out his sermons, but only wrote them in outline form with words he wanted to emphasize typed in red. Genester Nix, email message to author, November 15, 2020.

176. Rosenberg, *Art of the American Folk Preacher*, 30.

177. Mitchell, *Black Preaching*, 78.

178. Genester Nix, email message to author, November 15, 2020.

179. Elwood Nix, interview with author, November 21, 2020.

180. John Wilson, interview with author, January 20, 2021.

181. Ashon T. Crawley, *Blackpentecostal Breath: The Aesthetics of Possibility* (New York: Fordham University Press, 2017), 7.

182. Crawley, *Blackpentecostal Breath*, 87–88.

183. See, for example, Bishop Elijah Hankerson (https://youtu.be/cj4grHgz330) and Pastor Nathan Simmons (https://youtu.be/oYGGMnnOdKg).

184. John Wilson, interview with author, January 20, 2021.

185. John Wilson, interview with author, January 20, 2021.

186. Melvin L. Butler, "Performing Pentecostalism: Music, Identity, and the Interplay of Jamaican and African American Styles," in *Rhythms of the Afro-Atlantic* World, ed. Mamadou Diouf and Ifeoma Kiddoe Nwankwo (Ann Arbor: University of Michigan Press), 47.

187. "Kirk Franklin," accessed December 23, 2020, https://www.kirkfranklin.com/bio.

188. Butler, "Performing Pentecostalism," 49, 175.

189. John Wilson, interview with author, January 20, 2021.

190. Alisha Lola Jones, *Flaming? The Peculiar Theopolitics of Fire and Desire in Black Male Gospel Performance* (New York: Oxford University Press, 2020), 29–30.

191. John Wilson, interview with author, January 20, 2021.

NOTES 301

CONCLUSION

1. It is possible that white consumers sometimes purchased Nix's records, especially "Black Diamond," as novelties. "Black Diamond" was released in Great Britain, for example.

2. Schenbeck, *Racial Uplift*, 249.

3. Du Bois, *Souls of Black Folk*, 2.

4. Paul Gilroy, *The Black Atlantic: Modernity and Double Consciousness* (Cambridge, MA: Harvard University Press, 1993), 101.

5. Radio and television eventually became important mediums for Black and white preachers.

6. Martin, "Selling to the Souls of Black Folk," 212.

7. "Universal Fire in 2008 Estimated to Have Destroyed 500,000 Iconic Master Recordings," *Billboard*, accessed July 31, 2019, https://www.billboard.com/articles/business/8515469/universal -fire-in-2008-estimated-to-have-destroyed-500000-iconic-master.

8. Ewan Gibson Music, accessed June 2, 2017, https://ewangibsonmusic.com/music/.

9. "How Ketch Secor Started Wild Roots Band Old Crow Medicine Show," *Rolling Stone*, accessed June 2, 2017, http://www.rollingstone.com/music/news/how-ketch-secor-started-wild -roots-band-old-crow-medicine-show-20140721.

10. Max Nelson, "'This Barren Land': Bob Dylan's Gospel Variations," *Los Angeles Review of Books*, accessed June 2, 2017, https://lareviewofbooks.org/article/this-barren-land-bob -dylans-gospel-variations/.

11. Cross Rhythms, accessed June 2, 2017, http://www.crossrhythms.co.uk/articles/music/ Gospel_Roots/11534/p1/.

12. Radano, *Lying Up a Nation*, 98–100. Many African Americans had also recently served the country in World War I.

SELECTED BIBLIOGRAPHY

Abbott, Ernest Hamlin. "Religious Life in America: IV. Religious Tendencies of the Negro." *Outlook* (1893–1924) 69, no. 17 (December 1901): 1070–76.

Alexander's Magazine 2, no. 4 (August 15, 1906): 8.

Allen, William Francis, Charles Pickard Ware, and Lucy McKim Garrison. *Slave Songs of the United States*. New York: A. Simpson & Co., 1867.

Bacon, Alice Mabel. "Work and Methods of the Hampton Folklore Society." *The Black Perspective in Music* 4, no. 2, Bicentennial Number (July 1976): 151–55. Reprinted from a paper read at the Ninth Annual Meeting of the American Folk-Lore Society, Baltimore, 29 December 1897; published in *Journal of American Folk-Lore* 11 (January–March 1897): 17–21.

Baker, Houston A., Jr. "Completely Well: One View of Black American Culture." In *Key Issues in the Afro-American Experience*, edited by Nathan I. Huggins, Martin Kilson, and Daniel M. Fox, 20–33. San Diego: Harcourt Brace Jovanovich, 1971.

Ball, Fleetwood. "Southern Baptist Convention." *Baptist and Reflector* 25, no. 40 (May 20, 1915): 1–9.

Bennett, John. "A Revival Sermon at Little St. John's." *Atlantic Monthly* 98 (1906): 254–68.

Boehm, Henry. *Reminiscences, Historical and Biographical, of Sixty-Four Years in the Ministry*. New York: Carlton & Porter, 1865.

Bohlman, Philip V. *Music, Nationalism, and the Making of the New Europe*. 2nd ed. New York: Routledge, 2004.

Bohlman, Philip V. "Returning to the Ethnomusicological Past." In *Shadows in the Field: New Perspectives for Fieldwork in Ethnomusicology*, 2nd ed., edited by Gregory Barz and Timothy J. Cooley, 246–70. Oxford: Oxford University Press, 2008.

Boisen, A. T. "Religion and Hard Times." *Social Action* 5, no. 3 (March 15, 1939): 8–35.

Brackett, David. *Interpreting Popular Music*. Berkeley: University of California Press, 2000.

Brackett, David. "James Brown's 'Superbad' and the Double-Voiced Utterance." *Popular Music* 11, no. 3 (October 1992): 309–24.

Brennan, Sherry. "On the Sound of Water: Amiri Baraka's 'Black Art.'" *African American Review* 37, no. 2/3 (Summer–Autumn 2003): 299–311.

Brewer, J. Mason. *The Word on the Brazos: Negro Preacher Tales from the Brazos Bottoms of Texas*. Austin: University of Texas Press, 1953.

Brooks, Tim. *Lost Sounds: Blacks and the Birth of the Recording Industry, 1890–1919*. Urbana: University of Illinois Press, 2004.

SELECTED BIBLIOGRAPHY 303

Brooks, Tim. Liner notes to *Lost Sounds: Blacks and the Birth of the Recording Industry, 1891–1922*. Champaign, IL: Archeophone Records, 2011. CD-ROM.

Brooks, Tim. "'Might Take One Disc of This Trash as a Novelty': Early Recordings by the Fisk Jubilee Singers and the Popularization of 'Negro Folk Music.'" *American Music* 18, no. 3 (Autumn 2000): 278–316.

Brothers, Thomas. "Ideology and Aurality in the Vernacular Traditions of African-American Music." *Black Music Research Journal* 17, no. 2 (Autumn 1997): 169–209.

Brown, John Mason. "Songs of the Slave." *Lippincott's Magazine of Literature, Science, and Education* 2 (1868): 617–23.

Bureau of Labor Statistics, Consumer Expenditure Survey, and U.S. Census Bureau. *Statistical Abstract of the United States, 1918–1919*, sheet 9. Accessed May 15, 2018, https://www.bls.gov/opub/uscs/1918-19.

Burgett, Paul. "The Writings of Alain Locke." In *Black Music in the Harlem Renaissance: A Collection of Essays*, edited by Samuel A. Floyd Jr., 29–40. Knoxville: University of Tennessee Press, 1993.

Burnim, Mellonee. "Spirituals." In *African American Music: An Introduction*, 2nd ed., edited by Mellonee V. Burnim and Portia Maultsby. New York: Routledge, 2015.

Burnim, Mellonee V., and Portia Maultsby, eds. *African American Music: An Introduction*. 2nd ed. New York: Routledge, 2015.

Butler, Melvin L. "Performing Pentecostalism: Music, Identity, and the Interplay of Jamaican and African American Styles." In *Rhythms of the Afro-Atlantic World: Rituals and Remembrances*, edited by Diouf Mamadou and Nwankwo Ifeoma Kiddoe, 41–54. Ann Arbor: University of Michigan Press, 2010. doi: 10.2307/j.ctvc5pf5f.5.

Calt, Stephen. "The Anatomy of a 'Race' Label, Part II." *78 Quarterly* 1, no. 4 (1989): 9–30.

Carter, Scott A. "Forging a Sound Citizenry: Voice Culture and the Embodiment of the Nation, 1880–1920." *The American Music Research Center Journal* 22 (2013): 11–34.

Charters, Samuel B. *The Country Blues*. New York: Rinehart & Company, 1959.

Chesnut, Mary Boykin. *A Diary from Dixie*. New York: D. Appleton and Company, 1905.

The Chicago Commission on Race Relations. *The Negro in Chicago: A Study of Race Relations and a Race Riot*. Chicago: University of Chicago Press, 1922.

Cleveland, J. Jefferson, and Verolga Nix, eds. *Songs of Zion*. Nashville: Abingdon Press, 1981.

Colbert, William. *A Journal of the Travels of William Colbert, Methodist Preacher thro' Parts of Maryland, Pennsylvania, New York, Delaware, and Virginia in 1790–1838*. Vol. 5.

Cook, Nicholas, and Daniel Leech-Wilkinson. "A Musicologist's Guide to Sonic Visualiser." CHARM, accessed December 19, 2017, http://charm.cch.kcl.ac.uk/redist/pdf/analysing_recordings.pdf.

Cotton, Sandra. "Fach vs. Voice Type: A Call for Critical Discussion." *Journal of Singing* 69, no. 2 (November/December 2010): 153–66.

Courlander, Harold. *Negro Folk Music, U.S.A.* New York: Columbia University Press, 1963.

Cox, Thomas C. *Blacks in Topeka Kansas, 1865–1915: A Social History*. Baton Rouge: Louisiana State University Press, 1982.

Craddock, Van. *Longview*. Charleston, SC: Arcadia, 2010. https://books.google.com/books?id=YSE_TCA21PoC&printsec=frontcover#v=onepage&q=pleasant&f=false.

Crawley, Ashon T. *Blackpentecostal Breath: The Aesthetics of Possibility*. New York: Fordham University Press, 2017.

Curtis-Burlin, Natalie. "Black Singers and Players." *The Musical Quarterly* 5, no. 4 (October 1919): 499–504.

Curtis-Burlin, Natalie. *Negro Folk-Songs.* New York: G. Schirmer, 1918.

Curtis-Burlin, Natalie. "Negro Music at Birth." *The Musical Quarterly* 5, no. 1 (January 1919): 86–89.

Darden, Robert. *Nothing But Love in God's Water.* Vol 1, *Black Sacred Music from the Civil War to the Civil Rights.* University Park: Pennsylvania State University Press, 2014.

Davis, Angela Y. *Blues Legacies and Black Feminism: Gertrude "Ma" Rainey, Bessie Smith, and Billie Holiday.* New York: Vintage Books, 1998.

Davis, Gerald L. *I Got the Word in Me and I Can Sing It, You Know: A Study of the Performed African-American Sermon.* Philadelphia: University of Pennsylvania Press, 1985.

Dett, R. Nathaniel, ed. *Religious Folk-Songs of the Negro.* Hampton, VA: Hampton Institute Press, 1927.

Discography of American Historical Recordings, s.v. "Griggs, Sutton E., Rev." Accessed October 2, 2015. https://adp.library.ucsb.edu/names/204059.

Discography of American Historical Recordings, s.v. "OKeh matrix W400351. Hush! Somebody's calling my name / Mississippi Juvenile Quartette." Accessed November 27, 2020. https://adp.library.ucsb.edu/index.php/matrix/detail/2000209120/W400351-Hush _Somebodys_calling_my_name.

Discography of American Historical Recordings, s.v. "Victor matrix BVE-38994. Hush! Hush! Somebody's calling my name / Sandhills Sixteen." Accessed November 27, 2020. https:// adp.library.ucsb.edu/index.php/matrix/detail/800013256/BVE-38994-Hush_Hush _Somebodys_calling_my_name.

Dixon, Robert, and John Godrich. *Recording the Blues.* New York: Stein and Day, 1970.

Dixon, Robert, John Godrich, and Howard Rye. *Blues and Gospel Records: 1890–1943.* 4th ed. Oxford: Clarendon Press, 1997.

Dolinar, Brian, ed. *The Negro in Illinois: The WPA Papers.* Urbana: University of Illinois Press, 2013.

Dowd, Jerome. "Sermon of an Ante-Bellum Negro Preacher." *The Southern Workman* 30, no. 11 (November 1901): 655–58.

Drake, St. Clair, and Horace R. Cayton. *Black Metropolis: A Study of Negro Life in a Northern City.* Chicago: University of Chicago, 1970.

Drowne, Kathleen Morgan. *Spirits of Defiance: National Prohibition and Jazz Age Literature, 1920–1933.* Columbus: Ohio State University Press, 2005.

Du Bois, W. E. B. "The Negro in Literature and Art." *The Annals of the American Academy of Political and Social Science* 49, The Negro's Progress in Fifty Years (September 1913): 233–37.

Du Bois, W. E. B. *The Souls of Black Folk.* 1903. New York: Dover Publications, 1994.

Durham, Kenneth R., Jr. "The Longview Race Riot of 1919." *East Texas Historical Journal* 18, no. 2 (1980): 13–24.

Eidsheim, Nina Sun. "Voice as a Technology of Selfhood: Towards an Analysis of Racialized Timbre and Vocal Performance." PhD diss., University of California, 2008.

Epstein, Dena J. *Sinful Tunes and Spirituals: Black Folk Music to the Civil War.* Urbana: University of Illinois Press, 2003.

Evans, David. Liner notes to *Goodbye Babylon.* Dust-to-Digital, B0000DBOCB, 2003, 11.

Evans, David. Liner notes to *Rev. A. W. Nix*, Vol. 1, 1927–1928. Document Records, DOCD-5328, 2000.

Evans, David. Liner notes to *Rev. A. W. Nix and Rev. Emmett Dickinson*, Vol. 2, 1928–1931. Document Records, DOCD-5490, 2000.

Fales, Cornelia. "The Paradox of Timbre." *Ethnomusicology* 46, no. 1 (Winter 2002): 56–95.

Fenner, Thomas P. *Cabin and Plantation Songs as Sung by the Hampton Students*. New York: G. P. Putnam's Sons, 1876.

Filzen, Sarah. "The Rise and Fall of Paramount Records." *The Wisconsin Magazine of History* 82, no. 2 (Winter 1998–1999): 104–27.

Fisher, Miles Mark. *Negro Slave Songs in the United States*. New York: Citadel Press, 1981.

Fisher, William Arms, ed. *Seventy Negro Spirituals*. Bryn Mawr, PA: Oliver Ditson Company, 1926.

Floyd, Samuel A., Jr. "Black American Music and Aesthetic Communication." *Black Music Research Journal* 1 (1980): 1–17.

Floyd, Samuel A., Jr, ed. *Black Music in the Harlem Renaissance: A Collection of Essays*. Knoxville: University of Tennessee Press, 1993.

Floyd, Samuel A., Jr. *The Power of Black Music: Interpreting Its History from Africa to the United States*. New York: Oxford University Press, 1995.

Floyd, Samuel A., Jr. "Ring Shout! Literary Studies, Historical Studies, and Black Music Inquiry." *Black Music Research Journal* 11, no. 2 (Autumn 1991): 265–87.

Floyd, Samuel A., Jr. "Troping the Blues: From Spirituals to the Concert Hall." *Black Music Research Journal* 13, no. 1 (Spring 1993): 31–51.

Frazier, E. Franklin. *Black Bourgeoisie*. New York: Simon & Schuster, 1957.

Frazier, E. Franklin. *The Negro Church in America*. New York: Schocken Books, 1974.

Fuller, T. O. *History of the Negro Baptists of Tennessee*. Memphis, 1936.

Furness, Clifton Joseph. "Communal Music among Arabians and Negroes." *The Musical Quarterly* 16, no. 1 (January 1930): 38–51.

Gaines, Kevin K. *Uplifting the Race: Black Leadership, Politics, and Culture in the Twentieth Century*. Chapel Hill: University of North Carolina Press, 1996.

Gates, Henry Louis, Jr. *The Signifying Monkey: A Theory of African-American Literary Criticism*. New York: Oxford University Press, 1988.

Gates, Henry Louis, Jr. "The Trope of a New Negro and the Reconstruction of the Image of the Black." *Representations* 24, Special Issue: America Reconstructed, 1840–1940 (Autumn 1988): 129–55.

General Association of Colored Baptists in Kentucky. *Minutes of the Forty-Third Annual Session of the General Association of Colored Baptists in Kentucky*. Louisville, KY: American Baptist, 1911.

General Association of Colored Baptists in Kentucky. *Minutes of the Forty-Fourth Annual Session of the General Association of Colored Baptists in Kentucky*. Louisville, KY: American Baptist, 1912.

General Association of Colored Baptists in Kentucky. *Minutes of the Forty-Sixth Annual Session of the General Association of Colored Baptists in Kentucky*. Louisville, KY: American Baptist, 1914.

Gilroy, Paul. *The Black Atlantic: Modernity and Double Consciousness*. Cambridge, MA: Harvard University Press, 1993.

Gilroy, Paul. "Sounds Authentic: Black Music, Ethnicity, and the Challenge of a 'Changing' Same." *Black Music Research Journal* 11, no. 2 (Autumn 1991): 111–36.

Graham, Sandra Jean. "Spiritual." Grove Music Online. Accessed September 14, 2017. http://www.oxfordmusiconline.com.lp.hscl.ufl.edu/subscriber/article/grove/music/A2225625.

Graham, Sandra Jean. *Spirituals and the Birth of a Black Entertainment Industry*. Urbana: University of Illinois Press, 2018.

Graziano, John. "The Early Life and Career of the 'Black Patti': The Odyssey of an African American Singer in the Late Nineteenth Century." *Journal of the American Musicological Society* 53, no. 3 (Autumn 2000): 543–96.

Gregory, James N. *The Southern Diaspora: How the Great Migrations of Black and White Southerners Transformed America*. Chapel Hill: University of North Carolina Press, 2005.

Griggs, Sutton E. *The Hindered Hand: Or the Reign of the Repressionist*. 3rd ed. Nashville: Orion Publishing, 1905.

Grissom, Mary Allen. Foreward to *The Negro Sings a New Heaven*. Chapel Hill: University of North Carolina Press, 1930.

Harris, Michael W. *The Rise of Gospel Blues: The Music of Thomas Andrew Dorsey in the Urban Church*. New York: Oxford University Press, 1992.

Harrison, Peter T. *Singing: Personal and Performance Values in Training*. Edinburgh: Dunedin Academic Press, 2014.

Higginbotham, Evelyn Brooks. "The Black Church: A Gender Perspective." In *African American Religious Thought: An Anthology*, edited by Cornel West and Eddie S. Glaude Jr., 187–208. Louisville: Westminster John Knox Press, 2003.

Higginbotham, Evelyn Brooks. "Rethinking Vernacular Culture: Black Religion and Race Records in the 1920s and 1930s." In *The House That Race Built*, edited by Wahneema Lubiano, 157–77. New York: Pantheon Books, 1997.

Higginson, Thomas Wentworth. *Army Life in a Black Regiment*. 1869. Boston: Beacon Press, 1962.

Hildebrand, Jennifer. "'Two Souls, Two Thoughts, Two Unreconciled Strivings': The Sound of Double Consciousness in Roland Hayes's Early Career." *Black Music Research Journal* 30, no. 2 (Fall 2010): 273–302.

Hubbard, Dolan. *The Sermon and the African American Literary Imagination*. Columbia: University of Missouri Press, 1994.

Hughes, Langston. "The Negro Artist and the Racial Mountain." In *Let Nobody Turn Us Around: An African American Anthology*, 2nd ed., edited by Manning Marable and Leith Mullings, 253–57. Lanham, MD: Rowman & Littlefield, 2009.

Humphrey, Mark A. "Holy Blues: The Gospel Tradition." In *Nothing But the Blues: The Music and the Musicians*, edited by Lawrence Cohn, 107–49. New York: Abbeville Press, 1999.

Hurston, Zora Neale. *Mules and Men*. New York: HarperCollins, 1935.

Jackson, Duane Eric. "A Survey of Hymnody Usage in Selected African American Baptist Churches in the State of Florida." PhD diss., Florida State University, 2009.

Johnson, Clifton H., ed. *God Struck Me Dead: Voices of Ex-Slaves*. Cleveland, OH: Pilgrim Press, 1969.

Johnson, James Weldon. *The Autobiography of an Ex-Colored Man*. 1912. New York: Dover Publications, 1995.

Johnson, James Weldon. *The Book of American Negro Poetry*. New York: Harcourt, Brace, and Company, 1922.

Johnson, James Weldon. *God's Trombones: Seven Negro Sermons in Verse*. 1927. New York: Viking Press, 1969.

Johnson, James Weldon, and J. Rosamond Johnson. *The Books of American Negro Spirituals*. 1925. New York: Da Capo Press, 1969.

SELECTED BIBLIOGRAPHY 307

Jones, Alisha Lola. *Flaming? The Peculiar Theopolitics of Fire and Desire in Black Male Gospel Performance.* New York: Oxford University Press, 2020.

Jones, LeRoi. *Blues People: Negro Music in White America.* New York: Harper Perennial, 1963.

Kendi, Ibram X. *Stamped from the Beginning: The Definitive History of Racist Ideas in America.* New York: Nation Books, 2016.

Kennard, James, Jr. "Who Are Our National Poets?" *The Knickerbocker; or New York Monthly Magazine* (1833–1862) 26, no. 4 (October 1845): 331.

Kenney, William Howland. *Recorded Music in American Life: The Phonograph and Popular Memory, 1890–1945.* New York: Oxford University Press, 1999.

Kerlin, Robert T. *The Voice of the Negro: 1919.* New York: Arno Press, 1968.

Keyes, Cheryl L. "Sound, Voice, and Spirit: Teaching in the Black Vernacular." *Black Music Research Journal* 29, no. 1 (Spring 2009): 11–24.

Kilham, Elizabeth. "Sketches in Color: Fourth." *Putnam's Magazine.* Original Papers on Literature, Science, Art and National Interests (1868–1870) 5, no. 27 (March 1870): 304–11.

Knight, Arthur. *Disintegrating the Musical: Black Performance and American Musical Film.* Durham, NC: Duke University Press, 2002.

Lacey, Herbert J., C. Austin Miles, and Maurice A. Clifton, eds. *New Songs of the Gospel No. 2: For Use in Religious Meetings.* New York: Hall-Mack Company, 1905.

Laird, Ross. *Brunswick Records: A Discography of Recordings, 1916–1931.* Vol. 1: New York Sessions, 1916–1926. Westport, CT: Greenwood Press, 2001.

Laird, Ross. *Brunswick Records: A Discography of Recordings, 1916–1931.* Vol. 3: Chicago and Regional Sessions. Westport, CT: Greenwood Press, 2001.

Lanier, Sidney. *The Science of English Verse.* New York: Charles Scribner's Sons, 1911.

Laver, John. *The Phonetic Description of Voice Quality.* Cambridge, UK: Cambridge University Press, 1980.

Levine, Lawrence W. *Black Culture and Black Consciousness: Afro-American Folk Thought from Slavery to Freedom.* Oxford, UK: Oxford University Press, 2007.

Levine, Lawrence W. *Highbrow Lowbrow: The Emergence of Cultural Hierarchy in America.* Cambridge, MA: Harvard University Press, 1988.

Levine, Lawrence W. *The Unpredictable Past: Explorations in American Cultural History.* New York: Oxford University Press, 1993.

Locke, Alain. *The Negro and His Music.* Washington, DC: The Associates in Negro Folk Education, 1936.

Locke, Alain, ed. *The New Negro: Voices of the Harlem Renaissance.* New York: Touchstone, 1925.

Loftus, Donna. "The Rise of the Victorian Middle Class." BBC. Accessed October 16, 2016. http://www.bbc.co.uk/history/british/victorians/middle_classes_01.shtml.

Long, Christopher. "The Ridge, TX." In *Handbook of Texas Online.* Accessed August 18, 2017. http://www.tshaonline.org/handbook/online/articles/hrtfg.

MacLeod, R. R. *Document Blues-9:9.* Edinburgh: PAT Publications, 2002.

Marable, Manning, and Leith Mullings, eds. *Let Nobody Turn Us Around: An African American Anthology.* 2nd ed. Lanham, MD: Rowman & Littlefield Publishers, 2009.

Martin, Lerone A. "Selling to the Souls of Black Folk: Atlanta, Reverend J. M. Gates, the Phonograph, and the Transformation of African American Protestantism and Culture, 1910–1945." PhD diss., Emory University, 2005.

Maultsby, Portia. "Africanisms in African American Music." In *The African Presence in Black America*, edited by Jacob U. Gordon, 39–84. Trenton, NJ: Africa World Press, 2004.

Maultsby, Portia. "The Use and Performance of Hymnody, Spirituals, and Gospels in the Black Church." *Hymnology Annual* 2 (1992): 11–26.

McIlhenny, E. A. *Befo' de War Spirituals: Words and Melodies*. Boston: Christopher Publishing House, 1933.

McKinney, Richard I. "The Black Church: Its Development and Present Impact." *The Harvard Theological Review* 64, no. 4 (October 1971): 452–81.

Middleton, Howard Taylor. "Concerning the Black Race and Blue Records." *Talking Machine World* 9, no. 9 (September 15, 1913): 26.

Miller, Karl Hagstrom. *Segregating Sound: Inventing Folk and Pop Music in the Age of Jim Crow*. Durham, NC: Duke University Press, 2010.

Mitchell, Henry H. "African-American Preaching." *Interpretation* 51, no. 4 (October 1997): 371–77.

Mitchell, Henry H. *Black Preaching*. Philadelphia: J. B. Lippincott, 1970.

Mitchell, Henry H. *Black Preaching: The Recovery of a Powerful Art*. Nashville: Abingdon Press, 1990.

Monson, Ingrid. "Riffs, Repetition, and Theories of Globalization." *Ethnomusicology* 43, no. 1 (Winter 1999): 31–65.

Moses, Wilson J. "Literary Garveyism: The Novels of Reverend Sutton E. Griggs." *Phylon* 40, no. 3 (3rd Qtr., 1979): 203–16.

Murphy, Jeannette Robinson. "The Survival of African Music in America." *Appletons' Popular Science Monthly*, September 1899, 660–72.

Music Committee of the Sunday School Publishing Board. *Gospel Pearls*. Nashville: Sunday School Publishing Board, National Baptist Convention, 1921.

National Baptist Convention of the United States of America. *Journal of the Twenty-Fifth Session, 1905*. Nashville: National Baptist Publishing Board, 1906.

National Baptist Convention of the United States of America. *Proceedings of the Forty-First Annual Session of the National Baptist Convention: Held with the Baptist Churches, 1921*. The Burke Library at Union Theological Seminary, Columbia University, New York, NY.

National Jubilee Melody Song Book. Memorial Edition (In Memory of the Late Richard Henry Boyd). Nashville: National Baptist Publishing Board, 1923. Accessed September 28, 2021. https://babel.hathitrust.org/cgi/pt?id=mdp.39015057467329&view=1up&seq=7&skin=2021.

"Negro Minstrelsy—Ancient and Modern." *Putnam's Monthly Magazine of American Literature, Science, and Art* (1853–1857) 5, no. 25 (January 1855): 72–79.

The Negro Music Journal 1–2 (1902–1903). Westport, CT: Negro Universities Press, 1970.

Nix, A. W. *Black Religious Music, 1930–1956*. Document Records DOCD-5639, 1999, m4a.

Nix, A. W. *Rev. A. W. Nix, Vol. 1, 1927–1928*. Document Records, DOCD-5328, 2000, m4a.

Nix, A. W. *Rev. A. W. Nix and Rev. Emmett Dickinson, Vol. 2, 1928–1931*. Document Records, DOCD-5490, 2000, m4a.

Nix, Genester. Personal biography. Philadelphia, PA. Booklet.

Odum, Howard W. "Folk-Song and Folk-Poetry as Found in the Secular Songs of the Southern Negroes" (Concluded). *Journal of American Folklore* 24, no. 94 (October–December 1911): 351–96.

Odum, Howard W. "Religious Folk-Songs of the Southern Negroes." *American Journal of Religious Psychology and Education* 3, no. 3 (July 1909): 265–365.

SELECTED BIBLIOGRAPHY 309

Oliver, Paul. *Songsters and Saints: Vocal Traditions on Race Records*. Cambridge: Cambridge University Press, 1984.

Oliver, Paul, Max Harrison, and William Bolcom. *The New Grove Gospel, Blues and Jazz with Spirituals and Ragtime*. New York: W. W. Norton, 1986.

Olwage, Grant. "The Class and Colour of Tone: An Essay on the Social History of Vocal Timbre." *Ethnomusicology Forum* 13, no. 2 (November 2004): 203–26.

O'Neal, Jim, and Amy O'Neal. "Georgia Tom Dorsey." *Living Blues* 20 (March/April 1975): 17–34.

Parrish, C. H., ed. *Golden Jubilee of the General Association of Colored Baptists in Kentucky: The Story of 50 Years' Work from 1865–1915*. Louisville: Mayes Printing Company, 1915.

Parrish, Lydia. *Slave Songs of the Georgia Sea Islands*. Hatboro, PA: Folklore Associates, 1965.

Payne, Daniel Alexander. *Recollections of Seventy Years*. Nashville: Publishing House of the A.M.E. Sunday School Union, 1888.

Perkins, A. E. "Negro Spirituals from the Far South." *Journal of American Folklore* 35, no. 137 (July–September 1922): 223–49.

Pinckard, George. *Notes on the West Indies, Including Observations Relative to the Creoles and Slaves of the Western Colonies and the Indians of South America; Interspersed with Remarks upon the Seasoning or Yellow Fever of Hot Climates*. 2nd ed., Vol. 1. London: Baldwin, Cradock, and Joy, 1816.

Pipes, William H. *Say Amen, Brother! Old-Time Negro Preaching: A Study in American Frustration*. Detroit: Wayne State University Press, 1992.

Pitts, Walter F., Jr. *Old Ship of Zion: The Afro-Baptist Ritual in the African Diaspora*. New York: Oxford University Press, 1993.

Powdermaker, Hortense. *After Freedom: A Cultural Study in the Deep South*. Madison: University of Wisconsin Press, 1993.

Raboteau, Albert J. *Canaan Land: A Religious History of African Americans*. Oxford: Oxford University Press, 2001.

Raboteau, Albert J. *A Fire in the Bones: Reflections on African-American Religious History*. Boston: Beacon Press, 1995.

Raboteau, Albert J. Introduction to *God Struck Me Dead*, edited by Clifton H. Johnson, xxii. Cleveland, OH: Pilgrim Press, 1993.

Raboteau, Albert J. *Slave Religion: The "Invisible Institution" in the Antebellum South*. Oxford, UK: Oxford University Press, 2004.

Radano, Ronald. *Lying Up a Nation: Race and Black Music*. Chicago: University of Chicago Press, 2003.

Radano, Ronald. "Soul Texts and the Blackness of Folk." *Modernism/Modernity* 2, no. 1 (January 1995): 71–95.

Ramsey, Guthrie P., Jr. "The Pot Liquor Principle: Developing a Black Music Criticism in American Music Studies." *American Music* 22, no. 2 (Summer 2004): 284–95.

Ramsey, Guthrie P., Jr. *Race Music: Black Cultures from Bebop to Hip-Hop*. Berkeley: University of California Press, 2003.

Ramsey, Guthrie P., Jr. "Secrets, Lies and Transcriptions: Revisions on Race, Black Music and Culture." In *Western Music and Race*, edited by Julie Brown, 24–36. Cambridge, UK: Cambridge University Press, 2007.

Robinson-Martin, Trineice. *So You Want to Sing Gospel: A Guide for Performers*. Lanham, MD: Rowman & Littlefield, 2016.

310 SELECTED BIBLIOGRAPHY

Rosenberg, Bruce A. *The Art of the American Folk Preacher*. New York: Oxford University Press, 1970.

Schenbeck, Lawrence. *Racial Uplift and American Music: 1878–1943*. Jackson: University Press of Mississippi, 2012.

Seward, Theodore F., and George L. White. *Jubilee Songs: As Sung by the Jubilee Singers*. New York: Biglow & Main, 1884.

Shearon, Stephen, Harry Eskew, James C. Downey, and Robert Darden. "Gospel Music." Grove Music Online. Oxford Music Online. Oxford University Press. Accessed August 15, 2017. http://www.oxfordmusiconline.com.lp.hscl.ufl.edu/subscriber/article/grove/music/A2224388.

Simmons College of Kentucky Collection [State University]. Catalogue 1908–1909. University of Louisville Library, Louisville, KY.

Simmons College of Kentucky Collection [State University]. Catalogues 1908–1920. Digital Collections, University of Louisville Library. Accessed May 5, 2017. http://digital.library.louisville.edu/cdm/search/collection/simmons.

Sitton, Thad. "Freemen's Settlements." In *Handbook of Texas Online*. Accessed August 18, 2017. http://www.tshaonline.org/handbook/online/articles/uef20.

Smith, Warren Thomas. *Harry Hosier: Circuit Rider*. Nashville: Abingdon Press, 1981.

Sobel, Mechal. *Trabelin' On: The Slave Journey to an Afro-Baptist Faith*. Princeton, NJ: Princeton University Press, 1988.

Southern, Eileen. "The Antebellum Church." *Black American Literature Forum* 25, no. 1, The Black Church and the Black Theatre (Spring 1991): 23–26.

Southern, Eileen. "Hymnals of the Black Church." *The Black Perspective in Music* 17, no. 1/2 (1989): 153–70.

Southern, Eileen. *The Music of Black Americans: A History*. 3rd ed. New York: W. W. Norton, 1997.

Spear, Allan H. *Black Chicago: The Making of a Negro Ghetto, 1890–1920*. Chicago: University of Chicago Press, 1967.

Spearman, Rawn. "Vocal Concert Music in the Harlem Renaissance." In *Black Music in the Harlem Renaissance*, edited by Samuel A. Floyd Jr., 41–54. Knoxville: University of Tennessee Press, 1993.

Spencer, Jon Michael. "The Diminishing Rural Residue of Folklore in City and Urban Blues, Chicago 1915–1950." *Black Music Research Journal* 12, no. 1 (Spring 1992): 25–41.

Spencer, Jon Michael. *Sacred Symphony: The Chanted Sermon of the Black Preacher*. New York: Greenwood Press, 1987.

Stoever-Ackerman, Jennifer. "The Word and the Sound: Listening to the Sonic Colour-Line in Frederick Douglass's 1845 Narrative." *SoundEffects* 1, no. 1 (2011): 20–36.

Suisman, David. "Co-Workers in the Kingdom of Culture: Black Swan Records and the Political Economy of African American Music." *Journal of American History* 90, no. 4 (March 2004): 1295–324.

Sutherland, Robert Lee. "An Analysis of Negro Churches in Chicago." PhD diss., University of Chicago, 1930.

Svin'in, Pavel Petrovich. *Picturesque United States of America, 1811, 1812, 1813, Being a Memoir on Paul Svin'in, Russian Diplomatic Officer, Artist, and Author, Containing Copious Excerpts from His Account of His Travels in America with Fifty-Two Reproductions of Water Colors in his Own Sketch-Book*. New York: W. E. Rudge, 1930.

SELECTED BIBLIOGRAPHY

Tabernacle Baptist Church. "A Brief History of the Life of Our Pastor, Rev. A. W. Nix." Anniversary Book, Pittsburgh, Pennsylvania, 1936.

Taylor, Elizabeth Dowling. *The Original Black Elite: Daniel Murray and the Story of a Forgotten Era*. New York: HarperCollins, 2017.

Thurman, Howard. *Jesus and the Disinherited*. New York: Abingdon-Cokesbury Press, 1949.

Thygesen, Helge, and Russell Shor. *Vocalion 1000 & Brunswick 7000 Race Series*. Overveen, The Netherlands: Agram Blues Books, 2014.

Titon, Jeff Todd. "Ethnomusicology of Downhome Blues Phonograph Records, 1926–1930." PhD diss., University of Minnesota, 1970.

Titon, Jeff Todd. "From the Record Review Editor: African American Religious Music." *Journal of American Folklore* 96, no. 379 (January–March 1983): 111–13.

Titon, Jeff Todd. "North America/Black America." In *Worlds of Music: An Introduction to the Music of the World's Peoples*, edited by Jeff Todd Titon, 145–204. Belmont, CA: Schirmer, 2009.

Titon, Jeff Todd. "'Tuned Up with the Grace of God': Music and Experience among Old Regular Baptists." In *Music in American Religious Experience*, edited by Philip V. Bohlman, Edith L. Blumhofer, and Maria M. Chow, 311–34. Oxford, UK: Oxford University Press, 2006.

Townsend, Mrs. A. M., ed. *The Baptist Standard Hymnal with Responsive Readings: A New Book for All Services*. Nashville: Sunday School Publishing Board, 1924.

Tracy, Steven C. "Saving the Day: The Recordings of the Reverend Sutton E. Griggs." *Phylon* 47, no. 2 (2nd Qtr., 1986): 159–66.

Trotter, James M. *Music and Some Highly Musical People*. Boston: Lee and Shepard Publishers, 1880.

Tucker, David M. *Black Pastors and Leaders: Memphis, 1819–1972*. Memphis: Memphis State University Press, 1975.

Turino, Thomas. *Music as Social Life: The Politics of Participation*. Chicago: University of Chicago Press, 2008.

United States Department of Commerce, Bureau of the Census. Census of the United States: 1870. Population Schedule. Barnwell County, South Carolina, sheet 7.

United States Department of Commerce, Bureau of the Census. Census of the United States: 1910. Population Schedule. Gregg County, Texas, Justice Precinct 2, Enumeration District 4, sheet 10.

United States Department of Commerce, Bureau of the Census. Tenth Census of the United States: 1880. Population Schedule. Rusk County, Texas, Enumeration District 75, sheet 89.

United States Department of Commerce, Bureau of the Census. Twelfth Census of the United States: 1900. Population Schedule. Gregg County, Texas, Justice Precinct 2, Supervisor's District 7, Enumeration District 33, sheet 3.

United States Department of Commerce, Bureau of the Census. Fourteenth Census of the United States: 1920. Population Schedule. Cook County, Chicago, Illinois, District 5.

United States Department of Commerce, Bureau of the Census. Fifteenth Census of the United States: 1930. Population Schedule. Cook County, Chicago, Illinois. 13th Precinct, Enumeration District 16–901, Supervisor's District 6, Sheet 9A.

United States Department of Commerce, Bureau of the Census. Sixteenth Census of the United States: 1940. Population Schedule. Philadelphia County, Philadelphia, Pennsylvania. 22nd Ward, Block 39–40, Supervisor's District 7, Enumeration District 51–546, Sheet 1B.

Walker, Wyatt Tee. *Spirits That Dwell in Deep Woods: The Prayer and Praise Hymns of the Black Religious Experience*. New York: Martin Luther King Fellows Press, 1987.

Walton, Jonathan L. "The Preachers' Blues: Religious Race Records and Claims of Authority on Wax." *Religion and American Culture: A Journal of Interpretation* 20, no. 2 (Summer 2010): 205–32.

Washington, Booker T. "Atlanta Exposition Address." In *Let Nobody Turn Us Around: An African American Anthology*, edited by Manning Marable and Leith Mullings, 175–77. Lanham, MD: Rowman & Littlefield, 2009.

Washington, Booker T. "My View of Segregation Laws." In *Let Nobody Turn Us Around: An African American Anthology*, edited by Manning Marable and Leith Mullings, 177–80. Lanham, MD: Rowman & Littlefield, 2009.

Washington, Booker T., Fannie Barrier Williams, and Norman Barton Wood. *A New Negro for a New Century*. Chicago: American Publishing House, 1900.

Weidman, Amanda. "Gender and the Politics of Voice: Colonial Modernity and Classical Music in South India." *Cultural Anthropology* 18, no. 2 (May 2003): 194–232.

Weisenfeld, Judith. *Hollywood Be Thy Name: African American Religion in American Film, 1929–1949*. Berkeley: University of California Press, 2007.

Wheeler, Edward L. *Uplifting the Race: The Black Minister in the New South 1865–1902*. Lanham, MD: University Press of America, 1986.

Williams, Lawrence H. *A History of Simmons University: "Ole State University," 1873–1930*. Earlington, KY: General Association of Kentucky Baptists, 1977.

Williams-Jones, Pearl. "Afro-American Gospel Music: A Crystallization of the Black Aesthetic." *Ethnomusicology* 19, no. 3 (September 1975): 373–85.

Wilson, Olly. "Black Music as an Art Form." *Black Music Research Journal* 3 (1983): 1–22.

Work, Frederick J., ed. *Folk Song of the American Negro*. Nashville: Press of Fisk University, 1915.

Work, John W. *American Negro Songs: 230 Folk Songs and Spirituals, Religious and Secular*. Mineola, NY: Dover Publications, 1998.

Young, Alan. *Woke Me Up This Morning: Black Gospel Singers and the Gospel Life*. Jackson: University Press of Mississippi, 1997.

Yurchenco, Henrietta. "'Blues Fallin' Down like Hail': Recorded Blues, 1920s–1940s." *American Music* 13, no. 4 (Winter 1995): 448–69.

Zaretsky, Irving I., and Mark P. Leone, eds. *Religious Movements in Contemporary America*. Princeton, NJ: Princeton University Press, 1974.

INDEX

Page numbers in *italics* refer to illustrations. Page numbers in **bold** refer to tables.

Abbott, Ernest Hamlin, 71, 72, 195, 206
African Americans: class structures among, 5, 6, 273n14; as consumers of recordings, 98–99, 265; and disenfranchisement during the modern era, 64; dualities in experience of, 265–66; economic conditions for, 37–38, 278nn121–22; and new societal image of, 93; popular church denominations for, 69; purchase of recorded sermons by, 102–3; racist images of, 281n1; religious revival traditions of, 3. *See also* Black churches; Black ministers; Black vocal traditions; racism
African American Vernacular English (AAVE), 190, 214–16, 217, 218
Allen, Richard, *A Collection of Spiritual Songs and Hymns Selected from Various Authors*, 42
"Amen corner," 194, 293n21
antinomianism, 66
Armstrong, Louis, 33, 270
assimilation into dominant culture: and elite classes, 7–8, 265; and European aesthetics, 9–10, 87–88; reflected in Griggs's sermon, 104–6; through European aesthetics, 7, 70. *See also* elite/upper class African Americans; European cultural aesthetics; middle-class African Americans; racial uplift

Associated Negro Press, 9
A. W. Nix & Rev. Emmett Dickinson, Vol. 2, 1928–1931, 115

Ballard, Earl A., 49
Baptist and Methodist churches, 4, 73, 76, 77, 78, 81–82, 203
Baptist Standard Hymnal, The, 18, 226, 227, 279n136
Behnke, Emil, 89
Belt Sacred Quartet, 234
Berlin, Irving, songs of, 48–49, 54
biblical themes: Isaiah 28:20, 235; Psalm 23, 237; Song of Solomon 2:1, 235
Black Baptists: and Nix's recorded sermons, 13; self-governance for, 67–68; and storefront churches, 77; style of worship favored by, 39. *See also* Baptist and Methodist churches; Nix, Andrew William (A. W.)
Black churches: Christian morality as primary goal of, 175; class divisions in, 12, 71, 72–76; as community centers, 36; denominational criticism in, 184; differences in vocal expressions among, 4; emotional inspiration in, 69–70, 259; expectations of performers in, 263; loudness of, 202, 203; manhood and attendance at, 20; participatory performance in, 5; and racial uplift, 9;

313

scholarly study of, 273n24; secularization of, 74

"Black Diamond Express to Hell" (Nix sermons): advertising for, 111–12, *112*, 199, *200*; motivation for multipart recordings, 103, 154; and national recognition for Nix, 112, 113; Pt. I, 114–15, 116–19, 178–79, 204, 220–21, **221**; Pt. II, 119–22, 205, 208, 244, *244*; Part 3, 128–31, 213; Part 4, 131–34, 179, 180, 194, *194*; Part 5, 154–58, 177–78; Part 6, 158–62; rock band named after, 270; shouts in, *194*; spirituals and hymns in, 228–29, 232–33, 234; structure of, 290n64; and "The White Flyer," 288n29; train trope in, 240–41; Vocalion label titles for, 297n126; white purchasers of, 301n1

blackface minstrelsy, 9, 49, 64, 79, 90, 91–92, 107–8

Black folk traditions: African American disdain for, 3, 13, 70–71, 84; artistic value and pride in, 94, 265; continuous revision in, 239, 267; contrasted with high art, 91; records as preservers of, 99; spiritual frenzies, 3, 4. *See also* Black vocal traditions; oral traditions

Black Harry (Harry Hosier, Hoosier, or Hoshure), 67

Black ministers: borrowing of blues titles by, 153; as catalysts for progress, 103; class criticism by, 78–79; as community leaders, 176; in elite churches, 85; gravelly voices of, 69, 102, 206, 223, 261, 270; improvisation and spirituality of, 245; influence on musical style, 6, 270; jack-leg preachers, 79–80, 283n79; need for style-switching, 261–62; performative qualities of, 211–12; recording of sermons by, 3, 102–3; rural locations and, 287n13; scholarship on, 269–70; self-governance for, 68; and southern traditions, 269; topics addressed in sermons of, 175–76, 177; use of media, 301n5; vocal style and modern preaching of, 258–63

Black musicians, 87, 90, 99. *See also* blues and jazz music

Black Religious Music 1930–1956, 115

Black vocal traditions: Black preachers' use of their voices, 68; characteristics of, 189–90, 292n3; emergence of, 65; emotional expressivity in, 71–72, 78, 192, 271; as oral and auditory, 66; reflective of the rural South, 71–73; as resistance to racism, 271; technologies' role in disseminating, 6, 48, 54, 99–100, 103, 264; value and appeal of, 264; white and elite views of, 10. *See also* call-and-response; chanting; loudness; moans; shouts; vocalisms (style); vocal timbres

Black voices: biological differences with whites, 88–89; heterogeneity of, 4, 267; as indices of race and class, 7, 11; modern voices, 87–88; and vocal training, 89. *See also* Nix, Andrew William (A. W.): Voice of; vocal timbres

Blackwell, Scrapper, 144

Blakey, Johnnie (Son of Thunder), 289n36

Blues and Gospel Records: 1890–1943 (Dixon, Godrich, and Rye), 108, 197

blues and jazz music: in Bronzeville, 33; in contrast to high art, 47, 91; dangers of, 35; embellishment in, 43; gravelly voices in, 270; "how long" theme in, 144, 154, 290n59, 290n62; influence of chanted sermons on, 223; migrants' access to, 90; moans in, 196–97, **197**; musicians' religious recordings, 80; in Nix home, 226; personalization of lyrics in, 89; pride in, 94; recordings of, 98, *98*, 101, 264; and sinfulness, 179, 180; titles borrowed by Black ministers, 153; train theme in, 240–41

Bogle, Donald, 49, 50, 53

Bohlman, Philip V., 65

Brackett, David, 242

Bronzeville (Chicago), 33, 72–73, 80, 81, 184

Browne, Lennox, 89

Brown, James, 270

Brown, John Mason, "Songs of the Slave," 210
Brunswick-Balke-Collender Company, 96, 97, 101, 102
Brunswick Records: A Discography of Recordings, 1916–1931, Vol. 3, 108
Bryan, Andrew, 67
Burlin, Natalie Curtis, 195, 206
Burnett, J. C., "The Downfall of Nebuchadnezzar," 102, 287n183
Butler, Melvin L., 262

call-and-response: about, 204; in Black vocal traditions, 190; example of, 205; frequency of use of, 293n3; and lining out, 205; in Nix's sermons, 205; prayer bands' support through, 186, 231, 246; shouting as, 194; Wilson on meaning in, 261
Carr, Leroy, "How Long, How Long Blues," 144, 154, 242, 290n64
Cayton, Horace R. *See* Drake, St. Clair, and Horace Cayton
chanted sermons: characteristics of, 45, 68–69, 201–2, 204; commonalities with spirituals, 210; example of, *211*; form of, 113–15; influences on, 68; ministers' use of, 211; Nix's, 222–23; non-articulated sound in, 212–13; origins of, 53; as shared tradition, 67; similarities with blues, 223–24, *224*; speech-song in, 5
chanting: frequency of use of, 293n3; Nix's use of, 212; performative qualities of, 211–12; pitch centers in, 210; qualities in, 210–11; speech-song in, 210; traditions of, 209–10
Chesnut, Mary Boykin, 191
Chicago: adherence to Black vocal traditions in, 72; Black Belt in, 32; housing shortages in, 38; jack-leg preachers in, 80, 283n79; middle-class denunciation of low-class behavior in, 29–30; migration of southerners into, 30–31; racial tensions and riots in, 31, 32, 64, 188
Chicago Black churches: class divisions in, 72–76; growth in numbers of, 74; hybrid churches, 76; lower-class churches,

76–80, 81; middle-class and mixed churches, 76, 80–83, 273n15; upper-class/elite churches, 76, 83–86; vocal and musical practices in, 75–76
Chicago Commission of Race Relations (CCRR), 76
Chicago Defender: Ace's review of *Hallelujah*, 54; ads for Nix's sermons in, 112, 199; advice for migrants, 30–31, 75, 177, 178; on Bronzeville, 33; on importance of Black ministers, 176; on loudness, 29–30, 203; on lynching of Walters, 31; and marketing of records to African Americans, 97; phonograph advertisements in, 98; and proper behavior, 30
class: racial uplift and hierarchies of, 8, 10; as sermon theme, 183–84; and white cultural standards, 74. *See also* elite/upper class African Americans; lower-class African Americans; middle-class African Americans; musical expression, class differences in
Clayborn, Edward W., 299n165; "Your Enemy Cannot Harm You," 239–40
Cleveland Gazette, on the "New Negro," 90
Clinton, George W., 175
Colored American Opera Company, The, 87
Columbia Records, 96, 102, 287n10
conspicuous consumption, 80–81, 182–83
"coon songs," 90, 91, 95
Cosby, Marcus D., 260
Courlander, Harold, 195, 196, 206
Crawley, Ashon T., 260

dancing, 21, 53, 183
Davis, Angela, 179
Davis, Blind Willie: "Come and Go with Me to That Land," 299n150; "Dark Was the Night—Cold Was the Ground," 199, *199*; "Your Enemy Cannot Harm You," 240; voice of, 270
Davis, Gerald L., 212
"Deep Down in My Heart," 228
Dett, R. Nathaniel, *The Chariot Jubilee*, 92
Dixon, Calvin, 111, 234, 287n10; "As an Eagle Stirreth Up Her Nest," 102

INDEX

Dorsey, Thomas A.: as blues pianist, 33, 41; on the "cry" in the voice, 212–13; in Gospel Camp Meeting Singers, 234; "I Do, Don't You," 44; "If You See My Savior," 240; "It's Tight Like That," 144, 148; on moans, 196, 198; Mt. Zion's use of music by, 39; Nix brothers' influence on, 11, 40–41, 42, 48, 263, 279n134; second conversion of, 45–48; Vocalion recordings of, 46, 280n158

Downs, R. R., 79

Drake, St. Clair, and Horace Cayton: on class divisions in Chicago churches, 72–73, 76, 77, 79, 81; on gambling in Bronzeville, 184; on moans, 196; on public displays by the lower class, 183; on social clubs, 186

Du Bois, W. E. B.: and double consciousness, 266; education of, 8, 272n3; on generational split in church traditions, 71; on Griggs, 22; on loud shouting, 202; on moans, 195–96; proponent of classical liberal arts education, 8; and racial uplift, 7, 82; review of *Hallelujah* by, 50; *The Souls of Black Folk*, 3, 195; and spirituals, 90; view of Fisk Jubilee Singers, 10

Dylan, Bob, *Time Out of Mind*, 270

Edison, Thomas, 95

education, theme of, 187–88

elite/upper-class African Americans: attitudes toward storefront churches, 83, 183; decorum and restraint in worship, 72; denominations preferred by, 73–74, 83; and European aesthetics, 87–88; and hymn style, 47; musical preferences of, 84; Nix as part of, 19; Nix's challenge to cultural hegemony of, 94, 268; and racial uplift through assimilation, 7–8, 265; and State University's educational system, 25–27; views on migrants, 75. *See also* assimilation into dominant culture; racial uplift

Ellington, Duke, 97, 101

Epstein, Dena J., *Sinful Tunes and Spirituals*, 292n3

European classical music: Black singers' interest in, 273n20; in elite/upper-class churches, 84; and hymn style, 47, 231; as marker of respectability, 95; racial uplift through, 10; at State University, 24–25, 27; as tool against racism, 92

European cultural aesthetics, 10, 24–25, 87, 89, 190. *See also* Victorian ideologies

Evans, David, 110, 223, 239, 293n21

female voices in recorded sermons: call-and-response singing, 208, 230, 246; expectations for, 103; interjections by, 102, 213–14; Nix's sermons with, 288n22; prayer bands, 174, 194, 209; to represent classes, 217–18; to simulate live performance, 6, 108; singing of songs in, 232, 236, 237, 238, 247; soloists, 231. *See also* McKinney, Nina Mae

financial responsibility, theme of, 182

First Baptist Church (Georgetown, KY), 27

Fishback, C. G., 18–19

Fisk Jubilee Singers, 10, 42, 86–87, 92, 107

Floyd, Samuel A., Jr., 206, 241

Franklin, Kirk, 262

"Free at Last," 228

Freedman's Ridge, 14

Gaines, Kevin K., 7–8, 90, 181

gambling, theme of, 184

Gates, Henry Louis, Jr., 281n1

Gates, J. M.: "Death Might Be Your Santa Claus," 239; "Death's Black Train Is Coming," 52, 241; sermons by, 102, 288n23, 291n69; "These Hard Times Are Tight like That," 148; use of modern media by, 269

General Association of Colored Baptists, 19–20, 21, 27, 29–30, 177

Georgia Tom. *See* Dorsey, Thomas A.; "It's Tight like That" (Dorsey and Red)

Gilroy, Paul, 267

Godrich, John, 111, 234

Gospel Camp Meeting Singers, 234

gospel music: church performers of, 263; Dorsey's inspiration to write, 40–41; Dorsey's search for right voice for, 45–46, 47–48, 279n149; gospel music industry, 18

Gospel Pearls: Jesus-as-friend theme in, 299n167; publication of, 42; and *Songs of Zion*, 36; spirituals in, 227; William Nix Jr. and, 17, 18, 42–43, 226

Gray, Harry, 53

Great Depression, 34–35, 47, 64, 148, 188, 278n107

Great Migration, 6, 13, 23. *See also* migrants

Greenfield, Elizabeth Taylor, 87, 88

Gregg County (TX), 14, 15, *15*

Griggs, Sutton E.: *Collective Efficiency*, 23; as epitome of New Negro, 268; and European aesthetics, 107, 265; *Guide to Racial Greatness*, 22; "A Hero Closes a War," 104–8, 287n17; *Imperium in Imperio*, 22–23; influence on Nix's uplift principles, 177; intersection of Nix's career with, 21–23; photograph of, *22*; recorded sermons of, 103–4, *104*, 107, 287n17; use of standard English, 218; vocal delivery of, 2

Grissom, Mary Allen, 215; *The Negro Sings a New Heaven*, 229

Hall, E. H., 48, 280n163

Hallelujah (Vidor, 1929): modern women in, 139, 180–81; Nix sermon in, 11, 47, 52; Nix's influence on, 270; reviews of, 49–50; revival scene in, 52–53; significance of, 48; sin of city life in, 51; spiritual frenzy in, 50, 272n2 (Intro.); traditional Black voices in, 49

Hampton Institute, 9

Handy, W. C., 268

Harlem Renaissance, 10, 64, 65, 91, 92, 94

Harris, Charles K., "After the Ball," 239

Harris, Michael W.: on chanted sermons and the blues, 224; confusion of the Nix brothers by, 41, 44, 45; on Dorsey's gospel blues, 279n152; on Hall's voice, 48; and Nix's

personal-relationship-with-Jesus theme, 240; *The Rise of Gospel Blues*, 40–41

Harry T. Burleigh Choral Society, 185

Hatcher, William E., 215

Hayes, Roland, 92

Haynes, Daniel, 53

Haynes, Frederick Douglass, III, 260

Hester, Moses, 177

"Hide Me Over in the Rock of Ages," 228

Higginbotham, Evelyn Brooks, 185

Higginson, Thomas Wentworth, *Army Life in a Black Regiment*, 215

Holiness and Sanctified churches, 4, 21, 39, 76, 77, 78, 79

Hosier, Harry, 67

"how long" theme, 153–54, 196, 290n62

Hubbard, Dolan, 68

Hughes, Langston, 84, 94, 268

Hunter, Alberta, 97, 101; "How Long, Sweet Daddy, How Long," 153

Hurston, Zora Neale, 78, 94, 268

hymns, songs, and spirituals: "All o' My Sins" (and variant titles), 208, 228–29, 239, 297n122; "Amazing Grace," 125; "Come and Go with Me to That Land," 234, 299nn150–51; "Deep Down in My Heart," 231; "Done Found My Lost Sheep," 231–32; "Free at Last," 233–34, 297n122; "Great Change Since I Been Born," 232; "Hide Me Over in the Rock of Ages," 232–33, *233*, 297n122; "I Got Mah Swoad in Mah Han," 229; "I'm So Glad I Got My Religion in Time," 230–31, 297n122; "I Want Jesus to Walk with Me," 234–35; "Look for Me," 122, 125; "Look for Me!" (Miles), 230; "Nowhere to Hide," 229, 297n127; "O the Blood," 122, 229–30, 297n122; "Rock of Ages, Cleft for Me," 232, *233*; style of singing in hymns, 47; "Swing Low, Sweet Chariot," 205. *See also* spirituals

identity and vocal expression, 4–5, 215, 258, 264–65, 267

"I Do, Don't You?" (E. O. Excell), 17, 40–44

immoral women, theme of, 179–81

improvisation, 244–45, 293n3, 300n175
intertextuality: figurative tropes, 240–42; lyrical tropes, 239–40; Nix's use of, 239, 242; repetition, 242–44; tropes, 299n162
"It's Tight like That" (Dorsey and Red), 46–47, 290n55

Jasper, John, 215
Jazz Singer, The, 107–8, 288n19
Jefferson, Blind Lemon, 80, 206; "How Long, How Long," 290n59; "That Black Snake Moan," 197–98
Jessye, Eva, 50
Johnson, Bessie, 270
Johnson, Blind Willie, 270, 299n150; "Dark Was the Night—Cold Was the Ground," 199, *199*
Johnson, George W., 95
Johnson, James Weldon: on art, literature, and race consciousness, 93; attitudes toward slave era songs, 225; on attitudes toward slave songs, 84; *The Book of American Negro Spirituals*, 84; and "Free at Last," 233, 241; *God's Trombones*, 113; and Harlem Renaissance, 91; as song collector, 227, 228
Johnson, J. Rosamond, 93, 215, 225, 227, 228, 231, 233; *The Book of American Negro Spirituals*, 231
Jolson, Al, 108, 288n19
Jones, Matilda Sissieretta, 88

Kapp, Jack, 101
Keller, Louise, 47
Kennard, James, Jr., 219
Kenney, William Howland, 95, 286n157
Kilham, Elizabeth, 70, 191, 237
King Oliver, 33, 97, 101
Kingsley, Reverend, 76
Kruse, Harry, 52

Lanier, Sidney, *The Science of English Verse*, 210–11, *211*
Leadbelly (Huddie Ledbetter), 206
Levine, Lawrence, 239, 296n117
Lewis, Furry, "Sweet Papa Moan," 199, *200*

Liele, George, 67
Locke, Alain, 23, 91, 266, 287n183; *The New Negro*, 92, 288n23
Longview (TX), 14, 18, 31
loudness: as characteristic in Black vocal traditions, 201–3; and class affiliation, 29–30, 203–4; frequency of use of, 293n3; necessity for spiritual experience, 203; Nix's use of volume, 204, *204*; and power, 204; in "White Flyer to Heaven," 247, *248–57*
lower-class African Americans: appeal of recordings to, 95; attitude toward education, 77–78; conspicuous consumption of, 182–83; loudness in, 29–30, 203–4; spiritual frenzy in worship, 192; and traditional forms of worship, 73; and vernacular language, 215, 217–18; vocal style used in worship, 266–67

Mallard, R. Q., 202
Martin, Lerone A., 102–3, 183, 269
McIlhenny, E. A., 202, 225; *Befo' de War Spirituals*, 228
McKinney, Nina Mae: in *Hallelujah*, 48–49, 51, *52*, 53–54, 233, 234; in "The Black Diamond Express to Hell," 52, 54, 154, 156, 158, 160, 161, 180–81, 234
Memphis Times, on racial uplift, 9
middle-class African Americans: ambitions of, 80; criticism of lower-class vocal expressions, 3, 4, 29–30; decorum and restraint in worship, 72, 267; denominational preferences of, 73–74; and hymn style, 47; ministers as, 74; and proper behavior, 81; and racial uplift through assimilation, 7–8; and social clubs, 186; and standard English, 216, 217–18
migrants: alignment with Black folk traditions, 77; and familiar Southern traditions, 72–73; and loudness, 203–4; and migration of vocal characteristics, 189; Nix's advice and admonitions to, 176, 178, 182, 188; Nix's comments on, 183
Miles, Charles Austin, 230
Miller, Karl Hagstrom, 95

INDEX 319

minstrel performances. *See* blackface minstrelsy

Mississippi Juvenile Quartette, 231

Mitchell, Henry H., 66–67, 195

Mitchell, R., 20

moans: in blues, 196–99; importance in Black vocal traditions, 194–95; Nix's use of, 294n31; sacred moans, 195–96, 197, 199, 200–201, *201*; use in marketing, 199–200, *200*; in "White Flyer to Heaven," 247, *248–57*

modernity: Black folk voices and, 11, 264; consumerism and, 102–3; and modernized musical traditions, 86–87, 95, 107; the modern woman, 134, 179–80; musical voices as entrée into, 10–11; quietness as progress, 71–72; recorded sermons and ideas of, 4, 267; voices as conceptions of, 5

Morton, Jelly Roll, 33, 97

Moses, Wilson J., 22

Moton, Robert Russa, 70

Mt. Moriah Baptist Church (Harlem), *28*, 29, 277n93

Mt. Olive Baptist Church (Chicago), 33–34

Mt. Zion Baptist Church (Philadelphia), 35, 36, 38–39

Murphy, Jeannette Robinson, 196

musical assimilation, 9–10

musical expression, class differences in: modern Black voices, 87–94; modernized traditions, 94–100

National Association for the Advancement of Colored People, 9

National Association of Colored Women, 18

National Baptist Convention (1921): and Griggs' book, 22, 23; Nix brothers and Dorsey at, 17, 24, 40–41, 42–43, 279n134; William Nix Jr.'s contributions to, 18

National Jubilee Melody Song Book, 226–27, 228, 232, 297n122

National Urban League, 9

Negro Music Journal, The: on choral singing, 185; columns on singers' voices, 88; purpose of, 87–88

New England Conservatory of Music, *The Realm of Music*, 89

New Light Baptist Church (Cleveland), 35

"New Negro": aesthetics of, 10; artistic expressions of, 65; creation of, 64; as embodiment of Black sophistication, 90; and European aesthetics, 265; Griggs and, 268; Griggs's voice and, 22–23; and Harlem Renaissance, 91; use of term, 90–91

New Songs of the Gospel No. 2, 230

Nix, Andrew William (A. W.): alignment with both tradition and modernity, 266; death of, 39; early life and family of, 13–18, *16*; educational goals of, 37, 38, 85; education of, 19, 24–27, *26*, 187, 277n70; as exception to the rule, 83, 267; as father to his community, 185–86, 268; as fiery preacher, 35, 39; as great artist, 263; hybrid practices of, 9, 13, 49, 76, 85–86, 231, 247; income of, 34–35, 38, 278n120; influence on musical style, 6, 270; intersection with Griggs, 21–23; ministerial career of, 18–21, 27–29, 35, 79; misrepresentation of, 41, 268; move to Chicago, 29, 31, 32–33, 277n93; music in his churches, 82; philosophy of, 19; photograph with McKinney, 52, *52*; popularity of, 113; proponent of home ownership, 37–38, 80; residences of, 29, *34*; tombstone for, *40*; as trailblazer, 260, 263, 269, 270; use of Hebrew, 38–39; vocal traditions used by, 10, 264. *See also* Mt. Zion Baptist Church (Philadelphia)

Recordings of: analyses of, 12; choice of hymns and spirituals in, 225–28; descriptions of, 3, 110; discographies of, 55–63, *63*, 108; Dorsey inspired by, 41; improvisation in, 78; male voices in, 174; musical analyses of, 11; numbers of, 108, **109**; recording process for, 108, 109, **109**; significance of, 86; similarities with Dorsey's songs, 46; social context for, 107–8; success of, 46, 111–13, 154, 269; target audiences for, 77; time frame for, 34. *See also* hymns, songs, and spirituals; intertextuality; McKinney, Nina Mae; spirituals

Sermon themes: based on social issues, 288n23; biblical themes, 110, 178, 235–36; city life and sin, 50–51, 139, 179, 264; club membership, 81, 186–87; conspicuous consumption, 80–81, 143–44; education, 187; fire and brimstone, 177–78; gambling, 143, 184; immoral women, 134, 166, 179–81; marriage and family, 180–82; personal relationship with God, 240, 299nn166–67; personal responsibility, 185; racial uplift in, 174, 176–77, 187–88, 247, 266, 269; sexual themes, 148–49; storefront churches, 183–84; temperance, 184–85; thrift and financial responsibility, 139, 143–44, 149, 182, 218

Specific sermons of: "After the Ball Is Over," 115, **115**, 177, 178, 222–23, 224, 239; "Baseball Sermon" (not recorded), 244–45, *245*; "Begin a New Life on Christmas Day—Parts I and II," 183, 184, 232, *236*; "A Country Man in Town," 135–39, 180, 183; "Death Might Be Your Christmas Gift," 112, *112*, 115, 239; "The Dirty Dozen—No. 1," 162–67, 184, 185, 239, 240; "The Dirty Dozen—No. 2," 167–70, 180, 185; "Done Found My Lost Sheep," 231; "Generosity," 181, 239; "Goin' to Hell and Who Cares," 229; "Hang Out Your Sign," 179; "Hiding Behind the Stuff," 205, 216, 229; "How Long—How Long," 144, 149–54, 180, 186, 217, 240, 242–43, *243*; "How Will You Spend Christmas?," 182, 184; "Hush, Hush, Somebody's Callin' My Name," 44, *44*; "It Is a Strange Thing to Me," 230; "It Was Tight like That," 46, 47, 144–49, 187, 218, 240, 290n55; "Love Is a Thing of the Past," 181; "The Matchless King," 114, 187, 200–201, *201*, 235; note on transcription formats, 289n46; "Pay Your Honest Debts," 140–44, 182; "The Prayer Meeting in Hell," 114, 187, 213–14, *214*; "Robbing God," 177,

183; "The Seven Rs," 230; "Sleeping in a Dangerous Time," 178; "Slow This Year for the Danger Signal," 180; "That Little Thing May Kill You Yet (Christmas Sermon)," 184; "There's Something Rotten in Denmark," 170–75, 181, 187, 291n68, 291n69; "Too Much Religion," 234; "Watch Your Close Friend," 239–40; "Who Dressed You Up for Easter," 178; "You Got the Wrong Man," 181, 185; "You Have Played the Fool," 182; "Your Bed Is Too Short and Your Cover Too Narrow," 187, 235; "Your Time is Out," 177. *See also* "Black Diamond Express to Hell" (Nix sermons); "The White Flyer to Heaven" Parts I and II (Nix sermons)

Voice of: based on Black folk traditions, 5, 22, 260, 266; in chanted sermons, 222–23; and class differences among African Americans, 5, 216; compared to brother William, 44; to connect with people, 107, 190, 216–17, 259–60; emotional impacts from, 110; as exemplar of Black vocal traditions, 41, 267, 270; gravelly quality of, 11, 44, 190, 201, 207–9, 223, 230–31, 242; as hybrid form, 5, 107; power in, 86; the "screaming voice," 194; singing to introduce sermons, 297n142; style-switching of, 212, 216, 261, 262; use of call-and-response, 205; use of moans, 200–201, *201*; use of rhythm, 220; use of speech-song, 5; use of vernacular, 216; "White Flyer to Heaven—Part II" as example of, 247, *248–57*, 257–58, *258*

Nix, Andrew William, Jr. (son), 33

Nix, Elwood (son): about, 33, 35, 244; on Dorsey at services, 46; on father's Pentecostal style, 39; interviews with, 11; on jack-leg preachers, 79–80, 283n79; on loudness as power, 204; on modern-day preachers, 259; on Nix's alignment with Baptist church, 85; on Nix's big heart, 86; on Nix's voice, 110, 207; on preachers' moans, 196; on the sound of soul, 192

Nix, Emma (sister), 14, 16, *16*, 274n13, 275n18

Nix, Genester (daughter): about, 33, 35; banned activities in childhood home of, 77; on Black ministers' preaching, 193–94, 258–59; on church as an emotional experience, 39, 192–93; on church-sponsored musicales, 82; on Dorsey's friendship with Nix, 46; on elite-class church members, 85; on Holmesburg, 36–37; on home ownership of congregants, 37–38; on inspiration for Dorsey, 42; interviews with, 11; on the length of Nix's live sermons, 108; on Nix's hardships, 34; on Nix's improvisation, 244; on Nix's kindness, 86; on Nix's singing, 298n142; on Nix's vocal timbre, 207; on Sunday services, 36; on temperance at home, 184

Nix, Ida (mother, née Peterson), 14, 15–16, *16*, 274n12

Nix, Ida Anita (wife, née Burcher), *28*, 29, 32, 37, *40*, 238

Nix, Theophilus (son), 33

Nix, Verolga (daughter), 35, 36, 227–28

Nix, William, Jr. (brother): about, *16–17*, 16–18, 33; confusion with Andrew, 40–41, 269; and Dorsey, 11, 17, 41, 43, 48; and hymnals, 279n136; as renowned singer, 42, 43, 226; singing of "I Do, Don't You?," 17, 40, 43, 44; vocal qualities of, 43, 44; wives and children of, 17, 275n18, 275n21

Nix, William, Sr. (father), 14–16, *16*, 31, 274nn1–2

Norfolk Jubilee Quartet Singers, 232

normal schools, 24, 25

"Nowhere to Hide," 228

Odum, Howard W., 215, 228, 230

OKeh Records, 97, 98, *98*

Oliver, Paul, 209, 287n183, 288n23; *Songsters and Saints*, 41

Olivet Baptist, 81, 82

oral traditions: African American's reliance on, 103; in blues and jazz, 95; chanted sermons in, 209; Griggs and, 268; Nix's

inclusion of, 225, 238, 266; phonographs and, 99–100, 239; in preaching, 211; spirituals in, 296n117; vocal sound passed down through, 4, 99–100

participatory performance, 213–14, 224, 229

patriarchy, themes of, 181–82, 185–86

Patton, Charley, 206

Payne, Daniel A., 21, 70–71, 83, 175

Pentecostalism: attitudes toward, 260; growth of, 283n60; holy dancing in, 21; "holy hip-hop" in, 262; and speaking in tongues, 69; as storefront churches, 77; worship styles in, 39, 78–79

Perkins, A. E., 84

personal responsibility, theme of, 185

phonograph recordings: African American artists on, 95, 99; blues as authentic Black genre on, 98; as bridge between tradition and modernity, 6; and broadcasting of religion through, 269; consumption of, 90, 95; cultural uplift through classical music, 95; and dissemination of Black voices, 12, 87; electrical, 101, 287n6; of ethnic music, 96, 286n157; invention and appeal of, 95; as marker of modernity, 96, 264; as oral tradition, 99–100, 264; rehearsals for, 108; time limitations for, 103, 108. *See also* Nix, Andrew William (A. W.): Recordings of; race records; recorded sermons

Phonograph & Talking Machine Weekly, on Vocalion records, 99

Pinckard, George, 201

Pipes, William H., 154

Pitts, Walter F., Jr., 215, 219

Pittsburgh Courier: on musicale hosted by Nix, 82; on Nix and "Black Diamond Express to Hell," 111–12

Pleasant Hill Colored Methodist Episcopal Church, 15

Powdermaker, Hortense, 74, 273n14

prayer bands, 194, 293n21

preacher-congregation interaction, 213

Psalm 13:1, 153

Raboteau, Albert J., 68, 69, 71, 175, 211–12

race consciousness, 93, 98

race records: about, 6, 285n144; advertisements for, 199; and appeal of folk vocalisms, 265; and Black folk voices, 10; Black identity and experience in, 238–39; music and voices promulgated by, 97; pride in, 98; success of, 95

racial uplift: assimilation in, 20–21; and audience reaction to *Hallelujah*, 54; Black elite's focus on, 8–9; choral singing and, 185; citizenship as tool of, 20; creation of class hierarchies through ideologies of, 10; education and, 175, 176; home and family as symbols of, 181; and illiteracy, 103–4; and inclusion in American life, 187–88; institutional support of, 9, 27–29; "lifting as we climb," 18; and moral behavior, 175; Nix and, 13, 18–19, 27; as self-help mechanism to combat white racism, 7–8; social clubs and, 186; through musical assimilation, 9–10. *See also* assimilation into the dominant culture; Griggs, Sutton E.; Nix, Andrew William (A. W.): Sermon themes

racism: Black churches' education about, 36; Black leaders' work against, 270; and emotional expression, 192; great art as tool in battling, 91, 93, 94; internalization of, 8; Nix's experience with, 19; racial uplift as means to transcend, 7–8, 188; reform of Black folk culture to diminish, 92

Radano, Ronald, 67, 270–71

Rainey, Gertrude "Ma," 41, 45, 179; "Deep Moaning Blues," 197–98, *198*

Ramsey, Guthrie, 100

Randolph, Peter, 210

recorded sermons: blurring of class lines through, 6; changes to sermon form for, 113–14; and dissemination of Black vocal traditions, 102–3; emulation of live performance in, 5; as entrée into modernity, 11, 264; inclusion of songs and spirituals in, 225, 227–28; income from, 108; length limitations for, 288n20,

289n42; phonographs as oral tradition for, 100; popularity of, 4, 264, 287n10; and public awareness of Black vocal traditions, 6. *See also* hymns, songs, and spirituals; Nix, Andrew William (A. W.): Recordings of; spirituals

recording technologies, development of, 64. *See also* phonograph recordings; sound films

record manufacturers, 96. *See also* Vocalion label

Red, Tampa, 144, 148, 234. *See also* "It's Tight like That" (Dorsey and Red)

repetition, use of, 242–44

Rev. A. W. Nix, Vol. 1, 1927–1928, 115

revival meetings, 67

rhythm and meter, 218–21

Rijn, Guido van, 115

ring shouts, 71, 292n3, 293n10

Robeson, Paul, 94

Robinson, Bill "Bojangles," 53

Rusk County census (TX), 15, 274n1

Rye, Howard, 234

Sandhills Sixteen, 231

Schenbeck, Lawrence, 265

Second Baptist Church (Chicago), 33–34, *34*

Secor, Ketch, 270

sermons: climaxes in, 219–20, 222, 224, 247, 257; the Holy Spirit and emotion in, 66–67, 154; "intelligent" rhetoric in, 82, 284n91; lengths of, 288n21; Puritans and chanted sermons, 68, 113–15; racial uplift themes in, 82; rhythmic, chanting style of, 53; themes in, 175–76; traditional form, 284n93. *See also* chanted sermons; recorded sermons

Sherman, John T., 49

shouts: in Black vocal traditions, 4, 66, 71, 82, 189; and class associations, 78; distinction with talking back to the minister, 193; frequency of use of, 293n3; Nix's use of, 5, 11, 190; and participatory performance, 191, 193–94; the "screaming voice," 194; as spontaneous expression of the spirit, 191–93; in

"White Flyer to Heaven," 247, *248–57*. *See also* female voices in recorded sermons; Nix, Andrew William (A. W.): Specific recorded sermons of

Simmons, Nathan, 294n31

slave culture: and the Black experience, 5; Black folk traditions associated with, 3, 13, 65, 70; Black voices' agency in, 270–71; and Black worship practices, 65–68; and the chanted sermon, 53; cry of "How Long!" in, 154; loudness in singing, 201, 202; praise-house services, 191; revolt against, 225; songs in, 227; the voice and spiritual conversions in, 66

Slave Songs of the United States, 153, 202, 225

Smith, Bessie, 33, 94, 179, 270; "Back-Water Blues," 288n23

Smith, Clara, "Awful Moanin' Blues," 197

Smith, Lucy, 183

Smith, Mamie, "Crazy Blues," 97, 99, 287n183

social clubs, 186–87

social issues of 1920s, 64–65

Songs of Zion (ed. Cleveland and Nix), 36, 227–28, 234

Sonic Visualizer software, x, 207, 220, 269

sound films, 6, 49. See also *Hallelujah* (Vidor, 1929)

South, the, post-WWI conditions in, 30

Southern, Eileen, 42, 296n117

Speckled Red, "The Dirty Dozen," 239, 287n15

spectrogram graphs, *194, 201, 204, 207–9, 208*

speech-song, 5, 210, 262

Spencer, Jon Michael, 218–19

spirit possession, 68–69

spiritual conversions, 66, 67

spiritual experience and participatory performance, 213

spirituals: anthem spirituals, 283n88; arrangements of, 10–11; attention to, 4; Black colleges as advocates of, 285n122; chanting in, 210; characteristics of, 225, 237; chariot theme in, 241; contrasted with high art, 91; elite/upper-class attitudes toward, 84; "how long" theme in, 290n59; mystery spiritual, 236–39, *238*, 244, *248–57*, 257; new interpretations

of, 90, 92, 93–94; Nix's vocal characteristics compared to, 12; rejection by the middle class, 82; salvation through, 66; scholars on, 296n117; vernacular language in, 215

Spivey, Victoria, 47, 48, 51, *51*

State University (Louisville, KY): about, 19–20, 21, 24, 24–27, 276n60; influence on Nix's uplift principles, 177; Nix's education at, 19, 24–27

Still, William Grant, 94; *Afro-American Symphony*, 92

Stowe, Harriet Beecher, 70

style-switching, 212, 216, 261, 262, 296n96

Sunday School Publishing Board, 18, 42, 226, 233, 279n136

Sutherland, Robert Lee, 75, 76

Svin'in, Paul, 195

Tabernacle Baptist Church (Pittsburgh, PA), 29, 35

Talented Tenth, 8, 75, 82, 91

Talking Machine World, on race records, 96–97, 111

temperance, 20–21, 35, 176, 184–85

Topeka Plaindealer, on Nix's encounter with racial injustice, 19

tradition, in performance practice, 65–66. *See also* Black vocal traditions; oral traditions

Trotter, James M., 10; *Music and Some Highly Musical People*, 87, 88

Trotter, William Monroe, 25

Turino, Thomas, 213

Tuskegee Institute, 25

vernacular language, 215–18

Victorian ideologies, 20–21, 26, 27, 106–7

Victrola, 96

Vidor, King, 48, 49, 53, 54

Virginia Four, 232

Vocalion label: acquisition of, 97; advertisements for sermons by, 112; beginning of race record series on, 101; Brunswick's acquisition of, 97, 101; choice of Nix to record, 34; contact between Dorsey and

Nix through, 46; financial health of, 111; influence on sermon themes, 110; location of, 102; Nix's contact with Spivey through, 47; Nix sermons recorded on, 3, 13, 101; prices of records, 99, 278n107; sound quality on, 101; start of race record series, 101; and two-part recordings, 287n15

vocalisms (style): African American vocal characteristics since slavery, 189; Black history and development of, 5, 53; in gospel singing, 48; heterophany, *204*, 225, 231; improvisation, 244–45, 293n3, 300n175; participatory performance, 213–14, 224, 229; recorded sermons' highlighting of, 3–4; repetition, 242–44; rhythm and meter, 218–21; transcription of, 269; types of, 4; used by William Nix, 43, 44; vernacular language, 215–18; vocal layering, *246*, 246–47; wails in *Hallelujah*, 50, *50*. *See also* call-and-response; chanted sermons; chanting; loudness; moans; shouts; vocal timbres

vocal timbres: of Black voices, 4, 190, 206; of blues singers, 206; characteristics of, 207–8; and class affiliation, 206–7; as cultural construct, 4; gravelly voices, 69, 102, 206, 223, 261, 270, 293n3; of Nix's voice, 207, *208*, 208–9; and resonance in spiritual experience, 195; style-switching in, 261–62; sweetness, 88, 96, 193n3; in "White Flyer to Heaven," 247, *248–57*. *See also* Black ministers; blues and jazz music

vocal training, 89

Walker, Wyatt Tee, *Spirits That Dwell in Deep Woods*, 232

Walters, Lemmel, 31

Washington, Booker T.: challenges for southern migrants, 73; and industrial education, 8–9, 25; and new interpretations of spirituals, 90; *A New Negro for a New Century*, 90; proponent of economic segregation, 8–9; and racial uplift, 7; State University and philosophies of, 27; support for property ownership, 182; on vocal sophistication, 91

Waters, Muddy, "I Got My Mojo Working," 179

Weidman, Amanda, 107

Weisenfeld, Judith, 49

Wesley, Howard-John, 261

Western classical music. *See* European classical music

Wheeler, Edward L., 187–88

White, Clarence Cameron, "The American Negro in Music," 88

White, William, 202

Whitefield, George, 68

"White Flyer to Heaven, The" (Nix sermons): and "Black Diamond," 288n29; songs and spirituals in, 230, 238, *238*; textual analysis of, 122–28; train trope in, 241; vocalisms in, 222, *222*, 247, *248–57*; vocal layering in, 246, *246*

William, S. Laing, "The New Negro," 90–91

Williams, Bert (Elder Eatmore), popular songs of, 239

Williams, Eugene, 32

Williams, Fannie Barrier, *A New Negro for a New Century*, 90

Williams, J. Mayo, 99

Williams, L. K., 73

Wilson, John (grandson), 258, 259–61, 263

Wiseman Sextette, 231

women: challenges to ideal womanhood, 179; domination of churches by, 185–86; immoral, 134, 166, 179–81; modern, 180–81. *See also* female voices in recorded sermons; patriarchy, themes of

Wood, Norman Barton, *A New Negro for a New Century*, 90

Work, Frederick J., *New Jubilee Songs as Sung by the Fisk Jubilee Singers*, 42

Work, John W., 227, 228; *American Negro Songs*, 233

Work, John Wesley: *Folk Songs of the American Negro*, 42; *New Jubilee Songs as Sung by the Fisk Jubilee Singers*, 42

working class. *See* lower-class African Americans

Works Progress Administration (WPA), 73, 76, 183

ABOUT THE AUTHOR

Photo by Bozanich Photography

Terri Brinegar has presented her research on African American voices at numerous conferences, including the American Musicological Society, the Society for Ethnomusicology, and the Association for Recorded Sound Collections. She has performed for over twenty years in classic R&B and blues bands and has three professionally produced CDs of blues and jazz original compositions. She is author of *Voice and Stage Essentials for the Aspiring Female R&B Singer*.